GUARDIANS *of the* NORTH

GUARDIANS *of the* NORTH

Canadian Warships and Maritime Aircraft, 1910–2025

RICHARD H. GIMBLETT & KARL GAGNON

Publisher: Meghan Macdonald | Acquiring editor: Graham Matthews | Editor: Russell Smith
Cover designer: Laura Boyle
Interior design: Karen Alexiou

Library and Archives Canada Cataloguing in Publication

Title: Guardians of the north : Canadian warships and maritime aircraft, 1910–2025 / Richard H. Gimblett & Karl Gagnon.
Names: Gimblett, Richard Howard, 1956- author | Gagnon, Karl, author, illustrator.
Description: Includes bibliographical references and index.
Identifiers: Canadiana (print) 20250230410 | Canadiana (ebook) 20250230453 | ISBN 9781459755550 (hardcover) | ISBN 9781459755574 (PDF) | ISBN 9781459755567 (EPUB)
Subjects: LCSH: Canada. Royal Canadian Navy—Aviation—History. | LCSH: Canada. Royal Canadian Navy—Procurement—History. | LCSH: Canada. Royal Canadian Air Force—Procurement—History. | LCSH: Warships—Canada—History. | LCSH: Warships—Canada—History—Pictorial works. | LCSH: Airplanes, Military—Canada—History. | LCSH: Airplanes, Military—Canada—History—Pictorial works.
Classification: LCC VG95.C3 G56 2025 | DDC 359.9/40971—dc23

We acknowledge the support of the Canada Council for the Arts and the Ontario Arts Council for our publishing program. We also acknowledge the financial support of the Government of Ontario, through the Ontario Book Publishing Tax Credit and Ontario Creates, and the Government of Canada.

Printed and bound in Canada.

Dundurn Press
1382 Queen Street East
Toronto, Ontario, Canada M4L 1C9
dundurn.com, @dundurnpress

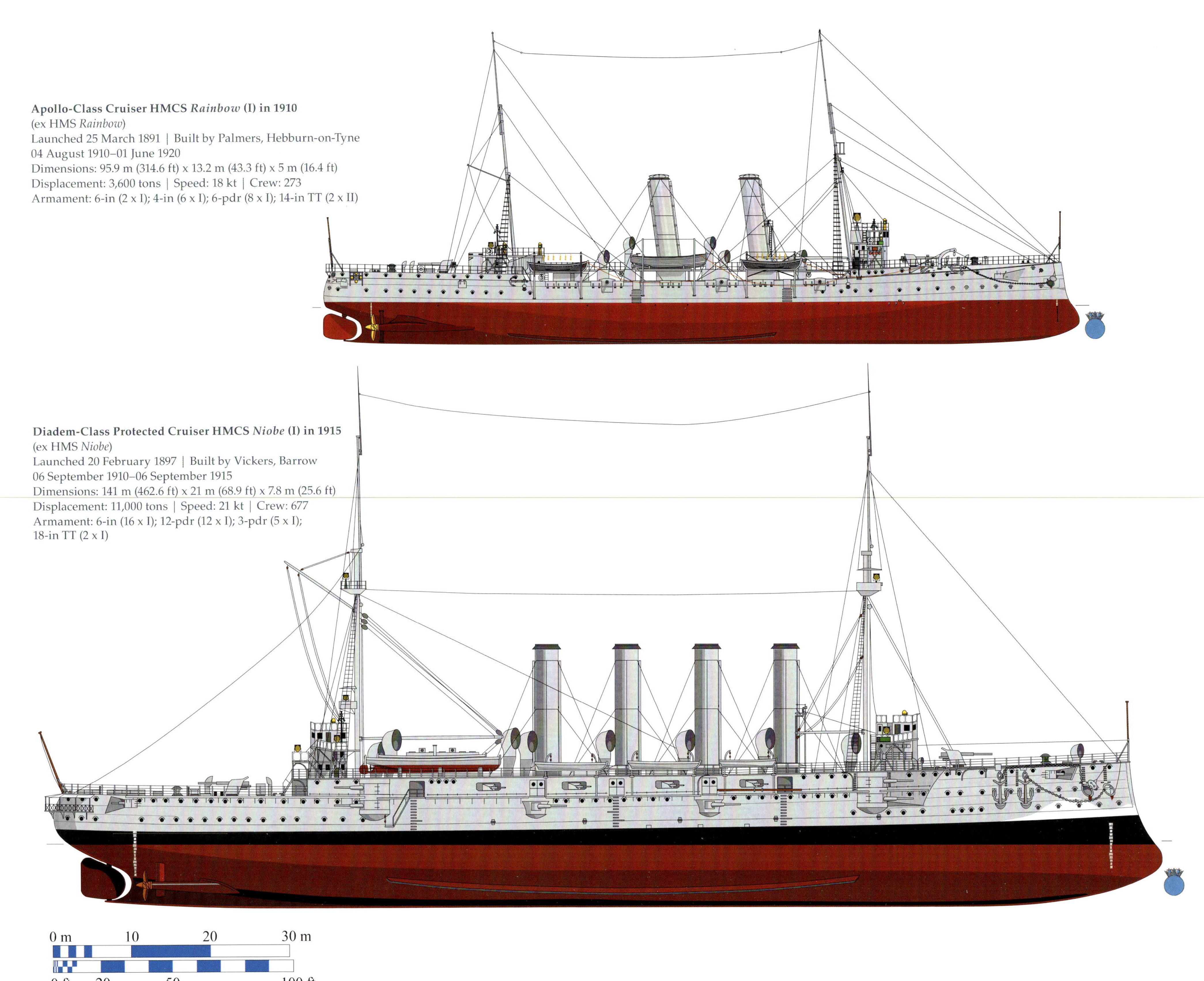

Apollo-Class Cruiser HMCS *Rainbow* (I) in 1910
(ex HMS *Rainbow*)
Launched 25 March 1891 | Built by Palmers, Hebburn-on-Tyne
04 August 1910–01 June 1920
Dimensions: 95.9 m (314.6 ft) x 13.2 m (43.3 ft) x 5 m (16.4 ft)
Displacement: 3,600 tons | Speed: 18 kt | Crew: 273
Armament: 6-in (2 x I); 4-in (6 x I); 6-pdr (8 x I); 14-in TT (2 x II)
Diadem-Class Protected Cruiser HMCS *Niobe* (I) in 1915
(ex HMS *Niobe*)
Launched 20 February 1897 | Built by Vickers, Barrow
06 September 1910–06 September 1915
Dimensions: 141 m (462.6 ft) x 21 m (68.9 ft) x 7.8 m (25.6 ft)
Displacement: 11,000 tons | Speed: 21 kt | Crew: 677
Armament: 6-in (16 x I); 12-pdr (12 x I); 3-pdr (5 x I);
18-in TT (2 x I)
0 m
10
20
30 m
0 ft
20
50
100 ft

2

THE BEGINNING: *RAINBOW* AND *NIOBE*

The notion of developing the FPS into a naval militia centred on CGS *Canada* got a significant boost in the spring of 1908, when Rear Admiral Charles Kingsmill, a Canadian-born officer serving in the RN, was hired by the Laurier government as part of a major reorganization of the Marine Department. Soon after assuming his new post as director of the Marine Services, Kingsmill undertook an assessment of the Dominion's naval requirements, and the report he presented on February 1, 1909, outlined a scheme for a modest coastal defence force that would "be confined to destroyers and scouts [small 2500-ton cruisers] for many a long day."[4] The timing was opportune, for the next month there erupted the so-called Dreadnought Crisis — the fear that the Imperial German Navy would outpace the RN in battleship construction — which raised calls throughout the Empire for cash contributions to Britain to augment its own building program. In Canada, when the House of Commons debated the issue on March 29, 1909, Laurier instead was able to revise the wording of the motion to align with his established policy, to call for "the speedy organization of a Canadian naval service." On April 19, Kingsmill presented a more detailed proposal that a pair of cruisers be obtained surplus from the RN to serve as training ships, one on each coast.

The type he had in mind was the Apollo class of "second-class" cruisers built for the RN under the 1889 *Naval Defence Act*. Twenty-one ships of the class had been built, beginning in 1889, with the last commissioned by the spring of 1893. Displacing 3,600 tons, they were armed with a combination of two 6-inch and six 4.7-inch guns and four 14-inch torpedo tubes. A pair of triple-expansion engines gave them a maximum speed of nearly 20 knots (37 kph), with a range of 8,000 nm at 10 knots (15,000 km at 19 kph).

Kingsmill was familiar with the Apollos, having served in near-sister cruisers *Blenheim* and *Mildura*, commanding the latter on the Australian Station (1900–03) and then also commanding *Scylla* (actually one of the class) for his return voyage to England in 1903–04. In the first decade of the twentieth century, the steam and weapon technologies they represented were still relatively new, and they had aged well: Their fairly simple machinery and armament, sturdy steel-hulled construction, and long range suggested they would be ideal for the intended training role in the remote and austere Canadian maritime environments. During negotiations with the Admiralty over the winter and spring of 1910, Kingsmill determined that the East Coast would be better served by the acquisition of a larger — but of similar lineage — Diadem-class protected cruiser of some 11,000 tons, constructed in the late 1890s but still sharing the same machinery and primary armament of 6-inch guns (sixteen of them). Explicitly, a vessel of this size could accommodate a much larger intake of trainees (ship's company of nearly 700, versus the 250 in an Apollo) that would hasten the readiness to crew the intended fleet.

The ships finally obtained were *Rainbow* (Apollo class) and *Niobe* (Diadem class). *Rainbow* had commissioned into the RN in 1892 and saw service on the China Station from 1895 to 1898, and then the Mediterranean (1898–1904) before being placed on reduced operations in home waters and finally paying off early in 1909. Still in fair shape just a year later, she required only a minor mechanical refit in addition to the modifications that *Niobe* also underwent to prepare for Canadian service: installation of a heating system and the new Marconi wireless device, and the stripping of unnecessary secondary armament to make space for an enlarged cadet gunroom and principal messdecks for trainees. *Rainbow* was commissioned on August 4, 1910, as the first "HMCS" and steamed from Portsmouth on the twentieth of that month. Sailing around South America by way of the Strait of Magellan, a distance of 15,000 miles (24,140 km) — because the Panama Canal was still under construction — eventually she arrived in Esquimalt on November 7, 1910.

Niobe's transfer was different only in degree. Commissioned into the RN in 1898, she saw action during the Boer War before returning to home waters, where she remained in service at the time of commissioning into the RCN on September 6, 1910. She sailed for Canada a month later, but with a shorter distance to transit, arrived off Halifax three weeks ahead of *Rainbow* in Esquimalt. *Niobe*'s entry into Halifax was carefully timed for October 21 (the 105th anniversary of the Battle of Trafalgar), to symbolize the transfer of the fighting tradition of Nelson to the new Dominion Navy.

Most histories are content to leave readers with the impression that Canada had inherited a couple of obsolete hulks, without appreciating the fact that ships then had a design life of twenty to twenty-five years, placing both within that time frame. Further, they had been acquired only to serve as training vessels pending the building of a proper fleet. The fact is that even as *Rainbow* and *Niobe* were settling into service in their new home ports, tenders were being prepared for a fully modern fleet to be constructed in Canada to encourage development of a domestic shipbuilding industry. These were finally promulgated in February 1911, calling for four Bristol-class light cruisers of the "improved Weymouth" design and six River-class destroyers of the "improved Acorn" design (not to be confused with the 1930–40s class of that name, discussed in Chapter 8). They were to be completed and in service within six years.

Then, in the summer of 1911, a pair of disasters struck the Canadian fleet. First, while returning from a training cruise into the Bay of Fundy, during the night of July 30–31, *Niobe* went aground off Cape Sable on the southern tip of Nova Scotia. Although she was floated off and able to make for Halifax, a lengthy repair period in dry dock was in store for her. Then Robert Borden's Conservatives won the general election on September 21, in part with the support of an anti-Navy coalition of Ontario pro-Empire imperialists and Quebec nationalists. The new government froze the Navy budget and cancelled the construction tenders. *Niobe*'s repairs did proceed, and *Rainbow* conducted a few training-fisheries patrols, but soon the ships were effectively laid up alongside, and desertions quickly outpaced recruitment. In the spring of 1914, money was allocated to make *Rainbow* seaworthy for a fisheries patrol into the Bering Sea, and her crew was brought up to strength through a combination of

Rainbow arriving in Esquimalt, November 7, 1910.

men transferred from *Niobe* and others raised through the Royal Naval Canadian Volunteer Reserve (newly established by Commander Walter Hose as captain of *Rainbow*). Before the cruiser could sail north, however, the government ordered her to Vancouver for a starring role in the infamous *Komagata Maru* immigration incident, which ended with *Rainbow* escorting that ship out of harbour on July 23.

Consequently, *Rainbow* was largely ready for action when war was declared a few days later. Her activities are fully covered in the recent official history (Johnston et al., *The Seabound Coast*) and need only be summarized here. *Rainbow* has the distinction of being the first Canadian military unit into action when, in the early hours of August 3, in anticipation of a declaration of war (which came the next day), she was ordered "to proceed

Niobe on arrival in Canada, October 21, 1910.

to sea forthwith to guard trade routes north of the equator."[5] Fortunately, the Canadian cruiser did not encounter the more modern and powerful German cruiser *Leipzig*, suspected to be in the vicinity, and when that ship was destroyed with the rest of Admiral Graf von Spee's squadron in the Battle of the Falklands in December 1914, the German threat in the Pacific effectively disappeared. *Rainbow* continued her patrols of the West Coast of North America without opposition, seizing a couple of German merchant schooners as prizes, and in 1916–17 transported $140 million in Russian bullion to Vancouver. That mission completed, and her crew desperately required on the Atlantic for the growing fight against the U-boats, *Rainbow* was paid off and deactivated on May 8, 1917. She recommissioned soon after as a depot ship alongside in Esquimalt and served as such until June 1, 1920, when sold for scrap to a Seattle shipbroker.

The declaration of hostilities in August 1914 found *Niobe* in bad shape from two years of laying alongside, and she had to be put into dry dock in Halifax for urgent repairs. This also gave time to begin reassembling a crew from available RN sailors (hers having been sent west in the spring, to *Rainbow*), buttressed by a contingent of 107 sailors from the Newfoundland Division of the Royal Naval Reserve. After escorting a troopship to Bermuda on September 11–13, carrying the Royal Canadian Regiment to take up garrison duties there, on October 6, *Niobe* joined the RN's Fourth Cruiser Squadron in patrolling off the New England seaboard for German contraband. Despite some successes in this, the winter cruising wore heavily on the vessel, which was prematurely aged owing to Canadian maintenance neglect, and after her final patrol of July 4–17, 1915, she was paid off to become a depot ship in Halifax. The Halifax Explosion on December 6, 1917, caused serious damage to her upper works and caused her to drag her mooring anchors (one of these was discovered in 2014 and now sits at the entrance to Halifax Dockyard). In 1920, she too was sold for scrap, to be broken up in 1922 in Philadelphia.

Against all expectations, both ships proved to be useful for the wartime roles they filled, for as long as they were required for them. One of the great "what ifs" of Canadian naval history is whether Canada's naval war

Niobe in final disposition as the depot ship in Halifax Dockyard, spring 1917.

would have been different if the proposed 1911 fleet were available for service in the Great War. Notwithstanding their poor reputation, but considering that their only intended role was to be training vessels, *Rainbow* and *Niobe* should, in fact, be remembered as having met the challenge of war and bringing honour to Canada's early maritime efforts in the Great War.

FURTHER READING

E.H.H. Archibald, *The Fighting Ship of the Royal Navy, 897–1984* (Military Press, 1984).

W.A.B. (Alec) Douglas, "Sir Charles Edmund Kingsmill," *Dictionary of Canadian Biography*, 2021, biographi.ca/en/bio/kingsmill_charles_edmund_16E.html.

Norman Friedman, *British Cruisers of the Victorian Era* (US Naval Institute Press, 2012).

Kenneth P. Hansen, "Kingsmill's Cruisers: The Cruiser Tradition in the Early Royal Canadian Navy," *The Northern Mariner/Le marin du nord* 12, no. 1 (January 2003): 37–52, tnm.journals.yorku.ca/index.php/default/article/view/553/529.

William Johnston et al. "The Naval Debates, 1909–1914," in *The Seabound Coast: The Official History of the Royal Canadian Navy, 1867–1939*, vol. 1 (Dundurn, 2010).

Mark Tunnicliffe, "The Fleet We Never Had," *Canadian Naval Review* 2, no. 2 (Summer 2006): 31–32.

HMCS *Margaret* in 1915
Completed in 1914 | Built by Woolton Works, Southampton
03 February 1915–03 April 1919
Dimensions: 62.7 m (205.7 ft) x 9.9 m (32.5 ft) x 3.4 m (11.2 ft)
Displacement: 756 tons | Speed: 15.5 kt | Crew: 36
Armament: 6-pdr (2 x I)

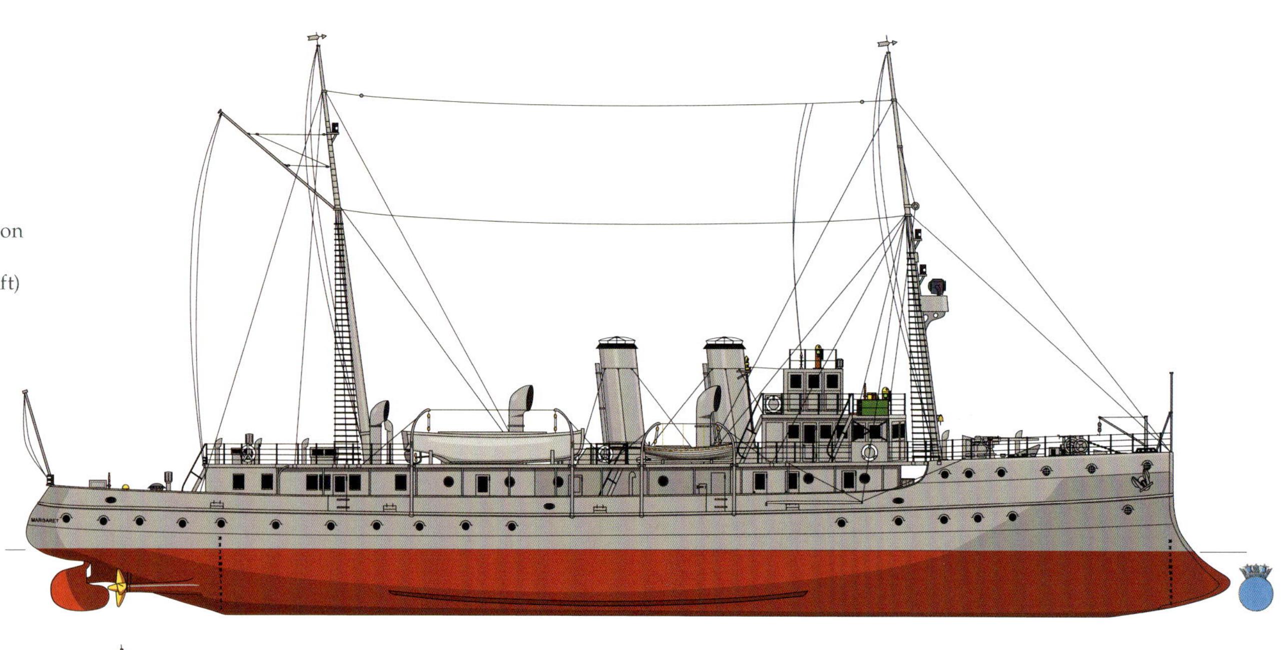

HMCS *Galiano* in 1918
Completed in 1913 | Built by Dublin Dockyard Co., Dublin
15 September 1917–30 October 1918
Dimensions: 49.5 m (162.4 ft) x 8.1 m (26.6 ft) x 3.8 m (12.5 ft)
Displacement: 393 tons | Speed: 11 kt | Crew: 39
Armament: 6-pdr (1 x I)

HMCS *Acadia* (I) in 1917
(ex CSS *Acadia*)
Launched 08 May 1913 | Built by Swan, Hunter & Wigham, Newcastle
16 January 1917–March 1919
02 October 1939–03 November 1945
Dimensions: 55.4 m (181.8 ft) x 10.2 m (33.5 ft) x 5.8 m (19 ft)
Displacement: 1,067 tons | Speed: 12.5 kt | Crew: 59
Armament: 4-in (1 x I)

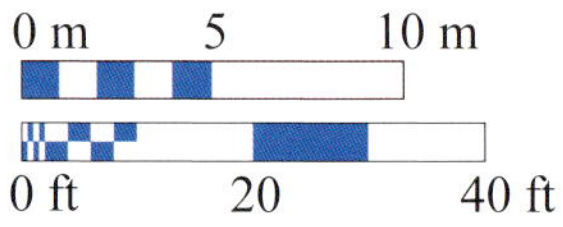

3

OTHER GOVERNMENT SHIPS OF THE FIRST WORLD WAR

In the years leading up to the Great War, while Borden's government allowed the Naval Service to languish, it did go to some lengths to improve the capabilities of the associated civil Marine and Fisheries Department as well as the Customs Service through an aggressive acquisition of modern vessels. Additionally, the *Naval Service Act* had transferred control of the Fisheries Protection, Hydrographic, Tidal and Current, and Wireless Telegraph Services to the Navy, and Kingsmill saw to their inclusion in the War Book for mobilization planning. Over the summers of 1912 and 1913, several of these vessels participated in exercises for the defence of Halifax Harbour, specifically *Canada* as a mini-destroyer, following her major refit (see Chapter 1), and also the smaller *Curlew* and *Petrel*, fitted out for minesweeping. Upon declaration of war in August 1914, many of these ships were transferred to the RCN, providing an immediate if modest augmentation to *Niobe* and *Rainbow* on their respective coasts.

Having generally been acquired individually for specific purposes, and as such having different specifications and dates of acquisition, they cannot be considered as a distinct "class" other than for our purposes of general discussion. A table is produced below with the full list of the ships with their pertinent specifications and naval employment, but only the more significant will be examined to illustrate their range of activities. With the FPS having been operated as a quasi-naval

Ship	Built	Specifications	RCN Service
Acadia	Swan, Hunter Newcastle, U.K., 1913	1,067 tons | 12.5 kts 1 × 4-inch, 1 × 12-pdr	Hydrographic survey, East Coast patrols and training
Canada	Vickers, Armstrong Barrow, U.K., 1904	557 tons | 14 kts 2 × 12-pdr, 2 × 3-pdr	FPS cruiser; see separate chapter
Cartier (*Charny*)	Swan, Hunter Newcastle, U.K., 1910	556 tons | 12 kts 3 × 12-pdr	Hydrographic survey, East Coast patrol; recommissioned Second World War as *Charny*
Constance, Curlew, Petrel	Polson Iron Works Toronto, Canada, 1891–92	185 tons | 10 kts 3 × light machine guns	FPS cruisers, East Coast mine-sweeping and patrol duties
Galiano, Malaspina	Dublin Dockyard Dublin, Ireland, 1913	393 tons | 11 kts 1 × 6-pdr	FPS cruisers, West Coast patrols
Gulnare	C. Connel Glasgow, U.K., 1893	262 tons | 10 kts No armament	FPS cruiser, East Coast patrols
Lady Evelyn	Tranmere, U.K., 1901	483 tons | 9 kts No armament	Mail ship, East Coast patrols
Margaret	Woolton Works Southampton, U.K., 1914	756 tons | 15.5 kts 2 × 6-pdr	Customs patrol cruiser, St. Lawrence patrols
Newington	Cook, Welton & Gremmell Hull, U.K., 1899	193 tons | u/k No armament	Lighthouse tender, West Coast Inside Passage minelayer and patrols
Restless	New Westminster, Canada u/k	76 tons | u/k No armament	Customs patrol ship, West Coast patrols and RNCC training

force since the 1890s, and with the recent experience of *Canada*, that transition was relatively smooth. Notably, there was some ambiguity as to the status of these other government ships — at first they remained under the command of, and were crewed by, their original officers and men and were identified in *The Canadian Navy List* as "Canadian Naval Auxiliaries," but certain of them, such as *Canada*, had long had Royal Naval Reserve officers in command. Then, through 1915 to 1916, as trained naval officers and ratings became available to fill out their complements, they came to be designated as HMC Ships.

Perhaps best known is the *Acadia*, which has the distinction of being preserved at the Maritime Museum of the Atlantic in Halifax, Nova Scotia (see image on page 67 in Chapter 11, "Corvettes: Flowers and Castles," where she is pictured co-located with HMCS *Sackville*). Built in 1913 specifically to survey Canada's northern waters, she was so engaged at the onset of the war and did not commission into the RCN until early 1917, when the German U-boat campaign required the expansion of inshore antisubmarine patrols off the East Coast. Reverting to the Hydrographic Survey in 1919, *Acadia* was recommissioned in October 1939 for service in the Second World War as a training ship but occasionally patrolled the approaches to Halifax Harbour. Paid off again in November 1945, she returned to hydrographic duties until disposal in 1969 to her present status.

Galiano and *Malaspina* were a pair of fisheries ships acquired in 1913 for the British Columbia coast (and hence having the same specifications). With their limited warfighting capabilities, and the quick reduction of any German threat on the Pacific, they alternated between civil and naval duties and had rather uneventful wars. Still, each is notable in a different fashion. *Galiano* has the distinction of being the only HMC Ship lost in the First World War, foundering in a gale while on patrol in Queen Charlotte Sound and sunk with all hands on October 30, 1918 (just a fortnight before the Armistice). *Malaspina*, like *Acadia*, was recommissioned in September 1939 for patrol and examination duties before being allocated as

RCN antisubmarine vessels at Halifax, probably mid-1918: (from left) *CD 16*, *CD 22*, Battle-class trawler *Givenchy*, and hydrographic survey vessel *Cartier*.

a training vessel to the RCN Naval College HMCS *Royal Roads*, from which she was paid off on March 31, 1945, and broken up the following year.

The most formidable of these various ships was the *Margaret*, built specifically for the Customs Preventive Service on the St. Lawrence River and Gulf. Newly delivered in summer 1914, she was taken up by the RCN soon after arrival in Canada and fitted with a pair of 6-pounder guns to continue patrol work in those waters. A fixture of the Navy's Gulf flotilla, her exploits, although uneventful, are described at length in the official history, *The Seabound Coast*. After the end of the war, she was returned to the Customs Service in February 1919.

FURTHER READING

Ken Macpherson and Ron Barrie, *The Ships of Canada's Naval Forces, 1910–2001*, 3rd ed. (Vanwell Publishing, 2002).

Charles D. Maginley and Bernard Collin, *The Ships of Canada's Marine Services* (Vanwell Publishing, 2001).

Roger Sarty, "The Army Origin of the Royal Canadian Navy: Canada's Naval Defences, 1855–1918," *The Northern Mariner/Le marin du nord* 30, no. 4 (Winter 2020): 341–78, tnm.journals.yorku.ca/index.php/default/article/view/41/92.

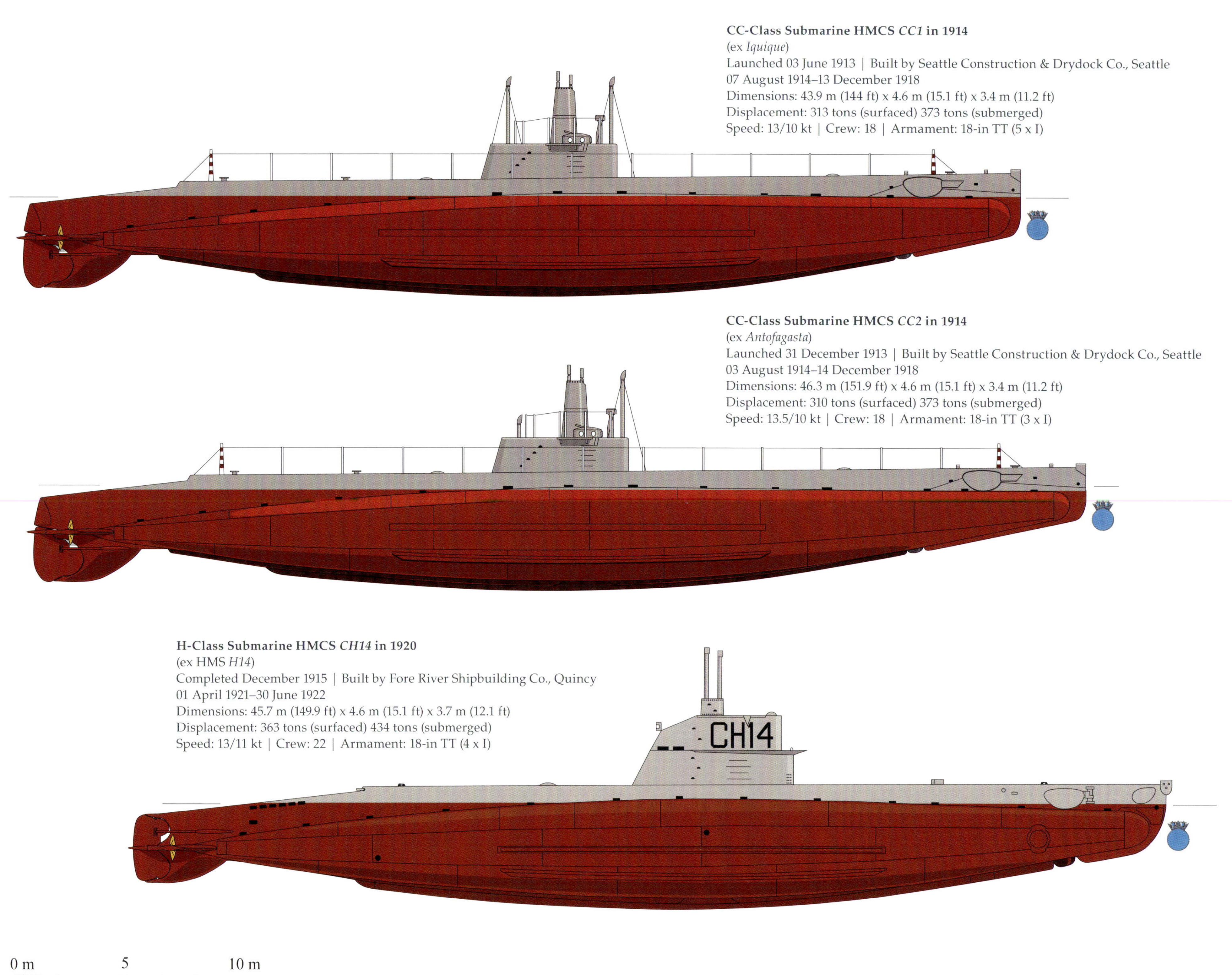

CC-Class Submarine HMCS *CC1* in 1914
(ex *Iquique*)
Launched 03 June 1913 | Built by Seattle Construction & Drydock Co., Seattle
07 August 1914–13 December 1918
Dimensions: 43.9 m (144 ft) x 4.6 m (15.1 ft) x 3.4 m (11.2 ft)
Displacement: 313 tons (surfaced) 373 tons (submerged)
Speed: 13/10 kt | Crew: 18 | Armament: 18-in TT (5 x I)

CC-Class Submarine HMCS *CC2* in 1914
(ex *Antofagasta*)
Launched 31 December 1913 | Built by Seattle Construction & Drydock Co., Seattle
03 August 1914–14 December 1918
Dimensions: 46.3 m (151.9 ft) x 4.6 m (15.1 ft) x 3.4 m (11.2 ft)
Displacement: 310 tons (surfaced) 373 tons (submerged)
Speed: 13.5/10 kt | Crew: 18 | Armament: 18-in TT (3 x I)

H-Class Submarine HMCS *CH14* in 1920
(ex HMS *H14*)
Completed December 1915 | Built by Fore River Shipbuilding Co., Quincy
01 April 1921–30 June 1922
Dimensions: 45.7 m (149.9 ft) x 4.6 m (15.1 ft) x 3.7 m (12.1 ft)
Displacement: 363 tons (surfaced) 434 tons (submerged)
Speed: 13/11 kt | Crew: 22 | Armament: 18-in TT (4 x I)

4

SUBMARINES OF THE FIRST WORLD WAR: *CC 1* AND *CC 2*, AND *CH 14* AND *CH 15*

One of the strangest episodes in Canadian naval history was the impromptu acquisition of a pair of submarines by the province of British Columbia at the onset of the Great War. As a lightly defended backwater of the British Empire, Canada's West Coast had always felt vulnerable to attack by a foreign raider, a sense heightened with the RN's closure in 1904 of the Esquimalt Dockyard as the base for the Pacific Squadron, and only slightly relieved by the arrival of *Rainbow* in 1910. Late in July 1914, when it appeared war was coming and *Rainbow* would be dispatched for patrols on the high seas, leaving the port undefended, the citizens of Victoria took matters into their own hands.

The story, replete with cloak-and-dagger elements, is fully told in the official history, *The Seabound Coast*, and Julie Ferguson's more popular (but still reliable) *Through a Canadian Periscope*, and so will be summarized here. Premier Richard McBride, as a keen follower of naval developments for many years, understood that an effective harbour defence included torpedo-boat destroyers and submarines, and he made arrangements with a Seattle shipbuilder to procure a pair of submarines that had just completed construction for the Chilean navy. Effecting a clandestine departure from American waters before U.S. President Woodrow Wilson could proclaim a declaration of neutrality that would make the submarines' sale illegal, they arrived in Esquimalt on the morning of

The submarines *CC 1* and *CC 2* alongside their tender, the former RN sloop HMCS *Shearwater*, which accompanied them on the transfer through the Panama Canal to Halifax in 1917.

August 5. The purchase was approved by federal Order in Council on August 7, and the RCN had its first "boats" (as submarines are known colloquially).

Built for the Chileans as *Iquique* and *Antofagasta*, they generally resembled the British C-class submarines and hence were commissioned into the RCN as *CC 1* and *CC 2* (for "Canadian C-class submarine"). There were, in fact, differences between the two, the most significant being that *CC 1* had five 18-inch torpedo tubes, four forward and one aft, while *CC 2* had only two tubes forward and one in the stern, and somehow this made the latter 8 feet (3.6 m) longer than her sister. It also turned out that they were available because the Chileans had refused to accept them owing to construction faults; it took some time to make these good, but this also allowed time to assemble and train Canadian crews for them. In due course (the date cannot be determined for certain), by the spring of 1915, they were conducting patrols of the Strait of Juan de Fuca, although by that time the German threat had diminished.

In spring 1917, they were ordered to Halifax, intended for service in European waters. Accompanied en route by their mother ship, the former RN sloop HMCS *Shearwater*, they became the first warships under the White Ensign to transit the Panama Canal (which had opened in 1914, and the no-longer neutral United States now allowed transit by Allied warships). The wear of the passage, however, made them unsuitable for a further transatlantic crossing, so they remained in Halifax for training other submariners and as practice "targets" for surface ships. Surviving the Halifax Explosion unscathed, they were put in reserve at the end of the war and sold for scrap in 1920.

Given the checkered employment of the CC boats, engineer-historian John Knox relates the great irony that their initial acquisition had inspired the RN to contract Canadian Vickers Ltd. to build several H-class submarines in Montreal in the fall of 1914. The shipyard had been established in the expectation it would be a major builder of Laurier's proposed 1911 fleet, which had not included submarines, on the thinking that such vessels would be too complex for a Dominion building program. However, with British shipyards now being too busy with other orders, beginning in January 1915, Canadian Vickers eventually assembled twenty-four of the type under the direction of the American Electric Boat Co. of Groton, Connecticut, fitting American machinery and equipment into Canadian manufactured hulls. Fitted with four 18-inch torpedo tubes in the bow and being mechanically reliable, the type proved successful — fifty-two in total entered service and saw good operational employment in European waters.

Ten of the type had also begun construction in 1915 at the Fore River Shipyard in Quincy, Massachusetts, in the then-neutral United States, but soon were impounded until after the U.S. entered the war in April 1917. Two of these were en route to Britain as hostilities ended and were rerouted to Halifax for presentation to the RCN in February 1919. They lay alongside there, unused, until being commissioned on April 1, 1921, as *CH 14* and *CH 15*. They made a series of port visits around the Maritimes and sailed to Bermuda for exercises over the winter of 1921–22 but were paid off on June 20, 1922, owing to budget cuts, and sold for scrap in 1927.

FURTHER READING

Julie Ferguson, *Through a Canadian Periscope: The Story of the Canadian Submarine Service*, 2nd ed. (Dundurn, 2014).

JHW Knox, "An Engineer's Outline of RCN History: Part 1 (1910–1968)," in *The RCN in Retrospect, 1910–1968*, ed. James Boutilier (UBC Press, 1982) 100–101.

J.D. Perkins, "The Canadian-Built British H-boats," last modified July 12, 1999, gwpda.org/naval/cdnhboat.htm.

Starr J. Sinton, "British Columbia's Submarine Fleet," 2025, navalandmilitarymuseum.org/archives/articles/defending-the-coast/cc1-and-cc2/.

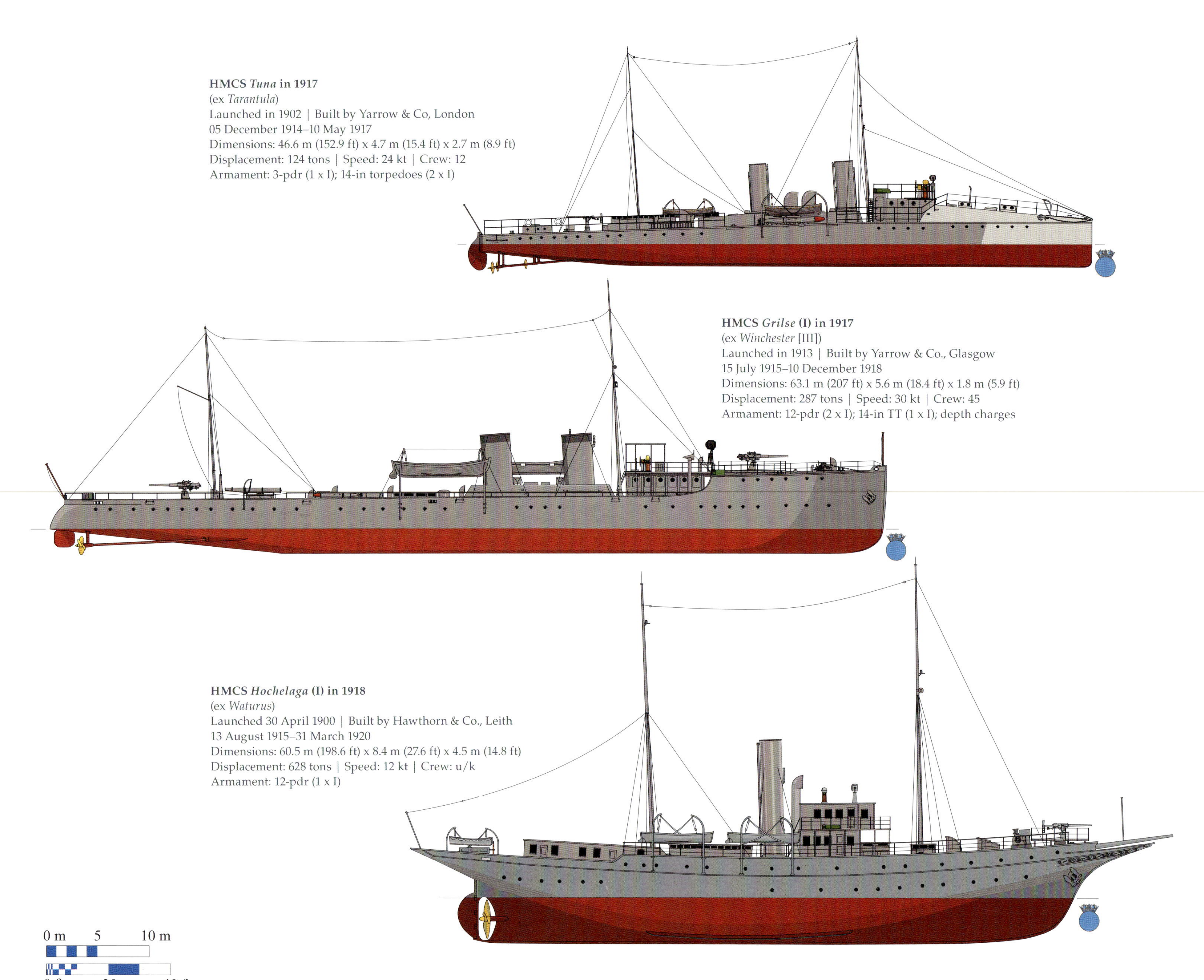
HMCS *Tuna* in 1917
(ex *Tarantula*)
Launched in 1902 | Built by Yarrow & Co, London
05 December 1914–10 May 1917
Dimensions: 46.6 m (152.9 ft) x 4.7 m (15.4 ft) x 2.7 m (8.9 ft)
Displacement: 124 tons | Speed: 24 kt | Crew: 12
Armament: 3-pdr (1 x I); 14-in torpedoes (2 x I)
HMCS *Grilse* (I) in 1917
(ex *Winchester* [III])
Launched in 1913 | Built by Yarrow & Co., Glasgow
15 July 1915–10 December 1918
Dimensions: 63.1 m (207 ft) x 5.6 m (18.4 ft) x 1.8 m (5.9 ft)
Displacement: 287 tons | Speed: 30 kt | Crew: 45
Armament: 12-pdr (2 x I); 14-in TT (1 x I); depth charges
HMCS *Hochelaga* (I) in 1918
(ex *Waturus*)
Launched 30 April 1900 | Built by Hawthorn & Co., Leith
13 August 1915–31 March 1920
Dimensions: 60.5 m (198.6 ft) x 8.4 m (27.6 ft) x 4.5 m (14.8 ft)
Displacement: 628 tons | Speed: 12 kt | Crew: u/k
Armament: 12-pdr (1 x I)
0 m
5
10 m
0 ft
20
40 ft

5

ARMED YACHTS OF THE FIRST WORLD WAR

In the absence of a coherent naval policy that would have allowed a Canadian shipbuilding program to provide the RCN with a fleet of proper warships to meet the demands of the war that erupted in the late summer of 1914, the Navy instead had to make do with (in the words of historian Ken Macpherson) a "motley assortment" of vessels taken up from a variety of other sources to fashion the semblance of a fleet.[6] Thus it came about that, in seeking vessels suitable for patrol service to supplement the other government ships pressed into service, the RCN became a yacht club in fact and not just in scornful name. The rationale was founded on the then-commonly understood principle that well-maintained civilian vessels could be suitable for conversion into naval auxiliaries. The RCN eventually acquired five privately owned yachts of assorted backgrounds and capabilities, each with an interesting tale illustrative of the Navy's challenges (a table listing the vessels in order of acquisition follows the discussion below). Only one was Canadian in origin, the remainder being procured surreptitiously by Canadian entrepreneurs from American owners to circumvent the U.S. neutrality proclamation.

That modus operandi was established with the very first vessel so acquired. Soon after hostilities broke out, early in August 1914, Canadian philanthropist JKL Ross, a captain in the militia deemed medically unfit for the Canadian Expeditionary Force, went to New York to buy the steam yacht *Tarantula* for presentation to the RCN, with the objective that he would then command the ship. *Tarantula* had been built in 1902 for American millionaire W.K. Vanderbilt, patterned after the British experimental

A contemporary colourized postcard of the armed yacht *Tuna.*

warship *Turbinia*, just recently launched by Yarrow as the first oil-fired, turbine-powered torpedo-boat destroyer for the RN. Successful in his mission, Ross delivered the ship to Halifax on September 10, 1914, and indeed was given command when she commissioned into the RCN on December 5. Renamed *Tuna*, in the words of the official history, "In an effort to make it more difficult for the Americans to trace the ship,"[7] her conversion was relatively simple, given her original construction intent, which primarily involved the fitting of a 3-pounder gun on the quarterdeck and a pair of 14-inch torpedoes that were slung from the sides. Because of her small tonnage, she was unsuitable for open-ocean work and instead was employed mostly for defence of the approaches to Halifax Harbour and other inshore work. After suffering an irreparable engine mount fracture, *Tuna* was paid off on May 10, 1917, and stripped for salvage. Her fate is unknown, although she reportedly remained as a hulk in Halifax's Northwest Arm into the 1930s.

Flushed with the successful circumvention of the American neutrality embargo, and with no good candidate vessels to be found in Canada, the RCN dispatched Ross to return to New York in June 1915 to purchase another turbine yacht. *Winchester* had been built more recently, in 1912, in Yarrow's new yard in Glasgow, and also along the lines of a naval torpedo boat, for the millionaire Charles Rouss to commute along the Hudson River. After arrival in Halifax, she was sent to Vickers in Montreal for conversion, with the addition of a pair of 12-pounder guns and a single torpedo tube. Renamed *Grilse*, she was commissioned into the RCN, again under the command of Jack Ross, on July 15, 1915. Double the size of *Tuna*, *Grilse* had much more interesting operational employment. Coming into service coincident with the laying up of the cruiser *Niobe*, she became the most powerful Canadian warship on the East Coast for the rest of the war. Loaned to the Gulf of St. Lawrence Patrol for the fall of 1915, but in expectation she would be unsuitable for winter patrol work in Canadian waters, she was sent to the Caribbean for the winter months. Repeating this pattern the next year, *Grilse* was again en route to Bermuda on December 12, 1916, when she was caught in a gale off Sable Island. Severely damaged and with six sailors lost overboard, she limped back into harbour for major repairs and did not re-enter service until spring 1917. With the rise of U-boat activity after that time, *Grilse* spent the rest of the war on antisubmarine patrol but never got positioned well enough to make an interception. Paid off on December 10, 1918, she was sold to an American millionaire for reconversion into a yacht (Solomon Guggenheim, as *Trillona*) and finally foundered in Long Island Sound in another nor'easter, the New England Hurricane of September 21, 1938.

The next pair to be acquired abroad were of the more conventionally understood yacht type, with a "clipper" bow form and coal-fired triple-expansion steam engines, supplemented with a sail plan that allowed for long-range patrols. Following the pattern established by Ross, in the summer of 1915, the RCN sent another naval enthusiast to seek suitable vessels in the United States. Aemilius Jarvis styled himself "Commodore," having skippered in every Canada's Cup yachting competition since its inauguration in 1896 through 1907, and after the war would become a fixture of the Navy League. The fruits of his labours were the *Walrus* and *Columbia*, acquired through the New York shipbroker Cox & Stevens. Renamed HMC Ships *Hochelaga* and *Stadacona*, respectively, they were commissioned into the RCN on August 13, 1915. Arming them with only a single 12-pounder gun forward was considered sufficient for their employment as East Coast Patrol vessels, which they continued for the duration of the war. Each of them, however, are remembered in a very different fashion. *Stadacona* became the depot flagship for the East Coast Patrol, commanded by now-Captain Walter Hose from August 14, 1916, and in 1919 accompanied the transfer of several Battle-class trawlers to the West Coast by way of the Panama Canal. Paid off on March 31, 1920, her subsequent civilian career included being a rum-runner during American Prohibition, but her name has lived on in the RCN as the East Coast shore establishment in Halifax.

In her turn, *Hochelaga* is notorious as the only HMC Ship to encounter the enemy during the Great War, only to refuse combat: On sighting the better-armed *U 156* on August 21, 1918, but without Marconi radio gear fitted, her captain turned away to seek reinforcements, for which he was court-martialled and dismissed in disgrace from the service. Perhaps in an effort to redeem her reputation and serving the purpose for which she originally had been built, in July 1919, she embarked a delegation consisting of the Prince of Wales (the later King Edward VIII), Governor General the Duke of Devonshire, and Admiral Kingsmill for a voyage along the St. Lawrence and Saguenay Rivers. Paid off on October 30, 1920, and sold for civilian use, her subsequent career ended when she was seized off Haifa in 1946 during an unsuccessful attempt to run Jewish Holocaust survivors into Palestine. She was impounded in Cyprus, fate unknown. Her name was later revived in RCN service as that of the naval supply depot near Montreal, 1955–66.

Ship	Built	Specifications	Commissioned/RCN Service
Tuna (ex-*Tarantula*)	Yarrow & Co. London Yard, U.K., 1902	124 tons | 24 kts 1 × 3-pdr, 2 × 14-inch TT	Dec 5, 1914 | East Coast, Torpedo boat destroyer
Grilse (ex-*Winchester*)	Yarrow & Co. Glasgow, U.K., 1912	287 tons | 30 kts 2 × 12-pdr, 1 × 14-inch TT	July 15, 1915 | East Coast, Torpedo boat destroyer
Hochelaga (ex-*Walrus*)	Hawthorn & Co. Leith, U.K., 1900	628 tons | 12 kts 1 × 12-pdr	Aug 13, 1915 | East Coast, Patrols
Stadacona (ex-*Columbia*)	Crescent Shipyards Elizabeth, NJ, 1899	682 tons | 12 kts 1 × 4-inch	Aug 13, 1915 | East Coast, Patrols
Florence (ex-*Emeline*)	Crescent Shipyards Elizabeth, NJ, 1903	257 tons | 12 kts 1 × 3-pdr	July 19, 1915 | East Coast, Patrols

The final yacht taken on by the RCN in the Great War was the only one to come directly from an original Canadian owner, although she also was an American-built vessel, from the same shipyard that had produced *Columbia* (*Stadacona*). In the summer of 1915, John Eaton also presented his *Emeline* to the Navy, which renamed her *Florence*, for employment on East Coast patrols. But

The armed yacht *Hochelaga*.

she proved unseaworthy in heavy weather, and after a brief spell as guard-ship in Saint John, New Brunswick, she was paid off in September 1916, sold to a trading company in Martinique, and lost in the Caribbean Sea the following year.

FURTHER READING

Keith Calow, "Rough Justice: The Court Martial of Lieutenant Robert Douglas Legate," *The Northern Mariner* 15, no. 4 (October 2005): 1–17, cnrs-scrn.org /northern_mariner/vol15/tnm_15_4_1-17.pdf.

S.D. Campbell, "Prologue: HMCS *Grilse*," in *Tin-Can Canucks: A Century of Canadian Destroyers* (Kay Cee Publications, 2017), 8–13.

Fraser McKee, *The Armed Yachts of Canada* (Boston Mills Press, 1983).

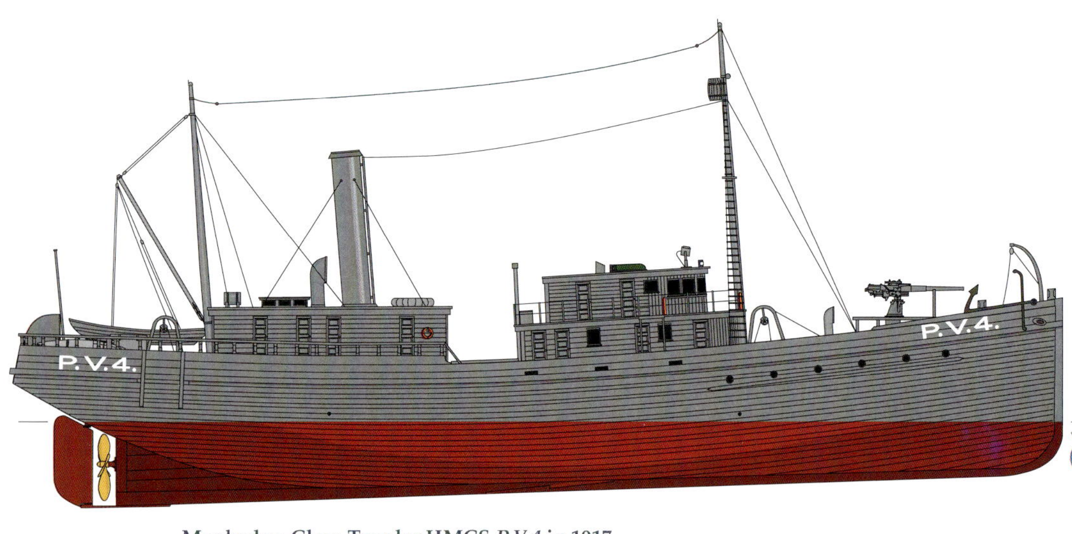

Menhaden-Class Trawler HMCS *P.V.4* in 1917
(ex *Martin J. Marran*)
Launched in 1911 | Built by Cobb, Butler & Co., Rockland
March 1917–April 1919
Dimensions: 46.2 m (151.5 ft) x 7.3 m (24.1 ft) x 2.8 m (18.8 ft)
Displacement: 323 tons | Speed: 8 kt | Crew: u/k
Armament: 12-pdr (1 x I)

TR-Class Trawler HMCS *TR 9* in 1918
Completed 16 May 1918 | Built by Collingwood Shipbuilding Ltd., Collingwood
16 May 1918–February 1919
Dimensions: 40.9 m (134.2 ft) x 7.2 m (23.6 ft) x 4.1 m (13.5 ft)
Displacement: 360 tons | Speed: 10 kt | Crew: 10
Armament: 12-pdr (1 x I)

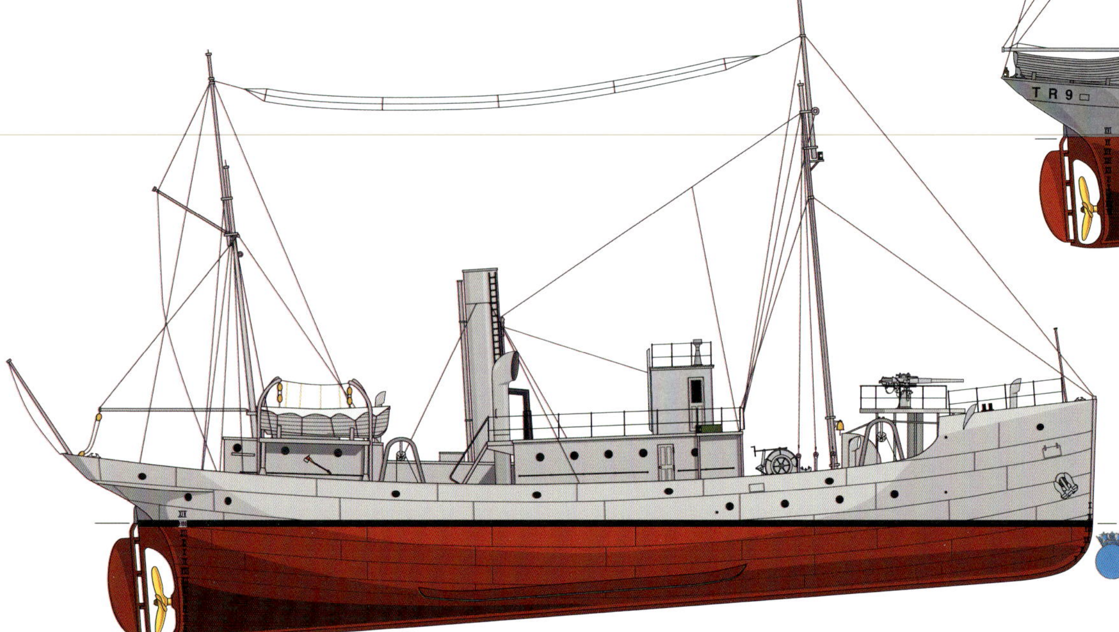

Battle-Class Trawler HMCS *St. Julien* in 1917
Launched 06 June 1917 | Built by Polson Iron Works Ltd., Toronto
13 November 1917–1920
Dimensions: 45.1 m (148 ft) x 7.2 m (23.6 ft) x 4.1 m (13.5 ft)
Displacement: 320 tons | Speed: 10 kt | Crew: 17
Armament: 12-pdr (1 x I)

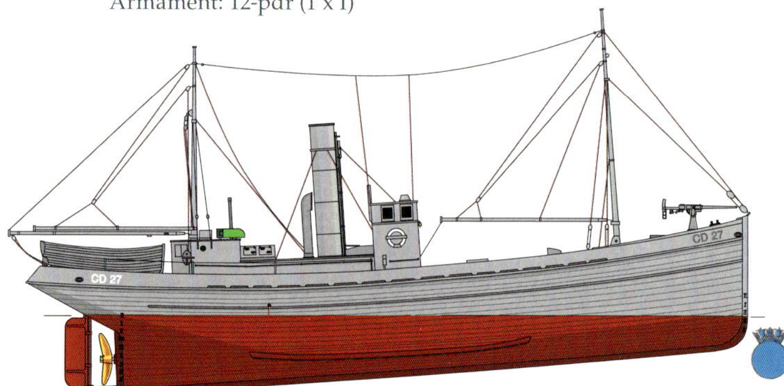

CD-Class Drifter HMCS *CD 27* in 1918
Completed 19 November 1917 | Built by Davie Shipbuilding Co. Ltd., Lauzon
19 November 1917–February 1919
Dimensions: 28.7 m (94.2 ft) x 6.1 m (20 ft) x 3.1 m (10.2 ft)
Displacement: 99 tons | Speed: 9 kt | Crew: 15
Armament: 6-pdr (1 x I)

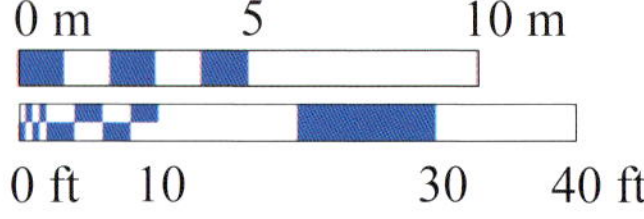

6

TRAWLERS, DRIFTERS, AND THE BATTLE CLASS

The documentary evidence as to the precise origins of the Battle-class trawlers has been lost to time, which is unfortunate, given the distinction of these vessels as the first warship construction program to be undertaken in Canadian yards for the RCN. What is known is that on February 8, 1917, the Borden government signed Order in Council PC 339, authorizing the building of twelve steel-hulled "North Sea trawlers" that would become known as the Battle class. In a clearly related but separate move just two days later, on February 10, the government appointed a Director of Ship Construction to oversee the large-scale assembly for the RN of minor warship trawler (TR) and drifter (CD) types that were similarly within the production capacity of the then-modest Canadian shipbuilding industry.

The context for this sudden burst of construction activity was the appreciation, in the fall of 1916 — following the failed Somme offensive — that the continuing stalemate on the Western Front promised a lasting war, and an expanded German U-boat campaign was anticipated to reach into Canadian waters in the summer of 1917. With reinforcements from the RN not available, it appears that over the winter of 1916–17, Kingsmill was finally able to convince the Borden government to begin a modest domestic warship-building program. At the same time, the British Admiralty was undertaking its own expansion of antisubmarine vessels. Before May 1917, when it finally implemented convoys as the primary defence against U-boats, the belief had been that the threat could be managed by "mass" — that is, the sheer volume of Allied warships in a patrol area would keep the enemy at bay. The corollary was that the vessels did not have to be especially large or well armed to accomplish the goal; rather, their mere presence would be sufficient deterrence (and being small in tonnage and crew, frankly, could be considered expendable). The Admiralty had begun by requisitioning and arming the trawlers of the British fishing fleet; by the fall of 1916, not only was this clearly not sufficient to accomplish the objective, but the redirection of those vessels from their primary occupation had caused the British fishing catch to decline considerably. Changing tack, the Admiralty now directed small British yards not capable of building complex major warships to undertake a large-scale trawler-building program that was within their technical capacity. Known as the Castle-class trawlers, of the 500 vessels ordered, some 280 would be completed by war's end.

It was to supplement this program that the Admiralty contracted Canadian yards to build thirty-six steam steel-hulled trawlers and one hundred wooden drifters, with the intention that they would be given over for employment by the RCN in the anticipated summer U-boat campaign. The trawlers were to be the same 285-tons displacement as the Castle class assigned to the British yards, armed with a single 12-pounder gun. Whereas the RN named each vessel, in Canada they were designated simply as "TR"; the order was subsequently increased in January 1918 from thirty-six to sixty, with the full class of vessels designated *TR 1* through *TR 60*. (As an indication of the Empire-wide scale of the project, another nine were built in India, although not completed until after war's end; in 1940, New Zealand built thirteen for domestic operations, choosing that design over modern alternatives for its simplicity of construction.) The TRs were built in yards along the St. Lawrence and on the Great Lakes, with the first coming off the slips in the spring of 1917. Fitting out for active service, however, was delayed by the entry of the United States into the war in April 1917 — otherwise a welcome addition to the Allied war effort, this resulted in a drain of skilled workers from Canada for higher-wage employment in the U.S., along with delays in acquisition of equipment required there. The last vessels produced were still being fitted out when the war ended. Seeing limited service owing to their late arrival, they all were sold off to the civilian fishing fleet without difficulty. Some were taken up in the Second World War by the RN as auxiliary minesweepers, and indeed two were engaged by the RCN as examination vessels in Halifax, finally getting proper names for the role: *Andrée Dupré* and *Macsin* (see Chapter 12).

The "drifters" were another type of fishing vessel, smaller than a traditional trawler, whose method of taking their catch by hauling drift nets was adapted by the RN to snag submerged submarines (there is no record of this having been accomplished, but it surely would have given U-boat commanders pause). Being of simpler wooden-hull construction and armed with a smaller 6-pounder gun, the one hundred vessels of this type were all quickly produced in Quebec yards along the St. Lawrence River and launched in the spring and summer of 1917. Again, the actual number entering service is difficult to determine, as the critical factor by then was

Esquimalt Harbour 1920: The Battle-class trawler *Thiepval* (right) and the armed yacht *Stadacona* astern constitute the bulk of the West Coast fleet; in the foreground is the two-masted schooner *Naden*, tender to the shore establishment.

to find sailors who were not required elsewhere to crew them; the generally agreed figure is fifty-three, some of which were fitted out for minesweeping and ranged as far as Bermuda, Gibraltar, and West Africa; eighteen were loaned to the United States.[8] An unknown number of these had the first recorded use of a green and black maple leaf affixed to the funnel to distinguish them overseas as Canadian vessels.

Meanwhile, to meet the immediate need, through the late winter of 1917, seven New England–built trawlers were acquired to form a minesweeping and patrol flotilla operating out of Sydney, Nova Scotia. Built before the war to roughly the same pattern, these small wooden vessels ranged in size from about 200 tons to nearly double that (390 tons) and, as they were considered auxiliaries like the TRs and CDs, were designated simply as "P.V."s (patrol vessels), although generally numbered with Roman numerals instead of Hindu-Arabic (and the naming convention curiously retaining the periods; the only known exception to this practice was the *P.V. 4*, pictured in the profile plate on page 32). Like the TRs, they were armed with a single 12-pounder gun, the smallest-sized weapon deemed capable of taking on a surfaced U-boat (the CDs could mount only a 6-pounder, as they were too lightly built for the heavier gun). Although performing able service, they never encountered an enemy and after the war were returned to their previous occupations.

Concurrent with but separate from the Admiralty orders for trawlers and drifters was the Borden government's determination to meet the U-boat challenge by building its own class of twelve steel-hulled vessels for patrol work by the RCN. The approved design was for a Mersey-class trawler similar to but slightly larger than the Castle-class TRs: At 148-feet (45 m) length overall versus the 134-feet (41 m) long Castle class, the primary visual distinction of the Battle class was the much larger midships "house" for a better enclosed bridge and crew accommodation spaces (once again, the origin of this design development is not known). Important further additions were that the entire Battle class was fitted with electrical lighting instead of the acetylene lamps standard in the TRs and also with hydrophones (an early form of Anti-Submarine Detection Investigation Committee [ASDIC], or sonar) for antisubmarine work. In the end, they were produced in two subtypes: The six contracted to Vickers in Montreal (of which two were

Class	#	Built	Specifications	Remarks
P.V. I–VII (Patrol vessels)	7	1903–12, New England (var.)	205–390 tons | 8 kts 1 × 12-pdr	
TR 1-60 (Castle-class trawlers)	60	1917–18, Great Lakes & Quebec (var.)	285 tons | 10 kts 1 × 12-pdr	
CD 1-100 (Drifters)	100	1917, Quebec (var.)	99 tons | 9 kts 1 × 6-pdr	
Battle-class trawlers	12	Polson Iron Works (Toronto)	320 tons | 10 kts 1 × 12-pdr	*Festubert, Messines, St. Eloi, St. Julien, Vimy, Ypres*
		Canadian Vickers (Montreal)	357 tons	*Arleux, Arras, Armentières, Givenchy*
		Kingston Shipbuilding	357 tons	*Loos, Thiepval*

further subcontracted to Kingston Shipbuilding) were some 357 tons displacement, while the six awarded to Polson Iron Works in Toronto were slightly smaller, at 320 tons (the difference in tonnage coming from slight reductions to beam and draft and their being constructed of iron instead of steel, which was in short supply). All were armed with the ubiquitous 12-pounder. Probably to distinguish them as true "Canadian" warships, and to bolster the image of the RCN with the Canadian public, they were assigned actual names for notable battles fought by the Canadian Expeditionary Force on the Western Front in France and Belgium (see table above). The hulls were completed by the summer of 1917, but fitting out was again delayed by the worker and equipment shortages arising from the U.S. entry into the war, so the Toronto-built ships did not commission until November 13, 1917 (all six on the same date). The first two Vickers-built commissioned only on June 5, 1918, and the remaining four on August 1, 1918. They did not assemble as a full class to join the East Coast Patrol until late August 1918, just in time to make their first patrols before the Armistice ended the war three months later.

Early in 1919, three of them (*Armentières*, *Givenchy*, and *Thiepval*) were transferred to the West Coast through the Panama Canal, accompanied by HMCS *Stadacona*. With the budget cuts of 1923, only *Festubert* and *Ypres* on the East Coast and *Armentières* and *Thiepval* on the West were kept on by the RCN as training vessels for the newly established Royal Canadian Naval Volunteer Reserve (RCNVR). The remainder were transferred to the Department of Marine and Fisheries for use as buoy tenders and lightships. Eight of the class were reacquired for service during the Second World War, most memorably *Givenchy* as the depot ship in Esquimalt, and *Ypres* as a gate vessel for Halifax Harbour — only for her to be rammed and sunk accidentally by the battleship HMS *Revenge* on May 12, 1940, the first RCN ship lost in the war. *Thiepval* had the most storied adventures, undertaking an epic trans-Pacific voyage in 1923 to Japan and the Soviet Union in support of a British round-the-world flight (ultimately unsuccessful; *Thiepval* ferried the aircraft wreck back to Canada). Later, while on a life-saving patrol in Barkley Sound on February 27, 1930, she struck a rock and sank in Thiepval Channel, which was thus named for her. Her 12-pounder was recovered and is on display in Ucluelet, British Columbia, while the wreck remains a popular attraction for sport divers.

The Battle-class trawler *Thiepval* returning from her epic 1923 trans-Pacific cruise, with the recovered British aircraft stowed on board.

FURTHER READING

F.J. Dittmar and J.J. Colledge, *British Warships, 1914–1919* (Ian Allan, 1972), 170–72 and 224–26.

Steve R. Dunn, ed., *British Naval Trawlers and Drifters in Two World Wars: From the John Lambert Collection* (Seaforth, 2021).

Daniel G. Harris, "Canadian Warship Construction 1917–19: The Great Lakes and Upper St. Lawrence River Areas," *The Mariner's Mirror* 75, no. 2 (1989): 149–58.

Roger Litwiller, "The Canadian Maple Leaf — A RCN Tradition Honouring Our Sailors Past," December 9, 2018, rogerlitwiller.com/2018/12/09/the-canadian-maple-leaf-a-rcn-tradition-since-wwii/.

Duncan McDowall, "HMCS *Thiepval*: The Accidental Tourist Destination," *Canadian Military History* 9, no. 3 (2000): 69–78, scholars.wlu.ca/cgi/viewcontent.cgi?article=1295&context=cmh.

Michael B. Moir, "Admiralty Orders for Canadian Shipyards: Trawlers, Drifters, and the Urgency of Coastal Defence During the Great War," *The Northern Mariner* 26, no. 3 (July 2016): 275–96, tnm.journals.yorku.ca/index.php/default/article/view/232.

Roger Sarty, "Hard Luck Flotilla: The RCN's Atlantic Coast Patrol, 1914–18," in *RCN in Transition, 1910–1985*, ed. WAB Douglas (UBC Press, 1988), 103–25.

Joseph Skentelbery, "Trawler and Drifter Construction in Canada for British Government, Through the Canadian Naval Service Department," *Canadian Railway and Marine World* (February 1919): 89–95.

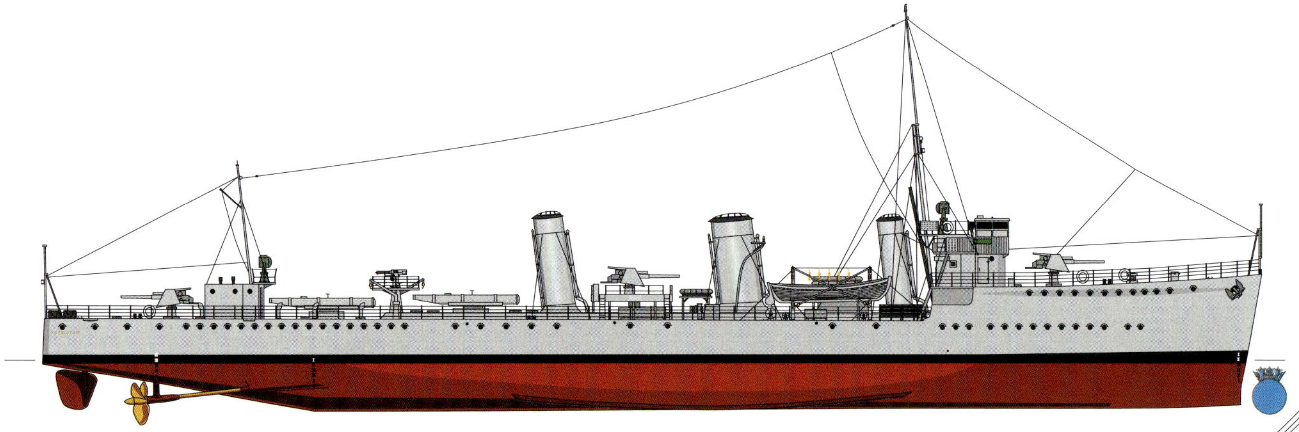

M-Class Destroyer HMCS *Patrician* in 1926
(ex HMS *Patrician*)
Launched 05 June 1916 | Built by Thornycroft, Southampton
01 November 1920–01 January 1928
Dimensions: 83.5 m (274 ft) x 8.4 m (27.6 ft) x 3.2 m (10.5 ft)
Displacement: 1,004 tons | Speed: 36 kt | Crew: 82
Armament: 4-in (3 x I); 2-pdr (1 x I); 21-in TT (2 x II); depth charges

Arethusa-Class Cruiser HMCS *Aurora* in 1921
(ex HMS *Aurora*)
Launched 30 September 1913 | Built by HM Dockyard, Devonport
01 November 1920–09 July 1922
Dimensions: 132.9 m (436 ft) x 11.9 m (39 ft) x 4.7 m (15.4 ft)
Displacement: 3,512 tons | Speed: 29 kt | Crew: 318
Armament: 6-in (2 x I); 4-in (6 x I); 3-in (1 x I); 21-in TT (4 x II)

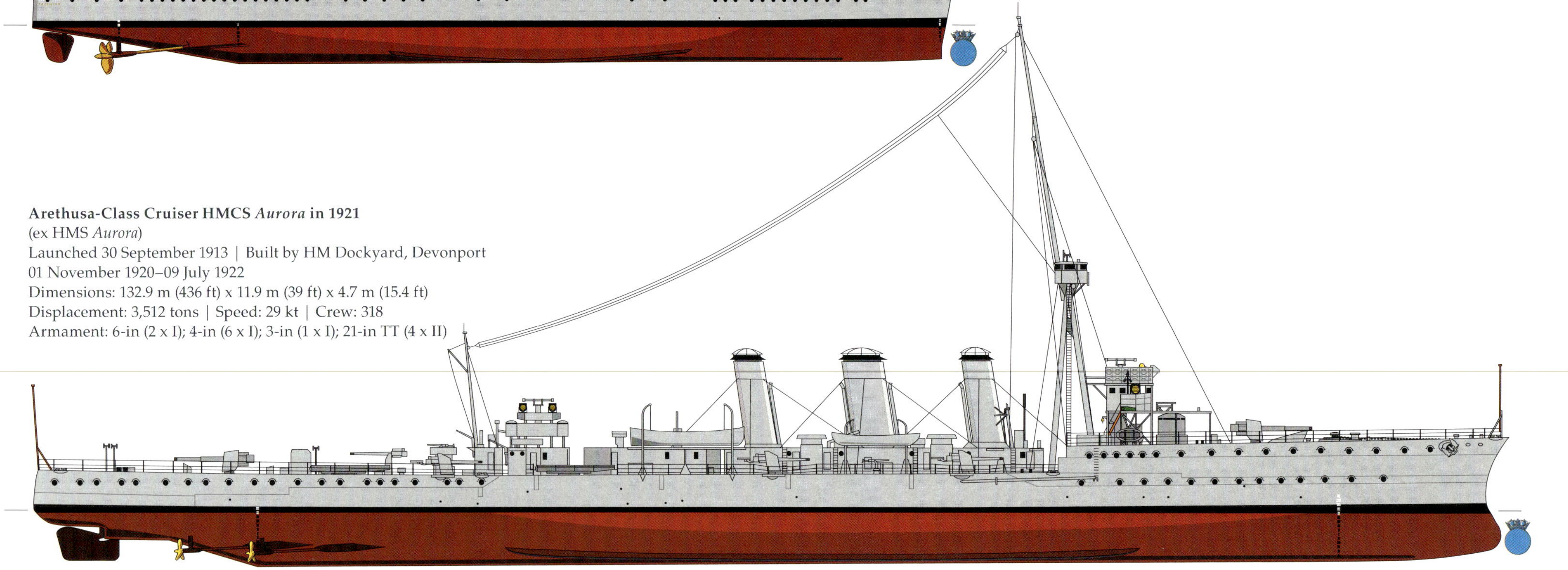

S-Special-Class Destroyer HMCS *Champlain* (I) in 1932
(ex HMS *Torbay*)
Launched 06 March 1919 | Built by Thornycroft, Southampton
01 March 1928–25 November 1936
Dimensions: 84.2 m (276.2 ft) x 8.3 m (27.2 ft) x 3.2 m (10.5 ft)
Displacement: 1,087 tons | Speed: 32 kt | Crew: 90
Armament: 4-in (3 x I); 2-pdr (1 x I); 21-in TT (2 x II); depth charges

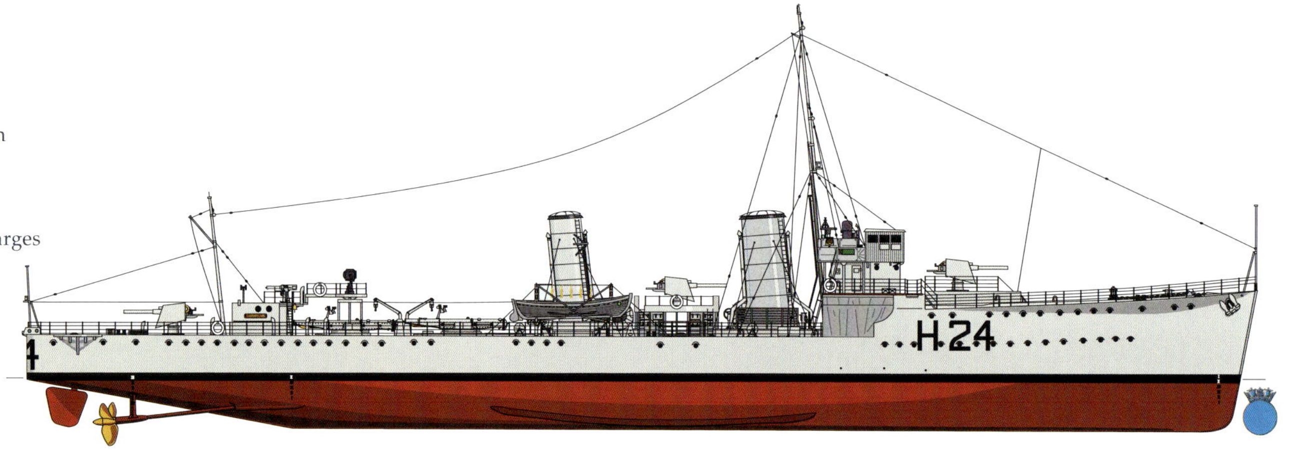

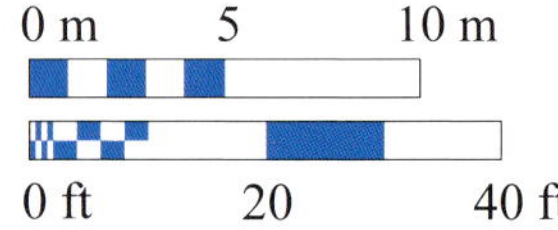

7

THE INTERWAR "OCCASIONAL" FLEET

In the wake of the Great War, the Borden government made an ambitious start on the revitalization and sustainment of a viable Canadian fleet. Even as East Coast waters were being ravaged, practically unopposed, by U-boats in the summer of 1918, Prime Minster Borden had agreed that Canada should be included as part of a postwar assessment of the naval needs of the empire, subsequently conducted through the course of 1919 by RN Fleet Admiral Sir John Jellicoe. Beginning with a stop in India in March, the Jellicoe Mission passed through Australia and New Zealand before arriving in Canada in November. In anticipation, a Naval Committee was struck in Ottawa to produce a series of "Occasional Papers" as a planning basis for discussions. The pertinent analysis on fleet composition was Occasional Paper No. 2, "Proposals for Canadian Naval Expansion," which envisioned the creation of a forty-six-ship navy over two seven-year building periods (1920–27 and 1927–34), consisting ultimately of seven cruisers, twelve destroyers, eighteen antisubmarine patrol craft, and three submarines, all to be crewed by 8,500 officers and ratings. It became the basis of Jellicoe's final recommendation, but by the time it got before Cabinet for discussion in March 1920, postwar budgetary retrenchment had set in. On March 25, Naval Minister C.C. Ballantyne told Parliament that a permanent naval policy was being deferred, and in the meantime, the RCN would be re-established along pre-war training lines, comprising a light cruiser and a pair of destroyers that were on offer from the RN.

The designated ships were the Arethusa-class light cruiser *Aurora* and Thornycroft M-class destroyers *Patriot* and *Patrician*. They were a logical combination, as the

Arethusas had been developed in 1912 as "scouts" to work with a destroyer flotilla. They were the first British cruisers to use destroyer-type oil-fired boilers and turbines, producing a top speed just short of 30 knots. Displacing 3,512 tons, and with a complement of 318 officers and men, they were armed with two single 6-inch and six single 4-inch guns and four double banks of 21-inch anti-ship torpedo tubes (eight total). *Aurora* completed in September 1914; her service in the war included action in the Battle of Dogger Bank in January 1915, and she was present at the surrender of the German High Seas Fleet in November 1918, following which she was placed in reserve with reduced manning.

The M-class destroyers also proved to be a very successful design. With the first laid down in November 1913, the class eventually comprised 103 ships (85 built to the original "Admiralty" specifications; the 18 more were only slightly different as built, 6 each in the Yarrow, Hawthorn Leslie, and Thornycroft yards) — hence, their names ran the gamut of the alphabet from *M* to *P*. Displacing 1,004 tons with a complement of eighty-two officers and men, their oil-fired turbines produced a speed of 36 knots. Main armament was three single 4-inch guns and two twin 21-inch torpedo tubes. *Patriot* and *Patrician* were ordered in February 1915, completed in June and August 1916, respectively, and both ended the war in the Fifteenth Destroyer Flotilla attached to the Grand Fleet. They were laid up in reserve in Portsmouth in November 1919.

The three ships were reactivated and commissioned into the RCN together in Portsmouth a year later, on November 1, 1920, and arrived in Halifax just before Christmas. Early in the new year of 1921, the little flotilla set off on a training cruise by way of the Caribbean Sea and Panama Canal to Esquimalt, making that harbour the backdrop for the only known photograph of the three ships together. By the time they returned to Halifax, the submarines *CH 14* and *CH 15* had been commissioned on April 1, 1921, and joined by the trawlers *Festubert* and *Ypres* (with *Thiepval* on the West Coast), Canada had the foundations for the fleet envisioned in Occasional Paper No. 2. That summer, the whole of the East Coast RCN participated in a history-making event, with the cruiser, destroyers, and trawlers constituting the "Red Force" in an exercise testing the defences of Halifax Harbour. The submarines joined a trio of Canadian Air Force (not yet "Royal") Curtiss HS-2L flying boats* and militia coastal defence artillery as the "Blue Force," in an event recounted in *The Seabound Coast* as the first known "Combined Exercises by Navy, Army and Air Force, 22–24 August 1921."[9]

It was not to last. In the general election of December 1921, William Lyon Mackenzie King formed his first ministry, elected on a platform of further retrenchment. Using the deliberations of the Washington Naval Arms Limitation Conference (November 1921 through February 1922) as a pretext, they slashed the Canadian naval budget. As the costliest single expense item, *Aurora*

* Note they originally had been acquired as for the Royal Canadian Naval Air Service of recent memory — see Chapter 48.

was laid up immediately to be de-stored and paid off on July 1, 1922; she remained alongside Halifax in deteriorating condition until sold for scrap and broken up in 1927. Paying off the submarines at the same time worked to ensure sufficient funds to save the two destroyers, with one to be based on each coast (*Patrician* was sent back to Esquimalt), joined by a rotating pair of Battle-class trawlers as the rump of a training force.

Despite its short-lived existence, the acquisition of the "occasional fleet" had two lasting effects for the RCN. First, the insistence of the Canadian naval staff that the cruiser be oil burning (the Admiralty had initially offered one of the older coal-burning Bristol class) led to the building in each harbour of permanent oil storage facilities, a measure that outlasted the budget cuts of 1922. Second, to crew the cruiser and destroyers upon commissioning for the voyage to Canada, the large number of Canadian officers and ratings who had served in RN ships during the war and were still in Britain were assigned to fill out their complements (not incidentally at great savings to the civilian passenger ship travel budget). A survey of *The Navy List* for 1921–22 shows their respective wardrooms populated by names familiar to students of Canadian naval history, including Leonard Murray, Godfrey Hibbard, and Harold Grant as lieutenants in *Aurora*; Charles Beard in command of *Patriot* (Ronald Agnew was his first lieutenant); and George Jones in command of *Patrician* (George Stephens was his engineer). The practice thus instituted, Canadian warships henceforth would generally be commanded and officered by Canadians (interrupted only and rarely by the demands of the Second World War).

The cruiser *Aurora* alongside with the destroyers *Patriot* and *Patrician* in Esquimalt Harbour during their over-winter visit in 1921.

During all this turmoil, Walter Hose replaced Kingsmill as director of the Naval Service at the end of 1920, and through the rest of the decade, he worked to convince Prime Minister King as to the need for a Canadian fleet. By 1927, when the destroyers had reached the end of their useful lives, the government agreed to the immediate acquisition of another pair of surplus RN destroyers pending the construction of new vessels. In rapid sequence, *Patriot* and *Patrician* were paid off over the new year of 1927–28 and their crews dispatched to Portsmouth to take possession of their replacements. On March 1, 1928, the former HM Ships *Torbay* and *Toreador* were recommissioned as HMC Ships, renamed *Champlain* and *Vancouver*, respectively. They had been laid down in 1917 as part of a sub-batch of S-class destroyers built by Thornycroft but launched only as the war concluded and almost immediately placed in reserve. It was another sizable class (total sixty-seven vessels), a displacement of 1,087 tons making them slightly larger than the earlier M-class destroyers, but with similar armament, and visually distinguishable from the earlier pair by having only two funnels (versus three) and a larger bridge that, in consideration of Canadian climatic conditions, was enclosed for the transfer.

In further consideration of the rough waters of the northern Atlantic, the ships made their way to Canada by way of the Azores, thence the West Indies. There they separated, *Champlain* making for Halifax and *Vancouver* for Esquimalt, where they spent the remainder of their careers dedicated to training. By the mid-1930s, their condition had deteriorated significantly, and they were paid off at their respective bases on November 25, 1935, and sold for scrap.

FURTHER READING

S.D. Campbell, "The Early Years: After the Great War," in *Tin-Can Canucks: A Century of Canadian Destroyers* (Kay Cee Publications, 2017), 14–23.

Norman Friedman, *British Cruisers: Two World Wars and After* (Naval Institute Press, 2022).

Norman Friedman, *British Destroyers: From Earliest Days to the Second World War* (Naval Institute Press, 2009).

Karl Gagnon, "Canada's First Destroyers, the M-Class," *Argonauta* XXIX, no. 1 (Winter 2012): 19–28, epe.lac-bac.gc.ca/100/201/300/argonauta/2012/argo_29_1.pdf.

Michael Whitby, "Learning Destroyers: Harry DeWolf and HMCS *Patriot*, 1925-26," *Canadian Naval Review* 19, no. 3 (2024): 11–15.

Ian Yeates, "Admiral Jellicoe Goes to Sea: The Naval Mission and the Ambition for an 'Imperial Navy,'" *The Northern Mariner/Le marin du nord* 33, no. 1 (Spring 2023): 43–80, tnm.journals.yorku.ca/index.php/default/article/view/1082.

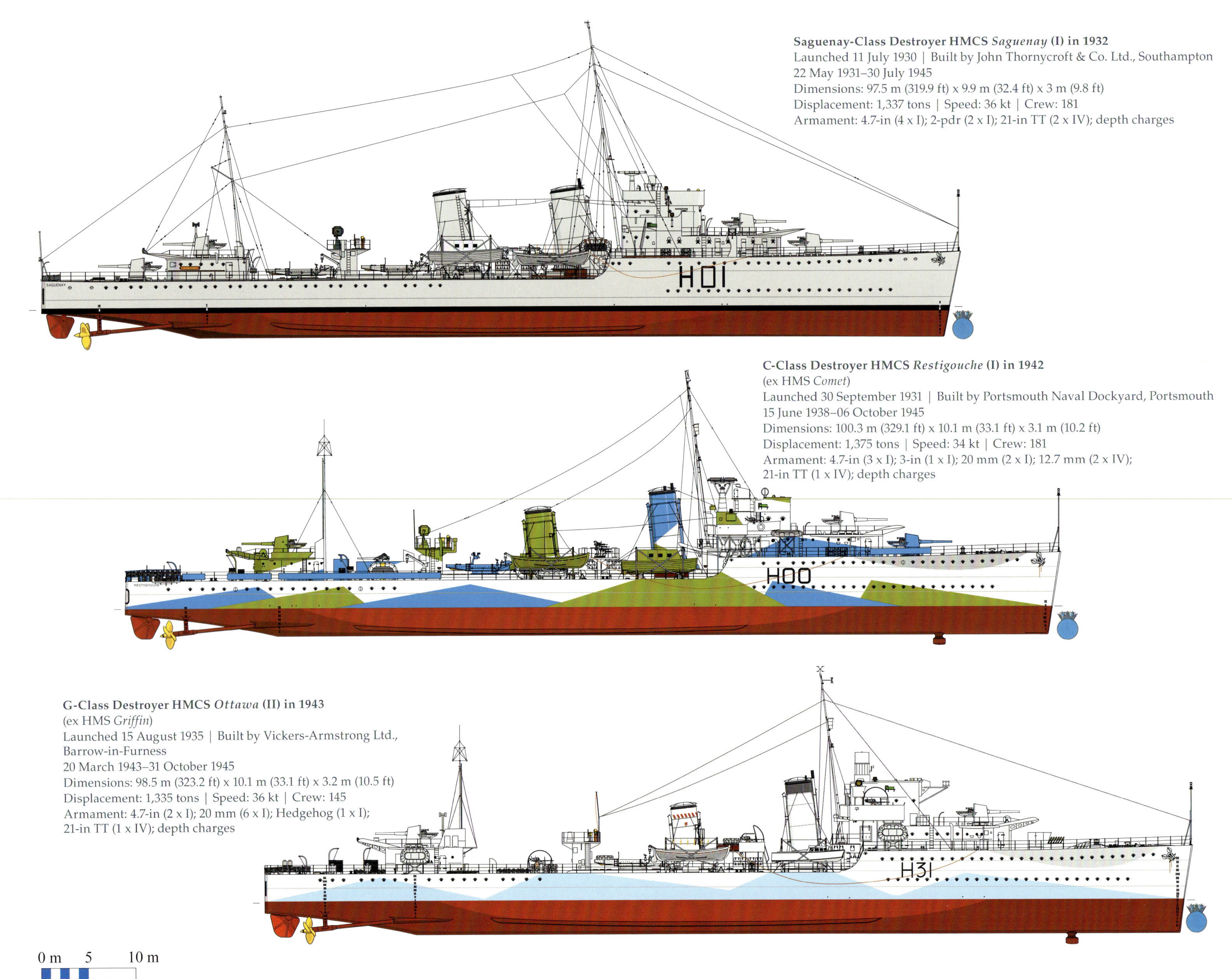

Saguenay-Class Destroyer HMCS *Saguenay* (I) in 1932
Launched 11 July 1930 | Built by John Thornycroft & Co. Ltd., Southampton
22 May 1931–30 July 1945
Dimensions: 97.5 m (319.9 ft) x 9.9 m (32.4 ft) x 3 m (9.8 ft)
Displacement: 1,337 tons | Speed: 36 kt | Crew: 181
Armament: 4.7-in (4 x I); 2-pdr (2 x I); 21-in TT (2 x IV); depth charges

C-Class Destroyer HMCS *Restigouche* (I) in 1942
(ex HMS *Comet*)
Launched 30 September 1931 | Built by Portsmouth Naval Dockyard, Portsmouth
15 June 1938–06 October 1945
Dimensions: 100.3 m (329.1 ft) x 10.1 m (33.1 ft) x 3.1 m (10.2 ft)
Displacement: 1,375 tons | Speed: 34 kt | Crew: 181
Armament: 4.7-in (3 x I); 3-in (1 x I); 20 mm (2 x I); 12.7 mm (2 x IV);
21-in TT (1 x IV); depth charges

G-Class Destroyer HMCS *Ottawa* (II) in 1943
(ex HMS *Griffin*)
Launched 15 August 1935 | Built by Vickers-Armstrong Ltd.,
Barrow-in-Furness
20 March 1943–31 October 1945
Dimensions: 98.5 m (323.2 ft) x 10.1 m (33.1 ft) x 3.2 m (10.5 ft)
Displacement: 1,335 tons | Speed: 36 kt | Crew: 145
Armament: 4.7-in (2 x I); 20 mm (6 x I); Hedgehog (1 x I);
21-in TT (1 x IV); depth charges

8

THE ROLLS-ROYCES: RIVER-CLASS DESTROYERS

The two new destroyers authorized by the Mackenzie King government in 1927 were the first major warships built specifically for the RCN. *Saguenay* and *Skeena* were early variants of the RN's modern postwar fleet destroyers then under construction in the U.K. That initial pair would be followed in Canadian service by an eventual further dozen of incrementally improved designs, all built through the course of the first half of the 1930s: Four were acquired in the process of peacetime rearmament, and the final eight were obtained to meet wartime expansion and replacement needs. As such, they were from various subclasses as designated by the RN, but being named for Canadian rivers, the full group are known in the RCN as the River class (see table on page 48 for the complete list).

In the mid-1920s, the RN embarked on the development of a new class of fleet destroyer, seeking to combine wartime experience with peacetime austerity while remaining within the tonnage and armament strictures of the Washington Naval Treaty. Notwithstanding these significant restrictions, the resulting compromise design proved quite successful — in total some eighty-three ships were built, generally in batches of eight organized as flotillas (the basic British operating formation). With only incremental improvements from the A through I classes, and as such an essentially homogeneous design throughout, all of them were built for the RN, other than the two

The four surviving RCN C-class River destroyers nested alongside Halifax in late summer 1942: (from inboard right) *Assiniboine*, *Ottawa*, *Restigouche*, and *St. Laurent* (missing is *Fraser*, lost in 1940). The image can be dated by the damage on *Assiniboine*'s bow, not yet repaired from her ramming of *U 210* on August 6, 1942.

early modifications for the RCN and four I-class for the Turkish Navy. Nearly half again larger than such earlier Great War staples as the M- and S-classes (see Chapter 7 on the "Occasional Fleet": *Patriot*, *Patrician*, *Champlain*, and *Vancouver*), at roughly 1,350-tons displacement, they carried much larger and improved main armament: initially, four single 4.7-inch guns and two quadruple 21-inch torpedo tubes (this would change during the war, as will be discussed below). Moreover, they were driven by more powerful oil-fired turbines, capable of speeds in excess of 35 knots.

The Canadian naval staff started from the presumption that their destroyers would most likely operate in a common flotilla with their British sisters, and as such should be generally similar to the RN types. By the time the orders were placed, the B-class was entering production, making that the design standard. A number of modifications were incorporated to meet Canadian environmental conditions: strengthened bows as protection against ice and greater flare to make for a drier foredeck; increased metacentric height (a measure of buoyancy) to allow for potentially 50–60 tons of ice and snow accumulation on the uppers; and steam heating for cold conditions, as well as better ventilation, considering the need for inter-coastal passage through the Panama Canal. These alterations were so substantial that the official Thornycroft company history noted, "On arrival at Portsmouth for working-up after delivery the ships were promptly dubbed the 'Rolls-Royce destroyers.'"[10]

Serious thought had been given to building *Saguenay* and *Skeena* under licence at Canadian Vickers in Montreal as part of a six-destroyer and four-minesweeper program to address naval defence needs while encouraging Canadian industry. However, the destroyer contract was awarded to Thornycroft in Southampton in consideration of that yard's familiarity with the new British destroyer design and therefore much lower cost of construction. In the end, the larger Canadian naval build program was forestalled by the onset of the Great Depression in October 1929 (the minesweeper contract was deferred and would not be completed until the late 1930s — see Chapter 9 on the Fundy class). And then there was a change of government: *Saguenay* was launched in July 1930, just a month before Prime Minister R.B. Bennett was elected on an austerity platform, with *Skeena* following off the slips in October. When they commissioned the next year, their standing as a notable advancement in Canadian naval capability was underscored with their first commanding officers being members of the original cohort of cadets who had entered in CGS *Canada* in 1909: *Saguenay* on May 22, 1931, under Commander Percy Nelles, and *Skeena* on June 10, under Commander Victor Gabriel Brodeur. Additionally, the sponsor for both ships was Mildred Bennett, sister of the prime minister. They sailed from Portsmouth on June 23 and entered Halifax on July 3, with *Skeena* leaving soon after to arrive in Esquimalt on August 7.

Mackenzie King's return to power in October 1935 coincided with a growing recognition of the global drift to war, but it is generally under-appreciated that the Navy was the initial focus of the broader Canadian rearmament program. With *Champlain* and *Vancouver* due to be discarded at the end of 1936 under the terms of the 1930 London Naval Treaty, but also aware it would take too long to replace them with newly ordered vessels, Nelles (now a commodore since becoming CNS on January 1, 1934) reminded Mackenzie King of his earlier agreement with Hose regarding the 1928 building program. Accordingly, the prime minister authorized the immediate transfer of two C-class destroyers from the RN; two more from the same class would be authorized in 1937. The commissioning of HMC Ships *Fraser* (ex-*Crescent*) and *St. Laurent* (ex-*Cygnet*) on February 17, 1937, and then *Ottawa* (ex-*Crusader*) and *Restigouche* (ex-*Comet*) on June 15, 1938, provided the RCN with a half flotilla of largely homogenous ships. Notably, the bulk of the Canadian fleet (*Fraser*, *St. Laurent*, and *Restigouche*, along with *Skeena*) were initially based on the West Coast, out of concern to have a force there to maintain the neutrality of Canadian waters in the event of war between the United States and Japan, which left only *Ottawa* with *Saguenay* on the Atlantic.

Although the naval staff had hoped to enter the war with a full flotilla and a leader (nine ships) on each coast, for a total fleet of eighteen destroyers, that did not come to pass before the outbreak of the European War in September 1939. Even as German forces were massing on the Polish frontier, the four West Coast destroyers were dispatched to Halifax for operations on the North Atlantic, where they would remain for the duration of the war. No RCN destroyers saw action in the Pacific, and other building programs (discussed in subsequent chapters) precluded the acquisition of any more than the fourteen Rivers. As their individual ship histories are covered elsewhere by other authors, there is no need to discuss them here, other than to provide a general summary and describe the acquisitions and modifications to the class brought about by the war.

Being the opening mainstay of the RCN, the River-class destroyers were the first to see action on many counts. *Saguenay* and *St. Laurent* escorted the first transatlantic convoy out of Halifax, HX-1, on September 16, 1939. When the whole force was rushed to European waters the next spring, in the wake of the invasion of France, *St. Laurent* became the first HMC Ship to engage the enemy, on June 11, 1940, shelling German forces ashore at Saint-Valery-en-Caux while covering the British withdrawal from the Continent. On November 6, 1940, *Ottawa* was the first Canadian unit to claim an Axis submarine, the Italian *Faa di Bruno* (credit shared

Ship/(ex-RN)	Launched/Class Commissioned RCN	Fate/Disposal	Pennant Number/Remarks
The Rolls-Royces			
Saguenay	July 11, 1930/B class[a] May 22, 1931	Paid off, July 30, 1945	D79/I79, constructive loss owing to collision Nov 15, 1942, thence tender *Cornwallis*
Skeena	Oct 10, 1930/B class[a] June 10, 1931	Wrecked, Oct 25, 1944	D59/159
Peacetime Rearmament			
Fraser (ex-*Crescent*)	Sep 29, 1931/C class Feb 17, 1937	Sunk collision, June 28, 1940	H48
St. Laurent (ex-*Cygnet*)	Sep 29, 1931/C class Feb 17, 1937	Paid off, Oct 10, 1945	H83
Ottawa (First) (ex-*Crusader*)	Sep 30, 1931/C class June 15, 1938	Lost in action, Sep 14, 1942	H60
Restigouche (ex-*Comet*)	Sep 30, 1931/C class June 15, 1938	Paid off, Oct 6, 1945	H00
Wartime Expansion			
Assiniboine (ex-*Kempenfelt*)	Oct 29, 1931/C class Oct 19, 1939	Paid off, Aug 8, 1945	D18/I18
Margaree (ex-*Diana*)	June 16, 1932/D class Sep 6, 1940	Sunk collision, Oct 22, 1940	H49, replaced *Fraser*; same fate 3 months later
Ottawa (Second) (ex-*Griffin*)	Aug 15, 1935/G class Mar 20, 1943	Paid off, Oct 31, 1945	H31, replaced *Ottawa* (First)
Kootenay (ex-*Decoy*)	June 7, 1932/D class Apr 12, 1943	Paid off, Oct 26, 1945	H75
Saskatchewan (ex-*Fortune*)	Aug 29, 1934/F class May 31, 1943	Paid off, Jan 28, 1946	H70
Gatineau (ex-*Express*)	May 29, 1934/E class June 3, 1943	Paid off, Jan 10, 1946	H61
Chaudière (ex-*Hero*)	Mar 10, 1936/E class Nov 15, 1943	Paid off, Aug 17, 1945	H99
Qu'Appelle (ex-*Foxhound*)	Oct 12, 1934/F class Feb 8, 1944	Paid off, May 27, 1946	H69

[a]Modified.

with her British H-class sister *Harvester*). From that point forward, antisubmarine operations became their primary employment, and over the years the class variously participated in the destruction of another eight German U-boats. A notable exception to the antisubmarine work came in the summer of 1944, when several of the class joined together in their original "anti-surface" purpose to cover the Normandy landings, one of their significant actions being in the early morning hours of July 6, 1944, when *Qu'Appelle*, *Restigouche*, *Saskatchewan*, and *Skeena* engaged German coastal forces in "The Battle of Pierres Noires" off Brest (see Milner in Further Reading).

The first wartime acquisition, HMCS *Assiniboine* (ex-C-class HMS *Kempenfelt*), was purchased in August 1939 and commissioned on October 19, intended to serve as a "leader" of the Canadian destroyer force (she had been built for that purpose, associated with the C-class half flotilla already transferred to the RCN). *Margaree* was the next acquired, in September 1940, to replace *Fraser* (see next paragraph). The further six were not commissioned until after March 1943, when the RCN began to take fuller responsibility for the transatlantic convoys and had need for additional Escort Group command ships. Those were all transferred from the RN, having been extensively upgraded for the role — most visibly, two of the 4.7-inch guns were generally replaced with Hedgehog antisubmarine mortars, better anti-aircraft gun mounts and more depth charges, along with radio direction-finding equipment and improved radars. All of these equipments were retrofitted at about the same time to the previous RCN destroyers, although there was no "standard" fit for the class — for example, in some instances, only one of the 4.7-inch guns was removed, while others lost one or both of the quadruple torpedo tube mountings.

Only one of the Rivers was lost to direct enemy action (*Ottawa*, September 14, 1942), although another two were lost in combat-related collisions (*Fraser* and, ironically, her replacement, *Margaree*). Neither of the two originals survived the war in fighting trim — *Saguenay*'s stern was blown off consequent to a collision in convoy in November 1942, following which she was eventually assigned as a stationary training ship at the RCN new entry school HMCS *Cornwallis*; *Skeena* was wrecked, having dragged her anchor in a gale off Reykjavik on October 25, 1944. The remaining nine all survived the war to be sold off for scrap within a year of Victory in Europe (VE) Day.

FURTHER READING

S.D. Campbell, "The First Rivers: Preparing for War," and "Later Rivers: Hostilities Only Destroyers," in *Tin-Can Canucks: A Century of Canadian Destroyers* (Kay Cee Publications, 2017), 24–55 and 80–117.

Norman Friedman, *British Destroyers: From Earliest Days to the Second World War* (Naval Institute Press, 2009).

JHW Knox, "An Engineer's Outline of RCN History: Part 1," in *The RCN in Retrospect, 1910–1968*, ed. James Boutilier (UBC Press, 1982), 101–103.

Ken Macpherson, *The River Class Destroyers of the Royal Canadian Navy* (Charles J. Musson, 1985).

Edgar J. March, *British Destroyers: A History of Development, 1892–1953* (Seeley Service, 1966).

Fraser McKee and Robert A. Darlington, *The Canadian Naval Chronicle, 1939–1945: The Success and Losses of the Canadian Navy in World War II* (Vanwell Publishing, 1998).

Marc Milner, "The RCN's Forgotten Surface Battles of 1944," *Canadian Naval Review* 19, no. 2 (2023): 14–18.

Fundy-Class Minesweeper HMCS *Fundy* (I) in 1938
Launched 18 June 1938 | Built by Collingwood Shipyards Ltd., Collingwood
01 September 1938–27 July 1945
Dimensions: 49.7 m (163.1 ft) x 8.4 m (27.6 ft) x 4.4 m (14.4 ft)
Displacement: 460 tons | Speed: 12 kt | Crew: 38
Armament: 4-in (1 x I); depth charges

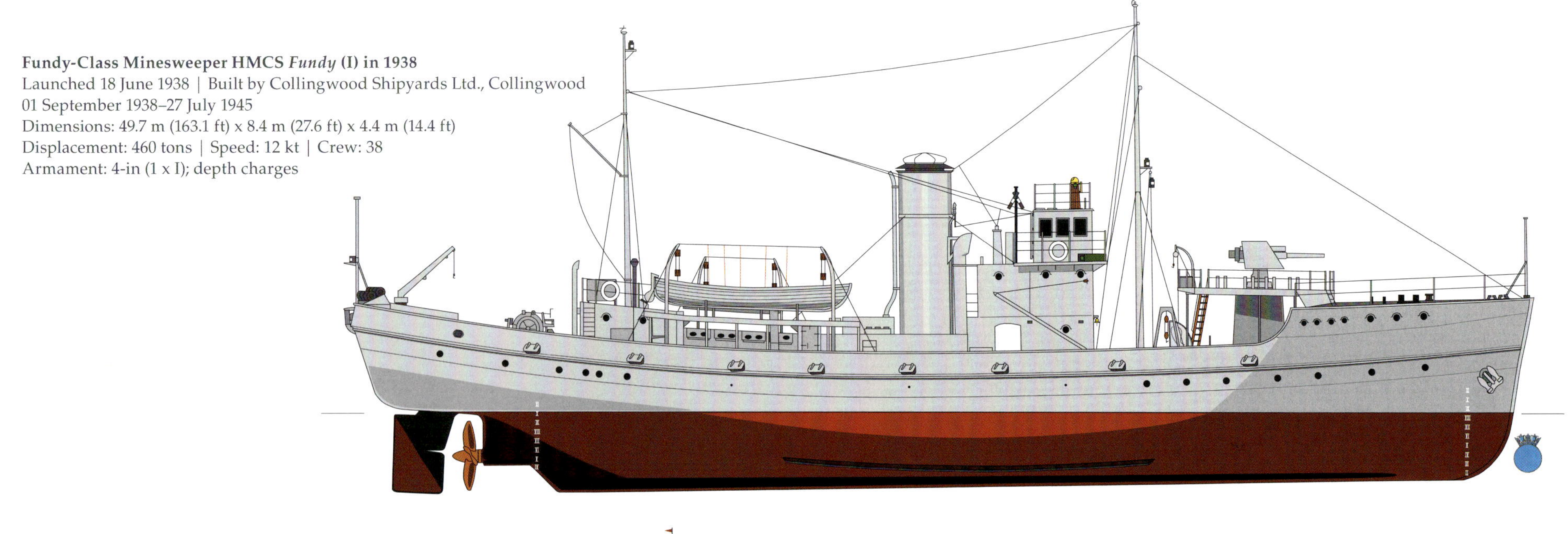

Llewellyn-Class Minesweeper HMCS *Daerwood* in 1945
Launched 14 August 1943 | Built by Vancouver Shipyards Ltd., Vancouver
22 April 1944–28 November 1945
Dimensions: 36.4 m (119.4 ft) x 6.7 m (22 ft) x 2.6 m (8.5 ft)
Displacement: 228 tons | Speed: 9 kt | Crew: 23
Armament: .50 MG (1 x II); .303 MG (2 x II)

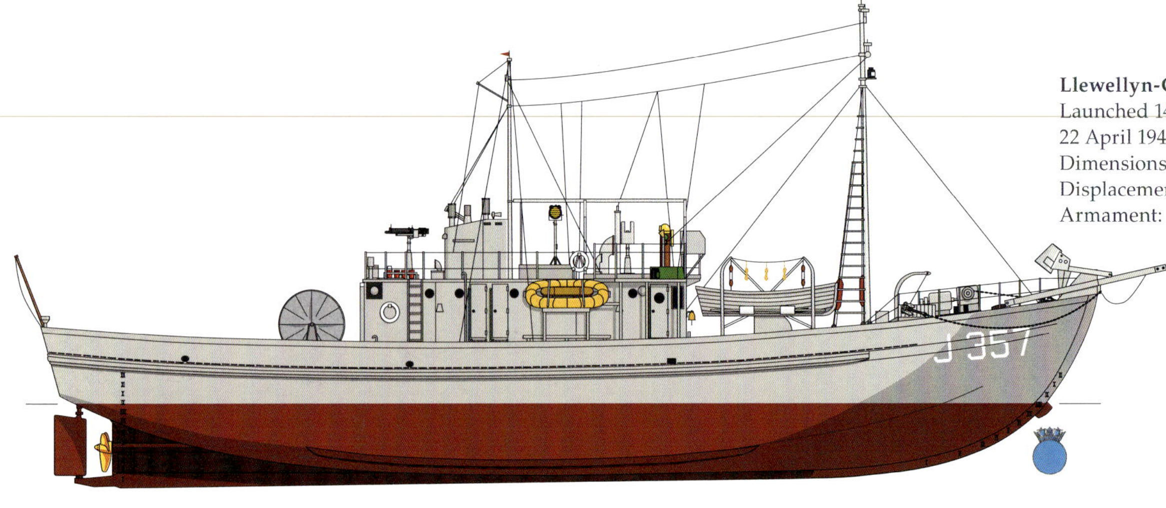

Llewellyn-Class Minesweeper HMCS *Llewellyn* in 1950
Launched 12 August 1942 | Built by Chantier Maritime, Ile d'Orléans
24 August 1942–14 June 1946
25 July 1949–31 October 1951
Dimensions: 36.4 m (119.4 ft) x 6.7 m (22 ft) x 2.6 m (8.5 ft)
Displacement: 228 tons | Speed: 9 kt | Crew: 23
Armament: nil

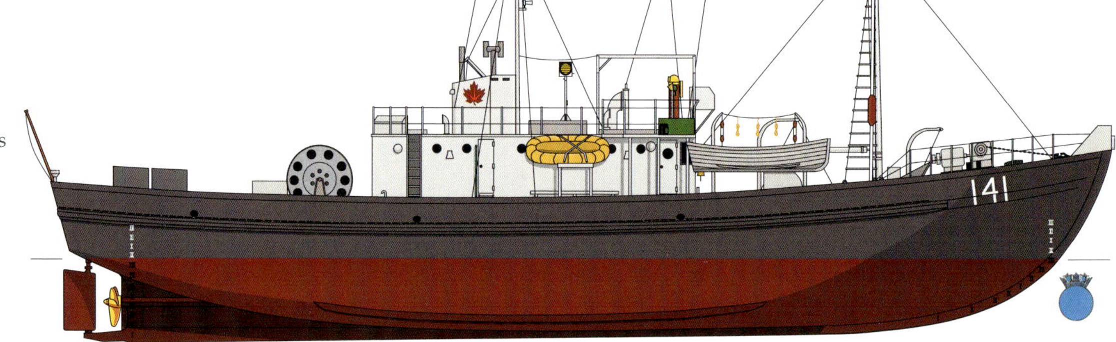

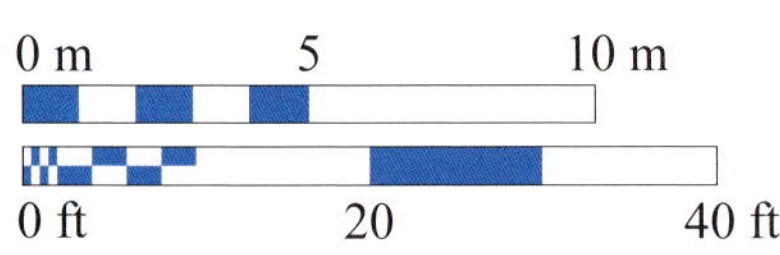

9

WARTIME INSHORE MINESWEEPERS

While destroyers were the focus of pre-war rearmament, minesweepers had been the other half of the proposal that Commodore Hose presented to Prime Minister Mackenzie King in 1928 and that Rear Admiral Percy Nelles (promoted to that rank in 1938) would prevail upon him in his turn. Provision for their building was begun in the 1936 estimates, and all four of the class were laid down and completed in 1938. Each was built in a different yard, two on each coast: the lead ship *Fundy* at Collingwood Shipyards in Ontario, *Gaspé* by Morton Engineering in Quebec City, *Comox* by Burrard at Vancouver, and *Nootka* in Yarrows at Esquimalt.

Other than being newly constructed, as copies of the British Basset class they varied little in appearance or capability from the Battle class they were meant to replace. At only 30 feet longer (163 ft/50 m overall) and 100 tons heavier displacement (460 tons), they also have the distinction of being the last ships built for the RCN to be propelled by coal-burning triple-expansion engines. But unlike destroyers, they could be constructed economically in Canada.

Upon the outbreak of hostilities in Europe in September 1939, while the West Coast destroyers began their rushed deployment to the Atlantic theatre, the early shipbuilding reassessment by the naval staff on September 6 (still before the Canadian declaration of war on September 10) was for an additional eighteen Fundy-class minesweepers. Over the next few days, this changed radically, and those plans were cancelled upon advice from the Admiralty that any new minesweepers should be of the oil-burning Bangor class that the RN

Minesweepers *Llewellyn* (J278, left) and *Suderoy V* (J05) seen steaming in close formation astern from *Lloyd George*.

itself was acquiring (see Chapter 16), augmented by the new whale-catcher-type patrol vessels (see Chapter 11 on the corvettes). In the event, another sixteen of the Basset/Fundy classes would be built in Canadian yards, although for the RN not the RCN. In the event, eight of these were loaned upon completion to the RCN for employment and, although remaining HM Ships, were given mostly Canadian names and were known as the Western Isles-class trawlers (see list in table at end of chapter).

With the initial focus of operations being the Atlantic, the two West Coast ships (*Comox* and *Nootka*) were transferred east in March 1940 for minesweeping duties in the Halifax approaches, in which they would be joined by the Isles-class trawlers built from early 1942. The one noteworthy wartime event for the class was the renaming on April 1, 1943, of *Nootka* to *Nanoose* to make her original name available for one of the four Tribal-class destroyers then building in Halifax (see Chapter 10). All four Fundy-class minesweepers were paid off in July 1945. *Fundy* remained in Canada in civilian guise, eventually to be broken up in 1987; the other three were sold to Chinese interests for use as tugboats. They disappeared from the Lloyd's Register in 1993, probably to be broken up.

An additional source of minesweepers arose after Norway was overrun and occupied by the Germans in April 1940, when six of their many nationally flagged whale catchers were left homeless in Halifax. These were immediately chartered for Canadian use and commissioned into the RCN in 1941 for minesweeping duties with the Halifax Local Defence Force as HMC Ships *Star XVI* and *Suderöy I, II, IV, V,* and *VI*. There is little more to note of them, and they were returned to their former owners after the war ended.

After the U.S. entry into the war, an assessment early in 1942 that the Germans could pursue an inshore campaign of laying magnetic-influence mines led to RCN interest in building several of the 105-foot Llewellyn-class wooden-hulled minesweepers, based on the successful British "small motor minesweepers" (MMS) class. That mining threat failed to materialize, and in the end only ten were built for the RCN. Two of those were on the East Coast, *Llewellyn* and *Lloyd George*, the names reflecting their being equipped with "double-L" magnetic sweeping gear. However, as Macpherson and Barrie note, "ingenuity seems to have failed when it came to naming the rest of the class"[11]: The other eight were all built on the West Coast in 1944 and named for British Columbia interior towns (see list in table below). They were employed for patrols between Esquimalt and Prince Rupert. With the end of the war, most of the class were sold off to various commercial interests. Two exceptions became tenders to Naval Reserve Divisions on the East Coast: *Llewellyn* to HMCS *Brunswicker* in Saint John, New Brunswick, and *Revelstoke* (transferred from the

Ship	Pennant	Ship	Pennant
Fundy (Basset)-Class Minesweepers			
Comox	J64	*Gaspé*	J94
Fundy	J88	*Nootka* (*Nanoose*)	J35
Western Isles–Class Trawlers (RN-Operated)			
Anticosti	T274	*Liscomb*	T285
Baffin	T275	*Magdalen*	T279
Califf	T276	*Manitoulin*	T280
Ironbound	T284	*Miscou*	T277
Ex-Norwegian Whalers			
Star XVI	Z16	*Suderöy IV*	Z02
Suderöy I	Z01	*Suderöy V*	Z05
Suderöy II	Z02	*Suderöy VI*	Z06
Llewellyn-Class Minesweepers			
Coquitlam	J364	*Llewellyn*	J278 (141)
Cranbrook	J372	*Lloyd George*	J279 (142)
Daerwood	J357	*Revelstoke*	J373
Kalamalka	J395	*Rossland*	J358
Lavallée	J371	*St. Joseph*	J359
Lake-Type Minesweepers (Transferred to Soviet Union)			
Alder Lake	J480	*Larch Lake*	J489
Beech Lake	J482	*Pine Lake*	J492
Cedar Lake	J484	*Poplar Lake*	J493
Elm Lake	J486	*Spruce Lake*	J494
Hickory Lake	J488	*Willow Lake*	J495

West Coast) to HMCS *Cabot* in St. John's, Newfoundland and Labrador. A third, *Lloyd George*, remained as a guard-ship in Halifax. All three were paid off in the mid-1950s for replacement by the Porte-class gate vessels (see Chapter 29).

A final footnote to this general type of vessel is that late in the war, the Navy had ordered sixteen of an enlarged development of the wooden-hulled minesweeper based on the British 126-foot MMS class. In the event never commissioned into the RCN, they are generally overlooked in discussions of Canadian warship types. Ten of them were completed, all built in Great Lakes yards. Given names of small lakes in turn named for Canadian trees, they were undergoing trials when the European war ended and were presented to the then-still-allied Soviet Union.

FURTHER READING

Steve R. Dunn, ed., *British Naval Trawlers and Drifters in Two World Wars: From the John Lambert Collection* (Seaforth, 2021).

Ken Macpherson, *Minesweepers of the Royal Canadian Navy, 1938–1945* (Vanwell Publishing, 1997).

"MMS-Type Minesweeper," Wikimedia Foundation, last modified April 1, 2024, 14:17 (UTC), en.wikipedia.org/wiki/MMS-class_minesweeper.

James Pritchard, *A Bridge of Ships: Canadian Shipbuilding During the Second World War* (McGill-Queens University Press, 2011).

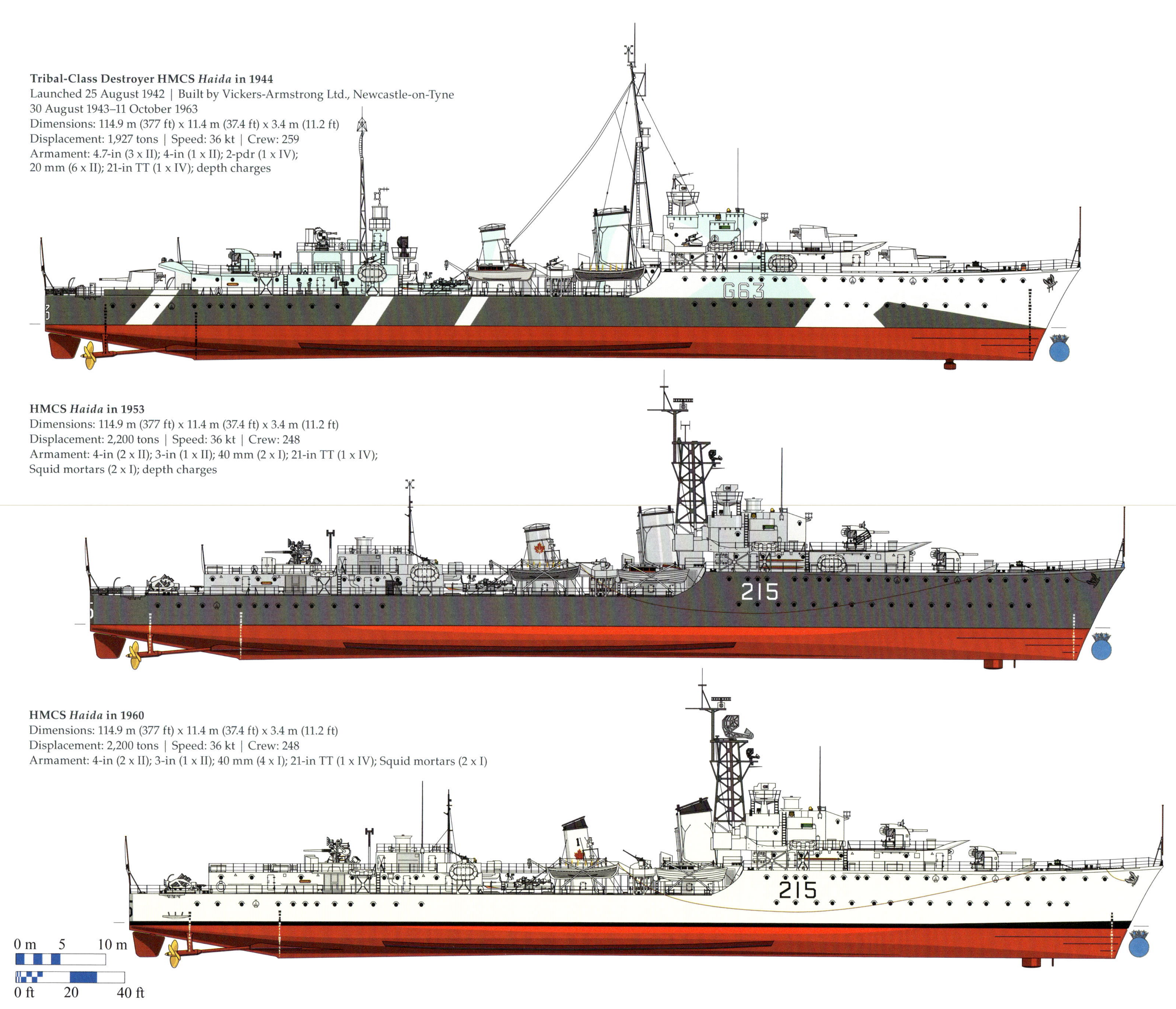
Tribal-Class Destroyer HMCS Haida in 1944
Launched 25 August 1942 | Built by Vickers-Armstrong Ltd., Newcastle-on-Tyne
30 August 1943–11 October 1963
Dimensions: 114.9 m (377 ft) x 11.4 m (37.4 ft) x 3.4 m (11.2 ft)
Displacement: 1,927 tons | Speed: 36 kt | Crew: 259
Armament: 4.7-in (3 x II); 4-in (1 x II); 2-pdr (1 x IV);
20 mm (6 x II); 21-in TT (1 x IV); depth charges
G63
HMCS Haida in 1953
Dimensions: 114.9 m (377 ft) x 11.4 m (37.4 ft) x 3.4 m (11.2 ft)
Displacement: 2,200 tons | Speed: 36 kt | Crew: 248
Armament: 4-in (2 x II); 3-in (1 x II); 40 mm (2 x I); 21-in TT (1 x IV);
Squid mortars (2 x I); depth charges
215
HMCS Haida in 1960
Dimensions: 114.9 m (377 ft) x 11.4 m (37.4 ft) x 3.4 m (11.2 ft)
Displacement: 2,200 tons | Speed: 36 kt | Crew: 248
Armament: 4-in (2 x II); 3-in (1 x II); 40 mm (4 x I); 21-in TT (1 x IV); Squid mortars (2 x I)
215
0 m
5
10 m
0 ft
20
40 ft

10

THE MIGHTY TRIBALS: TRIBAL-CLASS DESTROYERS

The story is quite probably apocryphal, but, as related by Michael Whitby in his definitive study of the RCN's acquisition of the Tribal-class destroyers (see Further Reading), it rings true: In 1938, when CNS Rear Admiral Percy Nelles saw a photograph of Britain's newly commissioned "super destroyers," he declared, "I want those for my navy!" As the immediate successor to Kingsmill and Hose, and the first to have risen through the ranks of the RCN to take its helm, he was quite attuned to the tentative and noncommittal idiosyncrasies of Canadian naval policy, so his reasoning was twofold: First, they looked to pack a powerful punch in a hull size appropriate to RCN capabilities, and so were quite likely to bring battle honour credit to the Navy in the looming European war; and second, once acquired, the cost of their building could make them too valuable for the government to scrap in any postwar retrenchment, as had happened at the end of the Great War. He would be proven right on both counts.

The British designed the Tribals in response to new, heavily armed destroyers being produced in the early 1930s by potential adversaries Japan, Italy, and Germany (as well as by friendly France and the U.S.) and which threatened to surpass the smaller-tonnage A through I classes — including the RCN Rivers — in the fleet protection role. More than a third larger than that previous generation, the Tribals as built displaced 1,957 tons. Most of that 600-ton increase was accounted for by four twin

4.7-inch gun mountings (versus the previous single 4.7s) and more powerful turbines that generated 44,000 shaft horsepower (up from 34,000 shp) to deliver a similar 36-knot top speed. Having evolved from a scaled-down light cruiser design, they quickly earned the moniker "pocket cruisers." The total RN order of sixteen ships was laid down over the course of the seven months between June 1936 and January 1937, with the lead ship, HMS *Afridi*, commissioned on May 3, 1938, and the last in March 1939, meaning all the British ships of the class were in service upon outbreak of the war.

In January 1939, Nelles first put forward to the government the requirement for ships more powerful than the Rivers to counter what was then believed would be the main threat in Canadian waters: enemy surface raiders such as the German pocket battleships, cruisers, and armed merchant cruisers — precisely what the British had designed the Tribals to meet. He argued that a flotilla of six on each coast would provide what he considered to be a reasonable naval defence. The home defence rationale aligned with the limited commitment rearmament aims of the Mackenzie King Liberals, and the government's defence estimates presented in the House of Commons on May 16, 1939, called for a force of eighteen destroyers for the RCN — the six Rivers then in service, plus the twelve proposed Tribals.

Their actual acquisition, however, soon fell afoul of the realities of warship building capacity. With British yards already challenged by their own emergency programs, and such complex designs being beyond the capacity then existing in Canadian yards, an intricate set of negotiations between the allies ensued. The details are not needed here (Whitby covers them quite adequately), but the result was a barter arrangement by which the British would lay down four Tribals for the RCN in the Vickers-Armstrong yard in Newcastle-upon-Tyne (two in each of 1940 and 1941) in exchange for ten of the new corvettes building in Canada to be directed for RN use (which ultimately ended up being commissioned into the RCN — see Chapter 11). An additional four Tribals would eventually be laid down in Halifax over 1942–43 so that Canadian industry would benefit from the wartime mobilization, serendipitously in the shipyard located in the riding of new Minister of the Naval Service Angus L. Macdonald, who had been appointed in July 1940. Acquisition of the additional final four destroyers to make up the dozen was deferred, and by mid-1943, the focus of that discussion had shifted to the "intermediate/emergency" types (which will be covered in Chapter 23). The total number of Canadian Tribals would remain at eight.

The first RCN Tribal, HMCS *Iroquois*, commissioned in Newcastle on November 30, 1942. A transatlantic shakedown cruise to Canada followed in February–March 1943, to allow naval and shipyard officials in Halifax an opportunity to view first-hand a completed example of the type, which by then was under construction there, the first pair having been laid down on May 20, 1942, and the final two to follow in May and October 1943, respectively. *Iroquois* returned to Europe in time to be joined by her sister, *Athabaskan*, for the Bay of Biscay antisubmarine offensive through the summer of 1943, during which *Athabaskan* suffered damage from a German glider-bomb attack that required repairs until the end of November. But by then, *Huron* and *Haida* had joined the fleet, and all four British-built Canadian Tribals were part of the screening force for the Murmansk convoy that witnessed the destruction of the German battleship *Scharnhorst* off North Cape, Norway, on December 26, 1943. Over the next year and a half, through to the end of the war in Europe, they would be fully engaged in earning the battle honours so coveted by Nelles: They operated out of Plymouth as part of the Tenth Destroyer Flotilla, clearing the Channel to cover the Normandy landings, and returned to the Bay of Biscay and the Murmansk Runs and general escort duties in the Western Approaches. The heavy price paid for those honours, regrettably, was the loss of *Athabaskan* in the early morning of April 29, 1944 hit again, this time fatally, in a surface action off the Île de Batz that itself became a touchstone to that fighting tradition.

The other downside was that the four Tribals being built in Canada did not figure into those actions. The first, *Micmac*, did not commission until September 12, 1945, just after Japan's surrender, and the others staggered at roughly one per year thereafter (see table below). The delays in completion were due to a combination of factors, principally the higher wartime priority given over to repair and refit work in the Halifax yard, and then general postwar retrenchment of the defence budget. Still, the work progressed to date had indeed made them too valuable to scrap, so they became part of the peacetime establishment, although completed to wartime specifications, including armament, to save the costs of retooling and purchasing new material. However, within the year of the last of them entering service (a second *Athabaskan*, on January 20, 1948, perpetuating the name of her lost sister), the naval staff assessment in the fall of 1947 that would result in development of the St. Laurent class and the Prestonian conversions (see Chapters 25 and 26, respectively, on those types), determined also the need to convert the whole of the Tribal class to similar "destroyer-escort" (DDE) standard. Prioritizing the RCN for antisubmarine warfare (ASW) in the postwar period, this resulted in a fairly major makeover for the Tribals: principally, the fitting of a pair of Squid mortars in place of the "Y" mounting (along with high-powered sonars); improving their anti-aircraft defences by exchanging the two forward twin 4.7-inch mounts with twin 4-inch high angle/low angle (HA/LA) rapid-firing mountings and the "X" mounting astern with a twin 3-inch/50 secondary anti-aircraft armament; and a new stronger lattice mast provided better placement for improved radar sensors.

The decidedly odd-looking temporary repair to *Micmac*'s fo'c'sle following her tragic 1947 collision and before her ultimate DDE conversion.

Andrée Dupré, taken up as a Marine and Fisheries tug for RCN employment as an examination vessel at Halifax, was built in 1918 as a TR-class trawler but then substantially converted for her subsequent role.

FURTHER READING

Ken Macpherson, *Canada's Fighting Ships* (Hakkert, 1975/Canadian War Museum Historical Publication No. 12).

Ken Macpherson and Ron Barrie, *The Ships of Canada's Naval Forces, 1910–2001*, 3rd ed. (Vanwell Publishing, 2002).

Charles D. Maginley and Bernard Collin, *The Ships of Canada's Marine Services* (Vanwell Publishing, 2001).

Richard Mayne, "The Little Boat Has Just Put Her Lights Out:" The Life, Fate and Legacy of HMCS *Bras d'Or*," *The Northern Mariner/Le marin du nord* 24, no. 4 (October 2004), 25–40, tnm.journals.yorku.ca/index.php/default/article/view/532/507.

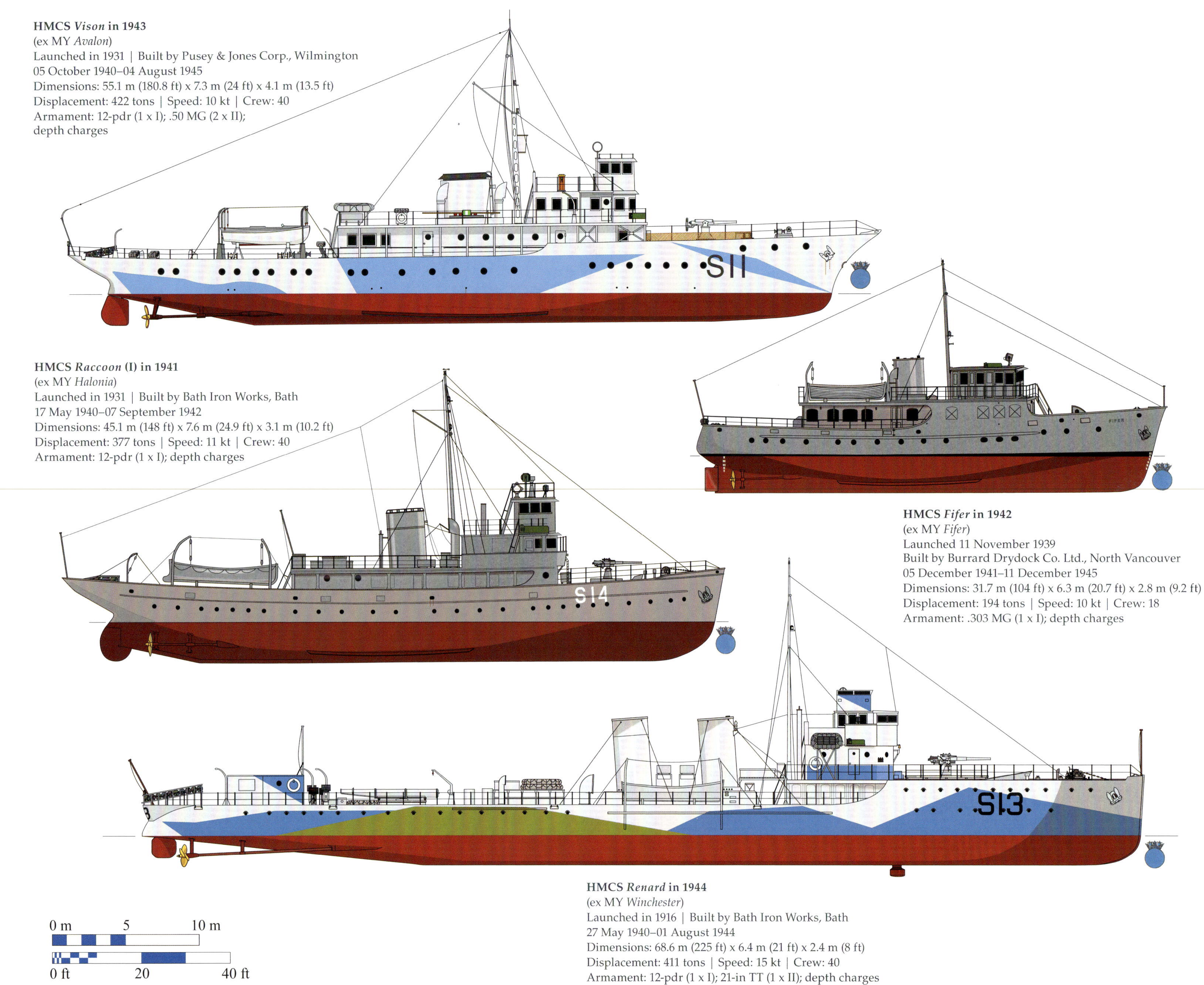

HMCS *Vison* in 1943
(ex MY *Avalon*)
Launched in 1931 | Built by Pusey & Jones Corp., Wilmington
05 October 1940–04 August 1945
Dimensions: 55.1 m (180.8 ft) x 7.3 m (24 ft) x 4.1 m (13.5 ft)
Displacement: 422 tons | Speed: 10 kt | Crew: 40
Armament: 12-pdr (1 x I); .50 MG (2 x II);
depth charges

HMCS *Raccoon* (I) in 1941
(ex MY *Halonia*)
Launched in 1931 | Built by Bath Iron Works, Bath
17 May 1940–07 September 1942
Dimensions: 45.1 m (148 ft) x 7.6 m (24.9 ft) x 3.1 m (10.2 ft)
Displacement: 377 tons | Speed: 11 kt | Crew: 40
Armament: 12-pdr (1 x I); depth charges

HMCS *Fifer* in 1942
(ex MY *Fifer*)
Launched 11 November 1939
Built by Burrard Drydock Co. Ltd., North Vancouver
05 December 1941–11 December 1945
Dimensions: 31.7 m (104 ft) x 6.3 m (20.7 ft) x 2.8 m (9.2 ft)
Displacement: 194 tons | Speed: 10 kt | Crew: 18
Armament: .303 MG (1 x I); depth charges

HMCS *Renard* in 1944
(ex MY *Winchester*)
Launched in 1916 | Built by Bath Iron Works, Bath
27 May 1940–01 August 1944
Dimensions: 68.6 m (225 ft) x 6.4 m (21 ft) x 2.4 m (8 ft)
Displacement: 411 tons | Speed: 15 kt | Crew: 40
Armament: 12-pdr (1 x I); 21-in TT (1 x II); depth charges

ARMED YACHTS OF THE SECOND WORLD WAR AND THE FISHERMEN'S RESERVE

The other acquisition program repeated from the Great War experience to fill the immediate expansion needs was to procure civilian yachts for conversion to naval purposes. This time the effort was undertaken more methodically, although in the end it proved to be little more productive than for the previous war.

For a start, the Canadian government was authorized by the Admiralty to requisition British-registered craft that could be put to use. However, that identified only a single vessel, *Trenora*, a large and fairly modern yacht owned by the Duke of Sutherland, who happened to be cruising off British Columbia in the summer of 1939. Renamed *Sans Peur* and initially fitted out for patrol duties at Esquimalt, she underwent an extensive refit in 1943 to make her suitable for antisubmarine training and soon after was transferred to the East Coast to perform that function, working with British submarines at HMCS *Cornwallis* in the Bay of Fundy. Next, the only Canadian-owned vessel that could be found in a suitable condition was the sturdy steel-hulled *Ambler* (which retained her name upon conversion), but she proved to be too slow for patrol work and spent most of the war as the Halifax-based tender to the shore establishment HMCS *Stadacona* (named for the Great War yacht).

But other Canadian yachts turned out to be "suitable" in different fashion. Macpherson and Barrie synthesize nicely how, in December 1939, the RCN made "a

The future armed yacht *Raccoon* in her pre-conversion life as the yacht *Halonia*.

discreet survey of the U.S. yacht market," which turned up a dozen vessels showing promise:

> Purchase seemed impossible without contravening neutrality regulations. It was accordingly arranged for a sufficient number of Canadian yachts, however inadequate, to be requisitioned from their owners, who then replaced them with yachts [they had then] purchased in the US. These replacements had, of course, already been selected with care by the RCN — which, "discovering" that the replacements were better than the yachts originally requisitioned, took over the replacements instead.[13]

Once in naval hands early in 1940, they were given new names — all for Canadian animals — in a modest attempt to disguise their origin. Then they were turned over to various yards along the East Coast and in Quebec for conversion, which typically involved building up and enclosing the wheelhouse, strengthening the hull, remodelling the interior for crew messdecks and a galley, and finally fitting out with the variety of available armament, largely leftovers from the Great War. The table at the end of this entry gives a sense of the hodgepodge assemblage (the listing gives the two actual "Canadian" acquisitions first, then the dozen American vessels). In this respect, *Renard* was unique in being equipped with a pair of 21-inch torpedo tubes; she was also the most warship-looking of the lot, with twin funnels, a long, low quarterdeck, and raised open-bridge arrangement, not much different from *Patriot-Patrician* and *Champlain-Vancouver* — but even only ten years on, quite obsolete and fortunately never called to action.

The relatively late date of their acquisition, compounded by the several-months length of the conversion process, meant that none of them would be ready for action before the summer of 1940. Fortunately, that corresponded to the end of the quiet "Phony War" phase of the war, after which they supported the makeshift local East Coast defence efforts until the corvettes became available to replace them in the spring and summer of 1941. In the event, none of the lot proved to be helpful for anything much more than the mundane but necessary tasks of harbour defence and training. The advances in naval technology over the interwar years had simply outpaced the scope for adaptation of civilian pleasure craft, which had hulls that were neither large enough to ship engines capable of generating any great speed nor sturdy enough to carry heavy armaments such as modern guns or depth charges. Still, along with the vessels taken up from other government departments (discussed in Chapter 12), the armed yachts performed yeoman service as the introduction to shipboard and naval life for a significant proportion of the some ninety thousand RCNVR recruits who joined the Navy through the course of the war, and the little "animals" were quite appropriate to their situation.

None of that made for operational stories as colourful as their Great War predecessors, although as if to underscore the dangers of wartime service, two of them came to be lost: *Otter*, in an accidental explosion leading to a fire in which two officers and seventeen men died; and *Raccoon*, pressed into service with the Gaspé Force in the desperate summer of 1942 when Germany brought the war into the Gulf of St. Lawrence, only to be torpedoed by *U 165* and lost with all hands (four officers and thirty-three men).

The other twelve that survived the war were paid off and put up for sale. Many returned to their previous employ, and at the time of writing (2024), at least one was still active as a private yacht — *Moose*, as the yacht *Uthingo* (details can be found on websites such as superyachttimes.com). The memory connection with the Navy continued over the years, through the perpetuation of many of the "animal" names, initially given to the several Fairmile motor launches reactivated for Reserve training in the 1950–70s, and currently to the eight Orca-class patrol training craft stationed in Esquimalt (see, respectively, Chapters 19 and 44).

Whereas all the above vessels were employed primarily on the Atlantic coast, another quite different group

This aerial view of the armed yacht *Wolf* shows her upper-deck arrangement, with an especially good angle of the depth charges on the quarterdeck aft.

of civilian vessels served exclusively on the Pacific. The Fishermen's Reserve had been formed before the war to meet the particular needs of the British Columbia coastline "with its hundreds of islands, inlets and channels,"[14] considered to be vulnerable to infestation by Japanese raiding parties. Assessing that the most competent group to patrol these remote waters would be those most familiar with them by the nature of their occupation, Commanding Officer Pacific Coast, Captain Victor Brodeur (who as a junior officer had been a major figure in Hose's 1923 reorganization of the RCNVR), instituted a training program in February 1939 to familiarize volunteer fishermen with basic naval duties. After the four River-class destroyers departed on their dash to the East Coast in September 1939, sixteen of these "skipper coxswains" reported for duty with their vessels at Esquimalt and Prince Rupert, and until the corvettes began to commission in numbers by late 1941, they were the only naval

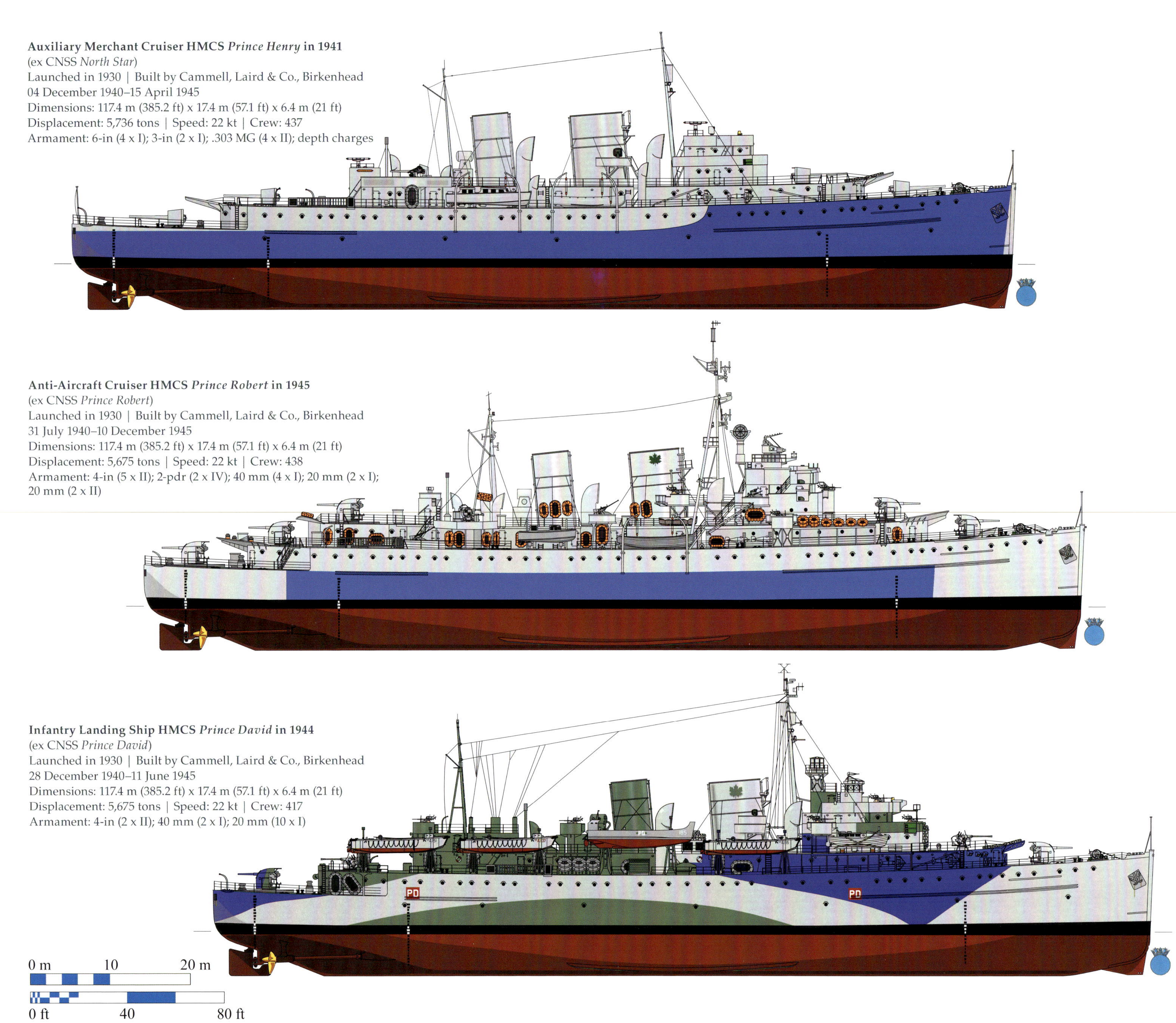

Auxiliary Merchant Cruiser HMCS *Prince Henry* in 1941
(ex CNSS *North Star*)
Launched in 1930 | Built by Cammell, Laird & Co., Birkenhead
04 December 1940–15 April 1945
Dimensions: 117.4 m (385.2 ft) x 17.4 m (57.1 ft) x 6.4 m (21 ft)
Displacement: 5,736 tons | Speed: 22 kt | Crew: 437
Armament: 6-in (4 x I); 3-in (2 x I); .303 MG (4 x II); depth charges

Anti-Aircraft Cruiser HMCS *Prince Robert* in 1945
(ex CNSS *Prince Robert*)
Launched in 1930 | Built by Cammell, Laird & Co., Birkenhead
31 July 1940–10 December 1945
Dimensions: 117.4 m (385.2 ft) x 17.4 m (57.1 ft) x 6.4 m (21 ft)
Displacement: 5,675 tons | Speed: 22 kt | Crew: 438
Armament: 4-in (5 x II); 2-pdr (2 x IV); 40 mm (4 x I); 20 mm (2 x I); 20 mm (2 x II)

Infantry Landing Ship HMCS *Prince David* in 1944
(ex CNSS *Prince David*)
Launched in 1930 | Built by Cammell, Laird & Co., Birkenhead
28 December 1940–11 June 1945
Dimensions: 117.4 m (385.2 ft) x 17.4 m (57.1 ft) x 6.4 m (21 ft)
Displacement: 5,675 tons | Speed: 22 kt | Crew: 417
Armament: 4-in (2 x II); 40 mm (2 x I); 20 mm (10 x I)

14

THE PRINCES: THE ARMED MERCHANT CRUISERS

A third option described by the naval staff in its September 18, 1939, recommendations to Cabinet for the rapid expansion of the Navy was one that had not previously been undertaken by the RCN in the Great War: the conversion of passenger liners into armed merchant cruisers. The notion, however, was quite familiar to Canadian naval professionals, having been a practice of the British RN since the late nineteenth century. Indeed, the RN already had several fitting out in Canadian yards at the beginning of the war. One was the SS *Letitia*, sister ship of *Athenia*, famous for being the first commercial ship sunk in the war, on September 3, 1939, thus marking the onset of the Battle of the Atlantic. Another well-known example was the 14,000-ton *Jervis Bay*, sunk while defending a convoy from the German pocket battleship *Admiral Scheer* in the mid-Atlantic on November 5, 1940. Indeed, that the German Kriegsmarine also had a number of the armed merchant cruiser type was part of the rationale for Canadian acquisition of the Tribal-class destroyers to counter them.

The three vessels that the RCN identified were somewhat smaller, at 5,600 tons, and so not a priority for the RN. The Steam Ships (SS) *Prince David*, *Prince Henry*, and *Prince Robert* had been built at Birkenhead, England, in 1930 for the Canadian National Steamship Company and were the most suitable Canadian-registered ships available for conversion. Although the company was government-owned, the ships' wartime acquisition was

A colourized postcard of SS *Prince Robert* in Canadian National livery before her acquisition and conversion by the Navy.

complicated in that *Prince Henry* had been sold to a private company in 1938 and also that the alterations were substantial enough to warrant their outright purchase rather than a charter-hire arrangement. As such, it was not until February 1940 that *Prince David* (which had been operating on the East Coast) and *Prince Robert* (on the West Coast) could be taken in hand for conversion at Halifax Shipyards and Burrard Dry Dock, respectively. *Prince Henry*, also based on the Atlantic, went in for conversion at Canadian Vickers in Montreal in mid-May. Pritchard describes the extent of the conversions: "Each of the three ships had its two upper decks removed as well as one funnel; they were then fitted with a cruiser-style superstructure and bridge and were armed with four 6-inch and two 3-inch guns, some light anti-aircraft guns, and a number of depth charges."[16] The pace of work varied greatly among the three yards, with *Prince Robert* completed and commissioned by mid-July 1940, but *Prince Henry* not until the beginning of December, and *Prince David* in Halifax slowest of all, commissioned at the end of that month.

Prince Robert was also quick to prove her worth, capturing the German freighter *Weser* off the west coast of Mexico in September 1940. She continued routine cruising, culminating in December 1941 with escorting the transport carrying the ill-fated Canadian garrison to Hong Kong. In May 1942, the other two ships were ordered to the West Coast to join *Prince Robert* in meeting the Japanese threat, ranging as far as the Aleutian Islands after their occupation. The operational conditions faced there, however, made it clear that armed merchant cruisers were no longer effective for the changed nature of naval warfare, and early in 1943, all three were paid off and handed over to Burrard Dry Dock for yet another major conversion to make them better suited for operations in the coming invasion of Europe.

The first to emerge was *Prince Robert*, recommissioned on June 7, 1943, as an auxiliary anti-aircraft cruiser, now sporting five twin 4-inch HA/LA dual-purpose guns, eight 2-pounder pom-poms, and twelve 20-mm Oerlikons. Transferred to British operational control, she arrived in the U.K. in late August and entered a dockyard on the Clyde for fitting of additional anti-aircraft equipment, including an improved Type 291 radar, a pair of Type 242 IFF (Identification Friend or Foe), and another six Oerlikons (for a total of eighteen), making her one of the most powerful anti-aircraft ships of her size afloat. In

November, she was assigned to Gibraltar Command and then in January 1944 to Plymouth Command but keeping the same duty to escort U.K.–Mediterranean convoys. She saw action on several occasions through the next ten months, in this fashion supporting the Normandy invasion from a distance, although unable to claim any enemy aircraft actually shot down. In September 1944, she was ordered to return to Esquimalt for a regular refit that lasted until June 1945. Sailing early the next month for service with the British Pacific Fleet (BPF), she arrived at Sydney, Australia, on August 10, and then went on to Hong Kong to represent Canada at the Japanese surrender ceremonies there. Embarking the released prisoners of war — many of them were men she had escorted there in late 1941 — she returned to Esquimalt, arriving on October 20.

In their turn, *Prince David* and *Prince Henry* were converted to Landing Ships Infantry (Medium; LSI[M]), each equipped to carry eight massive 20-ton landing craft hung on quadrangular davits, four per side along the upper deck. The 6-inch guns were removed and replaced with a pair of the twin 4-inch HA/LA mounts (one each forward and aft), two single 40-mm Bofors, and another ten 20-mm Oerlikons. Recommissioned over the new year of 1943–44, they were dispatched immediately to the United Kingdom for the coming invasion. *Prince Henry* embarked the eight Landing Craft Assault (LCA) of the 528th Flotilla and *Prince David* the six LCA of the 529th Flotilla (see listings in Chapter 20 on Coastal Forces [Overseas]). After landing Canadian troops at Juno Beach on D-Day, the ships were reassigned to take part in Operation Dragoon (the invasion of southern France) on August 15, and then onward for the liberation of Greece through the fall. *Prince David* struck a mine on December 10 and underwent temporary repairs in North Africa before carrying on for a fuller refit in Esquimalt. *Prince Henry* continued operations in the Mediterranean until March 1945, then proceeded to London for refit. During these respective refits, the RN requested that the pair be made available for operations in Southeast Asia, with the proviso that if the RCN could not crew them, the RN would take them on. The Canadian commitment to the BPF had already been determined to include just *Prince Robert*, so accordingly these others were paid off to be transferred to the RN and were still in dockyard hands when Japan surrendered.

Assault landing craft from *Prince David* head for the Normandy beaches.

After Victory over Japan (VJ) Day, all three were declared surplus. The armaments and landing craft of the two Princes still in Canadian hands (*David* and *Robert*) were removed as appropriate for future naval use (the twin 4-inch mounts found their way onto a couple of the Tribals for their conversion to DDE standard) and the ships sold off for mercantile purposes. Meanwhile, *Prince Henry*, in British hands, ended her days renamed as the North Sea troopship *Empire Parkston* and was the last to be broken up, in 1962.

The legacy of the Prince-class armed merchant cruisers is a mixed one. They filled a need identified early in the war for the protection of Canada's coasts against a threat that failed to materialize and, being unsuited for antisubmarine duty on the North Atlantic Run but with the exceptional range of an ocean liner, instead found employment in a variety of tasks mostly outside the accepted roles of the RCN. Especially once converted to the anti-air and landing ship configurations, they were productively engaged in European waters, assisting the various invasions for the retaking of the Continent. Fraser McKee gives the final word: "All who sailed in them are quite prepared to reminisce about the Princes with rarely a critical word."[17]

FURTHER READING

Robert A. Darlington and Fraser M. McKee, *Three Princes Armed: Luxury Liners to Warships* (2008).

Fraser McKee, "Princes Three: Canada's Use of Armed Merchant Cruisers During World War II," in *RCN in Retrospect, 1910–1968*, ed. James Boutilier (UBC Press, 1982), 116–137.

James Pritchard, *A Bridge of Ships: Canadian Shipbuilding During the Second World War* (McGill-Queens University Press, 2011).

C.R. Shelley, "HMCS *Prince Robert*: The Career of an Armed Merchant Cruiser," *Canadian Military History* 4, no. 1 (1995): 47–60.

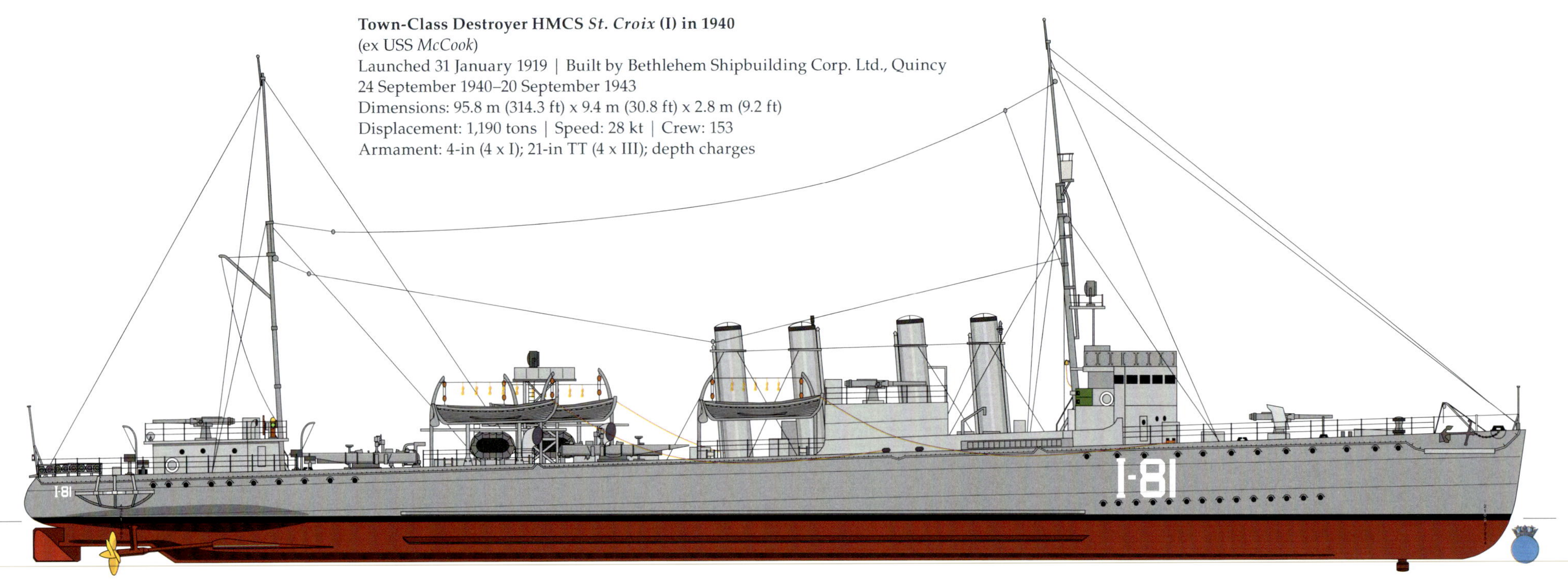

Town-Class Destroyer HMCS *St. Croix* (I) in 1940
(ex USS *McCook*)
Launched 31 January 1919 | Built by Bethlehem Shipbuilding Corp. Ltd., Quincy
24 September 1940–20 September 1943
Dimensions: 95.8 m (314.3 ft) x 9.4 m (30.8 ft) x 2.8 m (9.2 ft)
Displacement: 1,190 tons | Speed: 28 kt | Crew: 153
Armament: 4-in (4 x I); 21-in TT (4 x III); depth charges

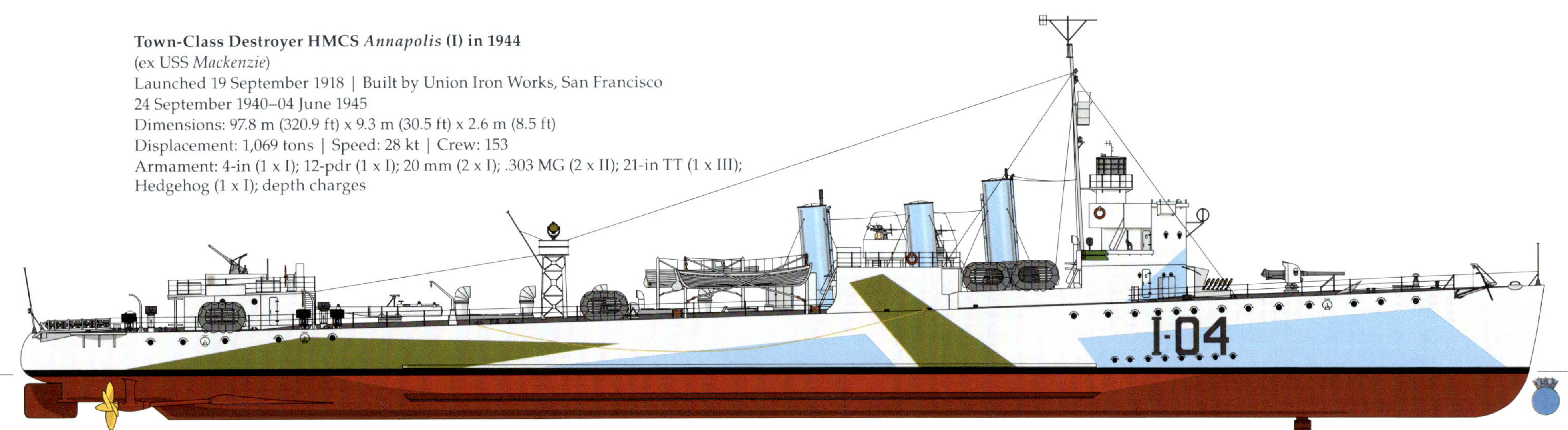

Town-Class Destroyer HMCS *Annapolis* (I) in 1944
(ex USS *Mackenzie*)
Launched 19 September 1918 | Built by Union Iron Works, San Francisco
24 September 1940–04 June 1945
Dimensions: 97.8 m (320.9 ft) x 9.3 m (30.5 ft) x 2.6 m (8.5 ft)
Displacement: 1,069 tons | Speed: 28 kt | Crew: 153
Armament: 4-in (1 x I); 12-pdr (1 x I); 20 mm (2 x I); .303 MG (2 x II); 21-in TT (1 x III); Hedgehog (1 x I); depth charges

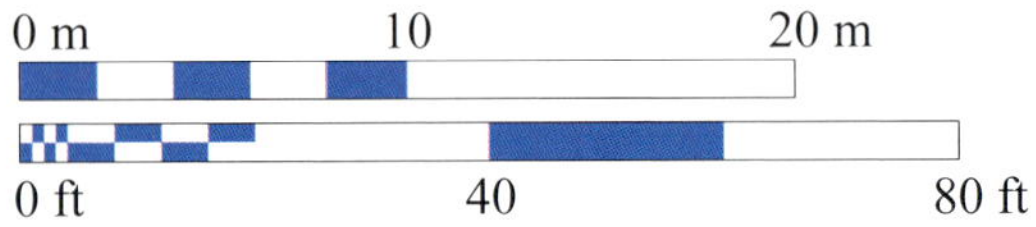

TOWN-CLASS (BORDER RIVER) DESTROYERS

In the late summer of 1940, a full year into the war, the RCN received an unexpected boost to its expansion effort. On September 2, with the Battle of Britain raging and defeat a real possibility, British Prime Minister Winston Churchill and American President Franklin D. Roosevelt confirmed a "destroyers-for-bases deal," whereby an emergency transfer was made to the RN of fifty surplus United States Navy (USN) destroyers in exchange for American access to various British bases ringing the North Atlantic. All the ships were delivered to Halifax through an RN section established to receive them, but the British were unable to crew all of them, so they convinced the Canadians to keep six. Renamed by the RN for towns found in both Britain and the U.S., in Canada — building upon the naming convention for destroyers — they were given names of rivers bordering or near the U.S. (see table below). As such, they were known interchangeably as the Town or Border River class, or more colloquially as "flush-deck destroyers" or "the four-stackers," in reference to their distinguishing upper deck and funnel arrangements.

Canadian naval staff were convinced to take them on with some reluctance, as the RCN was experiencing difficulties itself raising crews for the ongoing expansion programs of the armed yachts then commissioning, along with the Prince-class armed merchant cruisers and the first of the corvettes soon expected to enter service. Moreover, these were far from ideal warships — all had been built two decades previously as part of the USN expansion in the last year of the Great War, just in time to be put into reserve after the Armistice. And, although they had nice, long, sleek lines and could put in a good turn of

Name/Pendant # (ex-USS)	Built	Launched USN/Comm'd RCN	Fate/Remarks
Annapolis/I-04 (ex-*Mackenzie* 175)	Union Iron Works San Francisco, CA	Sep 19, 1918/Sep 24, 1940	Paid off June 4, 1945
Columbia/I-49 (ex-*Haraden* 183)	Newport News S.B. Newport News, VA	July 4, 1918/Sep 24, 1940	Paid off June 12, 1945
Niagara/I-57 (ex-*Thatcher* 162)	Bethlehem S.B. Quincy, MA	Aug 31, 1918/Sep 24, 1940	Paid off Sep 15, 1945
St. Clair/I-65 (ex-*Williams* 108)	Union Iron Works San Francisco, CA	July 4, 1918/Sep 24, 1940	Paid off Aug 23, 1944 Training hulk HMCS *Cornwallis*
St. Croix/I-81 (ex-*McCook* 252)	Bethlehem S.B. Quincy, MA	Jan 31, 1919/Sep 24, 1940	Torpedoed by *U 305* and sunk Sep 20, 1943
St. Francis/I-93 (ex-*Bancroft* 256)	Bethlehem S.B. Quincy, MA	Mar 21, 1919/Sep 24, 1940	Paid off June 11, 1945
Hamilton/I-24 (ex-*Kalk* 170) (ex-HMS *Hamilton*)	Bethlehem S.B. Quincy, MA	Dec 21, 1918/July 6, 1941	Paid off June 8, 1945
Buxton/H96 (ex-*Edwards* 265) (ex-HMS *Buxton*)	Bethlehem S.B. Quincy, MA	Oct 10, 1918/Nov 4, 1943	Paid off June 2, 1945

speed, at only 1,100 tons displacement (for comparison, about the vintage and size of *Patriot* and *Patrician*), they were not good open-ocean sea-keepers and, as would soon be discovered, were given to instability with any increased top weight; for example, owing to icing.

But they were "ships in hand" and, after being commissioned as a group on September 24, 1940, were distributed to various nearby shipyards for rather substantial modifications to bring their machinery and weapons up to date. Two of the four boilers were removed in favour of fuel tanks to greatly increase their range, albeit at the expense of speed (dropped from a maximum of 35 knots to 28 knots). Only the forward single 4-inch gun and a single bank of triple-21-inch torpedo tubes were kept, and the remaining original USN armament was replaced with one 12-pounder gun, four 20-mm Oerlikons, a pair of .50-cal machine guns, and depth-charge racks and throwers at the stern. New additions were British makes of radar and sonar; later in the war, from late 1943, Hedgehog was mounted just forward of the bridge.

After some initial shakedown issues, all were in service by March 1941. Over the course of the war, the RN would transfer two additional ships of the type to the RCN, both keeping their "new" RN names on commissioning as HMC Ships: *Hamilton* on July 6, 1941, and *Buxton* on November 4, 1943.

Even with the additional fuel storage, they still had relatively short "legs," and, compounded by their poor sea-keeping abilities, they tended to be assigned to near-offshore escort operations on both sides of the Atlantic, typically the Western Local Escort Force (from New England and Halifax to northeast of Newfoundland) or the Escort Groups operating in the Western Approaches of the British Isles. *St. Croix* was the only one of the class to have success against U-boats, sinking two of them (*U 90* on July 24, 1942, and assisting *Shediac* against *U 87* on March 4, 1943), before being sunk herself by *U 305* on September 20, 1943.

Most of the others soon developed significant engineering difficulties, and none were still fully operational by the last year of the war, all by then having been assigned to various training functions with HMCS *Cornwallis*. *St. Clair* suffered the worst indignity of being reduced

A pair of Town-class destroyers in the busy port of St. John's, Newfoundland and Labrador: *Columbia* alongside the jetty and *Niagara* outboard of her.

to a firefighting and damage control hulk in the Bedford Basin. All were paid off soon after VE Day for sale as scrap. Several would see their names perpetuated in the St. Laurent and derivative "River" classes of the 1950s (see Chapter 25).

FURTHER READING

S.D. Campbell, "Towns from America," in *Tin-Can Canucks: A Century of Canadian Destroyers* (Kay Cee Publications, 2017), 56–79.

John Henshaw, *Town Class Destroyers: A Critical Assessment* (The Crowood Press, 2018).

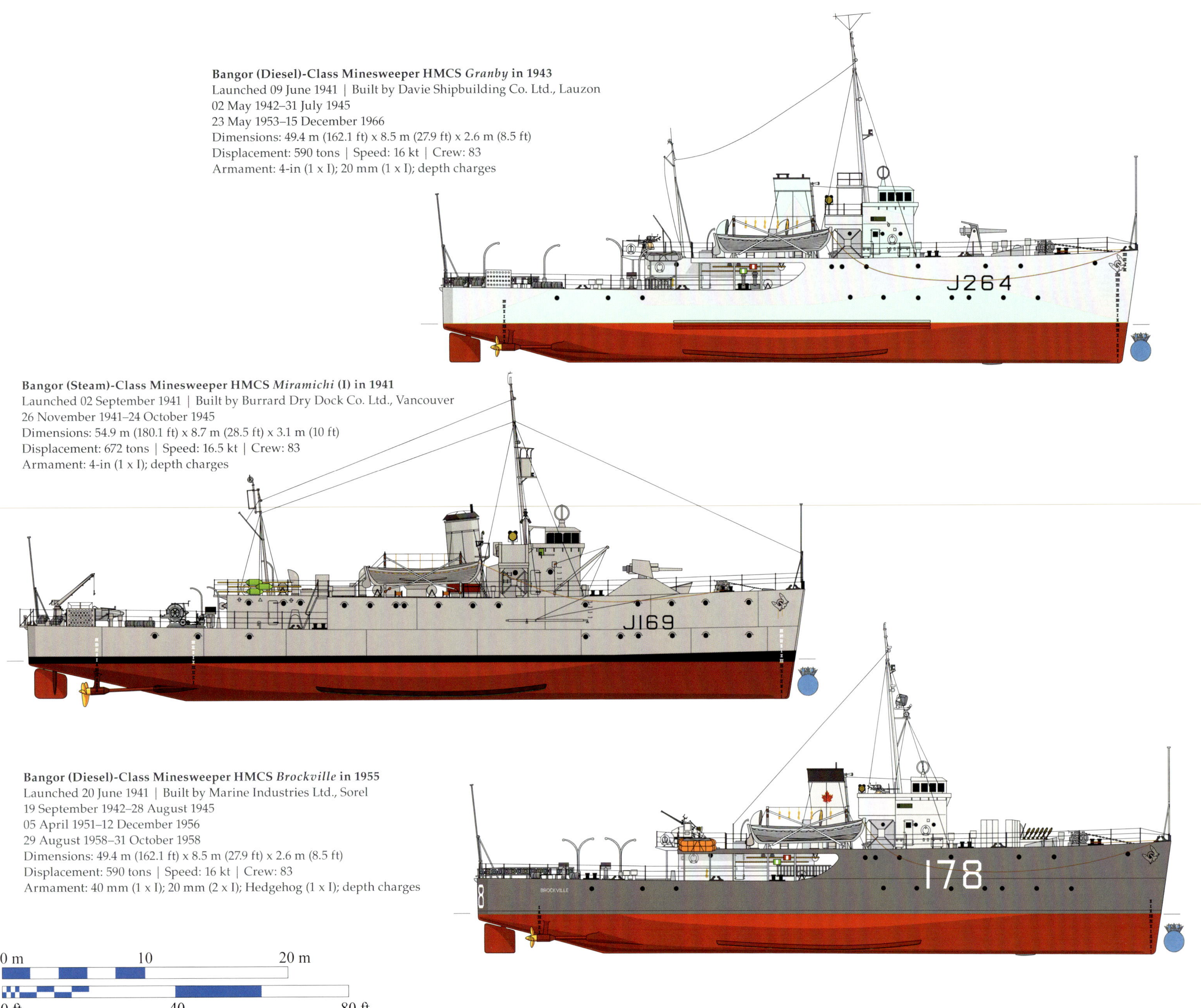

Bangor (Diesel)-Class Minesweeper HMCS *Granby* in 1943
Launched 09 June 1941 | Built by Davie Shipbuilding Co. Ltd., Lauzon
02 May 1942–31 July 1945
23 May 1953–15 December 1966
Dimensions: 49.4 m (162.1 ft) x 8.5 m (27.9 ft) x 2.6 m (8.5 ft)
Displacement: 590 tons | Speed: 16 kt | Crew: 83
Armament: 4-in (1 x I); 20 mm (1 x I); depth charges

Bangor (Steam)-Class Minesweeper HMCS *Miramichi* (I) in 1941
Launched 02 September 1941 | Built by Burrard Dry Dock Co. Ltd., Vancouver
26 November 1941–24 October 1945
Dimensions: 54.9 m (180.1 ft) x 8.7 m (28.5 ft) x 3.1 m (10 ft)
Displacement: 672 tons | Speed: 16.5 kt | Crew: 83
Armament: 4-in (1 x I); depth charges

Bangor (Diesel)-Class Minesweeper HMCS *Brockville* in 1955
Launched 20 June 1941 | Built by Marine Industries Ltd., Sorel
19 September 1942–28 August 1945
05 April 1951–12 December 1956
29 August 1958–31 October 1958
Dimensions: 49.4 m (162.1 ft) x 8.5 m (27.9 ft) x 2.6 m (8.5 ft)
Displacement: 590 tons | Speed: 16 kt | Crew: 83
Armament: 40 mm (1 x I); 20 mm (2 x I); Hedgehog (1 x I); depth charges

16

BANGOR-CLASS MINESWEEPERS

The Bangor class first came to the attention of the Canadian naval staff during the September 1939 planning for warship construction to build up the Canadian fleet. After destroyers to combat enemy surface raiders and coastal escorts for convoys, the next priority was for minesweepers, and the initial inclination was to build more of the recently acquired Fundy class (see Chapter 9), which was based on the British Basset class. The advice from the Admiralty, however, was that any further construction should be directed to a new design then being introduced into the RN, the Bangor class. Only slightly larger than the Basset/Fundy class, the Bangors had more efficient sweeping gear and burned oil instead of coal, resulting in much better endurance and speed. And they could be built without difficulty in Canadian yards.

The expansion program approved by Cabinet on September 19, 1939, therefore included an initial order for eighteen of the Bangor class (the same number that had been planned for a repeat of the Fundy class). In the event, the design would prove so successful to construct and operate that follow-on orders were approved for twenty more in 1940 and a final ten in 1941. With the RN also ordering a dozen in 1939, sixty were built in Canadian yards, spread across both coasts and on the Great Lakes (another 51 were built in British yards for the RN, for a total of 111 in the class). Of those ordered in Canada for the RN, the six built on the West Coast were transferred on loan to the RCN, for a total of fifty-four of the type commissioned as HMC Ships (see complete list below). In the RCN, the initial eighteen Bangors followed the convention of the Fundy class in minesweepers being

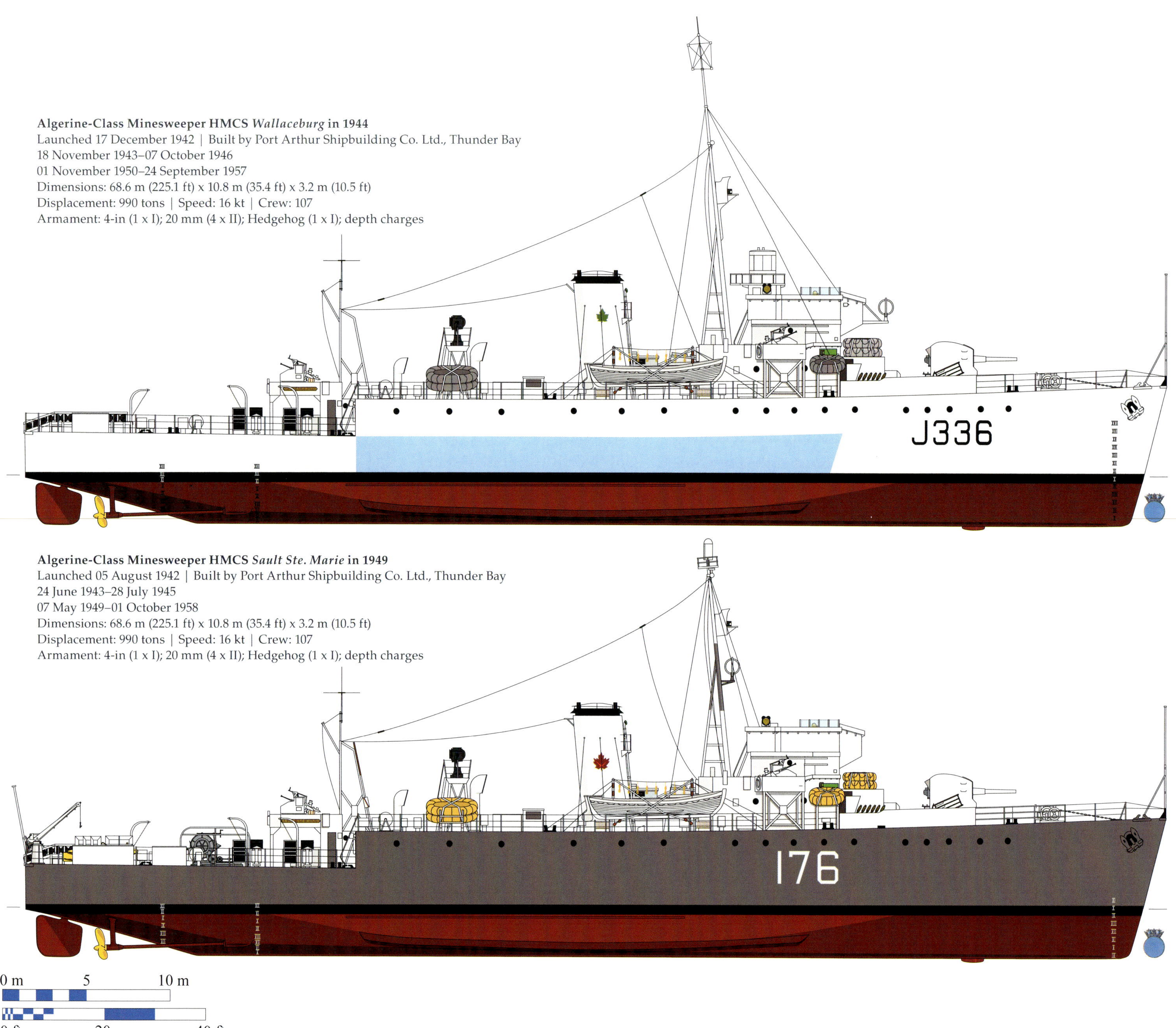
Algerine-Class Minesweeper HMCS *Wallaceburg* in 1944
Launched 17 December 1942 | Built by Port Arthur Shipbuilding Co. Ltd., Thunder Bay
18 November 1943–07 October 1946
01 November 1950–24 September 1957
Dimensions: 68.6 m (225.1 ft) x 10.8 m (35.4 ft) x 3.2 m (10.5 ft)
Displacement: 990 tons | Speed: 16 kt | Crew: 107
Armament: 4-in (1 x I); 20 mm (4 x II); Hedgehog (1 x I); depth charges
J336
Algerine-Class Minesweeper HMCS *Sault Ste. Marie* in 1949
Launched 05 August 1942 | Built by Port Arthur Shipbuilding Co. Ltd., Thunder Bay
24 June 1943–28 July 1945
07 May 1949–01 October 1958
Dimensions: 68.6 m (225.1 ft) x 10.8 m (35.4 ft) x 3.2 m (10.5 ft)
Displacement: 990 tons | Speed: 16 kt | Crew: 107
Armament: 4-in (1 x I); 20 mm (4 x II); Hedgehog (1 x I); depth charges
176
0 m
5
10 m
0 ft
20
40 ft

17

ALGERINE-CLASS MINESWEEPERS

In October 1941, as the war looked to be settling into a drawn-out campaign against the U-boats, the Canadian naval staff undertook a reassessment of the need for additional construction of ocean escorts and an improved minesweeper to counter the new type of magnetic mine the Germans were known to be developing. The Bangors were deficient in both respects — they were too small to handle the equipment associated with the new sweeping gear and were just then entering service and proving to be too poor sea-keepers for convoy work on the open Atlantic. The British Admiralty had identified the same issues with their Bangors and once again had a new design to fit the requirement for a replacement.

The Algerine-class minesweeper was essentially a stretched Bangor, at 45 feet (13.7 m) longer and with a slightly raked and flared bow, making them more seaworthy and providing additional space for new equipment, more crew, and extra fuel tanks for increased endurance. Having many of the same design elements as the Bangors also meant an easy transition for construction in Canadian yards, where 62 of the type would be built (another 48 were built in Britain, for a total of 110 in the class). The first were laid down in mid-1942, but as they were building, the RCN determined that the magnetic mine threat to Canadian waters was diminishing and cut back their orders to twelve. None of them were fitted with sweeping gear, but instead Hedgehog mortars and depth charges. The British used them only in the sweeping role, but their early experience confirmed the Algerines were no better suited than the Bangors for the ocean escort role, so a further sixteen building for the

The Algerine-class minesweeper *Oshawa* in her wartime colours.

RCN were exchanged with the RN for the dozen Castle-class corvettes (see Chapter 11).

The first to be completed and commissioned was *Sault Ste Marie*, at the end of June 1943, and the remainder followed at the rate of roughly one per six weeks, the last being *New Liskeard* in November 1944. All of them were assigned to the Western Escort Force off the Atlantic seaboard, but by that late stage of the war, that area of operations was seeing little action. The most noteworthy experience for the class was *Rockcliffe* accepting the surrender of *U 889* and escorting the submarine to Shelbourne, Nova Scotia, on May 10, 1945.

Border Cities	J344	*New Liskeard*	J397/168	*St. Boniface*	J332
Fort Frances	J396/170	*Oshawa*	J330/174	*Sault Ste Marie*	J334/176
Kapuskasing	J326/171	*Portage*	J331/169	*Wallaceburg*	J336/172
Middlesex	J328	*Rockcliffe*	J355/173	*Winnipeg*	J337/177

Because they had ended the war in fairly good condition, the bulk of the class was retained into the next decade for various training and oceanographic research duties (for which they were assigned new numeric pennant numbers, shown in the table this page). The last to pay off was *New Liskeard*, on May 1, 1969.

FURTHER READING

James Pritchard, *A Bridge of Ships: Canadian Shipbuilding During the Second World War* (McGill-Queens University Press, 2011).

River-Class Frigate HMCS *Beacon Hill* in 1944
Launched 06 November 1943 | Built by Yarrows Ltd., Esquimalt
16 May 1944–06 February 1946
21 December 1957–15 September 1967
Dimensions: 91.9 m (301.5 ft) x 11.1 m (36.4 ft) x 3.9 m (12.8 ft)
Displacement: 1,445 tons | Speed: 19 kt | Crew: 141
Armament: 4-in (1 x II); 12-pdr (1 x I); 20 mm (4 x II); Hedgehog (1 x I); depth charges

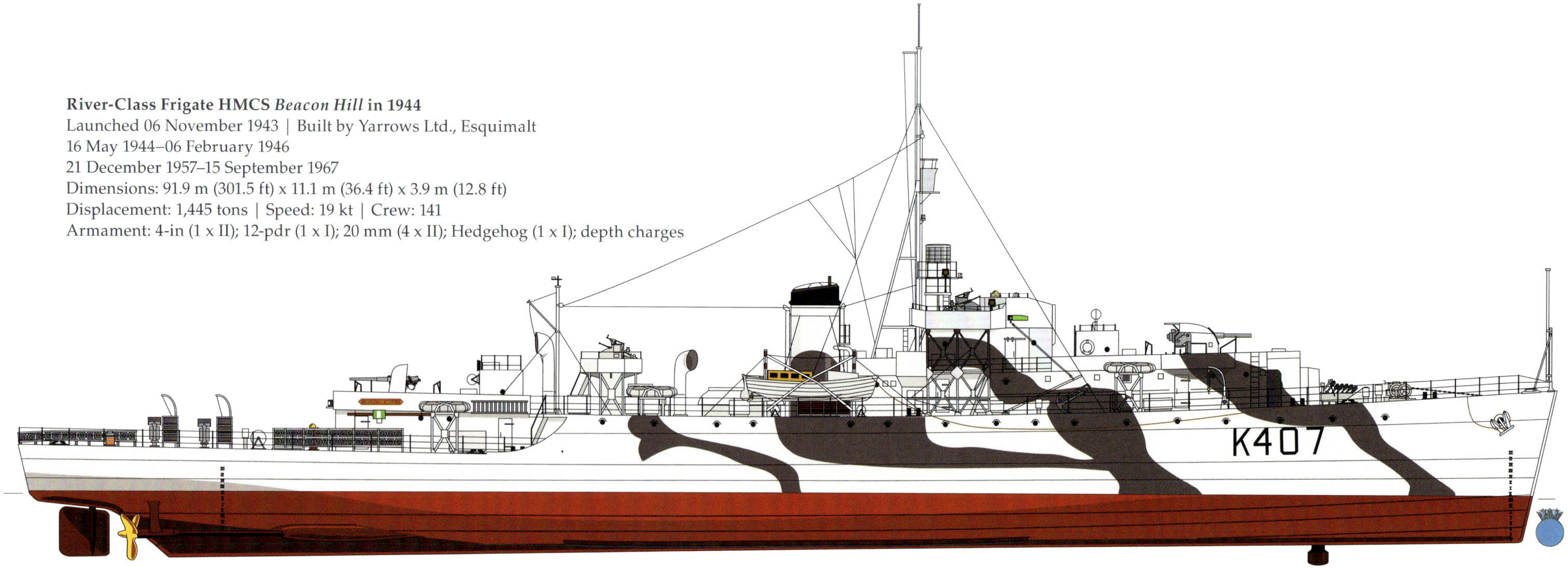

K407

Loch-Class Frigate HMCS *Loch Morlich* in 1944
(ex HMS *Loch Morlich*)
Launched 25 January 1944 | Built by Swan, Hunter & Wigham Richardson Ltd., Wallsend-on-Tyne
17 July 1944–20 June 1945
Dimensions: 93.6 m (286 ft) x 11.7 m (38.6 ft) x 2.7 m (9 ft)
Displacement: 1,435 tons | Speed: 19 kt | Crew: 141
Armament: 4-in (1 x I); 2-pdr (1 x IV); 20 mm (2 x II); 20 mm (2 x I); Squid mortars (2 x I); depth charges

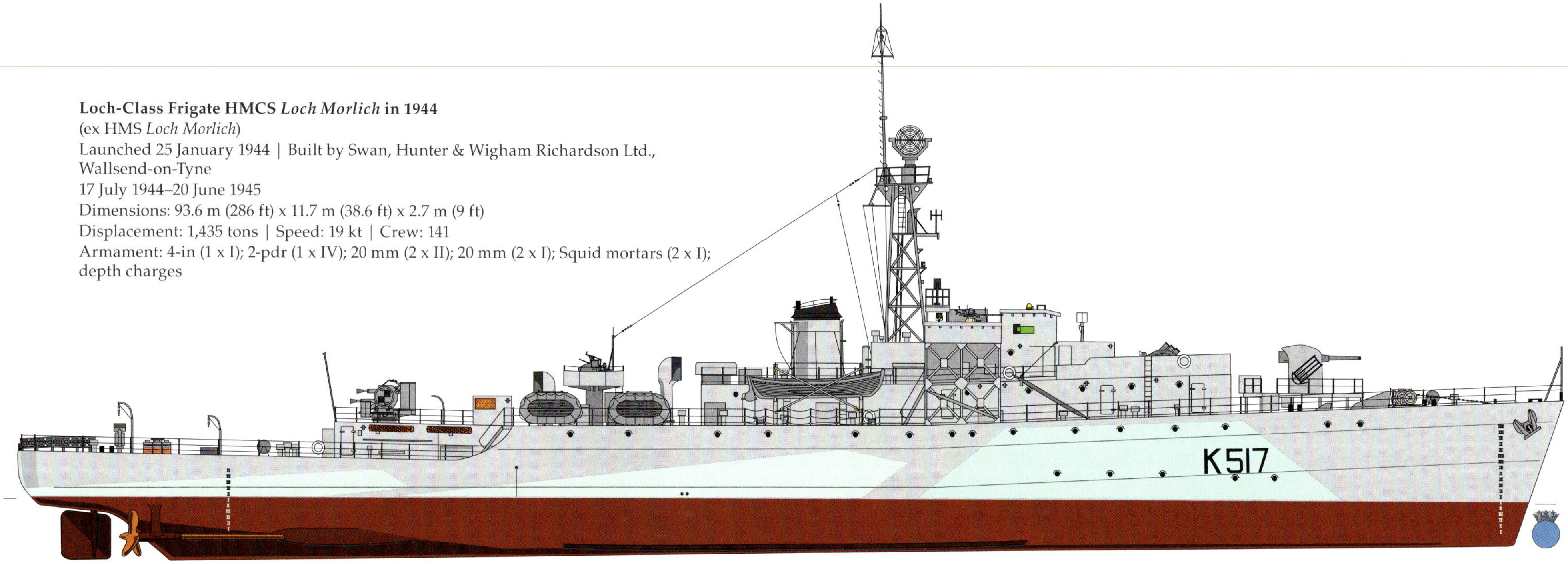

K517

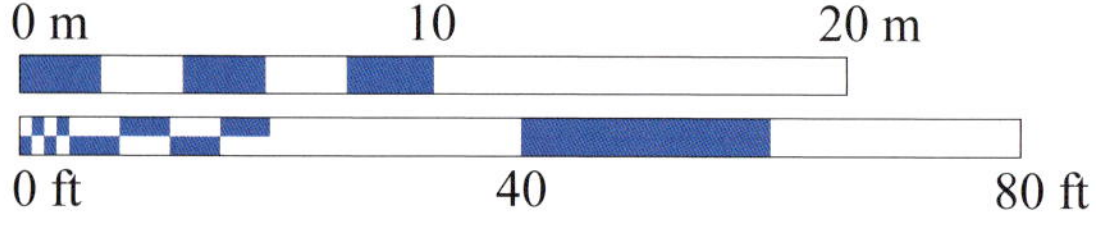

18

FRIGATES: RIVERS AND LOCHS

The Admiralty initiated the quest for a better open-ocean escort in November 1940, when the corvettes were proving unsatisfactory in having to be adapted to that role. Interestingly, Their Lordships turned to the originator of the corvette, William Reed of Smith's Dock Company, who proposed a design with lines clearly showing its heritage but that was a full third longer (301 feet/92 m, from 205 feet/62.5 m) and heavier (an added 500 tons, up to 1,445), making it a better sea-keeper and able to fit two of the "increased endurance" corvette reciprocating engines already in use, along with a pair of improved water-tube boilers. Reed unsurprisingly labelled it the "twin-screw corvette." It was really a whole new type, however, and to underscore the difference, Canadian CNS Rear Admiral Percy Nelles suggested reviving the out-of-use term "frigate," and the name took hold.[18] Wartime propagandists, using language in vogue elsewise, would later style them "pocket destroyers."

The several other advantages of the frigate over the corvette included increased speed of 19 knots, a critical 3-knot advantage when manoeuvring against U-boats whether they were surfaced or submerged; a range of 7,200 nm (13,300 km) at 12 knots, nearly double that of the original corvette; more space for better crew accommodation than the cramped and wet conditions of the original "whale catcher"; and better armament and sensors (discussed below). The RN ordered its first of the type in February 1941, but the greater complexity of the design required a longer build time, so did not commission the first, HMS *Rother*, until April 3, 1942. In total, British yards would build 73 of them, with a nearly equal number (70) in Canadian yards and 8 in Australia,

The congested Halifax waterfront confirms the bustle of activity in the wartime port. The censor has scratched out the pennant numbers, but most of the warships are River-class frigates (dating the image to probably sometime in 1944–45), and the majority of other craft are auxiliaries of various sorts.

for a total of 151 in the class. The British named them for rivers (hence the name given to the class), as did the Australians, whereas the Canadians — having already reserved that nomenclature for destroyers — gave these more of the now-commonplace names of cities and towns, popular for the war effort but making it impossible to distinguish most other wartime classes of HMC Ships by their names alone.

The RCN did not decide upon building the type until the October 1941 reassessment of its war needs, which also led to adopting the Algerine class (as discussed in Chapter 17), and Canada did not lay down the first of the initial order for thirty-three frigates until more than a half year later, in May 1942. Besides not identifying the need for a corvette replacement until some time after the British had, the Canadian delay was also driven by the unavailability of yards to build them in: The new design was too long to pass through the St. Lawrence River canals, eliminating production on the Great Lakes, and the East Coast yards were overburdened with repair and refit requirements, thus limiting frigate construction to builders along the lower St. Lawrence and the West Coast — and those were already at capacity with corvettes and other types on the slips. Hence, the first of the class to be laid down were *Waskesiu* and *St. Catharines* at Yarrows in Esquimalt on May 2, 1942, with the former being the first to commission on June 16, 1943, and her sister following a month later. The first in a Quebec yard were *Dunver* and *Cape Breton* at Morton Engineering & Dry Dock in Quebec City on May 3 and 5, 1942, commissioning in September and October 1943, respectively. By then, the design had proven itself in British hands, and in November 1943, the RCN got Cabinet approval to build another twenty-seven.

The pressing operational requirement then developing for more hulls to replace corvettes on the North Atlantic Run saw the transfer from the RN of seven River-class frigates over the winter and spring of 1944, and three of the very slightly larger but much improved Loch class as soon as they were completed, making for a total of seventy frigates seeing service as HMC Ships (see table at end of this chapter). The last Canadian frigate to commission was *Carlplace* on December 13, 1944 (the name was a contraction for the Ontario town of Carleton Place, "Carleton" already having been assigned to the Naval Reserve Division in Ottawa).

The major consequence of the later introduction of the Canadian frigates was that they all commissioned after the supposed defeat of the U-boats in the critical convoy battles of May 1943, following which the Battle of the Atlantic had entered a new phase. In truth, the German submarine threat was far from vanquished; rather, that date was a turning point at which the organization, tactics, and weapons employed by both sides changed. From the Canadian perspective, the RCN frigates were able to enter service fitted with the latest antisubmarine sonars and radars, as well as weapons such as the very effective Hedgehog ahead-throwing mortars, with which British ships had been equipped over the previous year, along with better gun armament and a larger store of the standard depth charges (the Canadian War Museum Fact Sheet in "Further Reading" has a very good description of these sensor and weapon fits, although the rest of its discussion is at odds with the research presented here).

Although the RCN operated only three of the Loch class, they (along with the dozen Castle-class corvettes being commissioned at the same time) served as the Canadian introduction to a significant technological development. The basic hull was just a slight stretch of 3 feet (0.9 m) over the preceding Rivers, owing to an increased sheer and flare of the bow to improve sea-keeping. Their fighting capability, however, was greatly improved in being based on the new Squid ahead-throwing antisubmarine mortar, which replaced the Hedgehog and its twenty-four small "spigot" explosives with a pair of three-barrelled units, firing a combined six 440-lb (200-kg) bombs to a fixed 275-yard (250-m) range ahead. It was a deadly and effective advance against submarines that would be retrofitted to the Canadian Tribal-class destroyers and the Prestonian-class frigates in their postwar modernizations (see Chapters 10 and 26). The Squid mounts, being much heavier than the Hedgehog, required a swap of the fo'c'sle armament arrangement; they were placed immediately ahead of the bridge and the single 4-inch gun was shifted closer to the bow. A further visual distinction was that the Lochs were also fitted with the better Type 277 radar, capable of detecting small targets, such as a snorkel, and requiring a sturdier lattice-style mast.

Another point often overlooked is that the Canadian frigates were captained exclusively by reservists, a healthy mix of RCNR and RCNVR officers who, by this stage of the war, had gained the necessary experience to assume that role effectively. Organizationally, a fair proportion of the new Canadian frigates worked in the intended role as ocean escorts, ensuring the safety of the large number of convoys crossing the Atlantic to feed the invasion forces; however, a great many more were now assigned to operate in the Western Approaches under general British control, but in Canadian hunter-killer Escort Groups. Overall, these better-armed and -crewed ships established the reputation chronicled by Marc Milner as "The U-Boat Hunters" — fittingly,

Dun-Class Oiler HMCS *Dundalk* in 1945
Launched in 1943 | Built by Canadian Bridge Co., Walkerville
13 November 1943–09 April 1946
Dimensions: 54.5 m (178.8 ft) x 9.8 m (32.2 ft) x 4 m (13.1 ft)
Displacement: 950 tons | Speed: 11 kt | Crew: 30
Armament: 12-pdr (1 x I); 20 mm (2 x I)

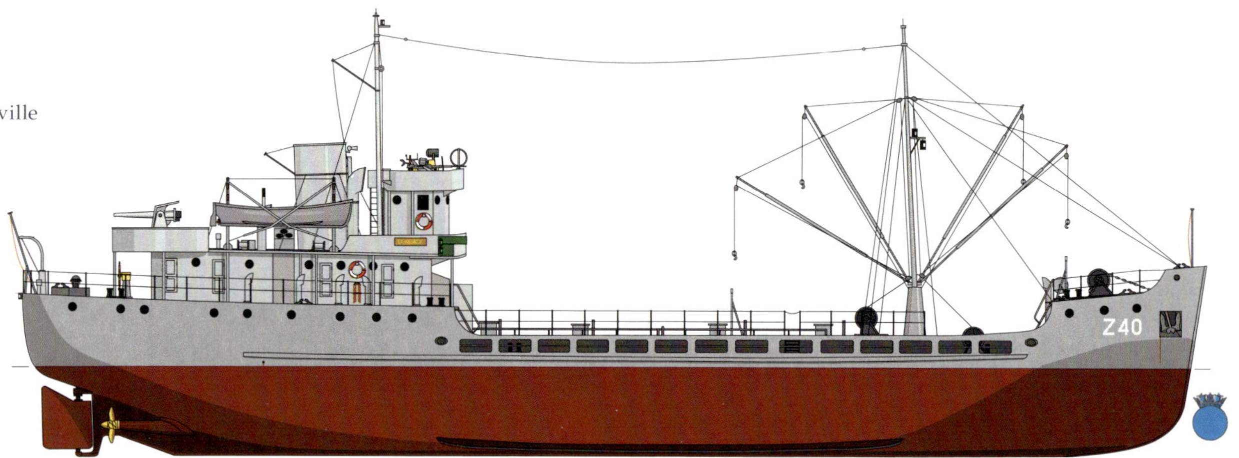

Preserver-Class Depot Ship HMCS *Provider* (I) in 1942
Launched in 1942 | Built by Marine Industries Ltd., Sorel
01 December 1942–22 March 1946
Dimensions: 81.8 m (268.4 ft) x 13.4 m (44 ft) x 5.4 m (17.7 ft)
Displacement: 4,670 tons | Speed: 10 kt | Crew: 107
Armament: 4-in (1 x I); 20 mm (2 x I)

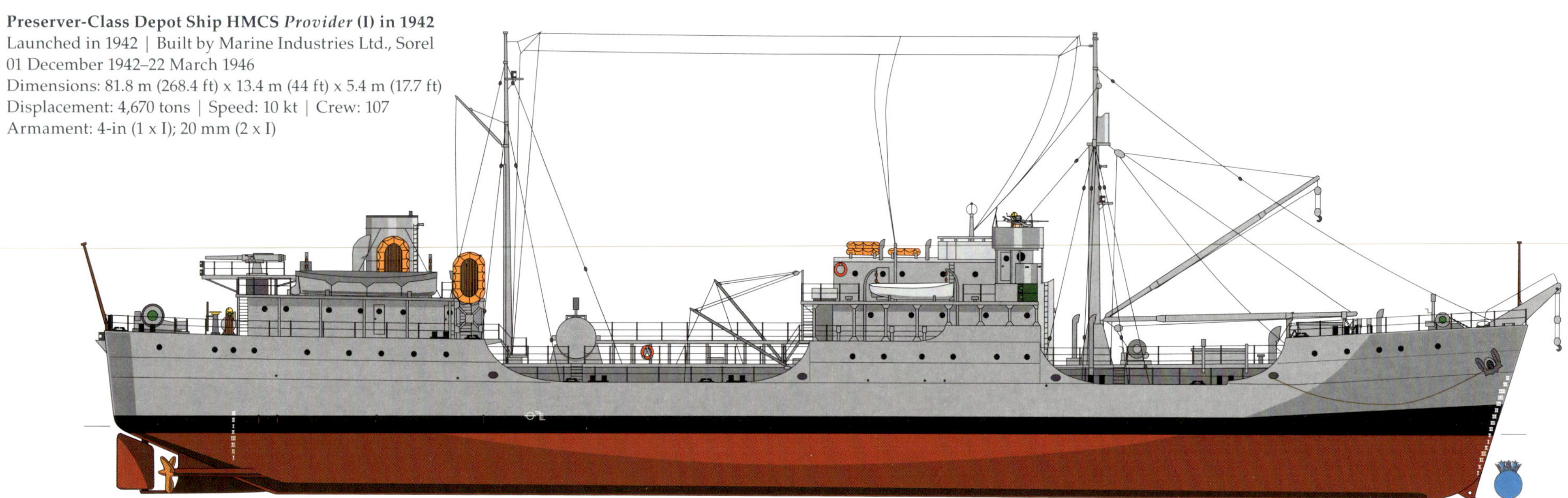

Fairmile B–Class Motor Launch HMCS *Q 060* in 1943
Launched 24 July 1941 | Built by Hunter Boats, Orillia
06 September 1941–20 June 1945
Dimensions: 34.1 m (111.9 ft) x 5.4 m (17.7 ft) x 1.5 m (4.9 ft)
Displacement: 79 tons | Speed: 20 kt | Crew: 17
Armament: 3-pdr (1 x I); .50 MG (1 x II); depth charges

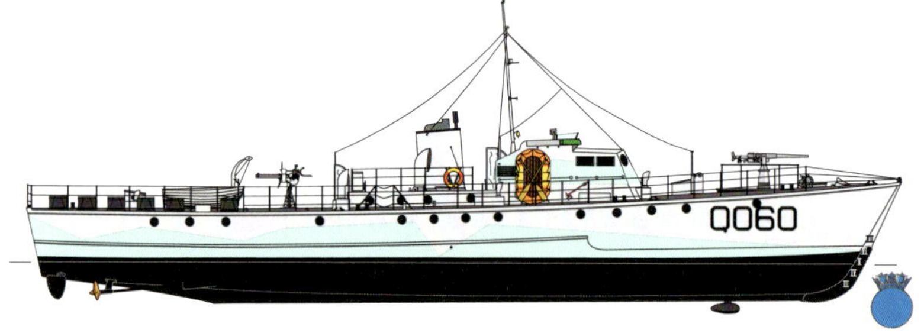

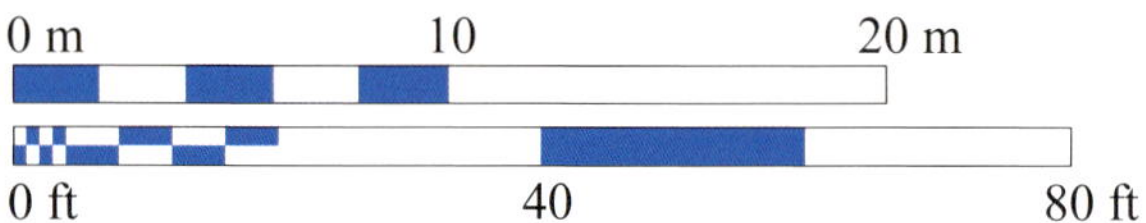

19

COASTAL FORCES (HOME WATERS): FAIRMILE Bs, DEPOT SHIPS, AND DUN-CLASS OILERS

The need for "motor boats fitted with torpedoes, or with ASDIC [sonar] and anti-submarine armament"[20] for local coastal defence against enemy attack was among the programs identified in the September 1939 assessment for the Navy's wartime expansion. The naval staff's thinking had originally focused on fast "motor torpedo boats" (MTBs), with which the RN was known to have been experimenting since 1937. By spring 1940, however, the Admiralty had determined that the type was not suited to carry ASDIC and depth charges against submarines, so the purely "MTB" development proceeded with a focus against surface craft, while the need for light coastal forces to deal with submarines would instead be better addressed through an entirely separate line of development styled the "motor launch" (ML). As a result, although the Canadian naval staff remained attracted by the concept of the fast MTB (see Chapter 20), they were coming to accept that the more immediate need was for inshore antisubmarine forces, and the initial authorization for thirty-two MTB was split, in May 1940, into two separate orders for twenty-four ML and twelve MTB.

The ML design developed in house by the Admiralty was directed to be produced by the Fairmile Company, where it was styled the Type B Motor Launch and took on the generic name of "Fairmile." As a 112-foot (34-m) wooden vessel driven by a pair of 650-hp gasoline engines giving a top speed of 20 knots, it was easily built

Fairmile B–Class Motor Launch HMCS *Q 105* in 1943
Launched 07 August 1943 | Built by Mac Craft, Sarnia
05 September 1943–16 September 1945
Dimensions: 34.1 m (111.9 ft) x 5.4 m (17.7 ft) x 1.5 m (4.9 ft)
Displacement: 79 tons | Speed: 20 kt | Crew: 17
Armament: 3-pdr (1 x I); 20 mm (2 x I); depth charges

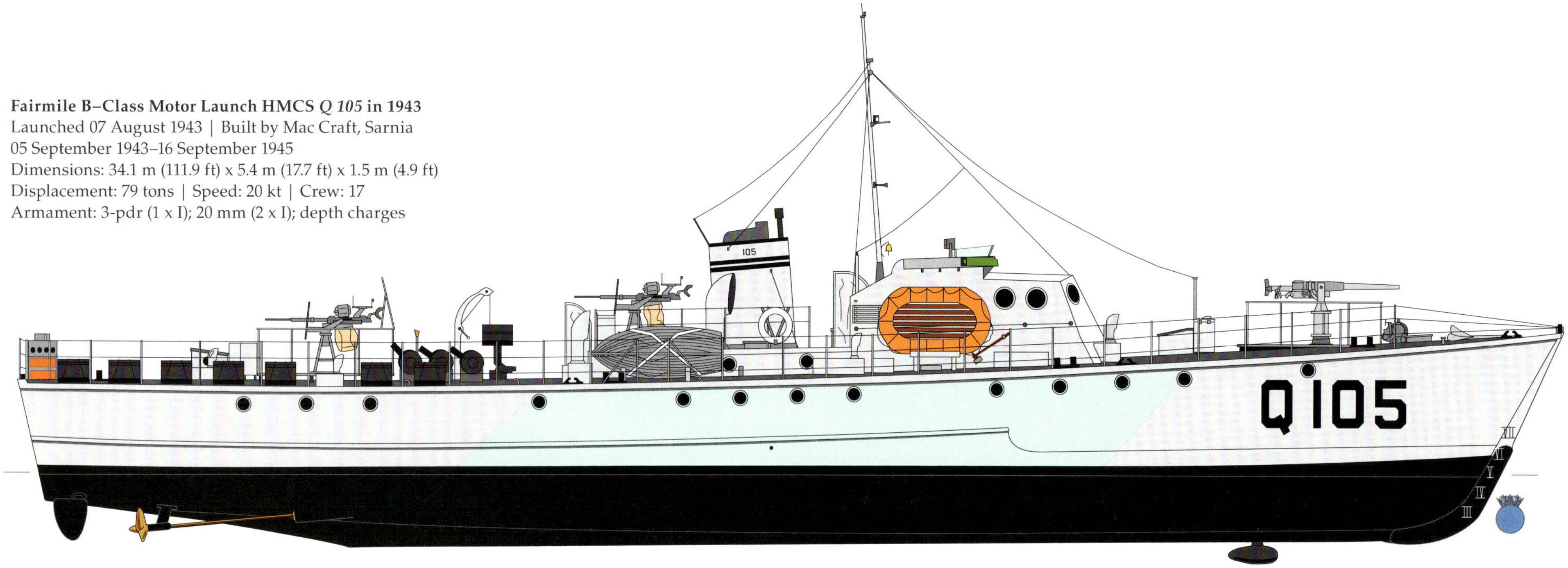

Fairmile B–Class Motor Launch HMCS *Beaver* (II) in 1954
(ex HMCS *Q 106*)
Launched 15 August 1943 | Built by Grew Boats Ltd., Penetanguishene
18 May 1954–13 November 1957
Dimensions: 34.1 m (111.9 ft) x 5.4 m (17.7 ft) x 1.5 m (4.9 ft)
Displacement: 79 tons | Speed: 20 kt | Crew: 17
Armament: 20 mm (1 x I)

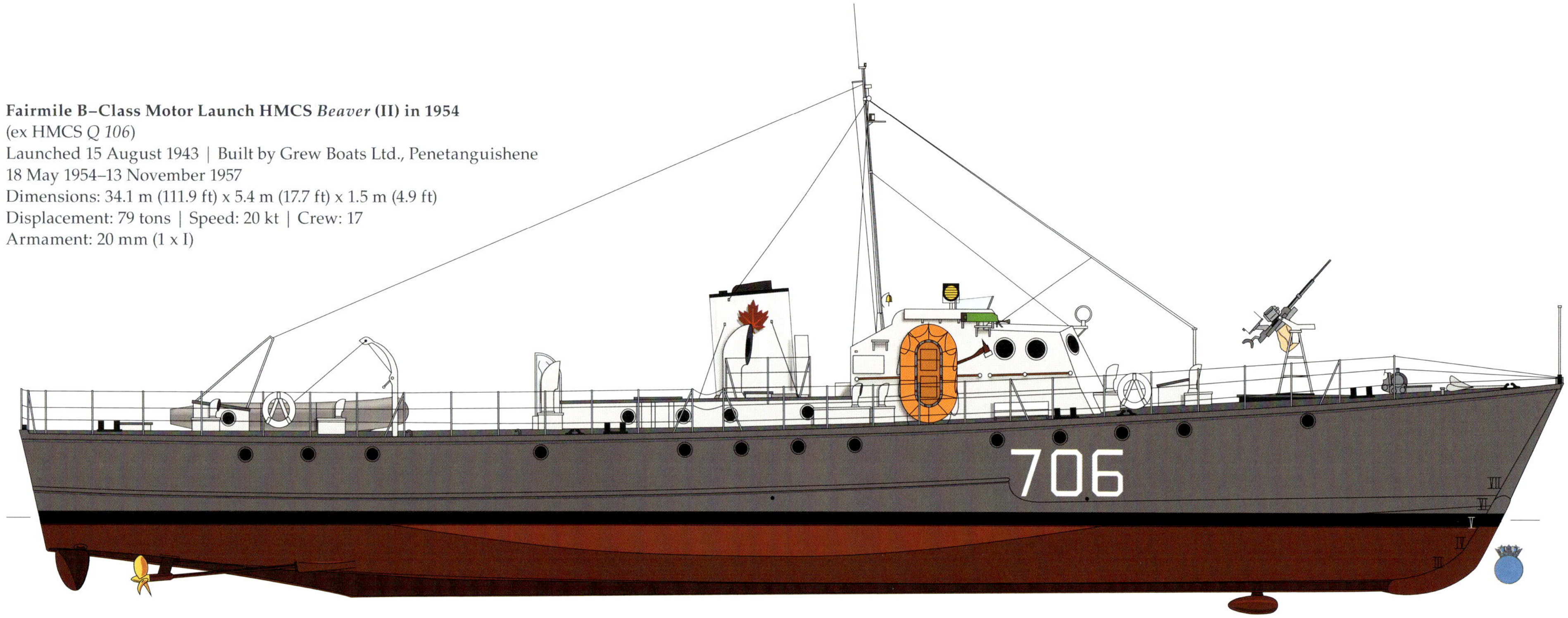

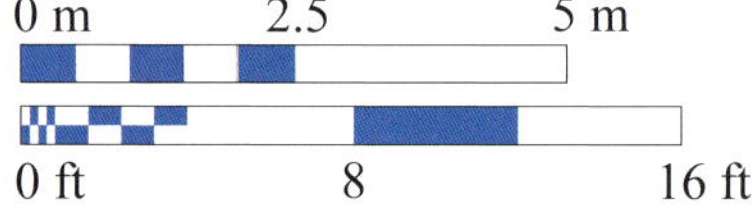

in Canadian yards, which in total produced eighty-eight of them, mostly on the Great Lakes (fifty-nine), but also fourteen on the West Coast and even fifteen in Weymouth, Nova Scotia, where they did not detract from refit and repair work. Other than eight of the Nova Scotia boats being assigned to the USN, all the rest were taken on by the RCN, which numbered them Q 050 through 129, and therefore they were sometimes referred to as "the Q Boats" — or, more commonly, simply "the Fairmiles." A final batch of eighteen built on the East Coast in 1943 (Q 112–129) had larger 700-hp engines, which achieved a marginally better top speed of 22 knots. The principal armament for both types was three single 20-mm Oerlikons (one each forward, midships, and aft) and twenty depth charges.

Since the ASDIC was not "trainable" (that is, it was fixed to "ping" pointed forward only), they were intended to operate in flotillas of six or eight vessels working together to locate and attack a submarine. In practice, because they were not that manoeuvrable at low speeds, this did not prove to be effective, and perhaps fortunately, the Canadian Fairmiles do not seem to have ever had occasion to come upon the enemy. Moreover, displacing only 79 tons, they did not handle well on open waters, but with a maximum continuous speed of 16.5 knots and economical endurance of 1,300 nm (2,400 km) were well suited to relatively enclosed areas. Accordingly, those built in Vancouver remained on the West Coast, to operate in the Strait of Juan de Fuca and the Inside Passage, while on the East Coast they tended to be based on the St. Lawrence River and the Gulf, as well as out of St. John's and Botwood, Newfoundland and Labrador. In the winter of 1942–43, with the Gulf frozen over, two flotillas of six boats each were dispatched to provide escort services in the Caribbean, where the Seventy-Third Flotilla moved about from Trinidad to Guantanamo Bay before settling in Key West with their depot ship, HMCS *Provider* (discussed below). The other flotilla, the Seventy-Second, had to turn back while on the southward journey, owing to bad weather. That southern deployment experience was repeated in the winter of 1943–44 by the Seventieth and Seventy-Eighth Flotillas operating out of Bermuda, again depoted by *Provider*.

Having never been formally commissioned into the RCN, at war's end the Fairmiles were not paid off as such; rather, most of them were simply sold to various commercial interests. Recently, at least one was still known to exist (ex-*Q 118*, as an excursion vessel in Ostend, Belgium). There were spasmodic attempts to restore an example in Canada, which regrettably ended unsuccessfully (*Q 105*, the ex-*Duc d'Orléans* in Sarnia; see "Further Reading"). The RCN did retain seven Fairmiles postwar as training vessels for reserves: a half dozen on the Great Lakes and another one on the West Coast. In 1954, these were finally commissioned and given names perpetuating the armed yacht "animals" whose training duties they had taken on: *Beaver* (ML 106), *Cougar* (ML 104), *Moose* (ML 111), *Raccoon* (ML 079), *Reindeer* (ML 116), and *Wolf* (ML 062) on the Lakes, with *Elk* (ML 124) in B.C. Seeing intermittent summer use only, they all were paid off and disposed of by the early 1970s.

Landing Craft Assault (LCA) in 1944
Dimensions: 12.6 m (41.3 ft) x 3.1 m (10.5 ft) x 0.6 m (2 ft)
Displacement: 9 tons | Speed: 9 kt | Crew: 4
Armament: .303 MG (1 x I)

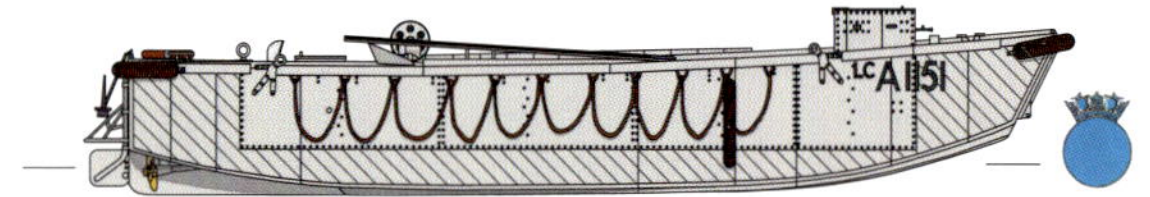

Landing Craft Infantry (Large) HMCS *LCI(L)-250* in 1944
Launched 16 December 1942 | Built by New Jersey Shipbuilding Corp., Barber
29 January 1944–31 August 1944
Dimensions: 48.3 m (158.5 ft) x 7.2 m (23.6 ft) x 2 m (6.5 ft)
Displacement: 390 tons | Speed: 16 kt | Crew: 28
Armament: 20 mm (4 x I)

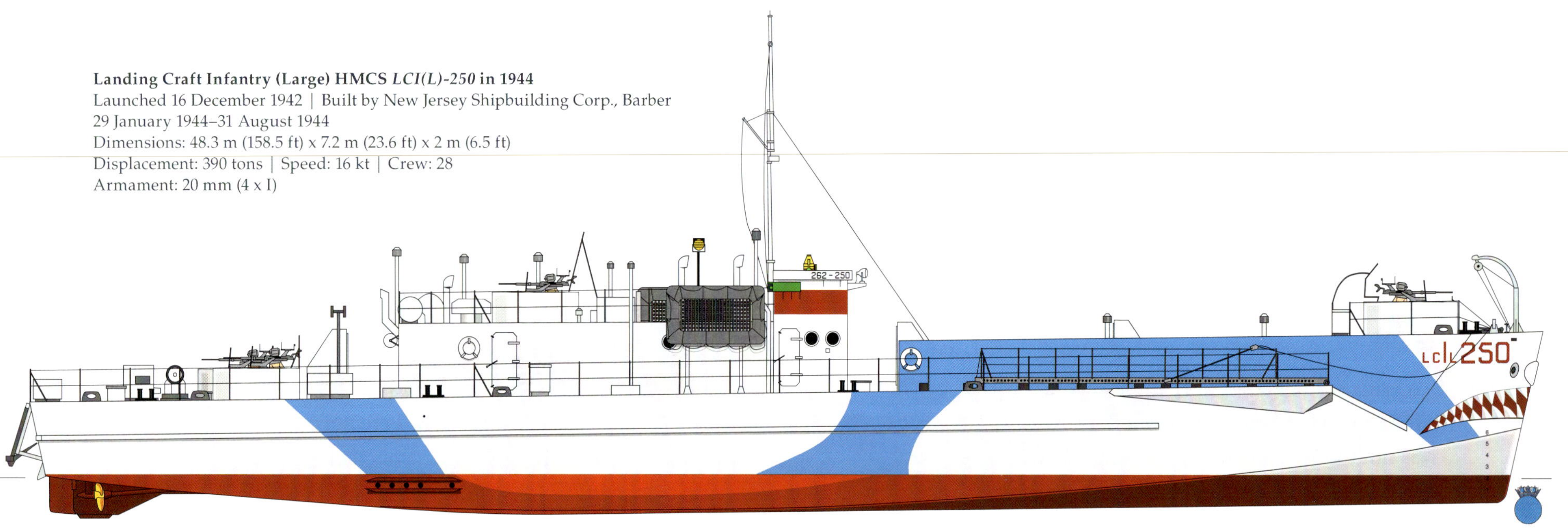

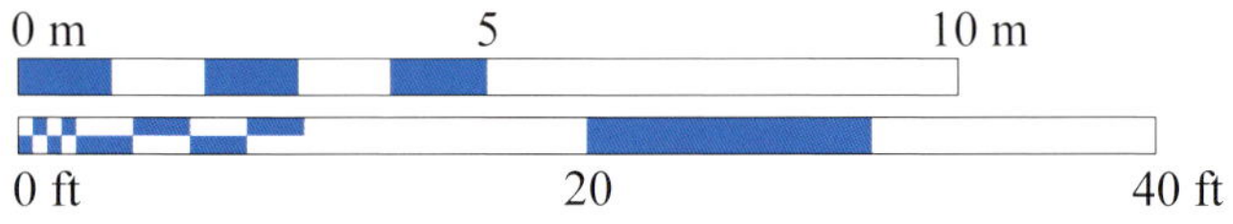

by the RN under Lend-Lease in 1941 were redirected to Canada, most serving with the RCAF as crash boats, but one, designated *S-09*, was commissioned into the RCN in September 1942 to patrol the St. Lawrence River between Gaspé and Quebec City. It relocated to Toronto in May 1944 to act as a firing range patrol vessel off Frenchman's Bay and was disposed of in June 1945.

The irony is that large numbers of Canadian sailors served in MTBs with the RN from early in the war. In the first years of Canadian naval expansion, when recruiting into the RCNVR sporadically outpaced the commissioning of HMC Ships into which they might serve, many of these men were loaned to the RN. Quite a few of them were directed into Coastal Forces and thence into the MTB flotillas operating in the Channel and the Mediterranean. The precise number is unknowable, with records lost over time, but the exploits of several have been recorded in volumes with fetching titles such as *White Plumes Astern* and *Champagne Navy* (see Further Reading). Tony German summarized their operations: "They snapped constantly at the enemy. They hit his convoys, defended their own from German E-boats; they landed and backed up raiding parties, attacking transiting U-boats and surface ships. There were countless fierce lightning-fast engagements."[23] A group of Volunteer Reservists from Vancouver (Cornelius Burke, Douglas Maitland, and Thomas Ladner) serving in the Adriatic were known as "The Three Musketeers," while another chap from Ottawa (Thomas Fuller) was styled "The Pirate of the Adriatic" (see "Further Reading" for Michael Braham's Canadian War Museum research paper and a survey of their exploits). As their experience and numbers grew, and as the RN began suffering its own but contrasting manning issue (too few men for the ships being produced in British yards), in the spring of 1943, the Admiralty proposed that Britain would supply boats for the RCN to establish its own little fleet. And so two Canadian flotillas of eight boats each were formed early in 1944 to operate in the English Channel, covering the planned Normandy invasion; each was led by an RCNVR veteran of coastal forces, although operating very different subtypes of vessels (see table at the end of this chapter).

A rare colour image of the 72-foot G-type MTBs at speed in the English Channel.

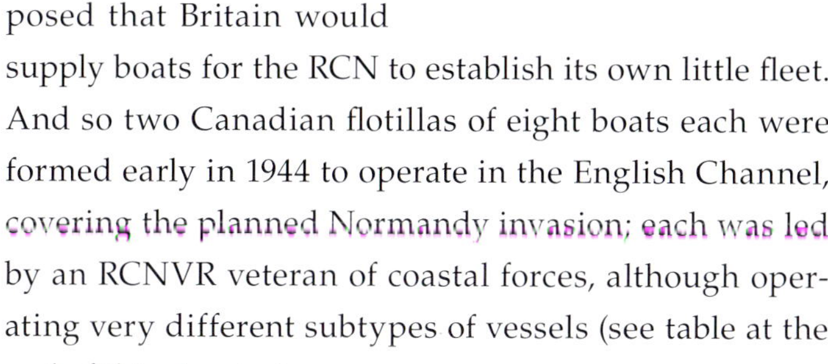

The Twenty-Ninth MTB Flotilla, under Lieutenant Commander Tony Law, was equipped with the 72.5-foot (22-m) G-type craft built by the British Power Boat Company, armed with a 6-pounder gun and a pair of 18-inch torpedo tubes, and driven by three V-12 supercharged high-octane gasoline-powered engines that produced a top speed over 40 knots. The short but distinguished history of the Twenty-Ninth included several successful engagements covering the gamut listed above by Tony German (Law wrote his own memoir, *White Plumes Astern*, and was also an accomplished war artist who vividly painted their actions). But the Twenty-Ninth suffered more than its share of tragedy. A pair of

Ruler-Class Escort Carrier HMS *Nabob* in August 1944
(ex USS *Edisto*)
Launched 22 March 1943 | Built by Seattle-Tacoma Shipbuilding Corp., Tacoma
07 September 1943–10 October 1944
Dimensions: 151.1 m (495.7 ft) x 32.7 m (107.3 ft) x 7.7 m (25.3 ft)
Displacement: 15,390 tons | Speed: 18 kt | Crew: 646
Armament: 5-in (2 x I); 40 mm (8 x II); 20 mm (27 x I); 20 aircraft

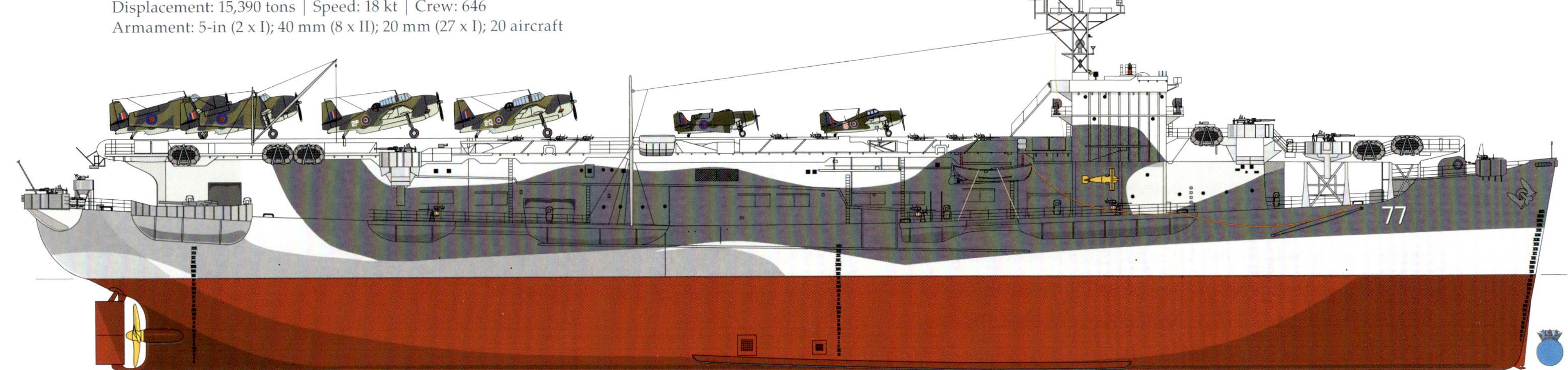

Ruler-Class Escort Carrier HMS *Puncher* in April 1945
Launched 08 November 1943 | Built by Seattle-Tacoma Shipbuilding Corp., Tacoma
05 February 1944–16 January 1946
Dimensions: 150 m (492.1 ft) x 33.1 m (108.6 ft) x 7.5 m (25.6 ft)
Displacement: 14,170 tons | Speed: 18 kt | Crew: 646
Armament: 5-in (2 x I); 40 mm (8 x II); 20 mm (14 x II); 20 mm (6 x I); 20 aircraft

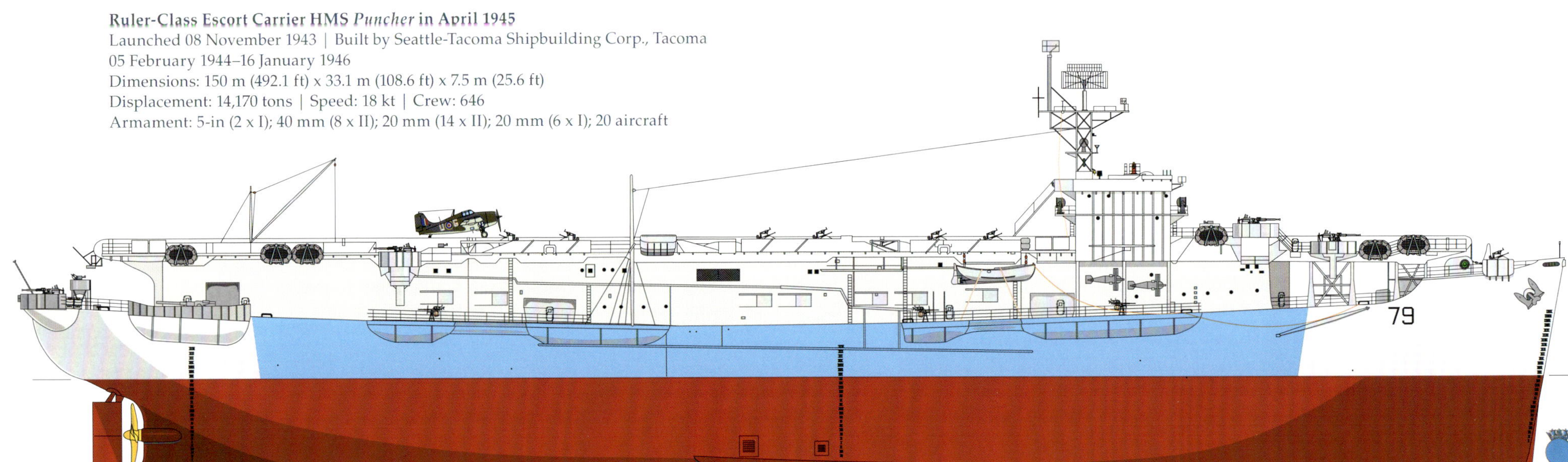

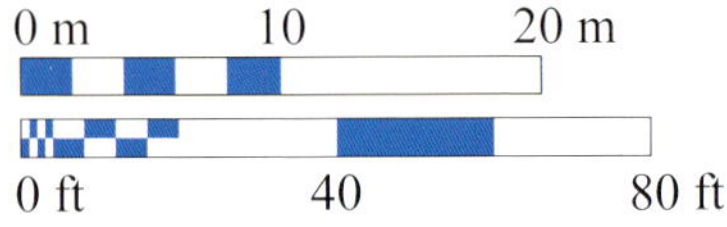

21

ESCORT AIRCRAFT CARRIERS

The escort aircraft carrier, or CVE (for "Carrier Heavier-than-Air [Aircraft] Escort," following the USN classification system) was a wartime expedient driven by the need to provide protection for convoys in the "black hole/air gap" of the mid-Atlantic beyond the range of shore-based aircraft. The concept was for a carrier deck to be fitted over top of a commercial ship hull, a conversion that could be fabricated much faster and more cheaply than constructing a new-build standard fleet carrier. Those savings, however, came at the cost of a CVE being about half the size of a fleet carrier, with no full hangar deck but only space for whatever aircraft could fit in the limited space of the standard ship's hold, and as such carrying relatively fewer aircraft. As well as being much slower and more lightly armed and armoured, these were all acceptable compromises for the North Atlantic threat environment, where enemy surface ships and attack aircraft were not a great concern by this stage of the war.

The RN had theorized the need in the 1930s, but continued adherence to the tonnage restrictions of the Washington Naval Treaty, coupled with the austerity of the Depression, prevented any actual development. The first of the kind turned out to be the conversion of a captured German freighter, commissioned on July 31, 1941, as HMS *Audacity*.* Although she was sunk by a U-boat

* An interesting Canadian aside is that the German merchant ship *Hanover* was captured off the Dominican Republic on March 6, 1940, by HMCS *Assiniboine* working in consort with the British light cruiser HMS *Dunedin*.

Puncher on passage to Casablanca, Morrocco, ferrying an upper-deck load of U.S. Army Air Force fighter aircraft: P-61 Black Widows (twin-boom aircraft) aft, and P-47 Thunderbolts and P-51B Mustangs forward.

barely five months later, on December 21, 1941, that was not before she had participated materially in the protection of four Gibraltar convoys. The concept proven, Britain requested the United States to purpose-build an eventual forty-three CVEs through the Lend-Lease program. The bulk of these were thirty-four ships of the Attacker and Ruler classes (derivatives of the USN's Bogue class), which could embark twelve to twenty-four aircraft, depending upon the operational need and type. The CVEs began coming into service late in 1942.

The RCN immediately appreciated the boost the CVE could provide to its efforts in defence of the North Atlantic convoys, which at the time was, frankly, not going very well, with such disasters as SC 107 (October 24–November 10, 1942, when fifteen of thirty-nine freighters were sunk in return for only two U-boats) and ONS 154 (December 18–30, 1942, when thirteen of fifty freighters were sunk for one U-boat), which "pointed to the Canadians as the weak link in the mid-ocean."[25] Therefore, early in 1943, the Canadian naval staff turned its attention to the matter, with Director of Operations Captain H.N. Lay and Director of Plans Acting Captain H.G. DeWolf producing "a joint memorandum on how the Navy could develop its own air policy ... including the gaining of experience at sea in a carrier."[26] Lay's subsequent investigation of American and British facilities recommended that the RCN establish a naval air service modelled on the RN Fleet Air Arm (FAA), which "should concern itself exclusively with carrier operations, leaving the RCAF to conduct coastal operations with shore-based aircraft."[27] In the short term, that effort came to naught, owing to two substantial obstacles: First, the Mackenzie King Cabinet was reluctant to take on the personnel and financial costs of running such large vessels, and second, Canada not being part of the Lend-Lease Agreement meant none of the vessels built in the U.S. for Britain could be taken over by the RCN.

By the fall of 1943, however, a confluence of other factors arose to make the effort viable. The main one was the RN manning crisis, described in Chapter 20; the British having built more ships than they could crew led the Admiralty to request the formation of Canadian MTB and landing craft flotillas with vessels loaned from the RN for them to crew. This request was now expanded to include an appeal for the RCN to bulk up the manning of a pair of CVEs being completed in the Burrard yard in Vancouver, for which the RN would provide the core engine room crews and FAA squadrons, allowing the vessels to remain as British "His Majesty's Ships" and avoid the complications of Lend-Lease. This solution proved workable, and so over the winter of 1943–44, the RCN began its first-hand experience of aircraft carrier operations.

Both ships had been built in Tacoma, Washington, initially laid down as merchantmen but converted while under construction to USN CVE configuration and subsequently identified for transfer to the RN under Lend-Lease. HMS *Nabob* (ex-*Edisto*, assigned RN pennant number D77), was the first commissioned on September 7, 1943, to be taken in hand by a skeleton British crew for transfer to the Burrard yard in nearby Vancouver for fitting out with British equipment. She was followed some months later by HMS *Puncher* (ex *Willapa*, D79), commissioned February 5, 1944, and not arriving in Vancouver until mid-March. It was while fitting out in Vancouver that the Canadian deck crews were embarked: *Nabob* from January 1944, under the command of Captain Lay, and *Puncher* from April, under Captain RES Bidwell. Although the two ships were notionally considered to be part of the same Ruler class of CVEs, there were slight differences between them — *Nabob* was 3 feet (1 m) longer and 800 tons heavier. As well, there were small differences in their final complement mix: *Nabob* is recorded, once her air squadrons were embarked, as having a ship's company of 500 RCN, 327 RN, and 9 Royal New Zealand Navy;[28] *Puncher*'s crew composition cannot be found with the same precision, other than it being "a smaller ship's company."[29] The British portions, of course, would vary with the number and type of aircraft embarked.

Nabob sailed from Vancouver in February 1944, bound for San Francisco to embark her first squadron, 852 Naval Air Squadron, equipped with Grumman Avenger torpedo bombers. Being the first into service, she almost immediately encountered a major personnel issue, arising from the fact that the entire mixed crew were paid at the lesser British rates of pay, received lower quality and quantity British food, and were subject to the harsher British discipline code, all leading to a minor revolt among the Canadians at a mid-March 1944 stopover in Norfolk, Virginia.[30] The resourceful Captain Lay recommended Canadian standards be put into effect in all respects for the entire crew, and this was also granted and implemented in *Puncher* by the time she was ready to sail (recall that she arrived in Vancouver only at about the time of this incident).

The operational careers of the two vessels are described in some detail by Leversedge and Martin in their respective books (listed in "Further Reading"), so will be only highlighted here. Both ships at different times operated a variety of British and American aircraft from a number of RN FAA squadrons and occasionally also ferried non-naval combat aircraft ranged on the flight deck destined for the fighting on the Continent. Most consequentially, by the time the Canadian CVEs arrived in the European theatre, the nature of naval operations had changed, with the U-boats having been driven largely from the mid-Atlantic back into coastal waters, so both ships conducted their most significant actions based out of Scapa Flow against German targets in the Norwegian littoral. During the ongoing Operation Goodwood attacks on the German battleship *Tirpitz* at anchor in the Kåfjord, on August 22, 1944, *Nabob* was torpedoed by *U 354* and was saved only by a Herculean damage control effort. Judged not worth repairing, she was cannibalized for parts and paid off on October 10, 1944. In due course, she was sold off after the war to a Dutch company for conversion into her original intention as a freighter, until finally being scrapped in 1977. *Puncher* also undertook a variety of strikes against Norwegian targets, as well as overseeing several Murmansk convoys, all without incident. After VE Day, her aircraft were landed ashore and the hangar fitted instead with bunks to transport soldiers back to Canada. Paid off in February 1946, she too was converted for mercantile service until being scrapped in 1973.

Although the embarked air squadrons were all RN FAA units that counted very few Canadians in their ranks, the sailors crewing the vessels gained experience in aircraft carrier operations that would be put to good effect in the postwar Canadian fleet. Indeed, both ships' captains (Lay and Bidwell) would go on to RCN flag rank in capacities that would have major impacts on Canadian naval aviation.

FURTHER READING

Norman Friedman, *British Carrier Aviation: The Evolution of the Ships and Their Aircraft* (Naval Institute Press, 1988).

JDF Kealy and E.C. Russell, *A History of Canadian Naval Aviation 1918–1962* (Queen's Printer, 1967).

TFJ Leversedge, *Aircraft Carriers in Royal Canadian Navy Service* (Kestrel Publications, 2023).

Thomas G. Lynch, "The Origins of Canadian Carrier Aviation: Canadian-Manned Escort Carriers of the Royal Navy, 1943–5," in *Warship 1994*, ed. John Arthur Roberts (Naval Institute Press, 1994).

Patrick Martin and Leo Pettipas, "Escort Carriers," in *Royal Canadian Navy Aircraft: Finish and Markings, 1944–1968* (pub. by author, 2021), 214–29.

Uganda-Class Cruiser HMCS *Uganda* in 1945
(ex HMS *Uganda*/future HMCS *Québec*)
Launched 07 August 1941 | Built by Vickers-Armstrong Ltd., Newcastle-on-Tyne
21 October 1944–13 June 1956
Dimensions: 169.4 m (555.8 ft) x 19.2 m (63 ft) x 5 m (16.4 ft)
Displacement: 8,800 tons | Speed: 30 kt | Crew: 730
Armament: 6-in (3 x III); 4-in (4 x II); 2-pdr (2 x IV); 40 mm (2 x IV); 20 mm (4 x II); 20 mm (2 x I); 21-in TT (2 x III)

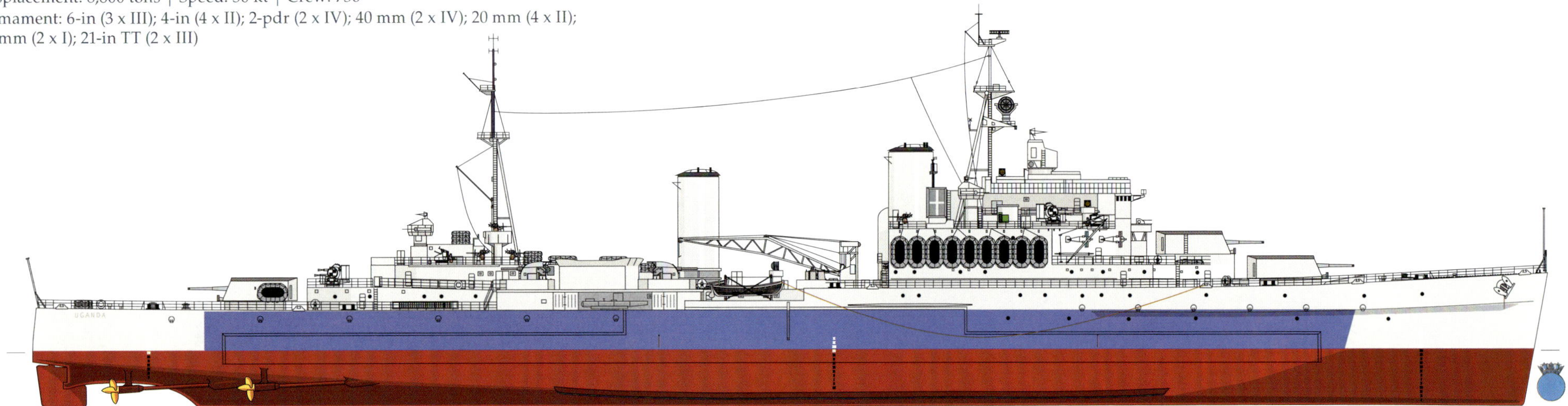

Minotaur-Class Cruiser HMCS *Ontario* in 1952
(ex HMS *Minotaur*)
Launched 29 July 1943 | Built by Harland & Wolff Ltd., Belfast
26 April 1945–15 October 1958
Dimensions: 169.4 m (555.8 ft) x 19.2 m (63 ft) x 5 m (16.4 ft)
Displacement: 8,800 tons | Speed: 30 kt | Crew: 730
Armament: 6-in (3 x III); 4-in (5 x II); 40 mm (3 x IV); 40 mm (3 x I); 21-in TT (2 x III)

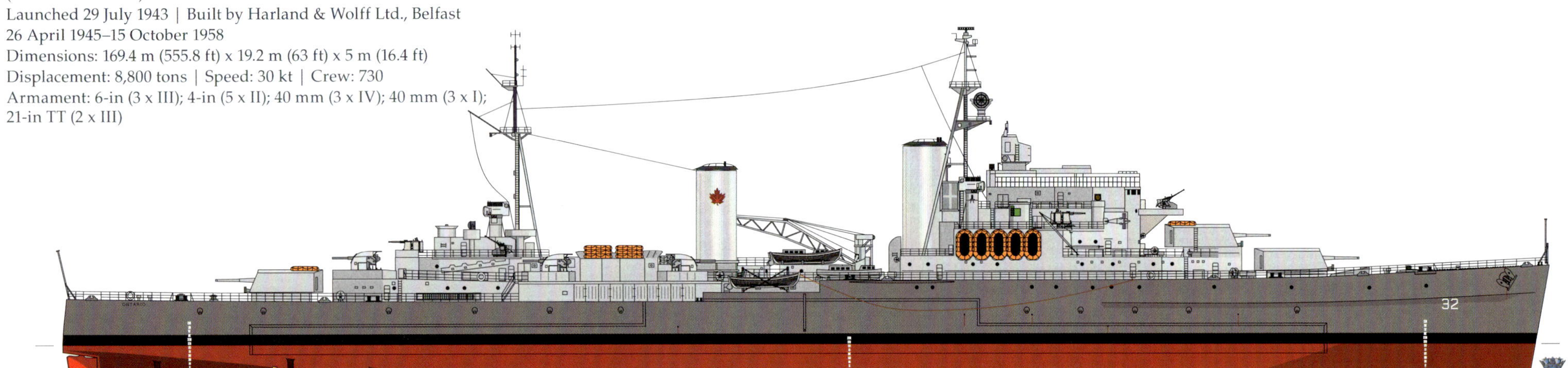

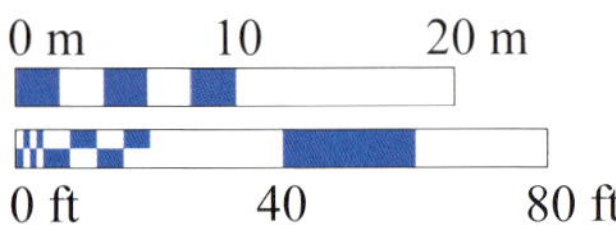

22

THE LAST CRUISERS

The definition of "cruiser" has evolved over the years, having different meanings across various eras, but that offered by Norman Friedman in his book *British Cruisers: Two World Wars and After* applies reasonably well, both for our subject and the time frame:

> The name implies a ship capable of cruising independently on a [far-off] station, which in the age of steam machinery entailed an ability to make running repairs far from home, as well as a long radius of action. Behind this name was the idea that the cruiser was smaller or more weakly armed than a battleship, yet still protected against enemy fire to some extent.[31]

This describes the operational conditions of vast and austere offshore waters that confronted the Canadian naval staff, and as such, cruisers (as we have seen) had been the unrequited ambition of the RCN from its very inception. *Rainbow* and *Niobe* were never meant as more than training vessels but were pressed into wartime service. Laurier's plan for a fleet with four of the Bristol class as its core was abruptly cancelled by a change in government. And then the commission of *Aurora* in the wake of the Great War was cut short as retrenchment set in. All these attempts ended without realizing their hoped-for potential. If the "occasional fleet" of the 1920s had been achieved (see Chapter 7), the RCN could have entered the Second World War as a significant force with seven of the type. Instead, the closest the Canadian naval staff came to its goal in the late 1930s was the rearmament promise for a flotilla of the Tribal-class destroyers described as "pocket cruisers." As fate would have it, just as the British-built foursome of Tribals were fully joining operations in the summer of 1943, an opportunity arose for the RCN to embark upon another flirtation with cruisers. This endeavour would last longer but end no happier and has not been repeated since.

The catalyst was the Quebec Conference of August 1943, at which Prime Minister William Lyon Mackenzie King hosted American President Franklin Roosevelt and British Prime Minister Winston Churchill. The tide of the war had changed dramatically in the previous six months, with Allied victory now a more certain thing, and it was time to plan for the invasion of France in 1944 and the subsequent war against Japan. A primary British naval objective at Quebec, for the RCN to help the RN with its personnel issues, resulted as desired in the formation of the Canadian MTB and LCI(L) flotillas discussed in Chapter 20. But in the course of discussions, the British request was broadened to include that the Canadians also crew two cruisers and a pair of fleet destroyers (the latter will be covered in Chapter 23). History has shown that this was all part of a plot by the Canadian naval staff to finally acquire cruisers so that the RCN could emerge triumphantly into the postwar era as a big ship navy (the official history, *A Blue Water Navy*, details the machinations[32]). Unaware of this background, and because all sides supported the ultimate goal of prosecuting the war to a successful conclusion, the Canadian Cabinet accepted the British gift of the pair of cruisers as part of the overall package.

The vessels initially allocated were then building as the Minotaur class HM Ships *Minotaur* and *Superb*, powerful designs developed from the latest wartime experience, with a displacement of some 8,000 tons, a main armament of nine 6-inch (152-mm) guns on triple mountings, and impressive secondary anti-aircraft weapons. Each required a complement of more than 850 officers and ratings. They were anticipated to be completed late in 1944, but when it appeared that *Superb* would be delayed and with the crews already assembling, the Admiralty suggested she be replaced with the slightly older but very similar Colony-class cruiser *Uganda*, which had been badly damaged in a glider-bomb attack and was being repaired in Charleston, South Carolina. The deal was struck, the crew redirected to that American port, and with the timeline back on schedule, "HMCS" *Uganda* was officially transferred to Canadian possession on October 21, 1944. Her commissioning wardroom indeed was a great breeding ground for the postwar Navy, including many names recognizable to students of Canadian naval history: Captain Rollo Mainguy, Commander (Executive Officer) Hugh Pullen, Paymaster Commander Henry McCandless, Engineer Commander John Caldwell, Gunnery Officer Bill Landymore, and Navigator John Littler — all would achieve flag rank in the postwar RCN (and Ontarians will recognize the name of Aircraft Recognition Officer John Robarts RCNVR as a future premier).

Minotaur would not be completed and commissioned into the RCN for another six months (May 1945), but her future captain was already experiencing his forthcoming employment. Harold Taylor Grant had been one of the lieutenants in *Aurora* and, like all of his contemporaries, had served in British "big ships" in the interwar period. In March 1943, having been identified by Nelles for a future senior role in the RCN (he indeed would become CNS in 1947), Grant was loaned to the RN to command the old Danae-class light cruiser *Diomede* (completed in 1918 as a near-contemporary of *Aurora*) as a preparation billet. In July (about the time of the Quebec Conference), he shifted to take command of HMS *Enterprise*, another vintage light cruiser (Emerald class, launched December 1919) but still in fighting trim and earmarked to participate in covering the Normandy invasion. Grant saw extensive action in her, including engaging a superior force of eleven German destroyers on December 28, 1943 (sinking three of them and damaging several others), for which he was awarded the Distinguished Service Order, and later being wounded during the bombardment of Cherbourg on June 25, 1944, for which he was awarded the Bronze Star Medal. As recorded by his biographer, Wilf Lund, "In the eyes of officers such as Harry DeWolf and Ken Dyer [another future CNS], he was a hero, but his illustrious war record remains little known to Canadians."[33] After convalescing, Grant was sent to stand by *Minotaur*, now renamed to be commissioned as HMCS *Ontario* on May 25, 1945, within two weeks following VE-Day.

Uganda would not be renamed until much later, out of wartime consideration to not offend that other colony for which she was named. By May 1945, she was already heavily engaged in action, having arrived in Australia in early March. Assigned to Task Force 57 of the BPF, the Canadian cruiser suffered kamikaze attacks, was involved in the bombardment of Japanese-held Truk and Formosa (now Taiwan) and the home island of Sakishima Gunto, and earned the battle honour "Okinawa" for operations during the invasion of that island in April. This fighting legacy, however, was tarnished by the fact that the ship's crew would soon effectively vote themselves out of the war in protest against the Mackenzie King government's policy that only renewed volunteers would continue in fighting the war against Japan. As one of the men recalled later, "I was one of the ones who did *not* volunteer. I was prepared to stay there, but if they were going through this nonsense of volunteering (which was all it was), I wasn't going to volunteer again."[34] Still, *Uganda* remained in theatre through completion of this first phase of operations, departing Task Force 57 on July 27 to make for home and a fresh crew of volunteers. She arrived in Esquimalt on August 10 to learn of the impending Japanese surrender.

Nor was *Ontario* able to salvage the day by delivering any illustrious war action herself. Commissioning in late May 1945, she at least had the opportunity to swap out non-volunteers for Pacific service before sailing from the U.K. on July 2. But at almost the same moment that her sister was reaching Esquimalt, on August 10, the second Canadian cruiser was only passing through the Suez Canal, still making her way to join the BPF. With the war over, *Ontario* participated in the continuing postwar recovery operations throughout Southeast Asia before finally entering Esquimalt on November 27, 1945.

Uganda enters Esquimalt Harbour on completion of an early postwar training cruise.

Having got at least a start on its cruiser force, albeit without the desired strong fighting record, the naval staff was left to determine what to do with the cruisers in peacetime. The understandable first step was to employ them in the fashion most familiar to those now-senior officers who had done their "big ship time" in the type in the RN. Turning the cruisers over to the role of training ships for new entries presented a golden opportunity to "Canadianize" the process of initial indoctrination into naval life. But the peacetime establishment of the RCN was soon reduced to a so-called Interim Force of ten thousand personnel, which neither needed nor could sustain two ships of that size. So, while *Ontario*, on arriving in Canada, went into an extended refit to prepare for her new role, *Uganda* picked up the immediate slack and then was paid off into reserve when her sister was reactivated in the spring of 1947.

The next couple of years saw thousands of young ratings and junior officers pass through first *Uganda* and later *Ontario*, and this practical experience of the training role suggested several improvements that could be made, especially for the purpose of junior officer training. In October 1950, work commenced to improve the layout of *Ontario*, mostly removing unnecessary secondary armament to allow more space for accommodation and upper-deck seamanship activity. One of the most visible and interesting changes was the installation of a new gunroom-style "house" on the upper deck between the funnels as a space for midshipmen to take their meals (the capacity of the wardroom was strained, and it was not considered appropriate for junior officers to eat "broadside messing" with the hands from the galley). With three long tables seating twenty-four and a dumb waiter to bring up meals from the galley below, it was styled "Dunc's Diner" after the ship's popular commander (executive officer), Duncan Raymond. The purpose — and the iconic name — fit, and similar structures would be retrofitted over the years to other classes of ships as they too transitioned into the training role (see the chapters on the Prestonian-class frigates, the Porte-class gate vessels, and the Bay-class minesweepers).

Training may have been the cruisers' primary postwar function, but it was not the only role in which they were engaged. The rising tensions in Europe and the outbreak of the Korean War lifted the establishment ceiling on the forces, and in 1951, *Uganda* went into refit in Esquimalt to be modernized and reactivated as part of Canada's commitment to NATO. This was also the occasion to rename her in line with her sister, and she was recommissioned on January 14, 1952, as HMCS *Québec*. Dispatched to her new home port of Halifax, she ended the year having participated in the first major NATO naval exercise, Mainbrace. The following year, she would be the flagship of the Canadian contingent to the Fleet Review at Spithead, marking the Coronation of Queen Elizabeth II. With her sister *Ontario*, the aircraft carrier *Magnificent*, and destroyer *Sioux*, it was a powerful display of the RCN's pride of place in the postwar world.

With this new-found confidence, the Canadian cruisers were dispatched on goodwill tours combined with training cruises, showing the flag to faraway places (admittedly, still wearing the RN White Ensign at the stern, but at least the blue version of the Canadian Ensign was at at the bow to identify her as a government vessel). As examples, in 1952, *Ontario* circumnavigated South America, and in 1955, *Québec* did the same around the continent of Africa. Both ships frequently embarked Queen Elizabeth II and Prince Philip on their visits to coastal waters in Canada.

It was not to last. The nature of naval warfare was changing rapidly, and the antisubmarine role that the RCN was taking on could be better addressed by purpose-designed DDEs augmenting an aircraft carrier. Even the training role could be accomplished more cost-effectively in other fashions. *Québec* was paid off in 1956, with *Ontario* following her in 1958. Ironically, the two were sold for breaking up in 1960 in Osaka, Japan — the former enemy turned stalwart ally. The time of the Canadian "British" cruisers had passed.

FURTHER READING

WAB Douglas et al., "Towards a Balanced Fleet," chapter 15 in *A Blue Water Navy: The Official Operational History of the Royal Canadian Navy in the Second World War, 1943–1945* (Vanwell Publishing, 2007).

Norman Friedman, *British Cruisers: Two World Wars and After* (Naval Institute Press, 2022).

Stephen Conrad Geneja, *The Cruiser Uganda: One War — Many Conflicts: The First Documented and Eyewitness Account of Canada's Only Cruiser in World War Two and Her Part in the Pacific War* (Tyendinaga Publishers, 1994).

J.L. Granatstein, "HMCS *Uganda*: The Royal Canadian Navy Ship That Voted Itself Out of a War," *The Hub*, June 28, 2022, thehub.ca/2022/06/28/j-l-granatstein-hmcs-uganda-the-royal-canadian-navy-ship-that-voted-itself-out-of-a-war/.

"History of HMCS *Ontario*" (DND: Directorate of History and Heritage 8000, HP 180/62).

Richard H. Leir, "'Big Ship Time': The Formative Years of RCN Officers Serving on RN Ships," in *RCN in Retrospect, 1910–1968*, ed. James Boutilier (UBC Press, 1982), 74–95.

Bill Rawling, "A Lonely Ambassador: HMCS *Uganda* and the War in the Pacific," *The Northern Mariner/Le Marin du nord* 8, no. 1 (January 1998): 39–63, tnm.journals.yorku.ca/index.php/default/article/view/661/634.

David Zimmerman, *Maritime Command Pacific: The Royal Canadian Navy's West Coast Fleet in the Early Cold War* (UBC Press, 2015).

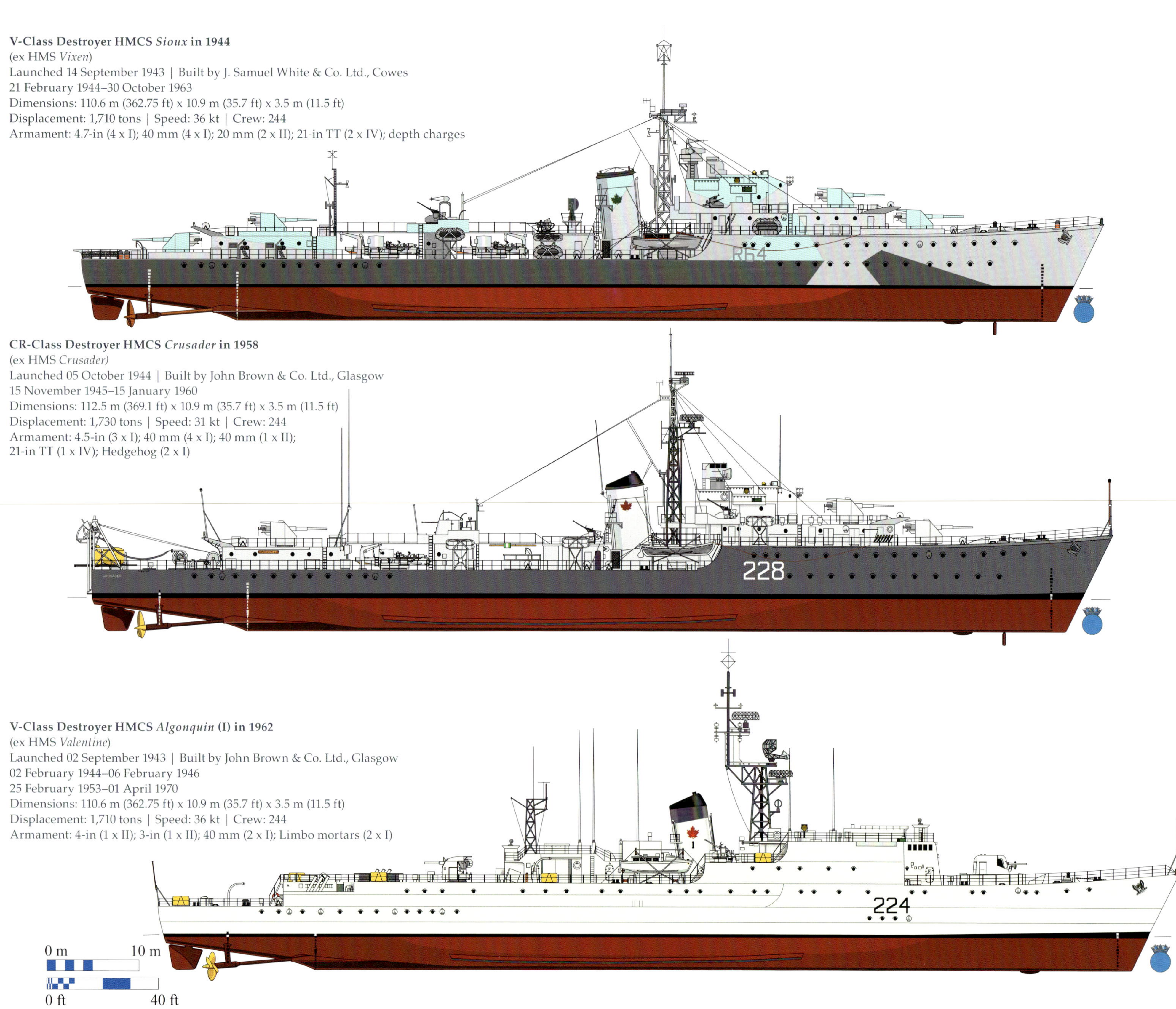

V-Class Destroyer HMCS *Sioux* in 1944
(ex HMS *Vixen*)
Launched 14 September 1943 | Built by J. Samuel White & Co. Ltd., Cowes
21 February 1944–30 October 1963
Dimensions: 110.6 m (362.75 ft) x 10.9 m (35.7 ft) x 3.5 m (11.5 ft)
Displacement: 1,710 tons | Speed: 36 kt | Crew: 244
Armament: 4.7-in (4 x I); 40 mm (4 x I); 20 mm (2 x II); 21-in TT (2 x IV); depth charges

CR-Class Destroyer HMCS *Crusader* in 1958
(ex HMS *Crusader*)
Launched 05 October 1944 | Built by John Brown & Co. Ltd., Glasgow
15 November 1945–15 January 1960
Dimensions: 112.5 m (369.1 ft) x 10.9 m (35.7 ft) x 3.5 m (11.5 ft)
Displacement: 1,730 tons | Speed: 31 kt | Crew: 244
Armament: 4.5-in (3 x I); 40 mm (4 x I); 40 mm (1 x II);
21-in TT (1 x IV); Hedgehog (2 x I)

V-Class Destroyer HMCS *Algonquin* (I) in 1962
(ex HMS *Valentine*)
Launched 02 September 1943 | Built by John Brown & Co. Ltd., Glasgow
02 February 1944–06 February 1946
25 February 1953–01 April 1970
Dimensions: 110.6 m (362.75 ft) x 10.9 m (35.7 ft) x 3.5 m (11.5 ft)
Displacement: 1,710 tons | Speed: 36 kt | Crew: 244
Armament: 4-in (1 x II); 3-in (1 x II); 40 mm (2 x I); Limbo mortars (2 x I)

23 THE EMERGENCY (INTERMEDIATE) DESTROYERS

By the time of the Quebec Conference of 1943, when the Admiralty proposed that the RCN crew a pair of destroyers as part of the arrangement covering cruisers and coastal craft flotillas, the Canadian naval staff had already given thought to the acquisition of additional destroyers. The RCN had never strayed from the desire expressed in the September 1939 submission on naval expansion for a force of eighteen of the type. Now the changing fortunes of the war offered, in the words of the official historian, "the opportunity to remodel the RCN from an antisubmarine escort force into a diversified, well-balanced fleet that could prove capable of meeting Canada's needs in the post-war period."[35] With the total of Tribal-class destroyers capped at eight (the four British-built ships then just entering service and the four building in Canada), and the 1930s-vintage River-class destroyers showing their age from years of hard action, the RCN was in the market for ten newer destroyers.

The staff had done its homework. From the perspective of the Admiralty, to meet the immediate requirement for the two to dispatch to the Pacific War, the most suitable solution seemed to be for the Canadians to take up another pair of Tribals that were completing refit (*Eskimo* and *Tartar*), which would make for a homogenous flotilla with the RCN Tribals already serving in U.K. waters. The Canadian preference, however, was for the slightly smaller but more modern "intermediate" fleet destroyers that were being built in British yards, primarily because these had greater endurance than the short-legged Tribals; also, when completed, they would be fitted with the very latest RN weapons and equipment. Since it

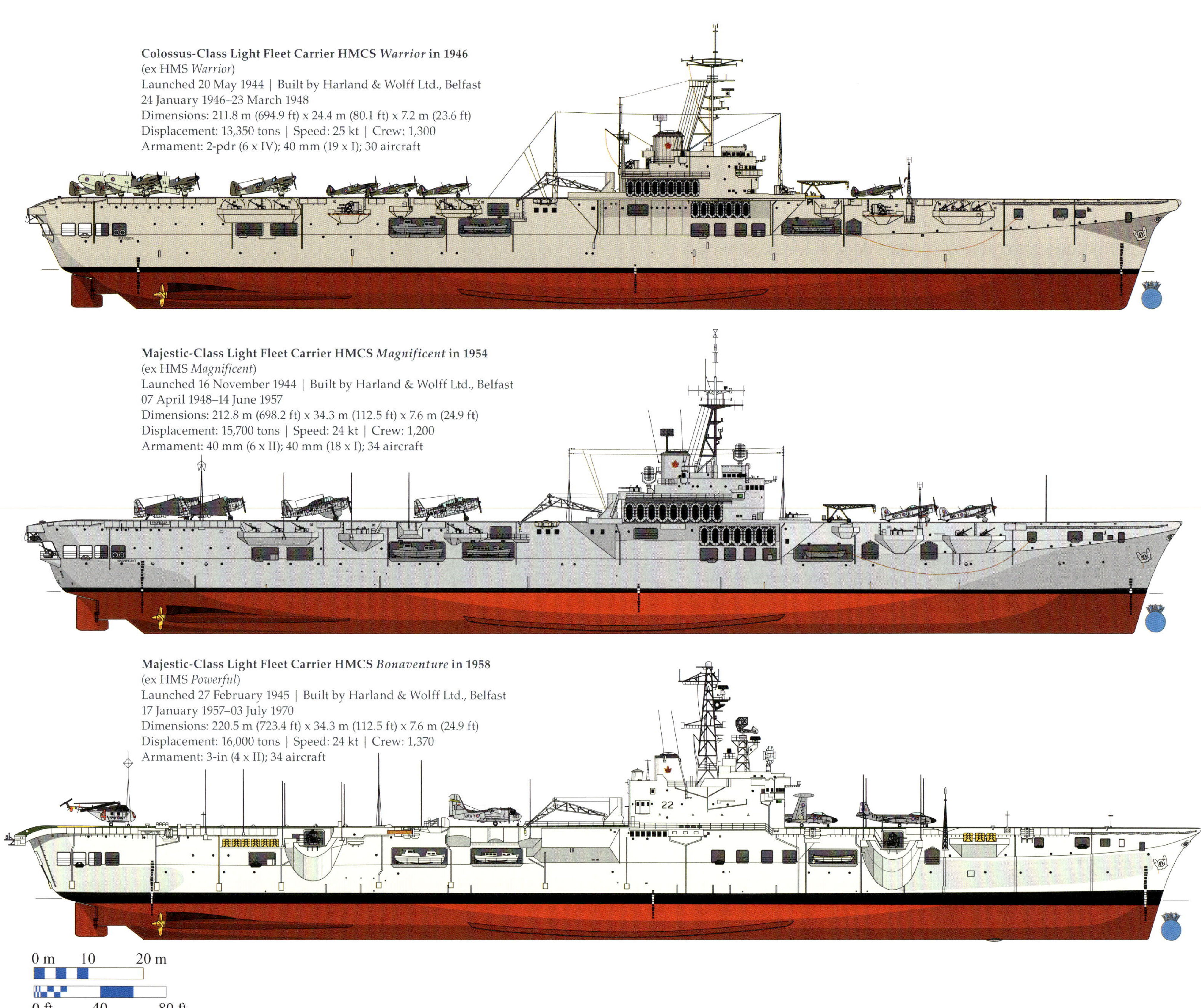
Colossus-Class Light Fleet Carrier HMCS *Warrior* in 1946
(ex HMS *Warrior*)
Launched 20 May 1944 | Built by Harland & Wolff Ltd., Belfast
24 January 1946–23 March 1948
Dimensions: 211.8 m (694.9 ft) x 24.4 m (80.1 ft) x 7.2 m (23.6 ft)
Displacement: 13,350 tons | Speed: 25 kt | Crew: 1,300
Armament: 2-pdr (6 x IV); 40 mm (19 x I); 30 aircraft
Majestic-Class Light Fleet Carrier HMCS *Magnificent* in 1954
(ex HMS *Magnificent*)
Launched 16 November 1944 | Built by Harland & Wolff Ltd., Belfast
07 April 1948–14 June 1957
Dimensions: 212.8 m (698.2 ft) x 34.3 m (112.5 ft) x 7.6 m (24.9 ft)
Displacement: 15,700 tons | Speed: 24 kt | Crew: 1,200
Armament: 40 mm (6 x II); 40 mm (18 x I); 34 aircraft
Majestic-Class Light Fleet Carrier HMCS *Bonaventure* in 1958
(ex HMS *Powerful*)
Launched 27 February 1945 | Built by Harland & Wolff Ltd., Belfast
17 January 1957–03 July 1970
Dimensions: 220.5 m (723.4 ft) x 34.3 m (112.5 ft) x 7.6 m (24.9 ft)
Displacement: 16,000 tons | Speed: 24 kt | Crew: 1,370
Armament: 3-in (4 x II); 34 aircraft
22
0 m 10 20 m
0 ft 40 80 ft

24

THE POSTWAR AIRCRAFT CARRIERS

Aside from the fact that the RCN operated light fleet aircraft carriers only in the postwar period, the title to this entry is misleading, as the primary consideration for their initial acquisition was to contribute to the war in the Pacific against Japan. But the second consideration indeed was that they be the basis of a well-balanced fleet structure for what the naval staff styled in its post-hostilities planning documents as "the continuing RCN" needed to meet the challenges of the postwar world. By the time of the second Quebec Conference in September 1944, at which the Pacific campaign was the focus of discussions, two factors had become apparent: Aircraft carriers were the clear capital ship successor to the big-gun battleship, and the Canadian naval contribution in the theatre was defined as being "2 cruisers and 2 light fleet carriers, the [armed merchant cruiser] *Prince Robert* re-armed as an anti-aircraft ship, 10 fleet destroyers, and about 40 frigates and corvettes."[37] Translated into a postwar fleet structure, if split neatly in half, that would allow for a carrier task force on each coast.

The British concept of a "light fleet" aircraft carrier (USN hull classification CVL) was framed in 1942 to meet the RN's need for a less expensive and more rapidly constructed version of the large Illustrious-class fleet carriers built in the late 1930s but not existing in sufficient numbers to sustain intense wartime combat operations and for which the Bogue-class "CVE" escort carriers (including the Canadian-crewed *Nabob* and *Puncher*; see Chapter 21) were not adequately equipped. As such, the initial tranche of CVL was the 13,350-ton Colossus class, which could embark up to fifty aircraft (depending upon

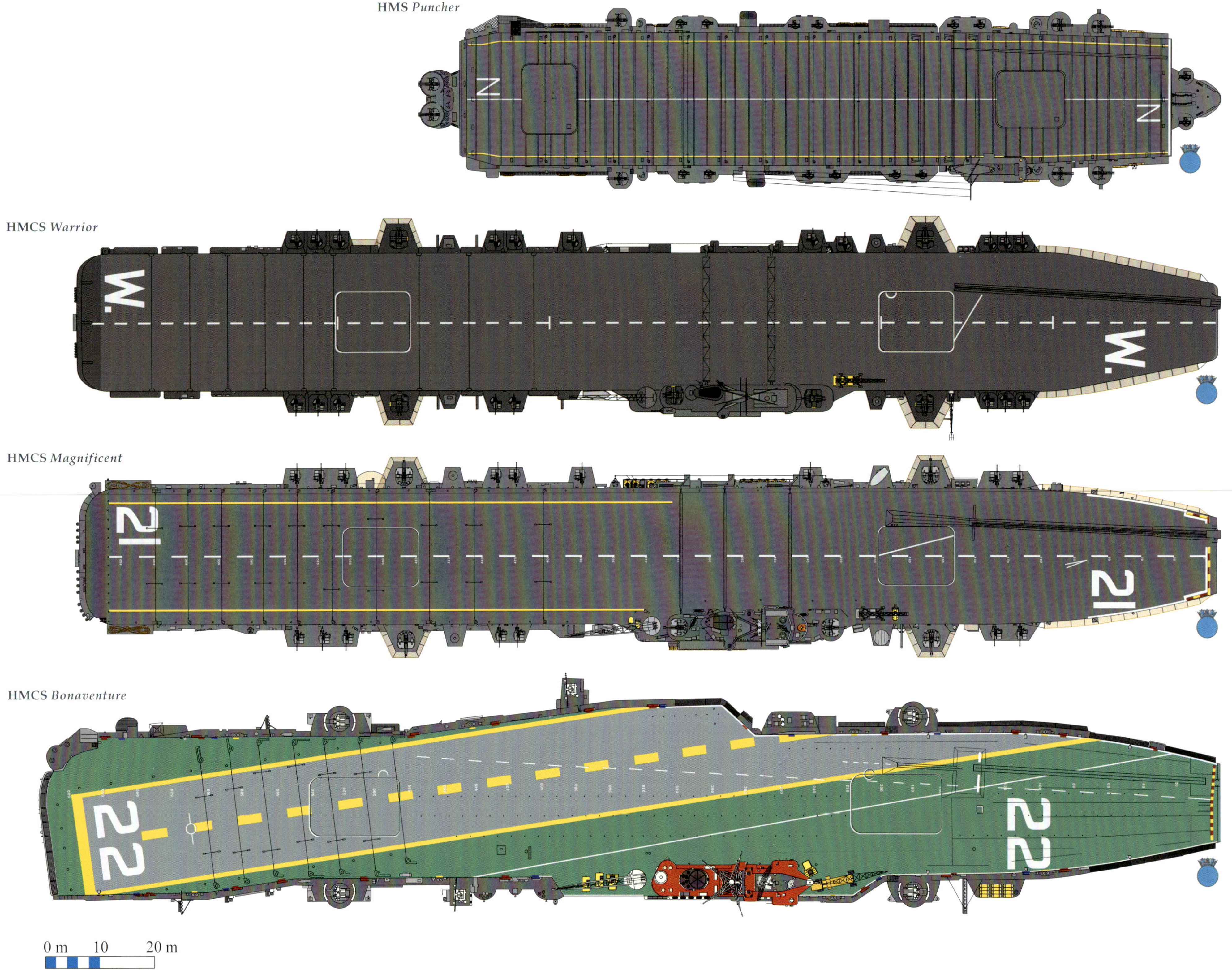
HMS *Puncher*
N
N
HMCS *Warrior*
W.
W.
HMCS *Magnificent*
21
21
HMCS *Bonaventure*
22
22
0 m
10
20 m
0 ft
40
80 ft

type), making it somewhat of an "intermediate" between the 23,000-ton *Illustrious* — with up to fifty-seven aircraft — and the "smaller" 14,000-ton Bogue-class CVE, which embarked only eighteen to twenty-four aircraft. (Note that, although the CVE displaced some 1,500 tons more than the CVL, the operational difference was in the latter's much longer flight deck and greater number of aircraft embarked. Friedman makes the difference specific in comparing the light fleet to the original British escort carrier: "[*Colossus*] was conceived as an *Audacity* with a hangar."[38]) Sixteen of the Colossus class were laid down during 1942 and 1943 in eight different British yards, with the expectation they would enter service in 1945–46. In November 1944, *Ocean* and *Warrior* were tentatively allocated for Canadian service; however, when the RCN experienced delays in gathering crews, the offer of *Ocean* was replaced with *Magnificent* as the second carrier.

Canadian crews were gathering to stand by *Warrior* at the Harland & Wolff builder's yard in Belfast, Northern Ireland, when the war ended in August 1945. The wholly unanticipated advent of atomic warfare threw postwar defence planning everywhere into disarray. By the end of September, the Canadian Chiefs of Staff Committee had determined the Interim Force manning level for the RCN to be ten thousand personnel, and in announcing the policy in the House of Commons on October 6, 1945, the minister of national defence described the Navy's requirement for what he called "a good workable little fleet."[39] The naval staff rapidly reassessed these factors as rationalizing a force of just a single CVL, supported by two cruisers (soon reduced to only the one) and nine fleet destroyers. *Warrior* was retained on loan from the RN and commissioned into the RCN on January 24, 1946, while the option for *Magnificent* was put on hold.

For the next quarter century, maintenance of a CVL would be the organizing principle for the RCN. Over that time span, the RCN would operate three CVLs in succession, each a progressive improvement over its predecessor. Importantly, the actual ship would be determined in a symbiotic relationship by the aircraft types it was planned to operate (these are all discussed in later chapters in Part 2), reflecting in turn the evolutionary advances in naval warfare through the period.

When *Warrior* sailed from Britain for Halifax in March 1946, she had embarked a pair of squadrons formed with the assistance of the RN FAA, being the Supermarine Seafire fighters of 803 Squadron and a strike variant of the Fairey Firefly with 825 Squadron. Designed as she was for tropical conditions in the Far East, *Warrior* soon proved unsuited for Canadian cold weather conditions, so in November, she transferred for an over-winter familiarization cruise to the Pacific coast, then returned to Halifax in March 1947. As will be seen in their respective chapters later in this book, the Seafires and early-model Fireflies were also determined to be inadequate to Canadian naval needs, so negotiations had already begun to exchange *Warrior* for an improved British CVL able to carry more capable aircraft types.

The RCN now exercised the option for the loan of *Magnificent*. Also constructed in Belfast and completed only six months after *Warrior*, she was of the slightly

A miscellaneous assortment of the classes portraying the RCN's "blue water navy" self-image in Halifax Dockyard in the early 1950s. Most recognizable are the carrier *Magnificent* in the foreground; immediately behind her, the cruiser *Québec*; and to the left, one of the Cape-class escort maintenance ships. Inside the camber can be seen a pair of Porte-class gate vessels and wartime Bangor-class minesweepers.

larger (15,700-ton) Majestic class. The Majestics were laid down as the last six of the Colossus class but with sufficient modifications made while building to constitute a class of their own. Mostly the extra tonnage was made up from strengthening the flight and hangar decks to be able to handle the heavier types of advanced aircraft that were being designed even as the war was still in progress. When HMCS *Magnificent* commissioned on March 21, 1948, these were the much higher-performance Hawker Sea Fury fighters and later-Mark IV Fireflies, with the latter replaced in 1950 by the durable workhorse Grumman Avenger torpedo bomber modified to conduct ASW. "Maggie," as she was affectionately known in the fleet, had a much more successful career in the RCN than her predecessor. Serving primarily as the core of the Canadian naval contribution to NATO while the destroyers constituted the commitment to Korea, she took part, for example, in the major exercises Mainbrace (1952) and Mariner (1953). Late in her commission, in 1955, she embarked the first HO4S-3 "Horse" antisubmarine helicopters, but her very last assignment was acting as a ferry transport for the Canadian ground forces sent to Egypt as part of the United Nations Emergency Force peacekeepers to resolve the Suez Crisis. She was paid off in Plymouth in June 1957 and returned to the RN for disposal.

Maggie's replacement, HMCS *Bonaventure*, had commissioned nearly a half year earlier, on January 17, 1957. "Bonnie," as she was quickly styled, had been constructed as HMS *Powerful*, also of the Majestic class and built by Harland & Wolff in Belfast. But she proved to be a very different type of carrier, completed with yet more improvements to accommodate the next generation of fighter and antisubmarine aircraft. The major new features required to operate these aircraft were an angled flight deck, steam catapults, and a mirror landing system, all the first to appear among Commonwealth navies. Her construction had been suspended after the war, and she was laid up in the yard, so when the RCN came looking in 1952 for a replacement for Maggie, she was available to be taken in hand to incorporate these advances. The scope of the changes, however, was such that the Canadian government had to purchase her (albeit at a discount) to have them undertaken. As for the aircraft to embark in her, the RCN turned now entirely to the United States, acquiring the jet-powered McDonnell F2H-3 Banshee fighters to give a limited all-weather air defence capability, the large Grumman CS2F Tracker twin-engined fixed-wing antisubmarine aircraft, and a full detachment of HO4S-3 antisubmarine helicopters with dipping sonars (see the respective chapters in Part 2). The embarked air group typically comprised sixteen Banshees, ten Trackers, and a half-dozen Horses.

The apex of the Canadian carrier experience did not last for long. The Trackers became fully operational at sea only in 1959, and the Banshees were phased out in September 1962 at the end of their service life — they had been acquired as surplus from the USN, and a fighter replacement that could operate from the now-considered-small Canadian deck was not possible within the Navy's budget. Under the premise of "Get Big or Get Out" (see Boutilier's article of that title, in Further Reading) the possibility was investigated of following Bonnie with an American Essex-class carrier — more than double the size of Bonnie, at 36,380 tons, and able to embark ninety to a hundred aircraft — but even at a generous American disposal offer, that was obviously also an unaffordable stretch. However, the phase-out of the Banshees came just as the Horses were being replaced by the much more capable CHSS-2 Sea King helicopter, and with the Trackers still being viable, from that point on, Bonnie was completely reroled as an antisubmarine carrier. In April 1966, she began a mid-life refit meant to enhance her capacity to perform that function through the next decade.

While she was out of service, events conspired against *Bonaventure*. The length of the refit stretched from a year to sixteen months, while the cost more than doubled from the projected $8 million to $17 million (a significant sum as inflation began to spiral in the mid-1960s). Not only was she unavailable to figure in the July 1, 1967, Centennial Fleet Review in Halifax Harbour, but the resulting scandal struck just as Prime Minister Lester Pearson's Liberal government began to look for spending cuts to put toward new welfare state funding. Keeping the carrier at sea was already consuming a full quarter of the Navy's annual budget, and wide-ranging belt-tightening measures — such as paying off the wartime Tribals and Intermediate destroyers, as well as the Prestonian conversions and laying up the Bay-class minesweepers (see the respective chapters) — were

The Atlantic fleet in 1968: In the centre are (left to right) the replenishment ship *Provider*, escort maintenance ship *Cape Scott*, and carrier *Bonaventure*; surrounding them are six St. Laurent–class DDHs ahead and a pair of Restigouche-class DDEs taking up the rear. Overhead are a flight of nine fixed-wing Trackers, preceded by three Sea King helicopters.

not keeping pace. Within the newly unified Canadian Armed Forces (CAF) — which in the first stages of "integration," beginning in 1964, had seen the disbandment of the individual service staffs for distribution into generic (read "army-centric") functions — members of the other former services were heard to observe that if the Navy had "made do" without Bonnie for so long, then why was a carrier needed at all? Without a proper naval staff to make the case for her retention, Bonnie was deemed surplus. She was paid off on July 3, 1970, sold for disposal, and soon after broken up in Taiwan in 1971.

With Bonnie's demise, so also went big-deck fixed-wing Canadian naval ambitions (the fate of the Naval Air Branch is explored more fully in Chapter 49; notably, after unification in 1968, there was no longer even an "RCN," until the symbolic restoration of the title in 2011). The Trackers, however, found new life ashore and the Sea Kings continued to operate for the rest of their service life from the small decks of the destroyer fleet converted to helicopter-carrying (DDH) configuration. Elements of Bonnie herself remain as described on the Wikipedia entry about the ship. Most poignantly, her starboard anchor is preserved in Halifax's Point Pleasant Park as the Canadian Peacetime Sailors' Memorial, colloquially known as "The *Bonaventure* Anchor Memorial," dedicated to Canadian Navy and Maritime Air Force personnel who have lost their lives at sea in the performance of their duty in peacetime.

FURTHER READING

"1942 Design Light Fleet Carrier" [Colossus Class], Wikimedia Foundation, last modified February 8, 2025, 02:14 (UTC), en.wikipedia.org/wiki/1942_Design_Light_Fleet_Carrier.

James A. Boutilier, "'Get Big or Get Out': The Canadian and Australian Decisions to Abandon Aircraft Carriers," in *Reflections on the Royal Australian Navy*, eds. T.R. Frame et al. (Kangaroo Press, 1991), 382–408.

William B. Christie, "Canadian Technical Involvement in the Design and Construction of HMCS *Bonaventure*," *Maritime Engineering Journal* (February 1997): 21–27.

WAB Douglas et al., "Towards a Balanced Fleet," chapter 15 in *A Blue Water Navy: The Official Operational History of the Royal Canadian Navy in the Second World War, 1943–1945* (Vanwell Publishing, 2007).

Norman Friedman, *British Carrier Aviation: The Evolution of the Ships and Their Aircraft* (Naval Institute Press, 1988).

Norman Friedman, *The Postwar Naval Revolution* (Naval Institute Press, 1986).

"HMCS *Bonaventure*," Wikimedia Foundation, last modified December 21, 2024, 01:27 (UTC), en.wikipedia.org/wiki/HMCS_Bonaventure.

JDF Kealy and E.C. Russell, *A History of Canadian Naval Aviation 1918–1962* (Queen's Printer, 1967).

TFJ Leversedge, *Aircraft Carriers in Royal Canadian Navy Service* (Kestrel Publications, 2023).

Norman Polmar, *Aircraft Carriers: A History of Carrier Aviation and Its Influence on World Events*, vol. 2, *1946–2006* (Potomac Books, 2008).

J. Allan Snowie, *The Bonnie: HMCS* Bonaventure (Boston Mills Press, 1987).

Michael Whitby, "Fouled Deck: The Pursuit of an Augmented Aircraft Carrier Capability for the Royal Canadian Navy, Part 1, 1945–56," *The Canadian Air Force Journal* 3, no. 3 (Summer 2010): 2–13, publications.gc.ca/collections/collection_2010/forces/D12-13-3-3-eng.pdf.

Michael Whitby, "Fouled Deck: The Pursuit of an Augmented Aircraft Carrier Capability for the Royal Canadian Navy, Part 2, 1956–64," *The Canadian Air Force Journal* 3, no. 4 (Fall 2010): 7–20, airforceapp.forces.gc.ca/CFAWC/eLibrary/Journal/Vol3-2010/Iss4-Fall/Sections/04-Fouled_Deck-Part_2_e.pdf.

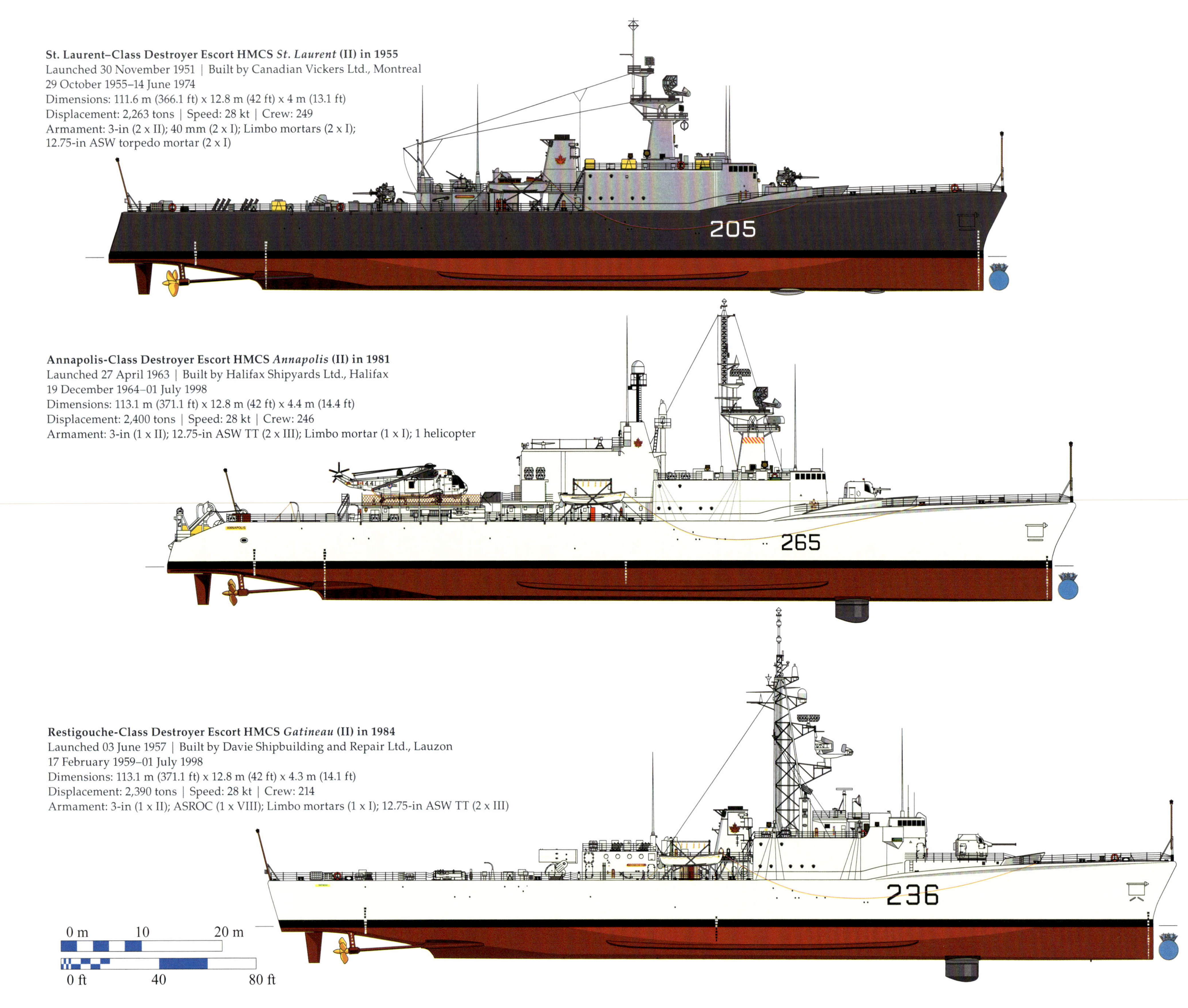
St. Laurent–Class Destroyer Escort HMCS *St. Laurent* (II) in 1955
Launched 30 November 1951 | Built by Canadian Vickers Ltd., Montreal
29 October 1955–14 June 1974
Dimensions: 111.6 m (366.1 ft) x 12.8 m (42 ft) x 4 m (13.1 ft)
Displacement: 2,263 tons | Speed: 28 kt | Crew: 249
Armament: 3-in (2 x II); 40 mm (2 x I); Limbo mortars (2 x I);
12.75-in ASW torpedo mortar (2 x I)
205
Annapolis-Class Destroyer Escort HMCS *Annapolis* (II) in 1981
Launched 27 April 1963 | Built by Halifax Shipyards Ltd., Halifax
19 December 1964–01 July 1998
Dimensions: 113.1 m (371.1 ft) x 12.8 m (42 ft) x 4.4 m (14.4 ft)
Displacement: 2,400 tons | Speed: 28 kt | Crew: 246
Armament: 3-in (1 x II); 12.75-in ASW TT (2 x III); Limbo mortar (1 x I); 1 helicopter
265
Restigouche-Class Destroyer Escort HMCS *Gatineau* (II) in 1984
Launched 03 June 1957 | Built by Davie Shipbuilding and Repair Ltd., Lauzon
17 February 1959–01 July 1998
Dimensions: 113.1 m (371.1 ft) x 12.8 m (42 ft) x 4.3 m (14.1 ft)
Displacement: 2,390 tons | Speed: 28 kt | Crew: 214
Armament: 3-in (1 x II); ASROC (1 x VIII); Limbo mortars (1 x I); 12.75-in ASW TT (2 x III)
236
0 m
10
20 m
0 ft
40
80 ft

THE CADILLACS: ST. LAURENT-CLASS DESTROYERS AND SUCCESSORS

The year 1947 was a turning point for the postwar RCN. The transition from war to peace was marked symbolically with the official end of "hostilities" as of June 30. More significantly, on September 1, Vice Admiral Harold Grant (previously seen in Chapter 22 as the highly decorated Canadian captain of the British cruiser HMS *Enterprise* and then of HMCS *Ontario*) became CNS, installed by Brooke Claxton, the dynamic new Liberal minister of national defence. As Grant's biographer concludes, "Grant became the pivotal figure in forging the postwar navy … [and] faced the Herculean challenge of rebuilding the navy.… Claxton brought energy and direction to the office and a determination to 'shake up' the department." For the RCN, this meant:

> strategy was to be reordered from an imperial to a North American orientation, and ASW was to replace the task-force concept.… In a war outside of Canada, the Navy would be employed in escort operations as in the Second World War.… Also, North America would become the primary source for material acquisition, and co-ordination with the United States forces became the priority.[40]

While the two men were often at odds over the social objectives of the Liberal government, on the broad outline of fleet structure they agreed. Together they would set in motion an unparalleled peacetime warship-building

The artist's conception of the antisubmarine escort vessel to be built in Canadian shipyards — released by the RCN on June 25, 1949, to coincide with the announcement of a contract award to German and Milne — bore little resemblance to Rowland Baker's actual proposal (probably to mislead Soviet intelligence) but is indicative of the design creativity he brought to the Canadian naval staff.

program that would establish the shape of the RCN for the duration of what was just then becoming known as the "Cold War" between the U.S.-led Western alliance and the communist east under the Soviet Union.

An RCN threat assessment prepared in January 1947 noted that the Soviet Navy was adapting advanced German U-boat technology into its rapidly expanding submarine force. In looking to reshape the Canadian fleet structure for the role of ASW, a naval staff survey of American and British warships revealed that no suitable advanced A/S (antisubmarine) frigate (as the type was still styled) was being planned. Concluding that "the escort of the future does not yet exist," in July 1948, the RCN obtained the loan of Constructor Captain Rowland Baker from the RN to establish a warship design authority on the Canadian naval staff.

Motivated by a growing sense of urgency, within months, Baker produced a preliminary sketch of a revolutionary flush-decked vessel, built around the innovative high-performance Y-100 steam propulsion plant. Continuing the rapid pace, the proposal was endorsed by the Naval Board on January 19, 1949, and only two months later, on March 26 (just over a week before the first meeting of the NATO Council on April 5), Prime Minister Louis St. Laurent's Cabinet approved construction of an initial three of the type. A year later, in August 1950, after the outbreak of the Korean War, a further four were authorized. As detailed design work progressed, it came to be appreciated this was a whole new class of ship: more capable than the wartime A/S frigates but not as large as a general-purpose postwar destroyer. The Naval Board restyled them "destroyer-escorts" or DDEs. They were to be named after previous RCN River-class destroyers and four-stackers to perpetuate battle honours earned in the Second Word War, and, with more than a passing nod to the prime minister who had approved their building, the lead ship of the class was named HMCS *St. Laurent*. Laid down on November 24, 1950, she was launched two years later and commissioned on October 29, 1955.

To build upon Baker's preliminary sketch, detailed design work was contracted in June 1949 to the Montreal naval architect firm German and Milne, and the final form of the ship quickly took shape, incorporating several pioneering features. As noted above, it was conceived around the Y-100 propulsion plant, a superheated-steam boiler and geared-turbine package with which Baker was familiar from his recent involvement in the preliminary design of the RN's Type 12 frigate. The fact of the Y-100 being British technology and ostensibly flying in the face of ministerial direction for North American equipment was overcome by the decision to fit only the lead ship *St. Laurent* with British machinery, provided by Yarrows; all follow-on ships would have a "Canadianized" version, built by a consortium of John Inglis (Toronto), Babcock-Wilcox (Galt, now Cambridge), and Canadian Westinghouse (Hamilton), among others (the full listing is provided by Good, "The Canadian Y.100," in Further Reading). This had the intended effect of progressing construction and testing of the lead ship more rapidly while the Canadian industries could get their footing. A welcome side benefit was that the redesign produced a number of innovations that were subsequently retrofitted to British plants. A longer-term consequence, however, was that *St. Laurent*'s engineering plant remained an "orphan" to the Canadian supply and maintenance chain. When the ship subsequently developed a major longitudinal crack in the mid-1960s — another result of her building to prototype engineering specifications — the decision was taken not to repair that, but rather to pay the ship off early, in 1974.

The Y 100 was unequalled in performance efficiency, taking up much less interior space than previous plants while generating 30,000 shp for a top speed in excess of 28 knots (52 km/hr) and a maximum endurance range of 4,500 nm (8,400 km) at 12 knots (22 km/hr). Twin screws and rudders made for exceptional manoeuvrability. With a length overall of 366 ft (111 m), the ship displaced 2,800 tons. The flush upper deck running the length of the ship was replicated inside one deck below with spaces opening onto an interior passageway named "Burma Road," which made this the first class of small warship in which it was possible to pass from bow to stern without having to venture outside. Other crew conveniences, as trialled in the Intermediate destroyer *Sioux*, included individual bunks, cafeteria messing, steam heating, and air conditioning. A novel and radical concept was that the bridge was enclosed and integrated with a large

Newly converted to helicopter-carrying destroyer configuration, *Assiniboine* conducts the initial trials embarking a Sea King in a moderate sea state.

operations room a deck below, from which the captain would "fight" the ship rather than conning (controlling) it from the bridge (which was also the basis of the Type 15 conversion made to the two other Intermediate destroyers, *Algonquin* and *Crescent*). These various "creature comforts" were immediately appreciated by their crews, who, in deference to the moniker given to the earlier original River-class of "Rolls-Royces," styled these "the Cadillacs." Later generations, after the introduction of gas turbine–powered ships, would come to know them affectionately as "the steamers."

Externally, the hull had a distinctive "round down" to enhance sea-keeping, and to counter the buildup of ice, the main mast was "plated" (enclosed, with interior ladders), and upper deck machinery was minimized — for example, with the anchors being handled inside below the fo'c'sle deck and stowed behind heated

The very different overhead aspects of the original Restigouche-class DDE *Kootenay* (258, upper inboard, before her IRE conversion) and *Saguenay* (206, lower outboard) after conversion to DDH configuration.

"anchor pocket doors." Such features also assisted in meeting the new requirement to operate the ship in a nuclear, biological, or chemical fallout area, with an exterior "pre-wetting" spray system to wash off contamination and the ability to maintain a positive pressure within an air-tight "citadel" in which the crew could live and operate, sealed off from the outside environment for at least a few hours.

The main armament was a pair of 3-inch/50-calibre radar-guided twin gun mounts primarily for protection against air attack, one each forward and aft, and a pair of the latest antisubmarine mortars, the 3-barrelled British Limbo Mk NC 10. This was a much-improved development of the Squid, in that it could be directed by sonar fire control systems from the operations room and fired in any direction out to 1,000 yards to bracket a submarine target with a six-bomb diamond pattern set to cover a range of depths.

The hull was built in sections for assembly construction so that in the event of an emergency, additional ships could be fabricated rapidly in the larger Canadian yards. To foster experience in the building techniques broadly across the industry, the work was also distributed among those seven yards: Marine Industries (Sorel, Quebec), Canadian Vickers (Montreal), Davie (Lauzon, Quebec), and Halifax Shipyards on the East Coast; and Burrard Dry Dock (Vancouver) and Victoria Machinery Depot (Victoria) in British Columbia (the ship size still precluded any being built on the Great Lakes, as the expansion of the St. Lawrence Seaway was only then in progress).

Although the St. Laurent class was originally expected to comprise fourteen ships, even as the original seven were building, a number of improvements in ASW technology had been developed. These were incorporated into the next seven ships to be laid down, so that even though they retained the same basic hull and power plant configuration, this next batch came to be called the Restigouche class. The most visible external difference was the fitting of a larger and more powerful wholly auto-loaded 3-inch/70-calibre gun forward, which necessitated the raising and enlargement of the enclosed bridge.

The promise of the Y-100 power plant and the other features of the St. Laurent class led to an aside investigation, commencing in 1953, into the design of a smaller

1,700-ton single-screw variant that could be produced more quickly and in larger quantities as a follow-on to the Prestonian-class conversions then under way (see Chapter 26). Designated the Vancouver-class frigate, it was cancelled two years later, owing to the advent of nuclear submarine technology, which made such a stripped-down design obsolete before it could be built. Research shifted instead to getting more "punch" from the existing hull with newer antisubmarine and anti-air technologies, and initial staff planning in 1956 proposed that a follow-on class to the Restigouches — designated the Mackenzie class — be equipped with a pair of state-of-the-art systems being introduced into the USN: the Anti-Submarine Rocket (ASROC) launcher and Tartar medium-range anti-air missiles (for the first time, staff planning also suggested the introduction of gas turbines into a Canadian warship as generators to provide the additional electrical power needed for those systems). However, analysis quickly revealed that all of this could not be made to fit into the existing hull, and design work progressed toward a larger vessel, 1000 tons heavier and 50 feet (15.2 m) longer, provisionally named the Manitoba class (see discussion in Chapter 38). This, in its turn, was cancelled in 1957 owing to budget pressures, with the naval staff deciding that the immediate needs for more escorts and to keep the shipyards engaged could be met economically by ordering a further six ships of very similar configuration to the established Restigouche design. In 1958, these were approved as the Mackenzie class that is better known to history.

To keep abreast of the rapidly changing nature of naval warfare, the RCN was experimenting with two separate concepts that would fundamentally alter the approach to shipboard ASW. The first was the capability to carry a large helicopter on the small DDE hull (this aircraft would prove to be the long-serving CH-124 Sea King, discussed in Chapter 53). The second was the development of the VDS to search for submarines attempting to evade detection below the surface sound layer (see discussion of VDS in Chapter 23 regarding the trials in the Intermediate destroyer *Crusader*). When both concepts proved immensely successful, over the period of 1962–64, all seven of the original St. Laurents underwent a major reconstruction, reconfiguring the aft half of the upper deck by the addition of a hangar and flight deck behind the funnels along with a "Beartrap" helicopter hauldown and rapid securing device, and removing one set of the Limbo mortars to make way for a VDS (see a fuller discussion in Chapters 52 and 53). Emerging with a distinctive new profile, they were reclassified as the Improved St. Laurent (ISL) DDH.

While these conversions were ongoing, in 1962, hulls 5 and 6 of the Mackenzies were redirected to be built from the keel up as DDHs of the two-ship Annapolis class. She and her sister, *Nipigon*, proved to be the end of the hull form, for a total of twenty ships. A follow-on class to incorporate yet more continuing improvements in ASW equipment was proposed soon after as "Repeat Nipigons"; however, the decision to change out the steam propulsion in favour of new gas turbine technology, and the fitting of a self-defence missile system, resulted in an entirely new design that came into being as the Iroquois-class destroyer (DDH-280; see Chapter 38, "Sisters of the Space Age").

Pending building of that entirely new class of ships, but with no funds for further DDH conversions, between 1968 and 1972, four of the seven Restigouches were converted to Improved Restigouche Escort (IRE) configuration, exchanging the aft gun for an ASROC launcher and one of the Limbo mortar mounts for a VDS. A distinctive lattice mast to host a variety of new radar and electronic warfare fits made for a unique visual profile. (The other three of the class were placed in long-term reserve and used as alongside training vessels. When *Kootenay* suffered a collision in June 1989, the replacement section for her bow was taken from *Chaudière*.)

In the early 1980s, a Destroyer Life Extension program was approved to maintain a minimal combat capability in the aging fleet, pending building of a replacement class (eventually the Halifax-class frigates described in Chapter 40). Under this refit, ten ships received varying upgrades of their combat sensors, command and control systems, and machinery control systems: All four IREs and the two Annapolis-class DDHs got a full upgrade, with four of the remaining original St. Laurents getting lesser modifications. Then, in the latter half of the decade, *Fraser*, *Annapolis*, and *Nipigon* had their VDS removed to be replaced with early models of the passive Canadian Towed Array Sonar System (CANTASS), which would be the primary antisubmarine sensor of the Halifax-class frigates then entering construction.

Since the Cold War never turned "hot," other than the near-run Cuban Missile Crisis in October 1962 (for which the original St. Laurents and Restigouches were available to play a major role), the only ship of the general type to see action was the IRE *Terra Nova* in the Persian Gulf War of 1990–91. Hasty upgrades required for this effort saw her ASROC launcher and remaining Limbo mortar replaced, respectively, with a pair of Harpoon antiship missile launchers and an anti-missile Phalanx CIWS "borrowed" from systems to hand for fitting in the Halifax-class frigates then under construction. In expectation of a prolonged conflict, *Restigouche* was similarly modified but never saw action.

The St. Laurents and Restigouches spent much of their early service generally divided between the coasts on which they were built. One of the consequences of the cost-cutting associated with unification of the armed forces in 1968 was redistribution of the fleet for concentration by type on the respective coasts. Because this also coincided with the DDH and IRE conversions, it was decided to port the more capable DDHs (the seven St. Laurents and the two Annapolis class) in Halifax, co-located with their Sea King helicopter detachments in nearby Shearwater Canadian Forces Base (CFB) to be available for NATO operations. Meanwhile, the IREs were transferred to the West Coast for operations, along with the Mackenzies, which became the backbone there of a training squadron. In anticipation of acquiring the Halifax-class frigates, in the late 1980s, the Navy was finally able to rebalance its force structure just as the Cold War was ending, with *Annapolis* transferring to the West Coast in 1989 (she had been preceded by the Iroquois-class destroyer *Huron* in 1987); there had been no helicopter-carrying Canadian ships on that coast until then, aside from the replenishment ship *Provider*. In consequence, to provide the air detachments now required, HS 443 Squadron was formed to reoccupy the former naval air station at Patricia Bay (Victoria International Airport).

St. Laurent was sold for scrapping in 1974 but foundered under tow in a gale off Cape Hatteras. Most of the others saw out the Cold War but were progressively removed from service as they were replaced by the Halifax-class frigates through the 1990s. Seven of them avoided the scrapyard to become artificial reefs for diving enthusiasts. The last of the general type to leave service was *Nipigon* on July 1, 1998; she remains as one of those diving reefs off Rimouski, Quebec. Controversially, the last of the type to be disposed of was *Fraser* — paid off on October 5, 1994, she was not sold until four years later, to become a floating museum in Bridgewater, Nova Scotia. Those plans fell through, and, after badly deteriorating, she was repossessed by the Department of National Defence (DND) to be broken up for scrap in 2011.

The St. Laurents were the first major warship class designed and built in Canada, notably ahead of any allied efforts to incorporate their many cutting-edge features. The resiliency of the design resulted in a total of twenty ships, built around the same distinctive general hull configuration and propulsion plant. With various conversions and modifications to maintain their fighting capabilities, these ships were the mainstay of the Canadian fleet from 1955 to 1995; indeed, the St. Laurent DDH pairing with the CH-124 Sea King helicopter was to become emblematic of the Canadian naval Cold War

Name	Pennant	Commissioned	Conversion Refit	Paid Off
St. Laurent Class (All Converted DDH)				
St. Laurent (Second)	205	Oct 29, 1955	Oct 1962–Oct 4, 1963	June 14, 1974
Saguenay (Second)	206	Dec 15, 1956	Aug 22, 1963–May 14, 1965	June 26, 1990
Skeena (Second)	207	Mar 30, 1957	July 26, 1964–Aug 4, 1965	Nov 1, 1993
Ottawa (Third)	229	Nov 10, 1956	Mar 25, 1963–Oct 28, 1964	July 31, 1992
Margaree (Second)	230	Oct 5, 1957	Sep 25, 1964–Oct 15, 1965	May 2, 1992
Fraser (Second)	233	June 28, 1957	July 2, 1965–Oct 22, 1966	Oct 5, 1995
Assiniboine (Second)	234	Aug 16, 1956	June 28, 1962–June 28, 1963	Dec 14, 1988
Restigouche Class (No Conversion)				
Chaudière (Second)	235	Nov 14, 1959	n/a	May 23, 1975
St. Croix (Second)	256	June 7, 1958	n/a	Nov 15, 1974
Columbia (Second)	260	Nov 7, 1959	n/a	Feb 18, 1974
Restigouche Class (IRE Conversion)				
Gatineau (Second)	236	Feb 17, 1959	Sep 9, 1969–Apr 14, 1971	July 1, 1998
Restigouche (Second)	257	June 7, 1958	Aug 3, 1970–May 12, 1972	Aug 31, 1994
Kootenay (Second)	258	Mar 7, 1959	Nov 28, 1969–Jan 7, 1972	Dec 18, 1996
Terra Nova	259	June 6, 1959	May 1965–Sep 1967	July 1, 1998
Mackenzie Class (No Conversion)				
Mackenzie	261	Oct 6, 1962	n/a	Aug 3, 1993
Saskatchewan (Second)	262	Feb 16, 1962	n/a	Apr 1, 1994
Yukon	263	May 25, 1963	n/a	Dec 3, 1993
Qu'Appelle (Second)	264	Sep 14, 1963	n/a	July 31, 1992
Annapolis Class (Built as DDH)				
Annapolis (Second)	265	Dec 19, 1964	n/a	July 1, 1998
Nipigon (Second)	266	May 30, 1964	n/a	July 1, 1998

experience. The Historic Sites and Monuments Board of Canada recognized the significance of the class with an historical plaque installed near *Fraser* in Bridgewater in 1997 (it was placed in storage when that ship was scrapped and is due to be revamped in the coming years). It reads:

> St. Laurent Class of Canadian Warship
>
> The pride of the Canadian Navy during the Cold War, these antisubmarine escorts were the first naval vessels conceived and built in Canada. Designed in 1948–1949, they influenced naval construction internationally with their smooth above-water surfaces and distinctive convex deck. They could also be sealed to protect crews against biological and radioactive threats. All seven St. Laurent–class ships were modified during the 1960s to carry helicopters and enhance their antisubmarine capability. Launched in 1953, HMCS *Fraser* is the last surviving example of this innovative class of warship.

FURTHER READING

R. Baker, "How to Build a Ship," *Crowsnest* 7, no. 2: 4–7, navalandmilitarymuseum.org/wp-content/uploads/2021/09/CFB-Esquimalt-Museum-Crowsnest-Volume07-Number-02-Dec-1954.pdf.

Ron Barrie and Ken Macpherson, *Cadillac of Destroyers: HMCS* St. Laurent *and Her Successors* (Vanwell Publishing, 1996).

D.K. Brown, *A Century of Naval Construction: The History of the Royal Corps of Naval Constructors* (Conway Maritime Press, 1983).

S.D. Campbell, "The Early Cadillacs" and "The Late Cadillacs," in *Tin-Can Canucks: A Century of Canadian Destroyers* (Kay Cee Publications, 2017), 169–248.

S. Mathwin Davis, "The '*St. Laurent*' Decision: Genesis of a Canadian Fleet," in *RCN in Transition, 1910–1985*, ed. WAB Douglas (UBC Press, 1988), 187–208.

E.B. Good, "The Canadian Y.100 ('St. Laurent' Class A/S/ Escorts)," *Journal of Naval Engineering* 9, no. 2 (April 1956): 164–177.

JHW Knox, "An Engineer's Outline of RCN History, Part 2 (1948-1968)," in *The RCN in Retrospect, 1910–1968*, ed. James Boutilier (UBC Press, 1982), 317–33.

Thomas G. Lynch, "Twilight of the St. Laurents," in *Warship 1990*, ed. Robert Gardiner (Naval Institute Press, 1991), 175–197.

The Atlantic fleet deployed to Bermuda Dockyard for Exercise WINTEX 60, January 1960. Left to right in three banks: (foreground) escort maintenance ship *Cape Scott* and Prestonian-class frigates *Cap de la Madeleine* and *La Hulloise*; (middle bank) Restigouche-class DDEs *Gatineau*, *Kootenay*, and *Restigouche*; (rear bank) Tribal-class destroyer *Micmac* and British A-class submarine *Auriga*.

named Vancouver class, a 1,700-ton scaled-down derivative of the St. Laurent design, essentially replacing the Prestonians' Squids with a pair of Limbo mortars and for propulsion having a single Y-100 boiler-turbine package. But it was shelved owing to appreciation that nuclear-powered submarine technology had progressed beyond the envisioned capability of that class. When the cruiser *Ontario* was paid off in 1958, the seven ships of the Fourth Escort Squadron (CORTRON 4) based on the West Coast found additional employment as training ships for junior officers and ratings and became visually distinguishable from their East Coast sisters by the fitting of an updated version of the "Dunc's Diner" that had been originated on the cruiser.

The whole of the class remained in service until budgetary pressures in the mid-1960s required they be paid off without replacement. The exception was the last of the class to be converted: *Victoriaville* was commissioned in 1959, only to be re-roled and renamed in 1966 as the diving tender *Granby* (taking on the name of the Bangor-class minesweeper she was replacing in the role). She was sold for scrap in 1974.

Three additional wartime frigates were transferred postwar to the Department of Transport for employment as Pacific Ocean "Station Papa" weather ships: the Coast Guard Ships (CGS) *Stone Town*, *St. Catharines*, and *St. Stephen*. They were given hull conversions in the early 1950s similar to those of the main Prestonian class, but without the upgraded sensors and weapons fits.

FURTHER READING

"First Converted Frigate Ready," *Crowsnest* 5, no. 11 (September 1953): 2, navalandmilitarymuseum.org/wp-content/uploads/2021/07/CFB-Esquimalt-Museum-Crowsnest-Volume05-Number-11-Sep-1953.pdf.

Harvey Johnson, "River/Prestonian Class Frigates — Backbone of Canada's Postwar Fleet," *Maritime Engineering Journal* 19, no. 1 (Spring 2000): 7–11, cntha.ca/static/documents/mej/mej-49.pdf.

Ken Macpherson, *Frigates of the Royal Canadian Navy, 1943–1974* (Vanwell Publishing, 1989).

Wind-Class Icebreaker HMCS *Labrador* in 1957
Launched 14 December 1951 | Built by Marine Industries Ltd., Sorel
08 July 1954–22 November 1957
Dimensions: 82 m (269 ft) x 19.2 m (63 ft) x 8.1 m (26.6 ft)
Displacement: 6,490 tons | Speed: 16 kt | Crew: 228
Armament: 40 mm (2 x I)

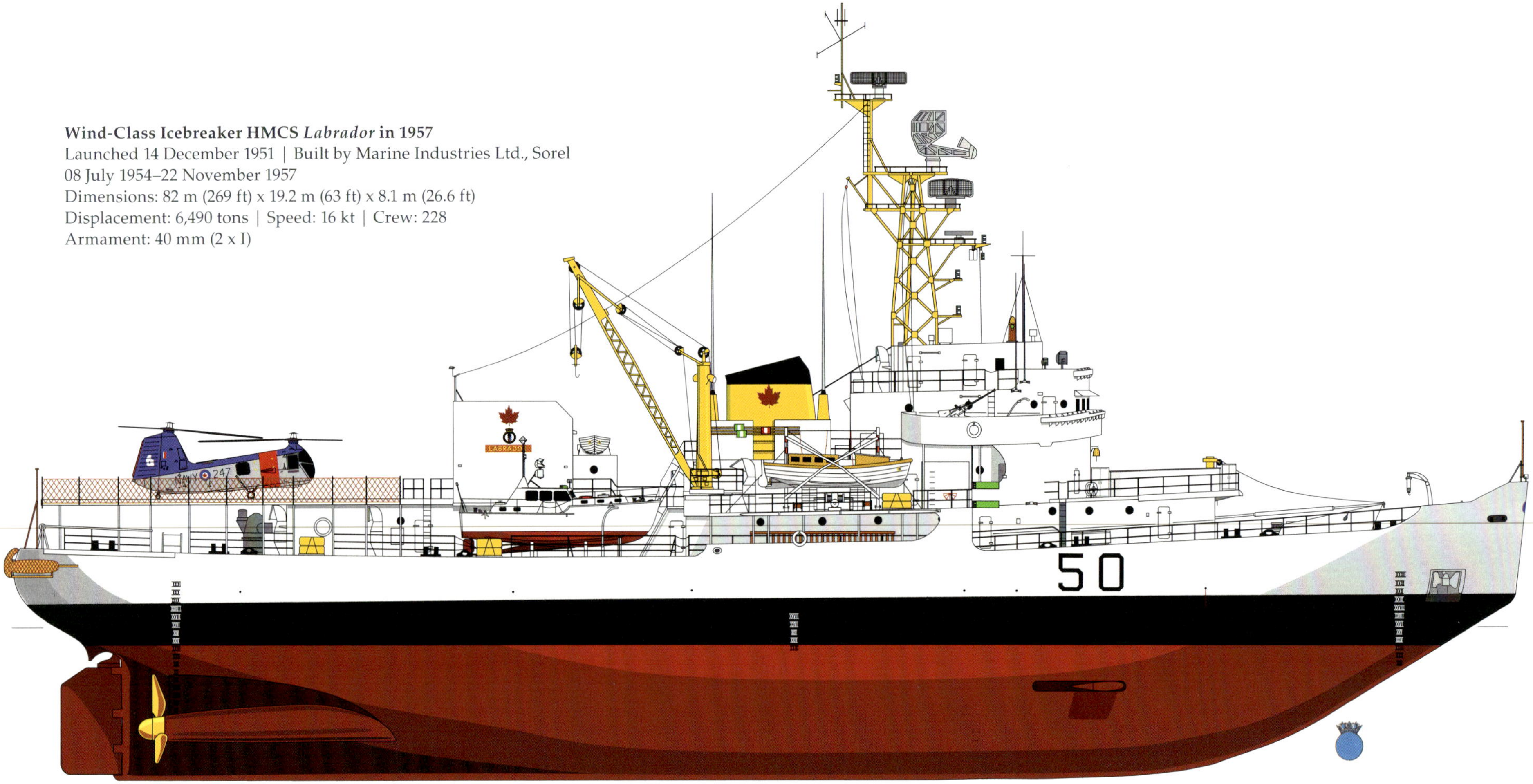

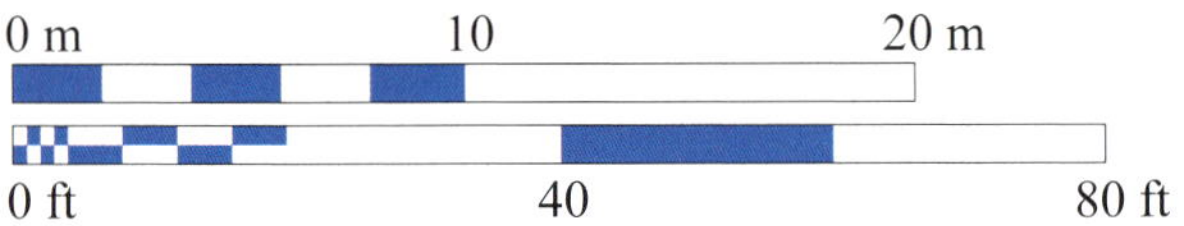

27

MODIFIED WIND-CLASS ICEBREAKER *LABRADOR*

Even as the Canadian naval staff was preparing to rejoin a Cold War Battle of the Atlantic against a potential Soviet opponent, its attention was also being drawn northward to the new theatre of the Canadian Arctic. There the Soviets remained the adversary, but the concern was equally for the activities of Canada's American allies, who recognized that the shortest route for a Soviet long-range atomic bomber attack was across our Arctic expanses, and this required the establishment of appropriate defensive measures. Following the practice established during the war for the building of the Alaska Highway, the Americans were willing to seek Canadian approval of any actions. But as Kikkert and Lackenbauer note, "Nightmares of American flags flying throughout the Arctic, with hundreds of U.S. servicemen flooding the region to challenge Canada's control, gravely concerned Ottawa."[41] Any American military presence necessitated corresponding Canadian forces being there as a demonstration of sovereignty in the region.

In the summer of 1948, both the USN and RCN made major deployments into the Canadian Arctic. Without any ice-capable ships, the Canadian Task Group was restricted to the waters south of Baffin Island: Indeed, while the Tribal-class destroyers *Nootka* and *Micmac* (supported by the oiler *Dundalk*, specially outfitted for the expedition) were able to foray into Hudson Bay down to Churchill, Manitoba, the carrier *Magnificent* was

Labrador with her near-sister USCGC *Eastwind* moored alongside. Note the pair of Bell 47 on her flight deck.

restricted from proceeding beyond Ungava Bay owing to treacherous currents in the poorly charted waters. Meanwhile, the Greenland-based American Wind-class icebreakers USCGC *Eastwind* and USS *Edisto* were able to penetrate much deeper into the archipelago, to the northern tip of Ellesmere Island and the far western reaches of Melville Island, respectively. Anticipating that that style of vessel would be much better adapted to the conditions, arrangements were made for Canadian observers from both the RCN and the Department of Mines and Resources to embark in the American ships.

Their various reports included, among other things, confirmation that a heavy icebreaker along the lines of the Wind class indeed was the type of vessel required for Canadian operations in the Arctic. In January 1949, Cabinet approved the contract for building such an Arctic patrol vessel, and work began almost immediately. But the observers had noted a number of shortcomings of the Wind class, which were passed to Captain Rowland Baker for review (recall this was the same naval constructor on loan from the RN, who was laying the groundwork for what would become the St. Laurent class and the Prestonian conversions). He determined several modifications to the basic design, detailed in a memorandum of May 13, 1949: The main improvements were a fuller form forward, with higher and flared bulwarks to keep the ship drier in a seaway; corresponding modification of the stern to push floating ice out of the wake; installation of heeling tanks to enable the ship to rock free if trapped in ice; removal of the 5-inch gun armament to make way for more storage space forward; enlargement of the hangar and flight deck half as big again to accommodate three helicopters (a combination of the Bell HTL-4 and Piasecki HUP-3 — see Chapter 52, "Early Naval Helicopters"); a revised mast arrangement for a Canadian radar and communications fit that was double that of the American; and the embarkation of a 36-foot all-aluminum hydrographic sounding craft named *Pogo* (which was maintained over the years and is presently in service with the Sea Cadet Corps in Gatineau, Quebec).

The incorporation of these many modifications required a longer than anticipated construction period, so it was not until July 8, 1954, that HMCS *Labrador* was commissioned, but no time was wasted thereafter in setting her to operational employment. After a brief stop in Halifax, *Labrador* sailed to meet with her American near-sisters, the US Coast Guard Cutters *Northwind* and

Burton Island, off Melville Island on August 25, 1954, making the point of escorting them through Canadian waters. *Labrador* then continued westward to conduct survey work in the Beaufort Sea before proceeding to Esquimalt on September 27, becoming the first warship to transit the length of the Northwest Passage. Returning through the Panama Canal to arrive in Halifax on November 21, 1954, *Labrador* also established herself as the first warship to circumnavigate North America in a single voyage — all on her maiden journey. After a quick over-winter refit, she spent the subsequent 1955 navigation season conducting work related to the survey and construction of the Distant Early Warning radar sites for NORAD, culminating in August with the escort of a sixty ship convoy of merchant vessels to locations along the length of the route.

The Canadian naval staff had not been keen on having the icebreaker on the Navy's books, as its cost would detract from the other building programs required to rejuvenate the fighting fleet. But CNS Harold Grant appreciated the argument that an American military presence should be met with a corresponding Canadian naval one, even as a symbolic statement of sovereignty, especially as the Liberal government was supportive of those other programs. But as circumstances changed, a reassessment was justified. Having made the point of exerting a Canadian naval presence in the Arctic, but with *Labrador* being relegated to more routine hydrographic survey and safety of navigation work in the following seasons, she was paid off on November 22, 1957, and transferred to the civilian Department of Transport. Although the transfer was made on the proviso that the icebreaker would be returned to naval service "if required," she never was. *Labrador* spent the next thirty years with the Canadian Coast Guard, finally being taken out of service in 1987 and broken up in Taiwan in 1989.

FURTHER READING

D.K. Brown, *A Century of Naval Construction: The History of the Royal Corps of Naval Constructors* (Conway Maritime Press, 1983).

Peter Kikkert and P. Whitney Lackenbauer, "Setting an Arctic Course: Task Force 80 and Canadian Control in the Arctic, 1948," *The Northern Mariner/le marin du nord* 21, no. 4 (October 2011): 327–358, tnm.journals.yorku.ca/index.php/default/article/view/302/284.

Adam Lajeunesse et al., eds., *HMCS* Labrador*: An Operational History* (Mulroney Institute of Government, 2017).

Michael Whitby, "Showing the Flag Across the North: HMCS *Labrador* and the 1954 Transit of the Northwest Passage," in *Northwest Passages: Navigating the Canadian Arctic from* Gjøa *to* Harry DeWolf, eds. P. Whitney Lackenbauer and Adam Lajeunesse (University of Calgary, Centre for Military and Strategic Studies, 2025), 99–105.

Bay-class minesweeper *Gaspé* under construction at Davie Shipbuilding in 1951, showing her composite mahogany and aluminum hull construction to reduce the ship's magnetic signature.

"MCB," they were given names perpetuating Bangor-class minesweepers with the common trait of Canadian bays and hence were known in Canada as the Bay class. Very soon after delivery in 1954, six of them were transferred to the French Navy under the NATO Military Defense Assistance Plan. A second building program to replace these was laid down in 1955–56 and took on the names of those that had been transferred. Another six were similarly transferred to Turkey in 1957 but without replacement.

These new six joined the remaining original four in being formed into two groups, one for each coast: the First Minesweeping Squadron (Atlantic) comprising *Chaleur, Chignecto, Fundy, Quinte, Resolute,* and *Thunder*; and the Second Minesweeper Squadron (Pacific) of *Cowichan, Fortune, James Bay,* and *Miramichi.*

In 1964, the whole lot were paid off as a cost-saving measure. The four remaining from the original program were sold outright to commercial interests, while the other six, slightly newer ships were laid up in reserve. These six were reactivated in 1972 as a subdivision of the reconstituted Training Group Pacific to conduct junior officer shiphandling and navigation training, where they were known colloquially as "The Woodpecker Squadron" in a nod to both their wooden construction and small-ship training function. Even with the sweeping gear and single Bofors 40-mm removed, living and classroom space was tight on the small vessels. In the early 1980s, this led to the installation on the quarterdeck of an additional accommodation space that quickly became known as the latest iteration of Dunc's Diner, although unlike the original in the cruiser *Ontario,* this had no "dining" facility but was given over entirely to accommodation, with bunks, heads and washplace, and chart table space. By the end of the decade, with the introduction of women into seagoing billets, it was redesigned to allow for separate gender accommodation spaces.

The end of the Cold War led, among other things, to a rethink of junior officer training. With the disbandment of Training Group Pacific in the mid-1990s, and the arrival into service of the Kingston class to take on their training duties (see Chapter 42), the Bay class were paid off and sold almost exactly four decades after their initial acceptance into service. Efforts were made to keep a couple of them going as commercial yachts, and as of the early 2020s, two were reported in use as 4,000-square-foot floating homes: *Fortune* in Vancouver, and *Cowichan* in Sooke.

Name	Pennant	Commissioned	Paid Off	Remarks
1951–52 Program (14)				
Chaleur	144	June 18, 1954	Sept 30, 1954	To France 1954
Chignecto	156	Dec 1, 1953	May 31, 1954	To France 1954
Comox	146	April 2, 1954	Sept 11, 1957	To Turkey 1957
Cowichan	147	Dec 10, 1953	Mar 31, 1954	To France 1954
Fortune	151	Nov 3, 1954	Feb 28, 1964	Sold commercial
Fundy	145	Mar 19, 1954	Mar 31, 1964	To France 1954
Gaspé	143	Dec 5, 1953	Aug 22, 1957	To Turkey 1957
James Bay	152	May 3, 1954	Feb 28, 1964	Sold commercial
Miramichi	150	July 30, 1954	Oct 1, 1954	To France 1954
Quinte	149	Oct 16, 1954	Feb 26, 1964	Sold commercial
Resolute	154	Sept 16, 1954	Feb 14, 1964	Sold commercial
Thunder	153	Dec 15, 1953	Mar 31, 1964	To France 1954
Trinity	157	June 16, 1954	Aug 21, 1957	To Turkey 1957
Ungava	148	June 4, 1954	Aug 23, 1957	To Turkey 1957
1955–56 Program (6)				
Chaleur (Second)	164	Sept 12, 1957	Dec 18, 1998	
Chignecto (Second)	160	Aug 1, 1957	Dec 19, 1998	
Cowichan (Second)	162	Dec 12, 1957	Aug 22, 1997	
Fundy (Second)	159	Nov 27, 1956	Dec 19, 1996	
Miramichi (Second)	163	Oct 29, 1957	Dec 16, 1998	
Thunder (Second)	161	Oct 3, 1957	Aug 22, 1997	

FURTHER READING

"Four Minesweepers, Gate Vessel Ordered," *Crowsnest* 1, no. 12 (October 1949): 2, navalandmilitarymuseum.org/wp-content/uploads/2021/09/CFB-Esquimalt-Museum-Crowsnest-Volume01-Number-12-Oct-1949.pdf.

Porte-Class Gate Vessel HMCS *Porte Saint Jean* in 1953
Launched 22 November 1951 | Built by George T. Davie & Sons Ltd., Lauzon
05 December 1951–31 March 1996
Dimensions: 38.3 m (125.7 ft) x 8 m (26.3 ft) x 4 m (13.1 ft)
Displacement: 429 tons | Speed: 11 kt | Crew: 23
Armament: 40 mm (1 x I)

Porte-Class Gate Vessel HMCS *Porte Saint Louis* in 1962
Launched 23 July 1952 | Built by George T. Davie & Sons Ltd., Lauzon
29 August 1952–31 March 1996
Dimensions: 38.3 m (125.7 ft) x 8 m (26.3 ft) x 4 m (13.1 ft)
Displacement: 429 tons | Speed: 11 kt | Crew: 23
Armament: nil

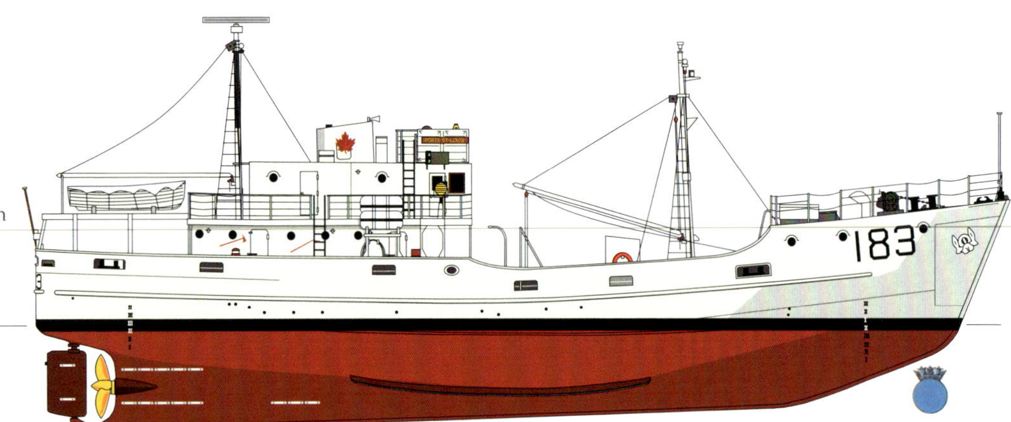

Porte-Class Gate Vessel HMCS *Porte de la Reine* in 1989
Launched 28 December 1951 | Built by Victoria Machinery Depot Co. Ltd., Victoria
07 October 1952–19 December 1996
Dimensions: 38.3 m (125.7 ft) x 8 m (26.3 ft) x 4 m (13.1 ft)
Displacement: 429 tons | Speed: 11 kt | Crew: 23
Armament: nil

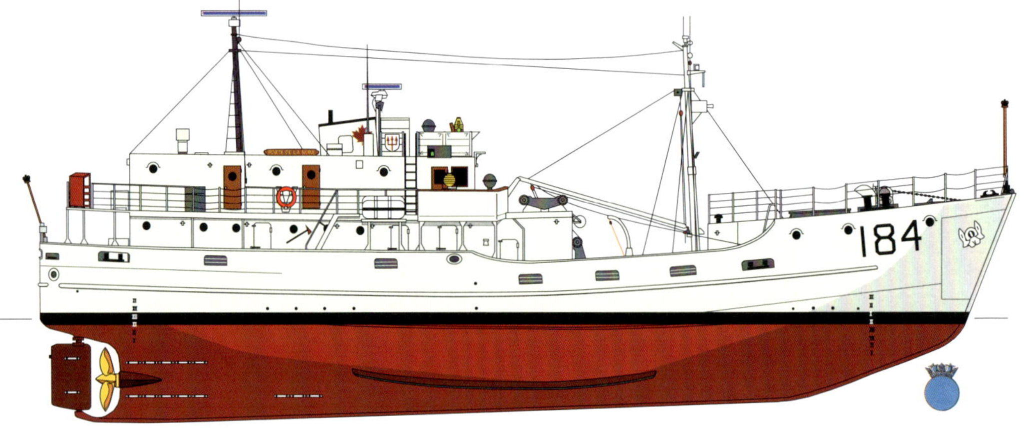

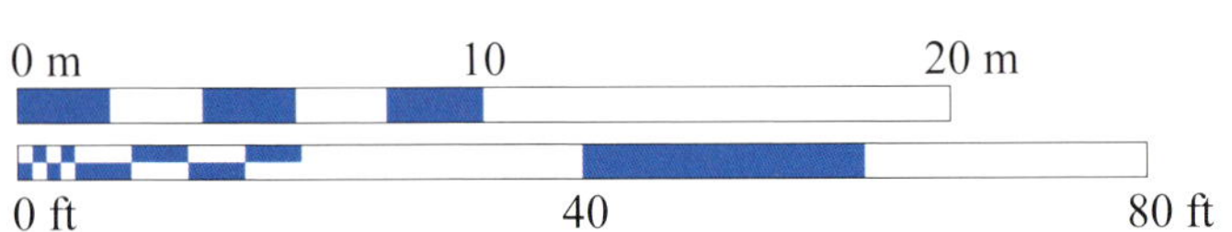

29

THE "PIG BOATS": PORTE-CLASS GATE VESSELS

The early Cold War appreciation of the need to redevelop the defences of Canada's harbours that resulted in acquisition of the Bay-class minesweepers also identified the requirement for a new class of antisubmarine boom or "gate" vessels to replace the First World War–vintage Battle class, which were finally worn out by the end of the Second World War. The basic design needed little improvement, however, and the concept for the new class, announced in September 1949, displayed the same trawler heritage, with a sturdy 430-ton, 125-foot (38-m) steel hull, powered now by a 600 brake-horsepower diesel engine. Five were built on the coasts where they were intended to operate (three on the East and two on the West), and they were named rather creatively for the gates or "Portes" of the French fortifications at Quebec and Louisbourg.

Porte de la Reine (pennant number 184) and *Porte Québec* (185) spent their entire service based in Esquimalt, while *Porte Saint Jean* (180) and *Porte Saint Louis* (183) did the same out of Halifax, with occasional summertime forays into the Great Lakes for Reserve training, based at HMCS *Star* in Hamilton, Ontario. *Porte Dauphine* (186) had a much more varied career, starting with the Navy in Halifax before being loaned from 1958 to 1974 to the Department of Transport as an environmental research ship, and then on return to the Navy, transferring to the West Coast.

Overhead view of the West Coast reserve training "Pig Boats" (from top to bottom), *Porte[s] de la Reine* (184), *Québec* (185), and *Dauphine* (186). The image nicely illustrates the variety of upper-deck arrangements of the mid-1980s.

The gate vessels were never employed in the anticipated harbour defence role, nor did they ever perform the mine-laying function for which they could also be fitted. Within a few years of commissioning in 1952, the original single 40-mm Bofors gun had been removed, and the vessels were given over full time to Reserve training. Although as a single-screw vessel they were not the best platform for preparing junior officers to handle the twin-screw ships of the rest of the fleet, their sturdy hull was most accommodating of the rigours put to them by neophyte shiphandlers, earning them the label of "pig boats." The designed accommodation for a crew of three officers and twenty ratings proved crowded for the training role, and more bunks were added over the years in a less than consistent fashion, but by the early 1980s, the class sported an enclosed area in the well-deck ahead of the bridge. They also had yet another variation of Dunc's Diner on the raised quarterdeck aft of the bridge, serving as a wardroom space (although it does not seem to have been called that in this class). Despite their top speed of only 11 knots, they ranged quite far afield, with *Porte Saint Jean* and *Porte Saint Louis* venturing as far as Bermuda and into the eastern Artic (the latter as recounted in the "Further Reading" article about long-time gate skipper Commander Hamish Berchem and as fictionalized by Fraser McKee), while the West Coast trio often forayed up the Inside Passage and around the Alaskan panhandle.

For the better part of forty years, the gate vessels were synonymous with the Reserve at-sea experience, until the entire group paid off over 1995–96, the Reserve training role thence given over to the Kingston class.

FURTHER READING

"Four Minesweepers, Gate Vessel Ordered," *Crowsnest* 1, no. 12 (October 1949): 2, navalandmilitarymuseum.org/wp-content/uploads/2021/09/CFB-Esquimalt-Museum-Crowsnest-Volume01-Number-12-Oct-1949.pdf.

Ian Holloway, "The Quest for Relevance," in *Citizen Sailors: Chronicles of Canada's Naval Reserve*, eds. Richard Gimblett and Michael Hadley (Dundurn, 2010), 93–108.

Fraser McKee, *Ellesmere Pickup: A Naval Novel* (SeaWaves Press, 2013).

George L. Zimmerman and Duff W. Crerar, "'The Gates' at Our Gates: F.R. (Hamish) Berchem and the Role of the Eastern Based Porte-Class Gate Vessels After Canadian Armed Forces Unification," *The Northern Mariner/Le marin du nord* 32, no. 3 (Autumn 2022): 315–40, tnm.journals.yorku.ca/index.php/default/article/view/998/1079.

Cape-Class Escort Maintenance Ship HMCS *Cape Scott* in 1959
(ex HMS *Beachy Head/Vulkaan*)
Launched 27 September 1944 | Built by Burrard Dry Dock Co. Ltd., Vancouver
28 January 1959–01 July 1970
Dimensions: 134.1 m (440 ft) x 17.4 m (57 ft) x 7.8 m (25.6 ft)
Displacement: 8,580 tons | Speed: 11 kt | Crew: 270
Armament: nil

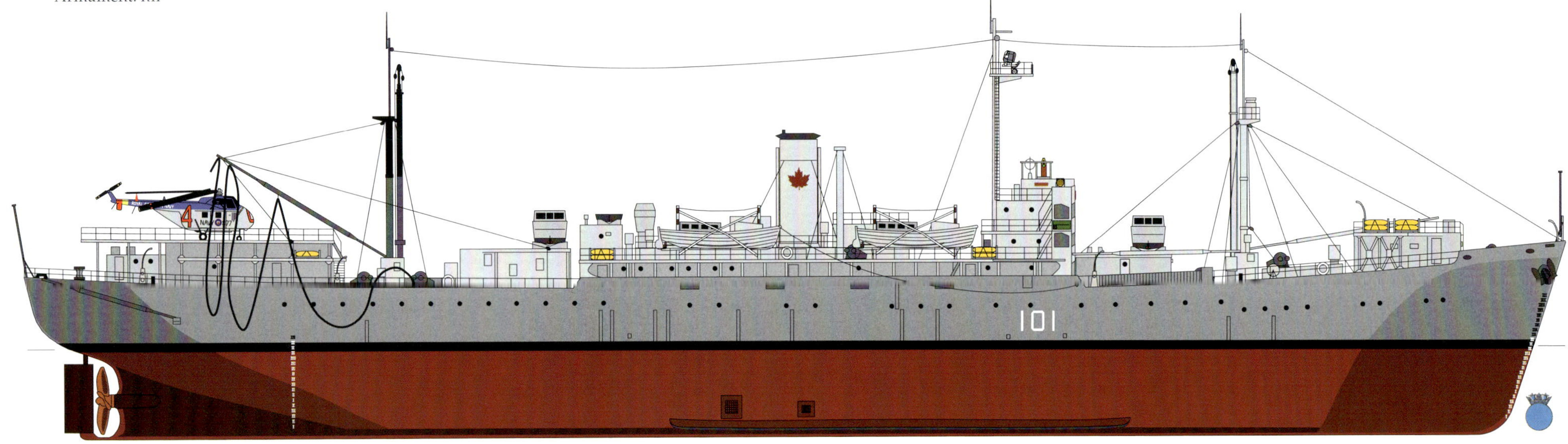

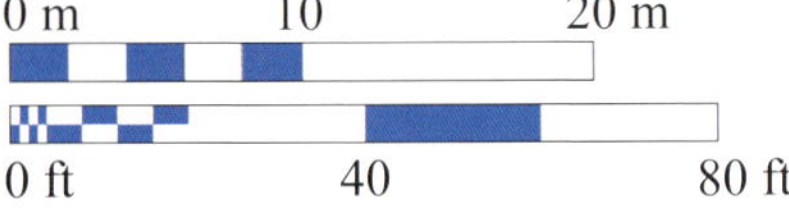

CAPE-CLASS ESCORT MAINTENANCE VESSELS

One of the new considerations for naval operations brought on by the advent of the atomic age was the requirement to disperse the fleet to secondary bases as a precaution against being caught at the "ground zero" targets that Halifax and Esquimalt were sure to become. To provide for ongoing routine maintenance of the fleet in the event of such an emergency deployment, the Canadian naval staff decided in the early 1950s to acquire a pair of Beachy Head-class "depot, maintenance, and repair" (NATO designation ARE) ships from the RN. That was a class of twenty-one vessels constructed in Canada during the war for the RN to act as part of the fleet train that would support the BPF for the war against Japan. Based on the 8,580-ton displacement Fort-class merchant ships of the "Victory" type, they were powered by an oil-fired reciprocating triple-expansion steam engine driving a single screw at a maximum of 11 knots. The two subsequently acquired for the RCN had both been built in the last half of 1944 by Burrard Dry Dock in Vancouver as HM Ships *Beachy Head* (lead of the class) and *Flamborough Head* and were now renamed *Cape Scott* and *Cape Breton*, respectively.

HMCS *Cape Breton* (ARE 100) was commissioned into the RCN on January 31, 1953, but does not seem to have ever deployed from her initial home port of Halifax, serving instead as a repair and training ship alongside until being transferred to the West Coast in 1958. On arrival in Esquimalt, she underwent refit for conversion as an "escort maintenance ship" with the installation of engineering and electrical workshops and the fitting of a helicopter landing pad, emerging to be recommissioned in November 1959. However, other than a shakedown

Cape Scott acting as a depot ship to the East Coast minesweeper squadron, deployed for exercise in the fall of 1960, in a scene that would be repeated "no duff" two years later, for the Cuban Missile Crisis of October 1962.

cruise to the exercise areas off San Diego in February 1960, she again did not ever deploy. She was paid off into reserve in February 1964 as a cost-cutting measure, becoming a fixture in Esquimalt Harbour as the supplementary workshop and accommodation vessel eventually named Fleet Maintenance Group (FMG) Pacific. With the opening in 1993 of a purpose-built building named Fleet Maintenance Facility Cape Breton in her honour, the former HMCS *Cape Breton* was sold to be sunk as a sports-diving wreck off Snake Island near Nanaimo, British Columbia. Her stern section had been kept on the North Vancouver shore for possible preservation as the centrepiece of a maritime museum, but it too was broken up in 2013–14.

In the meantime, *Cape Scott* (ARE 101) had not been commissioned on arrival in Halifax but was used through the 1950s as a classroom and for other auxiliary harbour services. Only upon the departure of her sister was she taken in hand for a similar conversion refit as an escort maintenance ship, finally being commissioned on January 28, 1959. From that point, however, she had a more eventful career. In January 1960, she deployed to Bermuda with the Atlantic Command fleet to act as the headquarters and maintenance ship for the annual WINTEX training exercise, and then, during the Cuban Missile Crisis, in October 1962, she was ordered to her dispersal station in Shelburne, Nova Scotia, to support the fleet during that active period of operations. In 1964, she was dispatched on the Medical Expedition to Easter Island, supporting a civilian anthropological mission to document the isolated island community in anticipation of its societal transformation with the building of an airport a few years later. Her then-Captain Tony Law — previously noted in Chapter 20 as the war artist commander of the Twenty-Ninth MTB Flotilla — captured this experience in paintings as well. HMCS *Cape Scott* was paid off on July 1, 1970, to parallel her sister as FMG Atlantic, but only until 1975, when the maintenance group moved ashore. Sold for scrap, the ship was broken up in Texas in 1978. Her memory is perpetuated with the new Fleet Maintenance Facility Cape Scott building, named for her.

FURTHER READING

Jacalyn Duffin, *Stanley's Dream: The Medical Expedition to Easter Island* (McGill-Queen's University Press, 2019).

Jordan J.D. Rowland, "The Final Days of HMCS *Cape Breton*," *Nauticapedia* (2016), nauticapedia.ca/Gallery/Cape_Breton_Scrapping.php.

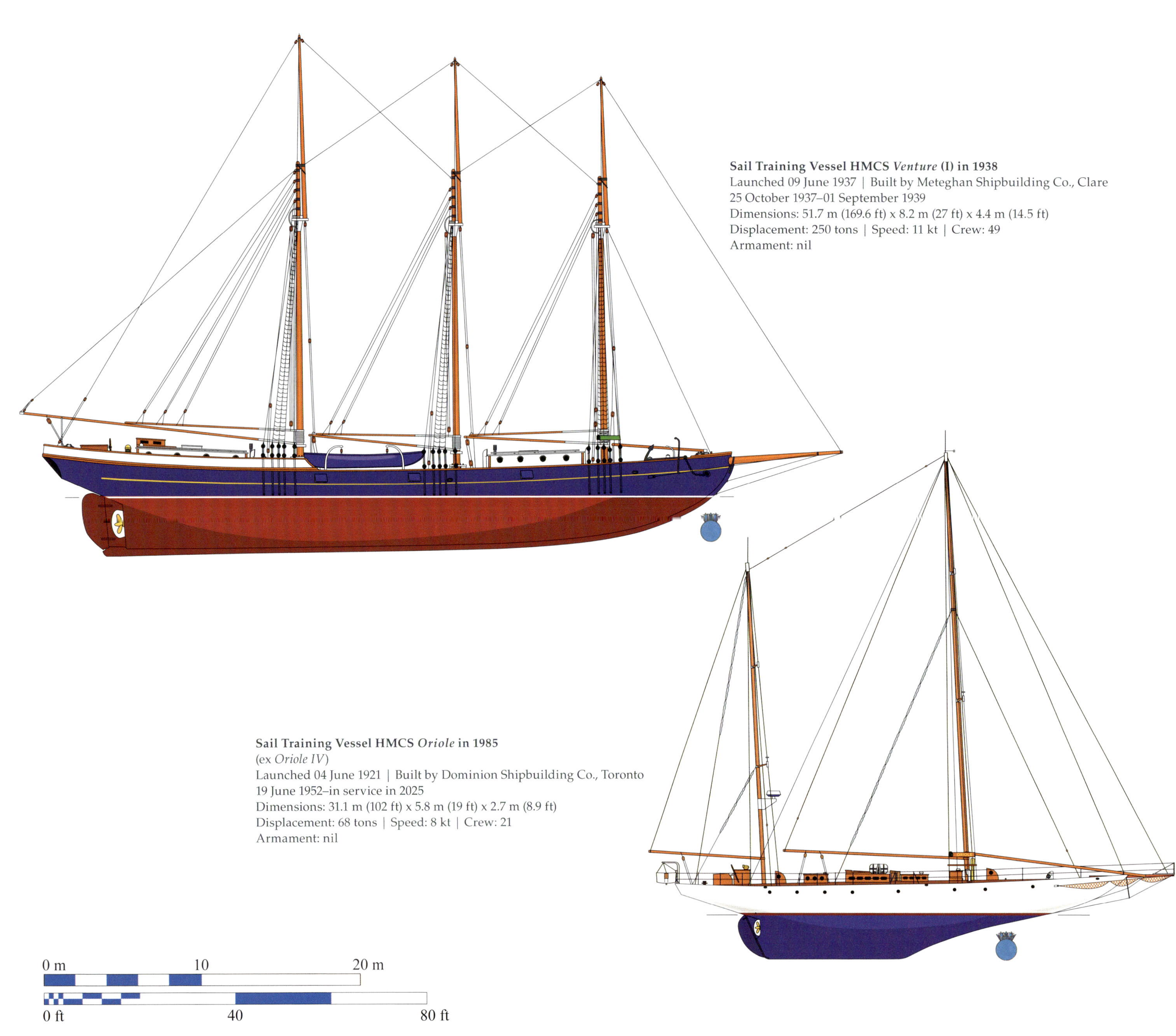

Sail Training Vessel HMCS *Venture* (I) in 1938
Launched 09 June 1937 | Built by Meteghan Shipbuilding Co., Clare
25 October 1937–01 September 1939
Dimensions: 51.7 m (169.6 ft) x 8.2 m (27 ft) x 4.4 m (14.5 ft)
Displacement: 250 tons | Speed: 11 kt | Crew: 49
Armament: nil

Sail Training Vessel HMCS *Oriole* in 1985
(ex *Oriole IV*)
Launched 04 June 1921 | Built by Dominion Shipbuilding Co., Toronto
19 June 1952–in service in 2025
Dimensions: 31.1 m (102 ft) x 5.8 m (19 ft) x 2.7 m (8.9 ft)
Displacement: 68 tons | Speed: 8 kt | Crew: 21
Armament: nil

31

SAIL TRAINING VESSELS *VENTURE* AND *ORIOLE*

Even though sail as a means of transport, let alone of warfighting, is long past, sail training remains a fundamental way for mariners to learn their profession through direct contact with the ways of the sea and to develop shiphandling and teamwork skills. To the present day, the tradition of large, square-sailed training continues with such representatives as the U.S. Coast Guard Cutter *Eagle*, the Italian Ship *Amerigo Vespucci*, the Federal German Ship *Gorch Fock*, and the Russian Navy Ship *Kruzenshtern*. As such, when the Royal Naval College of Canada was established in 1911, it was quite natural that it should acquire a pair of vessels as seamanship training tenders to cover that element of its curriculum: the schooner *Diana* and the sloop *Venture*. Both were probably destroyed in the Halifax Explosion of December 6, 1917 (or at least, nothing further was reported on them after that date), and no known record of them survives other than a photograph of *Diana* (see the January 1960 *Crowsnest* article in Further Reading; RCN sail training vessels were a popular theme in the newsmagazine at the time, with *Venture* and *Oriole*, described below, featuring on the covers of the May and March 1959 issues, respectively). But the earliest generation of "Canadian Flag Officers first learned the seaman's art in these vessels."[42] When rearmament in the mid-1930s offered the possibility to resume junior seamanship training in Canada, one of the RCN's first steps was to order a sail training vessel, which would be commissioned on October 25, 1937, as HMCS *Venture*, in memory of their own formative experience.

This second *Venture* was designed by the renowned Canadian naval architect W.J. Roué (famous as the

The three-masted training schooner *Venture*.

designer of the *Bluenose*) and built at Meteghan, Nova Scotia, as a 250-ton three-masted schooner with 12,000 sq. ft. (1,100 m^2) of sail. Armed with two 3-pounder guns, she carried a complement of forty, including twenty-four trainees. Her ambitious maiden voyage saw her departing from Halifax on January 1, 1938, for a winter cruise to Bermuda and into the Caribbean. With war imminent, she was paid off on September 1, 1939, and loaned to the RN as an accommodation tender for British ratings posted in Halifax for the war. She was taken back by the RCN as of November 1, 1941, to act as the Narrows guard-ship at the entrance to Bedford Basin, for which she was renamed *HC 190* to avoid confusion with HMCS *Venture II* (one of the ashore training establishments in Halifax). Her wartime duties completed, *HC 190* was struck off strength for disposal on April 1, 1945, then became a coal carrier in Newfoundland, only to be lost in an explosion and fire on October 3, 1951.

The name was revived yet again as part of the effort to Canadianize naval training in the early 1950s, when the RCN Junior Officer Training Establishment for short-service officer cadets not requiring career military college education was commissioned in Esquimalt on August 11, 1954, as HMCS *Venture*. Although the establishment was disbanded on unification of the services in 1968, the name was taken on informally for what continues presently as the Naval Officer Training Centre in Esquimalt, British Columbia (at the time of writing, it is understood that an effort is under way to recommission this training centre as HMCS *Venture*).

The sail training vessel attached to the shore training facility HMCS *Venture* in the mid-1950s was the 68-ton HMCS *Oriole*, ketch-rigged with 11,000 sq. ft. (1,000 m^2) of sail. She had been built in 1921 as a yacht for George H. Gooderham, commodore of the Royal Canadian Yacht Club in Toronto, purchased in 1941 by the Navy League of Canada for sea cadet training, and in 1943 was chartered by the RCN as a sail training tender to the Toronto Naval Reserve division HMCS *York*. At the end of the war, she was returned to the Navy League, only to be chartered by the Navy yet again from 1950 and assigned to HMCS *Cornwallis* when that establishment reopened as the Navy's new recruit training school. Officially commissioned as HMCS *Oriole* on June 19, 1952, she was

Oriole displaying one of her signature spinnakers, probably for the Swiftsure International Yacht Race in the Strait of Juan de Fuca in 1986.

purchased outright in 1956 for transfer to *Venture* on the West Coast. Unlike her predecessor, *Oriole* has steel hull construction, but otherwise teak deck and superstructure; all sails are operated manually (that is, without winches).

Unification had no impact on her general employment, and her training cruises have taken her across the Pacific and back and forth between Canada's coasts. Her latest return to the East Coast was in 2017 to be the Navy's official Tall Ship participant in Canada's sesquicentennial celebrations, following which Halifax became her present home port. *Oriole* has the double distinctions of being the RCN's longest-serving vessel and the only one with the unique battle honour "Dunkirk 1940," granted by perpetuation of her name from an RN ship that had won that honour.

FURTHER READING

Shirley Hewett, *The People's Boat: HMCS* Oriole*: Ship of a Thousand Dreams* (Heritage House, 2001).

"HMCS *Oriole*," Wikimedia Foundation, last modified January 20, 2025, 18:21 (UTC), en.wikipedia.org/wiki/HMCS_Oriole.

A.M. Hope, "The Royal Naval College of Canada," *Crowsnest* 12, no. 3 (January 1960): 5–9, navalandmilitarymuseum.org/wp-content/uploads/2021/10/CFB-Esquimalt-Museum-Crowsnest-Volume12-Number-03-Jan-1960.pdf.

"The *Venture* Story," *HMCS* Venture, *1954–1968*, accessed October 16, 2024, hmcsventure.com/Venture/Story/VentureStory.html.

Bird Class
66 tons | 28 m (91.9 ft) x 5.2 m (17.1 ft) x 1.6 m (5.3 ft) | 14 kt

75-foot YAG Class
71 tons | 22.9 m (75.1 ft) x 5.6 m (18.4 ft) x 1.3 m (4.3 ft) | 11 kt

Old Ville Class
18 tons | 12.2 m (40 ft) x 3.2 m (10.5 ft) x 1.4 m (4.6 ft) | 8 kt

75-foot Detachment Class
70 tons | 22.9 m (75.1 ft) x 5.2 m (17.1 ft) x 1.8 m (5.9 ft) | 15 kt

R Class
119 tons | 29.1 m (95.5 ft) x 6.1 m (20 ft) x 2.2 m (7.2 ft) | 20 kt

HMCS *Fort Steele* PB-140
85 tons | 36 m (118.1 ft) x 6.4 m (21 ft) x 2.1 m (6.9 ft) | 20 kt

65-foot Detachment Class
45.5 tons | 19.8 m (32.2 ft) x 4.5 m (14.8 ft) x 1.7 m (5.6 ft) | 10 kt

FROM SEAWARD DEFENCE TO RESERVE TRAINING: THE BIRD CLASS, YAGS, AND OTHERS

Canadian historian of the early Cold War period Sean Maloney has detailed how "the changing threat environment between 1952 and 1954 prompted both the United States and Canada to reassess measures taken to defend North America in the event of global war."[43] Beyond the expected need to protect the North Atlantic sea lanes of communication (or SLOCs, as they were becoming known in NATO parlance), the continent itself was now in danger of direct Soviet attack. The new Bay-class minesweepers already under construction could respond to the mining of harbour approaches, but with the St. Laurent–class DDEs committed to NATO use on the SLOCs, the near-offshore waters from which Soviet submarines could launch medium-range guided cruise missiles were suddenly perceived as vulnerable. A major review of "seaward defences" prepared over 1954–55 would have far-reaching consequences as the impetus for the establishment of close RCN-RCAF cooperation for ASW (see Chapter 55 on the early acquisitions of maritime patrol aircraft). But one of the first manifestations was far less dramatic: replacement of the Fairmile B motor launches that had performed the offshore defence role during the recent World War.

Bird-class patrol vessels *Cormorant* (left) and *Mallard* operating in the Halifax approaches.

This explains the sudden reactivation and commissioning in 1954 of the seven Fairmiles described in Chapter 19. But the bulk of the rest of those vessels had either already been disposed of or were no longer in condition for a renewed period of service. A clear sign of the sudden sense of urgency was the short period of time from concept through design to building of a replacement class for them: The first eight of an anticipated ninety vessels of the 92-foot, 66-ton Bird class of "Seaward Defence Patrol Craft" was ordered and launched in 1954. Another sign of the urgent need was that they were to be armed with the wartime Hedgehog — obsolete but readily available as surplus — for their primary antisubmarine weapon. In the end, just as quickly as the program had been undertaken, it was cut short, probably in the subsequent realization of how inadequate the vessels would be in the role of Soviet sub-hunter. Only four were built — all in lower Great Lakes yards that had been prime builders of the previous Fairmile Bs — and commissioned in 1955–56: HMC Ships *Loon* (PCS 780), *Cormorant* (781), *Blue Heron* (782), and *Mallard* (783) (the remaining four that had been ordered were cancelled, although their names had become known: *Arctic Tern*, *Sandpiper*, *Herring Gull*, and *Kingfisher*). Within a few years, the Hedgehogs would be removed, and all four were turned over from Regular Force service to the Naval Reserve to augment the Porte-class gate vessels in the training role (see Chapter 29). All were paid off as part of the mid-1960s budget cuts and sold in 1970–71.

Another class of vessels ordered at the same time, and which would become familiar to Canadian sailors through the last half of the twentieth century, were the ten "Yard Auxiliary, General" (YAG) built in small West Coast yards in 1954–55. As a common fixture supporting the movement of large groups of personnel around the confines and area of Esquimalt Harbour, they were known universally as the "Blue Boat" yard ferries. With the post-unification establishment of Training Group Pacific, seven of them were refitted with bunks, a galley, and additional basic navigation stations to support junior officer and reserve training and were unofficially given "animal" nicknames after the armed yachts of the Second World War (the Wikipedia entry in "Further Reading" gives the full list). They were disposed of between 2007 and 2013 in anticipation of acceptance of the Orca class patrol vessels (see Chapter 44); several remain in civilian guise.

The naval reserves have operated a broad range of vessels that are beyond the scope of this book, although two types are noted here owing to their prominent part in the Reserve Training Unit (Atlantic), which was set up in 1975 as the East Coast complement to Training Group Pacific. Its mainstays were the pair of Porte-class gate vessels *Porte Saint Jean* and *Porte Saint Louis*, augmented by several vessels transferred from other government departments: *Fort Steele* (from the RCMP, commissioned in 1975 and paid off in 1994) and *Rally* and *Rapid*, transferred from the Department of Transport (never commissioned, accepted in 1982, and retired in 1992). Co-author Gagnon has prepared the definitive survey of "Vessels of the Naval Reserve of Canada" referenced in Further Reading, and several others of that group are depicted in his profile drawing to this chapter.

FURTHER READING

Matthew Chapman, "Blue Boats: YFL/YFM/YFP/YFB Harbour Ferries," chapter 17 in *A History of the West Coast Canadian Forces Auxiliary Fleet: 60 Years of CFAV History* (Lookout Creative Services, 2008), 131–133.

Carl Gagnon, "Vessels of the Naval Reserve of Canada" and "International Radio Call Signs (IRCS) [of] Vessels of the Canadian Naval Reserve," in *Citizen Sailors: Chronicles of Canada's Naval Reserve*, eds. Richard Gimblett and Michael Hadley (Dundurn, 2010), 147–175.

Sean M. Maloney, "Parry and Thrust: Canadian Maritime Forces and the Defence of North America, 1954-62," *The Northern Mariner/le marin du nord* 18, no. 1 (January 2008): 39–54, tnm.journals.yorku.ca/index.php/default/article/view/347/328.

Michael Whitby, "A 'New Look' at Cold War Maritime Defense — The Royal Canadian Navy's Seaward Defence Report and the Threat of the Missile-Firing Submarine, 1955," *Naval War College Review* 73, no. 4, Article 8, digital-commons.usnwc.edu/nwc-review/vol73/iss4/8.

"YAG Training Vessel," Wikimedia Foundation, last modified October 24, 2024, 01:46 (UTC), en.wikipedia.org/wiki/YAG_training_vessel.

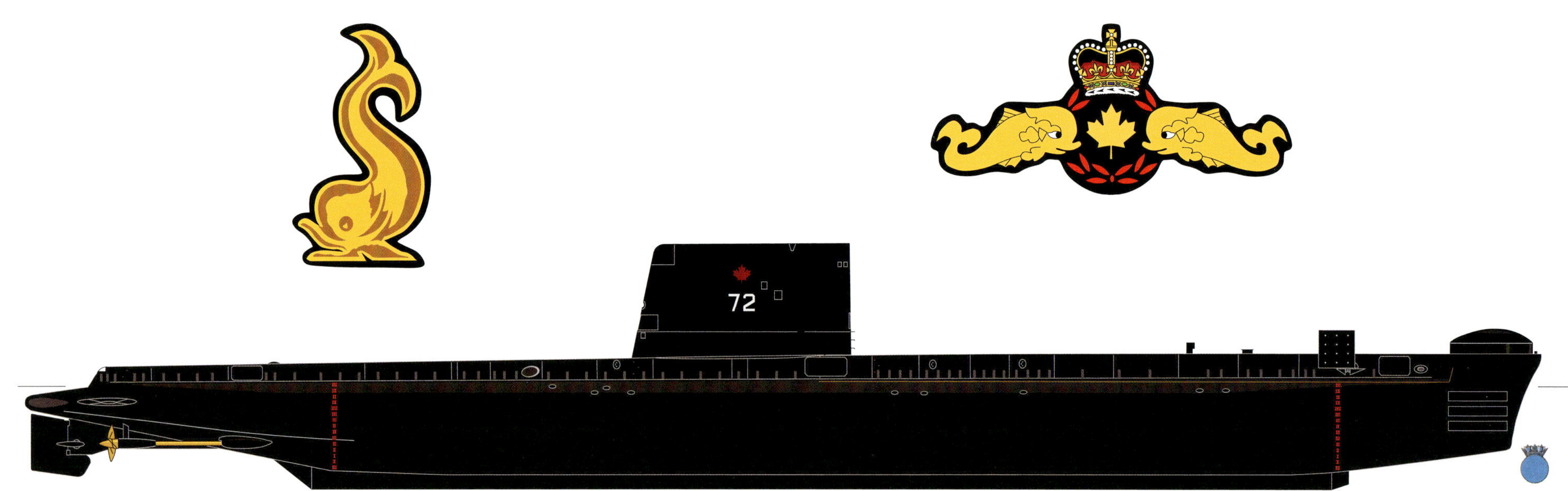

Oberon-Class Submarine HMCS *Ojibwa* in 1966
Launched 29 February 1964 | Built by HM Dockyard, Chatham
23 September 1965–21 May 1998
Dimensions: 90 m (295.28 ft) x 8.1 m (26.6 ft) x 5.5 m (18 ft)
Displacement: 1,610 tons (surfaced) 2,410 tons (submerged)
Speed: 12/17 kt | Crew: 68 | Armament: 21-in TT (8 x I)

Oberon-Class Submarine HMCS *Okanagan* in 1998
Launched 25 September 1967 | Built by HM Dockyard, Chatham
22 June 1968–30 September 1998
Dimensions: 90 m (295.28 ft) x 8.1 m (26.6 ft) x 5.5 m (18 ft)
Displacement: 1,610 tons (surfaced) 2,410 tons (submerged)
Speed: 12/17 kt | Crew: 65 | Armament: 21-in TT (6 x I)

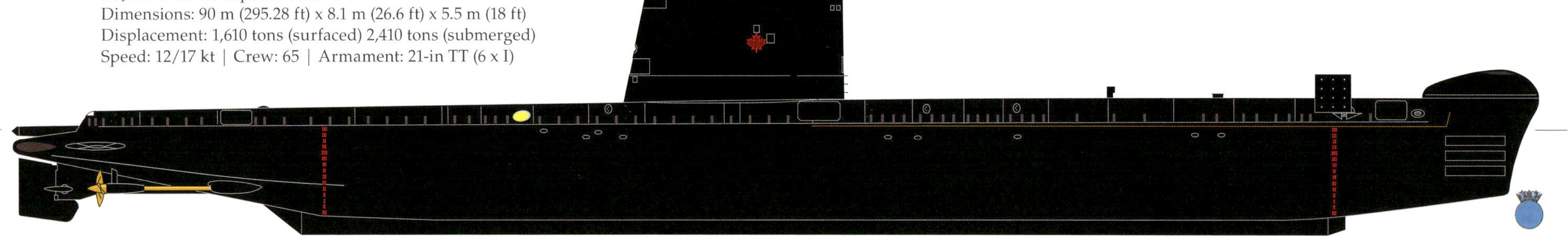

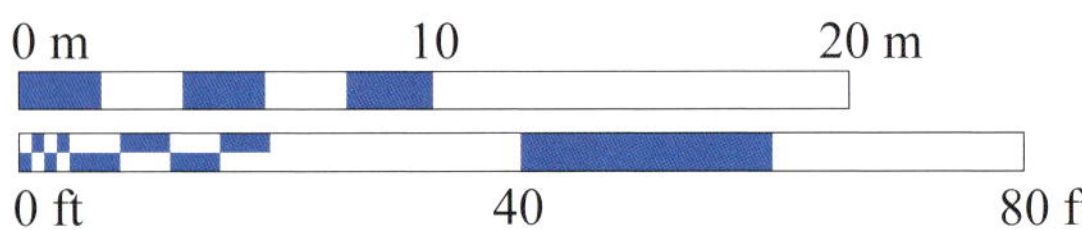

33

THE "O-BOATS": OBERON-CLASS SUBMARINES

Contrary to what they did in the Great War, the RCN did not operate submarines during the Second World War, although many RCNVRs served with distinction aboard them in the RN, and the British did loan several older boats for training purposes at the main Atlantic bases in Canada (none were stationed on the West Coast). Other than the very brief period of operating the surrendered German *U 190* and *U 889* out of Halifax from 1945 to 1947, the RCN had no regular underwater practice "targets" for the new generation of postwar sailors to hone their antisubmarine skills. Finally, in 1955, as the St. Laurent–class DDEs were poised to join the fleet, an arrangement was made for the RN to base its Sixth Submarine Squadron of three "A"-class boats in Halifax, pending the RCN's acquisition of its own submarine force. To further that end, Canadian sailors were sent on exchange postings with the RN in operational British submarines to build up their experience.

Concurrently, the Navy's Technical Services Branch had begun a feasibility study to ascertain future applications of nuclear power as a source of propulsion in warships generally. As Jason Delaney has demonstrated in a study of recently declassified files, "Efforts to acquire submarines followed two distinct objectives: acquiring submarines to establish a submarine service, and the investigation into nuclear propulsion."[44] But the general technical briefing to the Naval Board in August 1954 was followed just a month later, on September 20, with the commissioning of the USS *Nautilus* — the world's first nuclear-powered attack submarine (SSN) — and inevitably, "this initiative coincided with the efforts to establish a submarine service that resulted in the desire

Okanagan is launched at Chatham Dockyard on September 17, 1966.

to obtain nuclear-powered submarines."[45] Upon becoming CNS in 1956, Vice Admiral Harry DeWolf was a strong proponent of the acquisition of a projected force of nine Canadian SSNs to counter the Soviets in Arctic waters, and he established a Nuclear Submarine Survey Team while publicly declaring in May 1958 that "nuclear submarines will … make up half of Canada's fleet."[46] Ultimately, the quest was unsuccessful, cancelled formally by John Diefenbaker's Conservative government in 1962, having fallen upon the multiple obstacles of the sheer cost of the effort, the growing Canadian antinuclear movement, and — most critically — American refusal to share the secret details of nuclear technology beyond the British (interested readers should note Delaney's paper, augmented by Julie Ferguson's *Through a Canadian Periscope*, listed in Further Reading). Curiously, just two years later, the 1964 White Paper on Defence, promulgated by Lester Pearson's newly elected Liberal government, which controversially laid the groundwork for the integration and eventual unification of what would become the Canadian Armed Forces (CAF), also stated that "careful study [was] being given to the possibility of constructing two or three nuclear-powered submarines with powerful antisubmarine weapons."[47] But that investigation too was allowed to die quietly, and the subject of Canadian SSNs would not be resurrected for another two decades (see discussion in Chapter 43 on the Victoria-class submarines).

Meanwhile, the option for a conventionally powered attack submarine had continued and was now given new impetus. The preference of the naval staff was for the American Barbel class, laid down in 1956 and commissioned in 1959, which had many modern features, including a hydrodynamically efficient teardrop-shaped hull that allowed for a deeper diving depth and an unprecedented underwater speed of 23 knots. However, it was double the cost of its less capable but still viable British competitor, the Oberon class, which was available more cheaply through balance of trade offsets. With the operational requirement being reassessed back to the simpler training target role, the number had also been whittled down to three, as a straight Canadian replacement for the British A-boat squadron.

Although the RN commissioned its first of the Oberon class in 1960, in concept, looks, and general layout it constituted little more than the height of development from captured German wartime U-boat technology — which, in fairness, made it not unlike its conventional Soviet counterparts that constituted the bulk of that navy's attack force into the 1970s. Between 1957 and 1978, Britain built twenty-seven of the type for service with the navies of the United Kingdom (thirteen), Australia (six), Canada (three), Brazil (three), and Chile (two).

In keeping with British practice, the Canadian O-boats were named HMC Ships *Ojibwa* (pennant number 72), *Onondaga* (73), and *Okanagan* (74). All three were built in the British Chatham Dockyard, *Ojibwa* having been laid down for the RN as *Onyx* and acquired mid-build. As such she was commissioned in 1965, well ahead of the others in 1967 and 1968, respectively. All were retrofitted with Canadian communications and sonar equipment, larger air-conditioning units, a snorkel de-icer, and the USN Mark 37 heavy-weight torpedo.

A fourth O-boat, ex-HMS *Olympus*, was acquired in 1989 as an alongside training vessel, and upon being paid off in 1992, ex-HMS *Osiris* was shared by the RN for spare parts to keep the original three serviceable pending replacement, as the British were hoping, with their surplus Upholder class.

Among the notions pursued by the Canadian Navy in the late 1970s to overcome the obsolescence of the surface fleet was to upgrade their three original O-boats from simple training platforms into true hunter-killer attack submarines. The Submarine Operational Update Program (SOUP) was approved in 1979, incorporating new communications, active and passive sonars (including a towed array sonar), periscopes, fire control systems, and the USN heavy-weight Mk 48 torpedo. The SOUP was completed only in 1986, rather late in the Cold War, but in time for the upgraded Canadian O-boats to almost immediately enjoy some success tracking Soviet ballistic missile–firing submarines in the North Atlantic (see Whitby in Further Reading).

The O-boats spent most of their service based out of Halifax, Nova Scotia, initially for training and then to counter their presumed Soviet opponents. A rare exception was when *Ojibwa* accompanied *Athabaskan* on what was termed a "demonstration" cruise to the West Coast in 1977, the first for either of those classes. With the end of the Cold War, in 1990 *Okanagan* became the first Canadian submarine to undertake a cruise on the Great Lakes, while the others made brief deployments in rotation to the Pacific coast: *Onondaga* in 1994 and *Ojibwa* in 1997. During the so-called Turbot War in 1995, their presence monitoring the Spanish fishing fleet on the Grand Banks served as a deterrent in resolving the crisis. Then, in September 1998, *Okanagan* was engaged in the recovery effort of the Swissair Flight 111 crash in St. Margaret's Bay, Nova Scotia.

In anticipation of acceptance of the Victoria class, *Onondaga* was the last to be paid off, in Halifax on July 28, 2000. She is preserved as a museum ship at Rimouski, Quebec, as is *Ojibwa* in Port Burwell, Ontario, while *Okanagan* was broken up for scrap in 2011.

FURTHER READING

Jason Delaney, "On the Edge of Hubris: The 1959 Canadian Nuclear Attack Submarine Program," paper presented at the McMullen Naval History Symposium (2023), United States Naval Academy, Annapolis, MD.

Julie Ferguson, *Through a Canadian Periscope: The Story of the Canadian Submarine Service*, 2nd ed. (Dundurn, 2014), especially 259–309.

JDF Kealy, "The Development of the Canadian Navy, 1945–67" (DHH SGR II 223).

JHW Knox, "An Engineer's Outline of RCN History, Part 2 (1948–68)," in *The RCN in Retrospect, 1910–1968*, ed. James Boutilier (UBC Press, 1982), 325–26.

Michael Whitby, "Boomers, Draggers and Black Boxes: The Operational Legacy of Canada's Oberon Class Submarines, 1983–1998," *The Northern Mariner/Le marin du nord* 28 no. 4 (October 2013): 367–398, cnrs-scrn.org/northern_mariner/vol23/tnm_23_367-398.pdf.

Submarine *Grilse* entering Esquimalt Harbour while the Prestonian-class frigate *Sussexvale* exits (note the Dunc's Diner on Sussexvale abaft the funnel).

had also operated against Japan for the last year of the war but which in 1952 had undergone a "Fleet Snorkel Program" refit (a partial GUPPY [Greater Underwater Propulsion Power] conversion, adding a snorkel, streamlined sail, and more powerful electrical system, although without any increase in battery capacity). She was subsequently engaged in the "quarantine" against Cuba in 1962 and remained on active American service until sold to Canada. She was decommissioned from the USN on December 2, 1968, and recommissioned that same day as HMCS *Rainbow* (again second of name, pennant number 75). This time the Canadian Navy (by that date no longer "Royal" and now formally named Maritime Command, or MARCOM) bought her outright. Like her predecessor, *Rainbow* was crewed by Canadian sailors and performed her training role ably, although without any grand returns across the Pacific and soon showing her age. She was paid off only six years later, on December 21, 1974, as Ferguson observes, "officially … a casualty of the severe fuel crisis, and the fiscal restraint of the Liberal government, but her noisiness and the need for an expensive refit also hastened her demise."[48] CAF surface ships and patrol aircraft on the West Coast returned to their occasional exercise opportunities with USN units for the remainder of the Cold War, and aside from the brief deployments of the O-boats in the 1990s, there would be no further Canadian submarine presence in the Pacific until the arrival of HMCS *Victoria* in her namesake city in August 2003.

FURTHER READING

Julie Ferguson, *Through a Canadian Periscope: The Story of the Canadian Submarine Service*, 2nd ed. (Dundurn, 2014), especially 278–84 and 306–9.

JDF Kealy, "The Development of the Canadian Navy, 1945–67" (DHH SGR II 223).

JHW Knox, "An Engineer's Outline of RCN History, Part 2 (1948–68)," in *The RCN in Retrospect, 1910–1968*, ed. James Boutilier (UBC Press, 1982), 325–26

Provider conducts a side-by-side multi-point UNREP with *Huron* (left) and *Terra Nova* in 1988.

ship, the USS *Conecuh* (AOR-110), a war prize as the former *Kriegsmarine "Troßschiff"* (supply vessel) *Dithmarschen*, which had been built to support German surface raiders on extended deployments. After a brief pause in development, the Americans would settle on the "fast combat support ship," the first AOE-1 laid down in 1961 and commissioned in 1964 as the 30-knot, 54,000-ton USS *Sacramento*.

The Canadian variation on the operational concept for the ship was more modest in scale, displacing 22,700 tons fully loaded and 20 knots maximum speed. But it incorporated that same novel and fundamental difference from the practice to date of the Royal and United States navies. Where their "fleet trains" typically had a variety of purpose-built ships to deliver the several individual types of supplies, such as fuel (all three types: bunker, diesel, and aviation), ammunition, and food and other dry stores, the Canadian ships would carry all of those together in what would become known in the fleet as "one-stop shopping" (the phrase was a more colloquial variation on the "one-stop replenishment" slogan attributed to *Conecuh*). The design additionally included an eight-berth hospital facility instead of the standard sick bay. NATO would develop a new type designation to describe the concept: the AOR, short for Auxiliary Oiler Replenishment. Another conceptual difference was that, whereas most Allied ships were employed as auxiliaries with civilian crews (although under naval control), the Canadian ships would be commissioned ships crewed by Regular Force sailors. Notwithstanding the multi-delivery capability of the ships, they would be known affectionately throughout the fleet simply as "the tankers."

There were other distinctions from the original American design. The first devolved from the concurrent late-1950s Canadian naval technical investigation into nuclear propulsion, so that although fitted with the intended pair of oil-fired boilers driving a single-geared steam-turbine shaft, the aft section was given greater breadth to allow the second and third ships to be fitted with a nuclear reactor. And in recognition of another aspect of the new age of atomic warfare, the boilers and engine room were "boxed" with automatic and remote controls in a machinery control room within the pressurized citadel to permit the ships steaming "closed down" through a fallout zone. Finally, by the time her keel was laid, the RCN had completed its trialling of the employment of large helicopters at sea (see Chapter 52), and the capacity to operate a pair of those was incorporated into the design in the form of a large landing pad and hangar with second-line maintenance repair capacity, albeit without any associated hauldown system. The design was the first of any class in the RCN to be purpose built to operate rotary-wing aircraft (the earlier build of *Labrador* with a flight deck was the adaptation of an American design).

The first ship was ordered in 1958, laid down in 1961, and commissioned on September 28, 1963, as HMCS *Provider* (AOR 508). Although the need for the type had been proven by the Cuban Missile Crisis, which unfolded in October 1962 even while she was building, the budget crises of the mid-1960s postponed laying down the following two until October 1967. The interlude, however, was not without benefit, as it allowed time to assess the ship in operations and incorporate a number of design improvements: a higher freeboard, which made the open "jungle deck" with the pipes and valves below the fuelling stations less "wet"; a much larger forward "house," with a combined bridge and operations room complex; the single funnel now separated into two, allowing a wider hangar space for three embarked helicopters; a pair of 15-ton cranes aft and associated Landing Craft, Vehicle, Personnel (LCVP) landing craft to enhance an expanded sealift capacity; and provision for a 3-inch/50-calibre turret in the bow and a Sea Sparrow anti-aircraft missile launcher just ahead of the bridge (neither of these became standard fits: The 3-inch/50 was

Three Sea King helicopters embarked in *Preserver*'s hangar, early 1990.

discontinued after one got washed overboard in heavy seas and was fitted again for boarding operations only in the more placid waters of the Persian Gulf, 1990–91; as for the missile, while intended to be mounted similarly to that in the Iroquois-class DDH-280 destroyers, in the end, it was never fitted in the AORs owing to costs). It needs to be noted as well that by that time, the engineering flirtation with nuclear power had been put to rest, and these ships continued with the traditional steam-turbine configuration. For all that, the two new ships were only 2,000 tons heavier and barely 15 feet (3.9 m) longer than their near-sister. Most of the extra displacement was found in additional fuel oil capacity, for a new total of 14,000 tons of bunker oil; the other storage capacities were

A bird's-eye view of the various classes to be found in Esquimalt Harbour in 1993. Clockwise from left: research auxiliary *Endeavour*, replenishment ships *Protecteur* outboard of *Provider*, IRE *Kootenay*, maintenance ship *Cape Breton* with Restigouche-class *Columbia* outboard, and gate vessel *Porte Québec* outboard of the Bay-class minesweeper *Miramichi*; in the bottom right can be seen the stern of another of the Bay class, *Chaleur*.

roughly the same: 400 tons of aviation fuel, 1,050 tons of dry cargo, and 1,250 tons of ammunition.

Whereas *Provider* was built by Davie Shipbuilding in Lauzon, Quebec, the next pair were constructed at Saint John Shipbuilding in New Brunswick, commissioning, respectively, as HMC Ships *Protecteur* (AOR 509) in August 1969 and *Preserver* (AOR 510) in August 1970. More than half a century on, it is easy to forget just how innovative were the replenishment concepts presented in *Provider* and, soon enough, her near-sisters. They were the first of their kind in full-time commission to offer multiple stations permitting side-by-side, near-full-speed, simultaneous liquid fuel and solid stores UNREP. Their Canadian-designed quick-engage/disengage hoses and tensioned span-wire system quickly became a NATO standard and the model for modern navies around the world. The ultimate compliment is that the basic design was picked up as the pattern for the equally successful five-ship French Durance class, also sold onward to the Argentinian, Australian, and Saudi navies.

With *Protecteur* and *Preserver* entering service concurrent with the fleet redistribution after unification, they remained based in Halifax to support NATO operations, while *Provider* transferred to Esquimalt. All three ships ranged the breadth of their respective ocean areas, with both Halifax-based ships also taking advantage of their strengthened hulls to make occasional forays into the eastern Arctic in the 1970s. To accompany the Canadian Naval Task Group to the Persian Gulf in the summer of 1990, *Protecteur* finally received the significant anti-air defence of a pair of Phalanx CIWS and other upgrades. With *Preserver* getting the same treatment within a couple of years, both ships put the new systems to use in the RCN's return to the Gulf region for operations after the terror attacks of September 11, 2001 (9/11). In the meantime, *Protecteur* had exchanged coastal basing with *Provider* in 1996 in anticipation of the latter being paid off in 1998.

The hunt for replacements for all three tankers had begun soon after the Gulf War but was still not finalized when the remaining pair suffered separate but concurrent engineering failures a quarter century later: *Protecteur*'s engine room fire and breakdown in February 2014, some 390 miles (630 km) northeast of Hawaii, and *Preserver*'s extensive waterline corrosion brought on by the general wear and tear of age at about the same time. Neither ship could be repaired economically, and *Protecteur* was paid off in Esquimalt on May 14, 2015, with *Preserver* following in Halifax on October 21, 2016. That sudden suspension in national UNREP capability was the catalyst to finalize plans over 2015–17 for the restyled Joint Support Ship (JSS) project and to engage the services of a so-called interim AOR for an unknown period of time. That story, still unfolding at the time of writing, is told in Chapter 46.

FURTHER READING

Kenneth P. Hansen, "Canadian Naval Operational Logistics: Lessons Learned, Lost, and Relearned?," *The Northern Mariner/le marin du nord* 20, no. 4 (October 2010): 361–83, tnm.journals.yorku.ca/index.php/default/article/view/312/294.

JDF Kealy, "The Development of the Canadian Navy, 1945–67" (DHH SGR II 223).

JHW Knox, "An Engineer's Outline of RCN History, Part 2 (1948–68)," in *The RCN in Retrospect, 1910–1968*, ed. James Boutilier (UBC Press, 1982), 325–26.

Michael Whitby, "A 'New Look' at Cold War Maritime Defense — The Royal Canadian Navy's Seaward Defence Report and the Threat of the Missile-Firing Submarine, 1955," *Naval War College Review* 73, no. 4, Article 8, digital-commons.usnwc.edu/nwc-review/vol73/iss4/8.

Bras d'Or–Class Hydrofoil HMCS *Bras d'Or* (II) in 1969
Launched July 1968 | Built by Marine Industries Ltd, Sorel
19 July 1968–01 May 1972
Dimensions: 45.9 m (150.6 ft) x 20 m (65.6 ft) x 7.2 m (23.6 ft)
Displacement: 180 tons | Speed: 63 kt | Crew: 29
Armament: nil

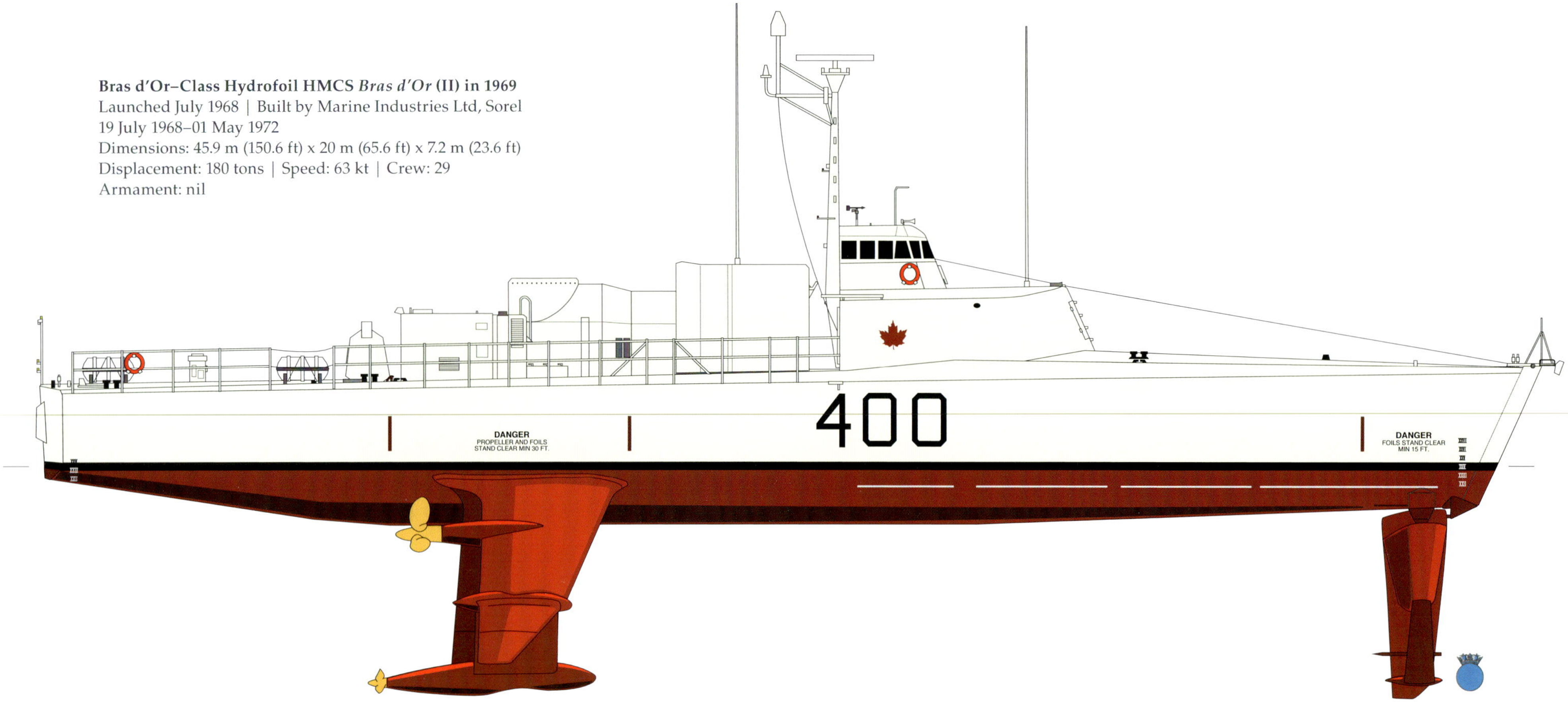

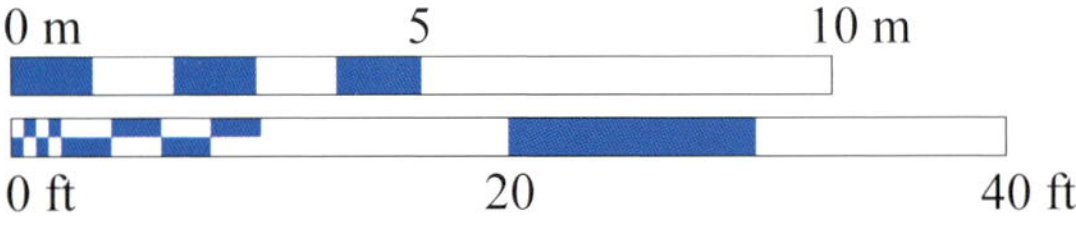

36

"THE FLYING 400": EXPERIMENTAL HYDROFOIL *BRAS D'OR*

Previous chapters have explored how the Canadian Navy's Cold War focus on ASW spurred a remarkable range of scientific research projects that developed into features that became standard fits in navies around the world, from the VDS and the Beartrap helicopter hauldown system for surface warships, to the replenishment-oiler concept. Another effort that was equally innovative, but alas did not translate into widespread use, was the fast hydrofoil escort (FHE). Harold Merklinger — a Canadian scientist-turned-historian of the Defence Research Establishment Atlantic — records, "The goal for hydrofoil design was to develop a fast 180-tonne ASW warship capable of operating in heavy seas in the open ocean."[52] The late-1950s operational concept was for a "sprint and drift" surface vessel able to replicate the capability of an aircraft to dash out to a search area, but with the loitering capacity of a warship; the Canadian innovation was appreciating that the wing-like structure of a hydrofoil could lift a hull out of the water, reducing drag to allow higher speed and less contact area for a smoother ride and greater fuel efficiency.

The full story of the development of the hydrofoil — from inception by Alexander Graham Bell and Casey Baldwin on the Bras d'Or Lakes of Cape Breton, Nova Scotia, in the years surrounding the Great War, through the renewed investigation by the British Admiralty in the early post–Second World War period — is a fascinating

Bras d'Or going foilborne during trials off Halifax in 1971; reportedly, this occurred at about 23 knots.

tale with too many details for this chapter (see instead Boileau in Further Reading). But the return of the notion to Canada was heralded on the aircraft carrier *Bonaventure*'s maiden voyage from Britain to Halifax in March 1957, when, instead of having embarked a conventional air group (her American-built Banshees and Trackers were awaiting in North America), lashed to the deck was a 17-ton experimentation prototype (unimaginatively named *R-103*) that had been built by Saunders-Roe in Britain. It was to be turned over to De Havilland Aircraft of Canada, working with Marine Industries Limited (MIL) in Sorel, Quebec, for completing the proof of concept.

Achieving sustained foilborne stability proved to be a challenge, but work advanced sufficiently quickly that by the end of 1962, the Naval Board gained Cabinet approval for the construction of a full-size prototype craft. The ship was designed to emerge progressively out of the water with speed and "fly" on a set of surface-piercing foils in a canard configuration (a small, steerable foil forward and a pair of larger load-carrying foils aft), powered when foilborne by a 25,000-hp Pratt & Whitney FT-4A gas turbine driving a pair of three-bladed supercavitating propellers (this was the same engine that would be featured in the Iroquois-class destroyers then in concurrent development). Hullborne propulsion was by a 2,400-bhp Davey Paxman diesel with a pair of variable-pitch propellers.

HMCS *Bras d'Or* (FHE 400) commissioned on July 23, 1968, and the Wikipedia entry on her notes that "the ship's helmsman had to be qualified as both a sea pilot and an aircraft pilot." Trials proceeded promisingly, with the vessel becoming foilborne for the first time on April 9, 1969, and demonstrating "extraordinary stability in rough weather."[53] On July 9, 1969, *Bras d'Or* became the world's fastest warship, with a speed of 62 knots (115 kph), a record exceeded only slightly and only recently by the Norwegian Skjold-class corvettes (275 tons, surface effect hull).

Although the feasibility of the FHE concept was proven, the planned fitting of a VDS and a fo'c'sle gun for operational trials never came to pass. The escalating costs of the program become a political liability, and the operational conditions in other aspects of ASW were shifting

Bras d'Or cruising hullborne in Halifax harbour.

development toward quick-response long-range patrol aircraft (see Chapter 57 on the Aurora) and passive towed array sonar-equipped surface vessels (see Chapter 40 on the Halifax class). Not unlike the RCAF's Avro Arrow a little over a decade earlier, the FHE program was abruptly cancelled by the minister of national defence (a Liberal this time) on November 2, 1971. At least in this instance, the vessel was laid up in a state of preservation pending disposal and was eventually donated to the Musée Maritime du Québec at L'Islet-sur-Mer, where to this day she remains on display and open to visitors.

FURTHER READING

John Boileau, *Fastest in the World: The Saga of Canada's Revolutionary Hydrofoils* (Formac Publishing, 2004).

Harold Merklinger, "Maritime Research and Development, 1960–68," in *Naval Service of Canada, 1910–2010: The Centennial Story*, ed. Richard H. Gimblett (Dundurn, 2009), 160–162.

JDF Kealy, "The Development of the Canadian Navy, 1945–67" (DHH SGR II 223).

JHW Knox, "An Engineer's Outline of RCN History, Part 2 (1948–68)," in *The RCN in Retrospect, 1910–1968*, ed. James Boutilier (UBC Press, 1982), 325–26.

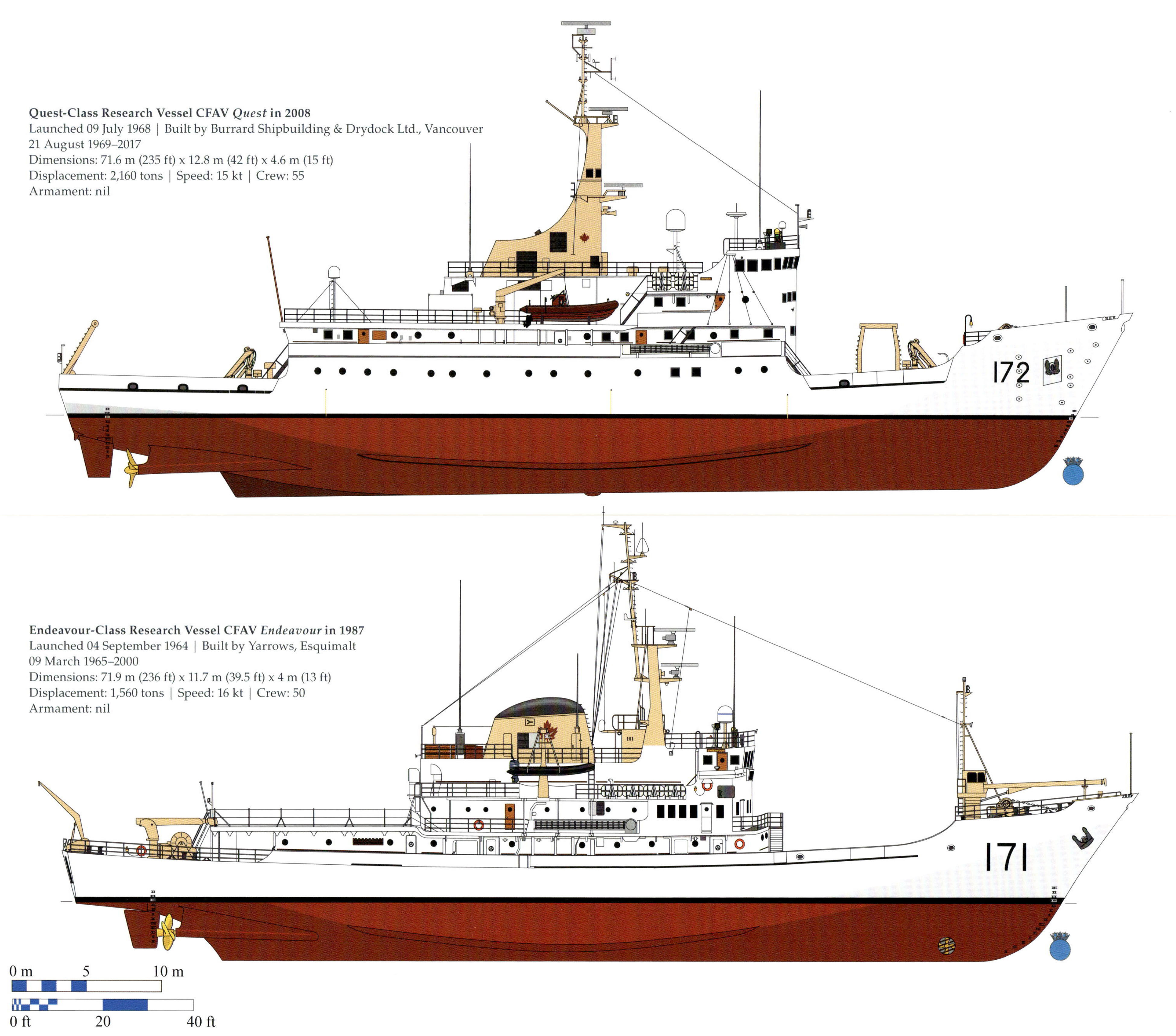

Quest-Class Research Vessel CFAV *Quest* in 2008
Launched 09 July 1968 | Built by Burrard Shipbuilding & Drydock Ltd., Vancouver
21 August 1969–2017
Dimensions: 71.6 m (235 ft) x 12.8 m (42 ft) x 4.6 m (15 ft)
Displacement: 2,160 tons | Speed: 15 kt | Crew: 55
Armament: nil

Endeavour-Class Research Vessel CFAV *Endeavour* in 1987
Launched 04 September 1964 | Built by Yarrows, Esquimalt
09 March 1965–2000
Dimensions: 71.9 m (236 ft) x 11.7 m (39.5 ft) x 4 m (13 ft)
Displacement: 1,560 tons | Speed: 16 kt | Crew: 50
Armament: nil

37

RESEARCH AUXILIARIES: CFAVS *QUEST* AND *ENDEAVOUR*

Many of the RCN's impressive research and development achievements through the 1950s, especially in the field of oceanographic research, had been accomplished with a variety of wartime vessels converted to the purpose. As described in Charles Maginley and Bernard Collin's chapter on "Naval Auxiliary Vessels" (see their encyclopedic *Ships of Canada's Marine Services* in Further Reading and the Select Bibliography), the list included several names from classes already encountered in these pages, reactivated some years after the war, typically with extensive modifications for their new functions: the Flower-class corvette *Sackville* (AGOR 113); the Western Isles trawlers *Whitethroat* (AGH 113) and *Bluethroat* (AGOR 114); the Algerine-class minesweepers *Oshawa* (AGOR 174), *New Liskeard* (AGOR 168), *Fort Francis* (AGOR 170), and *Kapuskasing* (AGOR 173). Another vessel taken on for such research work was unique in a couple of respects, being firstly a former Army Service Corps supply vessel (that is, not ex-RCN), and secondly commissioned into the RCN as HMCS *Cedarwood* (AGH 530); it consequently "stood out like a sore thumb in the Royal Canadian Navy's 1948 modern blue-water fleet."[54]

To explore fully the possibilities for new technologies that were becoming available in the early 1960s, the RCN's Pacific Naval Laboratory (subsequently renamed the Defence Research Establishment Pacific) made the case for a purpose-built ship, quieter and more stable than the aging previous assortment. The June 1964 issue of *Crowsnest* newsmagazine summed up the purpose for the new vessel as being to aid research and testing of "underwater detection techniques, underwater target identification and classification, underwater communications, noise reduction and antisubmarine weapons systems."[55]

Laid down at the Yarrows yard in Esquimalt in 1963 and entering service on March 9, 1965, as the Canadian Naval Auxiliary Vessel *Endeavour*, very soon after she was reclassified a CFAV. Mentioned in that same *Crowsnest* article was that "a somewhat larger research vessel … is planned for use by the Naval Research Establishment, Halifax." That ship was named *Quest*, built by Burrard Shipbuilding in Vancouver, entered service on August 21, 1969, and as such was a CFAV from the outset (she transferred immediately to the East Coast, where the Naval Research Establishment soon enough became the Defence Research Establishment Atlantic). Both ships had roughly similar overall dimensions, were originally fitted to embark a small utility helicopter, and were powered by the same twin-screw diesel-electric 5600-shp (4175-kW) engines with a small backup generator on which they could run "ultra quiet." *Quest*, however, was some 600 tons heavier than her near-sister, the main difference being she was ice-strengthened for anticipated operations in the varied conditions off the Atlantic coast and eastern Arctic.

Although not purely "Navy" vessels, both ships were fixtures on their respective coasts, often participating in exercises with the fleet as appropriate, especially in helping to develop tactics for the employment of towed array sonar.* Approaching the end of her service life, in 1995, *Endeavour* transferred to the East Coast (without replacement on the West Coast) to take over from *Quest* while the latter underwent a modernization refit. *Endeavour* continued working out of Halifax for the next five years, including for the recovery of the Swissair Flight 111 crash in 1998, and was subsequently disposed of in 2000. Meanwhile, *Quest* returned from refit to remain in service until disposed of in 2017, similarly without replacement of that unique and valuable research capability.

FURTHER READING

Matthew Chapman, "AGOR-171 *Endeavour*," chapter 10 in *A History of the West Coast Canadian Forces Auxiliary Fleet: 60 Years of CFAV History* (Lookout Creative Services, 2008), 71–80.

"CNAV *Endeavour*," *Crowsnest* 16, no. 6 (June 1964), navalandmilitarymuseum.org/wp-content/uploads/2021/10/CFB-Esquimalt-Museum-Crowsnest-Volume16-Number-06-Jun-1964.pdf.

Charles D. Maginley and Bernard Collin, *The Ships of Canada's Marine Services* (Vanwell Publishing, 2001), 255–63.

* Author Gimblett, as an antisubmarine specialist in the 1980s, recalls operating with each on their respective coasts in early experimental work on what would become the Canadian Towed Array Sonar — see discussion in Chapter 40 on the Halifax-class frigates.

A rare shot (taken in 1981) of all four Iroquois-class destroyers in their original configuration, steaming in formation in order of sequence number: (top to bottom) *Iroquois*, *Huron*, *Athabaskan*, and *Algonquin*.

Before actual design drawings could be completed, the investigation was cancelled in November 1957 owing to budget considerations.

Still, the requirement remained for a missile-equipped air defence vessel. The next proposal gained more traction when, in April 1962, the Conservative Diefenbaker government approved development of a General Purpose Frigate (GPF) to begin construction by the end of 1963. At 3,500 tons displacement, the GPF would be a third larger than the 2,400-ton St. Laurent class, with primary armament of a RIM-24B Tartar missile system, which had been developed to have a range extending to that of the earlier Terrier (20 miles/32.5 km). That would be augmented by a twin 5-inch main gun to retain the heavy anti-surface capability soon to be lost to the fleet with retirement of the wartime Tribal-class destroyers, and it would have enhanced antisubmarine capabilities with an embarked helicopter (no hangar but sheltered in the hull and serviced by an elevator) and new homing torpedoes being developed. Design was well under way when Lester Pearson's Liberals won the general election of April 1963. They installed a new minister of national defence, Paul Hellyer, who had his own notions as to how the three services should be reformed. For the Navy, that included cancellation of the GPF in October 1963, with direction to limit any new design to the antisubmarine specialty required to meet NATO force commitments. A year later, in December 1964, Hellyer announced the revised plan to construct four new DDHs that would essentially be "repeat *Nipigons*," incorporating incremental improvements as a modest continuation of the St. Laurent–class hull.

Historians still debate how this ministerial intent "grew" over the next four years to emerge as an entirely new warship, but much of the blame can be laid upon the other monumental changes Hellyer wrought upon the defence establishment. The integration (1964) and unification (1968) of the CAF did away with the former individual services and their staffs; for example, the "Head of Navy" responsibilities being distributed now between former CNS Vice Admiral Herbert Rayner — newly appointed chief of personnel for the CAF, with only a secondary responsibility as principal naval adviser — and

Rear Admiral William Landymore as commander of MARCOM but restricted to a purely operational focus on the coasts (it would become the now-familiar "vice admiral environmental commander" appointment combining policy and operations responsibilities only with the final unification reorganization in 1975). With little effective service or bureaucratic oversight and, frankly, lack of ministerial attention (in September 1967, Hellyer was replaced by Leo Cadieux and went on to become minister of transport), the naval architects carried on in the spirit of designing a ship they understood would meet the Navy's requirements, appearing to have started from the premise of adapting the GPF to include more of an antisubmarine focus.

The design that appeared in 1968 was revolutionary and incorporated several innovations that distinguished the ships as trailblazers in ASW. These ships were nearly twice the size of the St. Laurents, at 5,200 tons. The primary advances were the switch from steam-boiler to all-gas-turbine propulsion (the first such use among Allied navies, preceded only a little earlier by the Soviet Navy's Kashin class); variable-pitch propellers for rapid change of speed; space for two of the big new CH-124 Sea King helicopters; a groundbreaking computerized command and control system (CCS-280); powerful new Canadian-designed active sonars (the AN/SQS-505 in both hull-mounted and VDS versions); a heavier 5-inch gun;* and the RIM-7M Sea Sparrow point-defence surface-to-air missile system, which at 10-nm (19-km) range, offered a modest air defence capability to ships in close company. This missile system was fitted in a novel enclosed stowage configuration to protect it from harsh subarctic operating conditions, and though sometimes lampooned as a "totally wacky" mechanism, in practice it proved quite effective.

In hindsight, it is staggering how quickly such a major building program progressed, just shy of a decade from start to finish, but it was not without controversy. The final drawings were not finished when all four ships were laid down in 1969 (two each at Quebec shipbuilders Davie, in Lauzon, and Marine Industries at Sorel), and cost overruns of the program at a time of downsizing nearly led to its cancellation. Indeed, the supposedly poor management of the project prompted the Liberal government (now with Pierre Trudeau as prime minister) to establish the Management Review Group of 1971–72, which resulted in the fundamental reorganization of the structure of the defence department — not least the procurement process — familiar to this day. At the time, however, the project was rescued by the budget and personnel savings gained from scrapping the carrier *Bonaventure* and cancelling the hydrofoil project. It didn't hurt that the ships were being built in Quebec yards.

* It is an oddity of Canada's complex relationship with the imperial and metric systems of measurement that the gun obtained was from the Italian firm OTO Melara, which fabricated it as a 127-mm model made to be compatible with USN 5-inch/54-calibre ammunition. As such, it was always known in Canadian use as a 5-inch gun, even though the nation formally adopted the metric system in 1975, very soon after the class came into service.

Name (Pennant)	Commissioned	TRUMP Refit	Paid Off
Iroquois (280)	July 29, 1972	Nov 1989–July 1992	May 1, 2015
Huron (281)	Dec 16, 1972	July 1993–Nov 1994	Mar 31, 2005
Athabaskan (282)	Sep 30, 1972	Oct 1991–Aug 1994	Mar 10, 2017
Algonquin (283)	Nov 3, 1973	Oct 1987–Oct 1991	June 11, 2015

The lead ship of the class, *Iroquois* (pennant number 280), was commissioned on July 29, 1972, with the others following by the end of 1973 (see table above). Styled "Sisters of the Space Age" when they entered service (the title of a 1974 National Film Board production marking their introduction), they were known more colloquially within the Navy as the "280s" or "Tribals," to distinguish them from the older St. Laurent "steamer" classes that still constituted the bulk of the surface fleet. For most of their first two decades in service, which coincided with the last two decades of the Cold War, all four ships were home-ported in Halifax for operations in the anticipated primary battleground of the North Atlantic Ocean. A notable exception was a demonstration cruise made by *Athabaskan* to the West Coast in 1977, in company with the submarine *Ojibwa*. As part of the fleet redistribution with the commissioning of the Halifax-class frigates, *Huron* and *Algonquin* were finally transferred to the West Coast in 1987 and 1994, respectively.

When *Algonquin* made that coastal transfer, she did so in remarkably different guise. As part of the Mulroney government's revitalization of the CAF in the last half of the 1980s, and to complement the coming introduction of the Halifax-class antisubmarine frigates (see Chapter 40), the Tribal Update and Modernization Program (TRUMP) was undertaken to finally convert the Iroquois class into proper area air defence guided-missile destroyers. This involved a major reconstruction of the ships, replacing the original gun in the forward fo'c's'le with a 29-cell vertical launch system of the SM-2 Block 2 surface-to-air missiles (range approximately 90 miles/150 km) and a 76-mm rapid-firing gun where the Sea Sparrows had been. The distinctive original canted "bunny ears" funnels were replaced by one large, squared funnel with a forced-air cooling system to reduce the thermal infrared signature targeted by heat-seeking enemy missiles. A Phalanx CIWS was installed atop the strengthened hangar, and the operations room was totally reworked to incorporate a new CCS-280 computer system that modernized the ships' task group command and control capabilities. *Algonquin* was the first to be completed, being declared operationally ready in March 1993.

It was more good fortune than planning that the original introduction of the class had occurred so soon after the paying off in 1970 of *Bonaventure*, and they were able to take up that ship's role as flagship for fleet deployments. Indeed, this capacity was critical to the assignment of Canadian commodores to take command of Allied and coalition fleets in such operations as the Standing Naval Force Atlantic (all four ships at various points over the decades); the Persian Gulf War (*Athabaskan* and *Huron*, 1990–91); in the Adriatic against the Former Republic of Yugoslavia (*Algonquin*, 1993–94); and the post-9/11 war against terror (*Iroquois*, *Algonquin*, and *Athabaskan*, 2001–03 and 2008).

Huron was put into reserve in 2000 owing to personnel shortages and to meet defence cutbacks and was sunk by her sister *Algonquin* in a live-fire exercise on May 14, 2007; the event was captured in a History Television documentary, *Sinking a Destroyer*. When further cutbacks over the next decade would not allow for repair of various mechanical defects, *Algonquin* and *Iroquois* were taken out of service in the mid-2010s. *Athabaskan* was the last to be paid off, on March 10, 2017, and a portion of her bow forms the naval monument at the Carling Campus of National Defence Headquarters in Ottawa. No program for replacement of the class had been announced by that time, the gaps in task group command and control and air defence notionally being filled by a concurrent mid-life modernization of the Halifax class. Finally, in February 2019, a contract was signed with a consortium of BAE and Lockheed Martin to undertake final design of a development of the British Type 26 Global Combat Ship (see Chapter 47).

FURTHER READING AND VIEWING

J.W. Arsenault, "The DDH 280 Program: A Case Study of Governmental Expenditure Decision Making," in *Canada's Defence Industrial Base*, ed. David Haglund (Ronald. P. Frye, 1988), 118–36.

Ron Barrie and Ken Macpherson, *Cadillac of Destroyers: HMCS* St. Laurent *and Her Successors* (Vanwell Publishing, 1996).

S.D. Campbell, "A New Tribe: Enter the Bunny-Ears," in *Tin-Can Canucks: A Century of Canadian Destroyers* (Kay Cee Publications, 2017), 249–80.

Richard W. Greenwood, "An Engineer's Outline of Canadian Naval History, Part 3 (1970–2014)," *The Northern Mariner/Le marin du nord* 24, nos. 3 and 4 (Summer & Autumn 2014): 273–95, tnm.journals.yorku.ca/index.php/default/article/view/255/237.

JHW Knox, "An Engineer's Outline of RCN History, Part 2 (1948–68)," in *The RCN in Retrospect, 1910–1968*, ed. James Boutilier (UBC Press, 1982), 331–32.

"Manitoba Class Destroyer Escorts" (DHH 81/520/8885-DDE/MA).

Sinking a Destroyer, Parallax Films, 2007, parallaxfilm.com/episode/sinking-a-destroyer/.

Sisters of the Space Age Part 1: HMCS Iroquois, Athabascan, Huron, *&* Algonquin" (National Film Board, 1974), posted April 17, 2010, by Paul Quin, YouTube, 9 min., 54 sec., youtube.com/watch?v=WVMa01z1REo.

Cormorant-Class Diving Support Vessel HMCS *Cormorant* (II) in 1986
(ex *Vista Esterna*)
Launched in 1965 | Built by Cantiere Naval Apoania Marina, Carrara
10 November 1978–02 July 1997
Dimensions: 72 m (236.2 ft) x 11.9 m (39 ft) x 5 m (16.4 ft)
Displacement: 2,350 tons | Speed: 14 kt | Crew: 65
Armament: nil

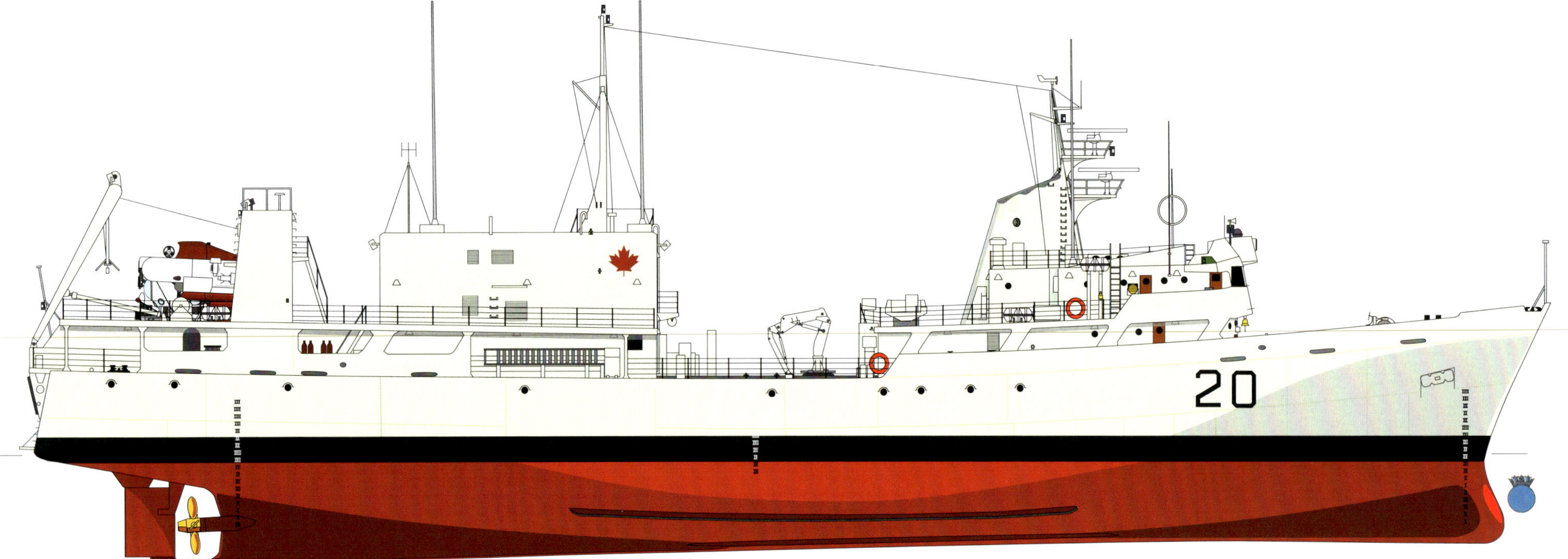

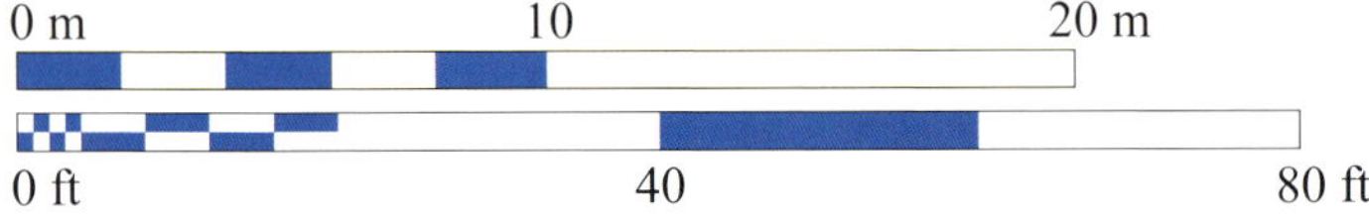

39

DIVING SUPPORT VESSEL *CORMORANT*

In 1970, the Canadian government acquired the "Submersible Diving Lockout" *SDL-1* as part of an effort to sustain the business of Vancouver-based Hyco International Hydrodynamics, manufacturers of the more widely known *Pisces* series of deep-diving manned submersibles built between 1965 and 1976 (*SDL-1* was the fourth in line of manufacturing, preceded by *Pisces I–III* and followed by *IV–XI*). Because of its bottom search and salvage capabilities, *SDL-1* was passed to the DND for evaluation by the clearance divers of MARCOM's Fleet Diving Unit Atlantic in Dartmouth, Nova Scotia. The submersible proved quite satisfactory in local harbour operations, and so the decision was made to acquire a "mother ship" to transport and support it in operations farther afield.

The Navy's earlier diving tenders, *Granby* and *Victoriaville* (in turn confusingly renamed *Granby*), had been conversions of Second World War–vintage warships: a diesel Bangor minesweeper and a Prestonian-class frigate, respectively (see Chapters 16 and 26). Once again, rather than purpose-build a new vessel, in 1975, the Navy acquired the Italian-flagged stern trawler *Aspa Quarto*, built by Cantiere Navale Apuania (Marina-Carrara, Italy) in 1965. The extensive conversion to the new role was conducted principally at Davie Shipbuilding in Lauzon, Quebec, with the resultant HMCS *Cormorant* (ASL 20) being commissioned on November 10, 1978. Most striking in her changed appearance was the large "hangar" aft, big enough to accommodate two submersibles, such that *Cormorant* occasionally embarked one of the *Pisces* in addition to *SDL-1*. They were launched by way of the

Cormorant deploying the SDL-1.

A-frame arrangement at the stern. To complement the diving function, the ship carried a doctor and had a full medical facility. The initial plan to fit a large recompression chamber in one of the former fish holds never materialized, with the large, empty space down low subsequently contributing to the ship's propensity to roll heavily. Her propulsion was also unique in the RCN, with three diesel engines driving a single controllable pitch propeller to make good only about 14 knots.

Before being paid off two decades later, on July 2, 1997, *Cormorant* ventured extensively throughout Canada's Atlantic, Arctic, and Great Lakes waters and as far afield as the Caribbean, conducting deep-water research. That activity was occasionally expanded to include surveys of a variety of high-profile sunken vessels, such as the *Irving Whale* oil barge off Prince Edward Island; the nineteenth-century British barque *Breadalbane*, which had sunk off Beechey Island, Nunavut, in 1853 while searching for the Franklin expedition; and recovery of the ship's bell of the SS *Edmund Fitzgerald* from Lake Superior. Within the Navy, *Cormorant* was just as significant for having been chosen to conduct the first mixed-gender crew trial from 1980 to 1984 and thereafter having a mixed-gender ship's company.

After being paid off in July 1997, she was sold to an American company, ostensibly for further diving operations, but was allowed to languish in Bridgewater, Nova Scotia, not far from her equally ignored former naval colleague, the DDE *Fraser*. *Cormorant* was also eventually repossessed by the Canadian government and broken up in Sheet Harbour, Nova Scotia, in 2020.

Anticosti-Class Minesweeper HMCS *Moresby* in 1991
(ex *Joyce Tide*)
Launched in 1973 | Built by Allied Shipbuilding Ltd., Vancouver
07 May 1989–10 March 2000
Dimensions: 58.2 m (190.9 ft) x 13.1 m (43 ft) x 5.2 m (17.1 ft)
Displacement: 2,205 tons | Speed: 13.5 kt | Crew: 25
Armament: 12.7 mm MG (2 x I)

Anticosti-Class Minesweeper HMCS *Anticosti* in 1999
(ex *Jean Tide*)
Launched in 1973 | Built by Allied Shipbuilding Ltd., Vancouver
07 May 1989–21 March 2000
Dimensions: 58.2 m (190.9 ft) x 13.1 m (43 ft) x 5.2 m (17.1 ft)
Displacement: 2,205 tons | Speed: 13.5 kt | Crew: 25
Armament: 12.7 mm MG (2 x I)

41

MINESWEEPING AUXILIARIES: *ANTICOSTI* AND *MORESBY*

After a decade of détente, in the early 1980s, the Cold War appeared to be entering a new and deadlier phase, characterized by U.S. President Ronald Reagan's so-called Star Wars initiative. The naval complement to this was the USN's Maritime Strategy, developed to emphasize forward operations against the Soviet Navy in its home ports and to strike its ballistic missile–firing nuclear submarines operating from Arctic bastions with a new generation of long-range intercontinental ballistic missiles. For its part, the Conservative government of Prime Minister Brian Mulroney produced its own "ambitious and expansive" 1987 White Paper on Defence. Titled *Challenge and Commitment: A Defence Policy for Canada*, it is remembered primarily as calling for a fleet of ten to twelve nuclear-powered submarines as the mainstay of what Defence Minister Perrin Beatty styled "a three-ocean Navy to protect our three-ocean country"[56] (see that discussion in Chapter 43 on the Victoria-class submarines).

With the reciprocal Soviet threat against North America also being renewed, one of the other directions in the White Paper was for the Canadian Navy to resurrect a mine warfare capability, a set of skills not seen in the fleet since the 1960s, when the Bay-class minesweepers were paid off into reserve. In the intervening decades, much had changed in the specialized field of mine clearance technologies: Systems such as side-scan sonar and remotely operated vehicles to locate and neutralize bottom-influence mines were now available for containerization and, as such, easily embarked in ships with sufficient open deck space. While a project for a purpose-built mine countermeasures ship was stood up (which would become the Kingston class, originally intended as mine warfare vessels, described in Chapter 42), the Navy sought to acquire an interim capability to begin training immediately.

The solution was a pair of offshore drill-rig supply vessels suitable for conversion as minesweeping auxiliaries (MSAs). They were assessed to be ideal for the purpose, having a large open deck area aft and a high degree of manoeuvrability, with twin shafts and a bow thruster. Built in Vancouver, British Columbia, in 1973 by Allied Shipbuilders Limited, the ships had operated in European waters as the Motor Vessels *Jean Tide* and *Joyce Tide* before being purchased by MARCOM in 1988 and commissioned together on May 7, 1989, as HMC Ships *Anticosti* (MSA 110) and *Moresby* (MSA 112), respectively. After a further fuller conversion to their new role at Marystown, Newfoundland, through 1990 to 1991, the pair set about a busy routine of experimentation and exercises. Both were initially based in Halifax, but *Moresby* was transferred to Esquimalt in 1997. Memorably, *Anticosti* assisted in the Swissair crash recovery operations in 1999. After completion of delivery of the Kingston class, the pair was paid off in March 2000 and sold to commercial interests. At the time of writing, *Moresby* is back to her original oil-rig supply purpose, based in Panama, and *Anticosti* is reported to be a research vessel working in Newfoundland.

FURTHER READING

Robert Smol, "Challenge & Commitment Lost: Part 1: Looking Back at the Defence White Paper of 1987 — A Made-in-Canada Policy," *Esprit de Corps* 24, no. 8 (October 12, 2017), espritdecorps.ca/perspectives-1/challenge-commitment-lost-part-1-looking-back-at-the-defence-white-paper-of-1987-a-made-in-canada-policy.

James D. Watkins, "The Maritime Strategy," *US Naval Institute Proceedings* 112, no. 1, 995 Supplement (January 1986), usni.org/magazines/proceedings/1986/january-supplement/maritime-strategy-0.

Glace Bay demonstrates a tight high-speed turn.

tasks to include general coastal patrol, fisheries duties, and constabulary support; it also allowed for construction of the ship to be done to commercial standards for better cost-savings, resulting in steel-hull fabrication. Bob Blakely, a former Commander of the Naval Reserve, noted that the steel hull was "an odd thing for [a ship] that would have to sweep magnetic mines."[58] The primary intent that they be crewed by the Naval Reserve remained throughout, although the Cold War vision for follow-on Batch 2 and 3 builds of, potentially, another twelve each was shelved, and the final construction remained at the contracted first twelve ships. An innovation to the contracting process was the incorporation of a follow-on in-service support contract for civilian extended maintenance of the vessels — although this arose from "lack of upfront commitment to support the MCDVs with existing resources, due to competing CPF, TRUMP, and submarine requirements,"[59] this subsequently became a standard feature of future building and modernization programs.

Historian Marc Milner has observed, "At 970 tons and nearly 200 feet [61 m] in length, the MCDVs [are] about the size of the Second World War corvettes."[60] The lead of the class, HMCS *Kingston*, was laid down in December 1994 and commissioned on September 21, 1996, with *Summerside* being the last to commission, on July 18, 1999. They were all built by Halifax Shipyards for subsequent distribution equally between coasts, as per the table below. Naming was a mix of tradition with acknowledgement to ongoing public relations engagement requirements: Following the lead set with the Halifax-class frigates (which were generally named for provincial capitals and major cities), all the Kingston class were named for "secondary" cities in each of the provinces and then-territories, attempting where possible to perpetuate ships with Second World War battle honours and, where that was not possible, to recognize the past practice of naming minesweepers for Canadian "bays."

Their introduction into service in the last half of the 1990s had always been intended as a replacement for the Porte-class gate vessels used for training reservists, but it being coincident with retirement of the Bay-class minesweepers led to the Kington class taking on the Bays' role as the vessels for all junior officer navigation and shiphandling training. Blakely makes another interesting observation: "The last gate vessels were decommissioned in December 1996 in Esquimalt; at the same time, and on the same day, HMCS *Ottawa*, the last of the patrol frigates (CPFs), and HMCS *Nanaimo*, the first West Coast maritime coastal defence vessel, joined the Pacific Fleet."[61] Although not the connection he intended to make, the fates of the two new classes would soon enough be intertwined. Before the first full decade of operating the Kingston class was over, it was apparent that their full-time core crewing by naval reservists could not be sustained by the small cadre of seagoing officers and ratings actually available to do so. The situation was becoming dire when there arose a separate, unintended consequence in the withdrawal of several of the Halifax class into their FELEX/HCM mid-life refits at the same time (see Chapter 40), reducing the seagoing bunks available for the Regular Force. The need to maintain fleet proficiency drove the resolution of both challenges being found in that, from the mid-2010s, the crewing of the Kingston class shifted to a shared Regular and Reserve responsibility.

Several oddities became apparent from the continual shifting of the intended role of the class. Early on, the desire for the design to incorporate a bow thruster to assist in "hovering" while employing mine countermeasure equipment was dropped as a cost-saving factor, compromising that aspect of their intended employment. More fundamentally, the unique Z-drive propulsion system is drastically different from the propulsion systems of all other HMC Ships, making the Kingston class not especially appropriate for training junior officers in shiphandling — the lessons they learn in the Kingstons are not applicable to driving the Halifax-class frigates.

East Coast		
Name	**Pennant**	**Commissioned**
Kingston	700	July 12, 1996
Glace Bay (Second)	701	Oct 26, 1996
Shawinigan (Second)	704	June 14, 1997
Goose Bay	707	July 26, 1998
Moncton (Second)	708	July 12, 1998
Summerside (Second)	712	July 18, 1999
West Coast		
Name	**Pennant**	**Commissioned**
Nanaimo (Second)	702	May 10, 1997
Edmonton	703	June 21, 1997
Whitehorse	705	July 18, 1997
Yellowknife	706	Apr 18, 1998
Saskatoon (Second)	709	Dec 5, 1998
Brandon (Second)	710	June 5, 1999

As well, the need for the Kingston class to pick up the slack in meeting fleet operational commitments led to their being deployed well beyond Canadian coastal waters. Initial participation in NATO mine countermeasures exercises in European waters expanded to practically every one of the Kingstons having been deployed abroad:

into the Baltic and Mediterranean to counter Russian expansionist aims as part of the two NATO Standing Mine Countermeasures Groups; to the shores of Africa's Gulf of Guinea for training the developing navies in the region; into the Caribbean and Central American waters on counter-drug operations; and to Hawaii for biannual multinational Rim of the Pacific exercises. Additionally, they have deployed regularly into Canada's Arctic as part of annual Operation Nanook activities.

Despite the class wearing their quarter-century age fairly well, all these newer missions demanded greater capabilities than what the vessels were designed with. Still, observers were caught by surprise with the announcement on July 24, 2025, that the class would begin to be taken out of service just a few months later, and in rather dramatic fashion: Through the course of the fall, fully two-thirds (eight ships) of the class would be paid off — HMC Ships *Shawinigan*, *Summerside*, *Goose Bay*, *Glace Bay*, and *Kingston* from Halifax, and *Saskatoon*, *Whitehorse*, and *Brandon* from Esquimalt. The four remaining in commission would be concentrated in Halifax for operational and maintenance considerations, comprising *Moncton* (originally from Halifax), joined by *Yellowknife*, *Edmonton*, and *Nanaimo* transferring from the west coast. How much longer they survive will in part be determined by the success in finding a replacement. At time of writing, that is understood to be narrowing to what is being described as a "continental defence corvette," with significant capabilities, including a gun of some firepower, an extended range surface-to-air ballistic missile defence system, the ability to conduct helicopter operations, and far better open-ocean sea-keeping characteristics (see Afterword).

FURTHER READING

Bob Blakely, "'This Ain't Your Dad's Naval Reserve Anymore': Sharp-End Missions and Total Force, 1989–2010," in *Citizen Sailors: Chronicles of Canada's Naval Reserve*, eds. Richard Gimblett and Michael Hadley (Dundurn, 2010), 109–23.

Government of Canada, *Challenge and Commitment: A Defence Policy for Canada* (June 1987), publications.gc.ca/collections/collection_2012/dn-nd/D2-73-1987-eng.pdf.

Richard W. Greenwood, "An Engineer's Outline of Canadian Naval History, Part 3 (1970–2014)," *The Northern Mariner/Le marin du nord* 24, nos. 3 and 4 (Summer & Autumn 2014): 273–95, tnm.journals.yorku.ca/index.php/default/article/view/255/237.

"Kingston-Class Patrol Ships," Naval Association of Canada, Naval Affairs Program Briefing Note #23, updated September 2022, navalassoc.ca/wp-content/uploads/2024/11/BN-Kingston-1.pdf.

F.W. McKee, "Maritime Coastal Defence Vessels," in *The Ships of Canada's Naval Forces, 1910–2001*, 3rd ed., eds. Ken Macpherson and Ron Barrie (Vanwell Publishing, 2002), 299.

Robert Smol, "Challenge & Commitment Lost: Part 1: Looking Back at the Defence White Paper of 1987 — A Made-in-Canada Policy," *Esprit de Corps* 24, no. 8 (October 12, 2017), espritdecorps.ca/perspectives-1/challenge-commitment-lost-part-1-looking-back-at-the-defence-white-paper-of-1987-a-made-in-canada-policy.

James D. Watkins, "The Maritime Strategy," *US Naval Institute Proceedings* 112, no. 1, 995 Supplement (January 1986), usni.org/magazines/proceedings/1986/january-supplement/maritime-strategy-0.

Victoria-Class Submarine HMCS *Victoria* in 2000
(ex HMS *Unseen*)
Launched 14 November 1989 | Built by Cammell Laird, Birkenhead
02 December 2000–in service in 2025
Dimensions: 70.3 m (230.6 ft) x 8.3 m (27.2 ft) x 3.2 m (10.5 ft)
Displacement: 2,215 tons (surfaced) 2,365 tons (submerged)
Speed: 12/20 kt | Crew: 45
Armament: 21-in TT (6 x I)

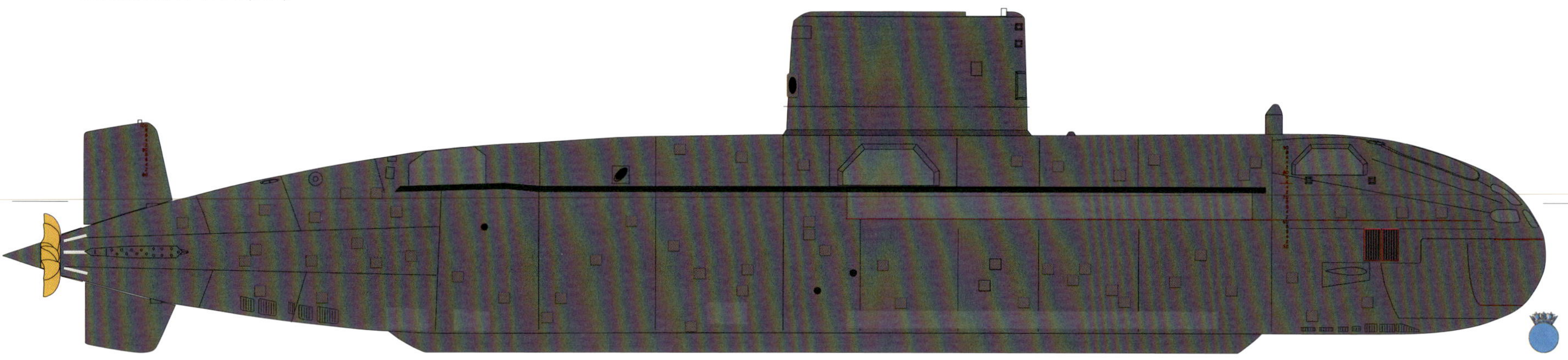

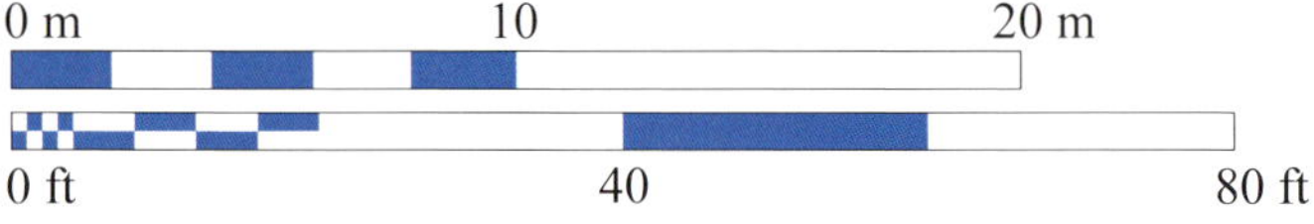

43

VICTORIA-CLASS SUBMARINES

The operational obsolescence of the Oberon-class submarines was understood even at the time of their introduction into Canadian service in the last half of the 1960s. The purchase, however, was rationalized as the means to acquire a homegrown antisubmarine training platform while simultaneously developing the expertise for a future hunter-killer submarine force. A program to replace them had begun with all this in mind in the early 1980s, proceeding in tandem with the SOUP mid-life refit described in Chapter 33 on the Oberons. The Canadian Submarine Acquisition Program (CASAP) was stood up early in 1983 following the appointment of former submariner Rear Admiral James Wood as Chief of Maritime Doctrine and Operations (CMDO, making him the senior naval officer in Ottawa in the unified National Defence Headquarters; a few months later in 1983, Wood would be promoted to vice admiral and take the helm in Halifax as commander MARCOM). The CASAP office soon joined efforts with its equivalent in the RAN, which was also looking to replace its Oberons, and together focused attention on three conventionally powered options: the Dutch Walrus class (a second-generation variant of the U.S. Barbel design) and the German Type 209, which were both just entering service, and the British Type 2400 Upholder class, beginning design development.

The story goes that in 1985, when the Ottawa CMDO staff (by then headed by another future commander of MARCOM, "Chuck" Thomas) briefed incoming Conservative Defence Minister Eric Neilson on CASAP, Neilson interrupted with the query: "Was nothing prepared on nuclear-powered submarines?"[62] Thus was

Windsor out of the water on the syncrolift in Halifax Dockyard, while *Victoria* (foreground) does a camber test dive.

born the Nuclear Submarine Option Study, which became the centrepiece of the 1987 White Paper, *Challenge and Commitment*. The nuclear submarine acquisition misadventure has been covered thoroughly elsewhere (see any of Delaney, Ferguson, Greenwood, and Wikipedia's "Canada-Class Submarine" in Further Reading). The important elements for this chapter are that CASAP was set aside in favour of the Nuclear Submarine Acquisition program, which was focused on a choice between the British Trafalgar class or French Rubis class SSNs, only to be cancelled abruptly in the government's belt-tightening budget of April 1989. The major sticking points were mostly familiar from the experiences of 1959–62 and 1964: the substantial costs involved, growing public opposition, the lessening of Cold War tensions with the collapse of the Soviet Union, the projected twenty-five to thirty years it would take to implement, and especially the intransigence of the USN in allowing the transfer of nuclear technology secrets. Perhaps the biggest "what if?" of Canadian naval history is that, had that acquisition gone ahead in the early 1990s, would the RCN today (2025) be well on the way to operating a fleet of ten to twelve nuclear-powered submarines? — a prospect bandied about recently as an option in the current search for a replacement submarine (see discussion in the Afterword).

The Nuclear Submarine Acquisition project that closed in 1990 resurfaced the following year as the Canadian Patrol Submarine Program. The office figuratively blew the dust off the previous CASAP contenders, adding two new ones into the mix for consideration: the Swedish Type 471 (a variant of which the Australians were developing by then, as their Collins class) and the French Amethyste (a conventional variant of the Rubis). Soon enough, however, the new submarine program office also had to close, a victim of the 1992 Conservative budget, which inflicted deep "peace dividend" cuts on defence spending. Determined to preserve some measure of hope for its revival, the Navy renamed the replacement search to "the intentionally ambiguous 'Submarine Capability Life Extension' Project," the acronym for which, as Greenwood observes, "was not taken to be especially propitious, [as] SCLE was commonly pronounced 'sickle' or 'sickly' according to the mood."[63] But as fate would have it, new life was given to the long-running quest by a change in government. Jean Chrétien's

Victoria class submarine *Windsor* doing a personnel transfer with the CH-124 Sea King from Halifax-class frigate *Ville de Québec*, in the background.

Liberals are remembered as coming to power in 1993 in part on their election platform to scrap the EH-101 helicopter as the replacement for the also overly obsolete Sea Kings (as will be discussed in Chapter 54, on the CH-148 Cyclone). With a small change of heart the next year, their own White Paper on Defence of 1994 adopted the premise of SCLE in announcing the intention to explore the purchase of the British Upholder class as an "interim" solution to retaining a submarine capability, pending definition of a formal conventional attack submarine replacement project.

The RN undertook design of the Type 2400 (denoting a submerged displacement of 2,400 tons) in the early 1980s as a conventional submarine replacement for the Oberon-class submarines in supplementing their otherwise primarily nuclear-powered attack submarine fleet. Aside from the power plant, the 2400s had large commonality of structural, sensor, and weapon systems with the RN SSNs, but, being non-nuclear and consequently shorter ranged, they were envisioned to conduct patrols in the nearby Greenland–Iceland–United Kingdom (GIUK) Gap, working in tandem with SOSUS against Soviet submarines. A class of twelve was planned, but in the end, only four were built. The lead vessel, named *Upholder*, was laid down in November 1983 and commissioned in June 1990. Before the last one (*Unicorn*) could even enter service, however, a post–Cold War British defence review determined the RN should shift to an all-nuclear submarine force. When subsequent attempts to sell the four vessels variously to Pakistan, Portugal, and Chile ran afoul of USN defence technology transfer restrictions, Britain faced limited options elsewhere. Canada, however — being a member of the "Five Eyes" defence intelligence-sharing community (Australia, Canada, New Zealand, the U.K., and the U.S.) — qualified for non-nuclear technology transfers. Moreover, Canadian Navy technical officers on exchange positions with the RN had been involved with the Upholder program from the earliest days. As such, it was not unnatural for the availability of the British boats — probably at a modest cost — to be made known to the Liberal government for inclusion in the 1994 White Paper. During the subsequent negotiation process, the RN maintained the Upholders in a "light mothball" status, until finally in April 1998, a deal was announced to acquire the four boats for $750 million (indeed a significant discount on the potential cost to build a full replacement class).

British Name	Laid Down	Launched	British Service	Cdn Name	Comm'd
Upholder	Nov 1983	Dec 1986	Jun 1990–Apr 1994	*Chicoutimi*	Sep 2015
Unseen	Aug 1987	Nov 1989	Jul 1991–Apr 1994	*Victoria*	Dec 2000
Ursula	Aug 1987	Feb 1991	May 1992–Jun 1994	*Corner Brook*	Jun 2003
Unicorn	Mar 1989	Apr 1992	Jun 1993–Oct 1994	*Windsor*	Oct 2003

The transfer was to be effected by their undergoing a reactivation work period paid by the RN (another substantial cost-saving to Canada), followed by safety trials and diving qualification in Britain by Canadian crews, which would culminate in an acceptance and renaming ceremony before sailing for Canada, where a further "Canadianization" work period would be conducted. This would incorporate exchanging British sensor and weapons systems with Canadian ones that had mostly been fitted in the Oberons through the 1980s under SOUP and were still in good condition, which primarily entailed replacing the RN Mk 24 Tigerfish torpedoes with USN Mk 48 heavy-weight torpedoes and fire control system, adding the Canadian SUBTASS, and taking care of various communications and periscope equipment fits.

The reactivation work in both Britain and Canada turned out to be much more of a challenge than anticipated, owing in equal measures to a variety of factors: the vessels not having fully completed their introduction into RN service before being mothballed; the lightness of the mothballing not anticipating the longer-than-expected time before reactivation and resulting in some corrosion issues; the complexity of submarine structural technologies new to Canadian industry; and other unanticipated demands on the RCN budget, such as the major post-9/11 deployment of practically the entire surface fleet to the Arabian Sea theatre of operations. The final acquisitions were accomplished in sequence (see table this page for full details), beginning with *Unseen* being accepted and renamed *Victoria* and commissioned as lead ship of the Canadian class in Halifax on December 2, 2000. All went well until the final vessel of the transfer — the original lead British ship, *Upholder*, renamed *Chicoutimi* — was struck with tragedy: On October 5, 2004, the day after sailing from Britain for Canada, while the boat was travelling on the surface during a gale, sea water entered through the conning tower, causing an internal explosion and fire that killed one officer and injured nine sailors and left the submarine wallowing dead in the water. After being rescued and towed back to Faslane, the badly damaged *Chicoutimi* was transported by heavy lift vessel, first to Halifax in January 2005 for a lengthy damage assessment, and then on to Esquimalt in April 2009 to undergo a major refit. She finally commissioned there on September 3, 2015, more than a decade later than intended.

Meanwhile, on completion of their Canadianization work periods, the other boats began to make up for lost time, as a quick survey reveals. In June 2005, *Windsor* commenced the first operational cycle for her class, participating in several international exercises, including the successful tracking of a USN SSN and assisting in the workups of an American carrier battle group. In the spring of 2007, *Corner Brook* participated in the NATO Exercise Noble Warrior, marking the first time in fifteen years that a Canadian submarine had been present in European waters, and in August later that year, she deployed to the Arctic in support of Operation Nanook. In March 2012, *Victoria* was declared fully operational after weapons certification and soon thereafter became the first RCN submarine to fire a warshot Mk 48 torpedo, sinking the ex-USNS *Concord* on July 17, 2012, during a Rim of the Pacific exercise near Hawaii. In 2015, *Windsor* achieved the original ambition for the Upholder class in tracking a Russian submarine while patrolling the GIUK Gap. In her turn, *Chicoutimi* deployed to the Far East in 2017–18 for an epic 197 days deployed, as part of Operation Neon, enforcing United Nations sanctions against North Korea.

Despite these accomplishments, the sad truth is that the class has never achieved the desired output of there being always at least one available for operational tasking. Instead, they have been the subject of media stories such as that headlined by the Canadian Broadcasting Corporation on February 11, 2020: "Canada's submarine fleet spent 'zero days' at sea last year [2019]."[64] In April 2015, the Conservative government of Prime Minister Stephen Harper announced plans for a major life extension for the class pending acquisition of a replacement, and this was confirmed in the Justin Trudeau Liberal government's 2016 defence policy statement, *Strong, Secure, Engaged*. In the summer of 2021, the RCN set up a team to begin (again) the acquisition process for a new vessel, now styled the Canadian Patrol Submarine Project. The ambition is to have a formal replacement of the Victorias complete early in the 2030s, and this iteration of the story is discussed in the Afterword.

FURTHER READING

"Canada-Class Submarine," Wikimedia Foundation, last modified December 14, 2024, 23:40 (UTC), en.wikipedia.org/wiki/Canada-class_submarine.

Jason Delaney, "The One Class of Vessel That Is Impossible to Build in ~~Australia~~ Canada," *The Northern Mariner/Le marin du nord* 24, nos. 3 and 4 (Summer & Autumn 2014): 260–72, tnm.journals.yorku.ca/index.php/default/article/view/251/233.

Julie Ferguson, *Through a Canadian Periscope: The Story of the Canadian Submarine Service*, 2nd ed. (Dundurn, 2014), 334–71.

Richard W. Greenwood, "An Engineer's Outline of Canadian Naval History, Part 3 (1970–2014)," *The Northern Mariner/Le marin du nord* 24, nos. 3 and 4 (Summer & Autumn 2014): 273–95, tnm.journals.yorku.ca/index.php/default/article/view/255/237.

Peter T. Haydon, "The *Chicoutimi* Accident: Lessons Learned and Not Learned," *Canadian Military Journal* 6, no. 4 (Autumn 2005): 15–25, journal.forces.gc.ca/vo6/no3/maritim-marin-eng.asp.

Paul T. Mitchell, "The 'Deal of the Century' or 'A Most Improbable Project': Acquiring the Upholder Submarines," Naval Association of Canada, Niobe Papers, no. 5 (August 2019), navalassoc.ca/wp-content/uploads/2020/09/Mitchell-Niobe-5.pdf.

"Submarines," Naval Association of Canada, Naval Affairs Program Briefing Note #5, updated October 2024, navalassoc.ca/wp-content/uploads/2024/11/BN-Submarines.pdf.

Orca-Class Patrol Craft Training PCT *Orca* in 2010
Launched 09 August 2006 | Built by Victoria Shipyards, Victoria
17 November 2006–in service in 2025
Dimensions: 33 m (108 ft) x 8.2 m (27.4 ft) x 2 m (8 ft)
Displacement: 210 tons | Speed: 18 kt | Crew: 4 + 16
Possible Armament: 12.7 mm MG (1 x I)

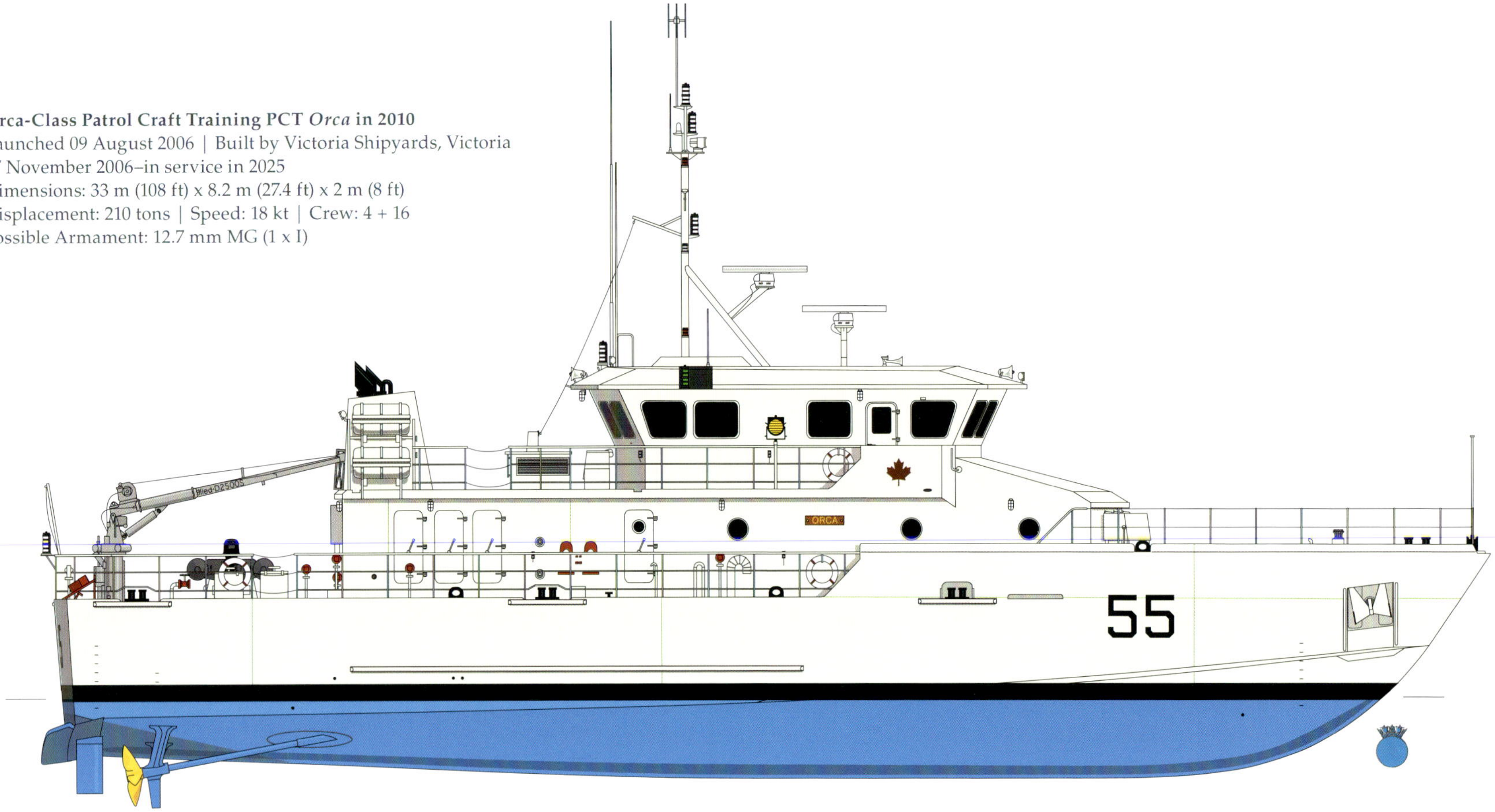

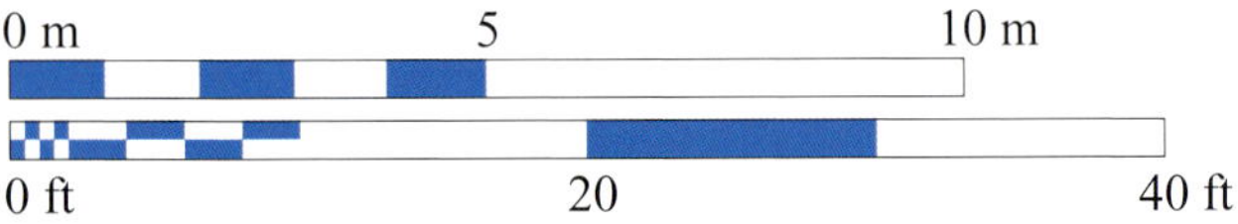

ORCA-CLASS PATROL/TRAINING CRAFT

In conjunction with initiating the project that delivered the Kingston class as replacements for the Bay-class minesweepers, the naval staff appreciated that a follow-on was also required for the Porte class, YAGs, and miscellaneous Naval Reserve division tenders employed as introductory training vessels (discussed in Chapters 29 and 32). What was initially designated the Harbour class was granted planning approval as the Naval Cutter Project in November 1992, only to be put on hold pending a defence review after the Chrétien Liberals were elected in 1993. While the project remained in limbo for the rest of that decade, the pressures to find sea time and training bunk spaces for junior officers in the rest of the fleet grew increasingly difficult until coming to a head against operational priorities in the aftermath of the 9/11 terrorist attacks. By that time, the envisioned numbers for the would-be Cutter type had been scaled back to a simple replacement of the half-dozen training YAGs on the West Coast (that is, not to also replace the reserve division tenders across the country, which by that time had been paid off). In due course named the Orca class and designated "Patrol Craft Training," such vessels would, however, be capable of performing other minor operational roles, such as port security, search and rescue, and general coastal patrol.

On November 8, 2004, a contract was awarded to Victoria Shipyards to build six vessels with an option for another two, for a total budget of just under $100 million. The Orca-class design that was selected was a development of the Pacific-class patrol boats built for the RAN between 1985 and 1997, taking into consideration the operational experience of the RAN with

The full division of Orca patrol craft conducting close-in, line-abreast manoeuvres; *Raven* in the foreground.

those vessels and the specific Canadian naval training requirements. The latter primarily included a larger bridge, configured to replicate the shore-based simulator at the Naval Officers Training Centre *Venture*, along with a shipboard training classroom one deck below it, and greater accommodation space for five crew and twenty-four trainees. Other changes for the Canadian Navy included strengthening the fo'c'sle for the mission-specific fitting of a 12.7-mm (.50-cal) machine gun and associated ammunition stowage modifications, as well as revised environmental stewardship requirements under the *Canada Shipping Act*. This all resulted in a ship somewhat larger than the Australian original (210 tons, up from the original 160), necessitating a more powerful pair of Caterpillar diesel engines to drive the twin shafts and fixed-pitch propellers, but with a compensating gain in maximum speed from 16 to 20 knots. Being much larger and longer than the YAGs they were to replace, the Orcas (210 tonnes/33 m versus the YAG 70 tonnes/23 m) created a strain on berthing space in the small Esquimalt Harbour, with a consequent infrastructure redesign that was not completed until the mid-2020s. However, in a rare instance for Canadian defence procurements, all of this was managed so effectively within the allotted budget that the option to purchase the additional pair could be exercised. In the end, wrote David Peer, "The final tally for the project was eight vessels, which exceeded contracted performance requirements that cost 1.1 percent below budget, and arrived fifteen months early."[65]

Like the YAGs before them, the Orcas are not commissioned ships of the RCN. However, in appreciation that their role hearkens back to that performed by the armed yachts of the Second World War and then by the Fairmiles used by the reserves in the 1950s, the class were given "animal" names with a connection to First Nations lore, perpetuating six of those former vessels. Two new names were chosen to cement a West Coast affiliation and given to the lead ship, *Orca*, and the second completed, *Raven*. The remainder are listed in the table below, along with their dates of entering service.

All are based in Esquimalt. Two of the class were armed for employment in Operation Podium, the Canadian Forces' contribution to security for the Vancouver 2010 Winter Olympics. Approaching nearly

Orca-class patrol vessels *Orca* and *Caribou*, armed for patrol at the 2010 Olympics.

two decades in service at the time of publication, the Orcas continue to prove their worth as the introductory vessel for Canadian naval new entries.

Name	Pennant	Service Entry
Orca	55	Nov 9, 2006
Raven	56	Mar 15, 2007
Caribou (Second)	57	July 31, 2007
Renard (Second)	58	Sep 13, 2007
Wolf (Third)	59	Nov 29, 2007
Grizzly (Second)	60	Mar 19, 2008
Cougar (Third)	61	Oct 2, 2008
Moose (Third)	62	Nov 27, 2008

FURTHER READING

David Peer, "The Orca Project: A Procurement Success," *Canadian Naval Review* 9, no. 2 (2013): 29–31, navalreview.ca/wp-content/uploads/CNR_pdf_full/cnr_vol9_2.pdf.

Harry DeWolf–Class Icebreaker HMCS *Harry DeWolf* in 2021
Launched 15 September 2018 | Built by Halifax Shipbuilding Ltd., Halifax
26 June 2021–in service in 2025
Dimensions: 103.6 m (339.9 ft) x 19 m (62.3 ft) x 5.8 m (19 ft)
Displacement: 6,615 tons | Speed: 20 kt | Crew: 65
Armament: 25 mm (1 x I); 12.7 mm MG (2 x I); 1 x helicopter

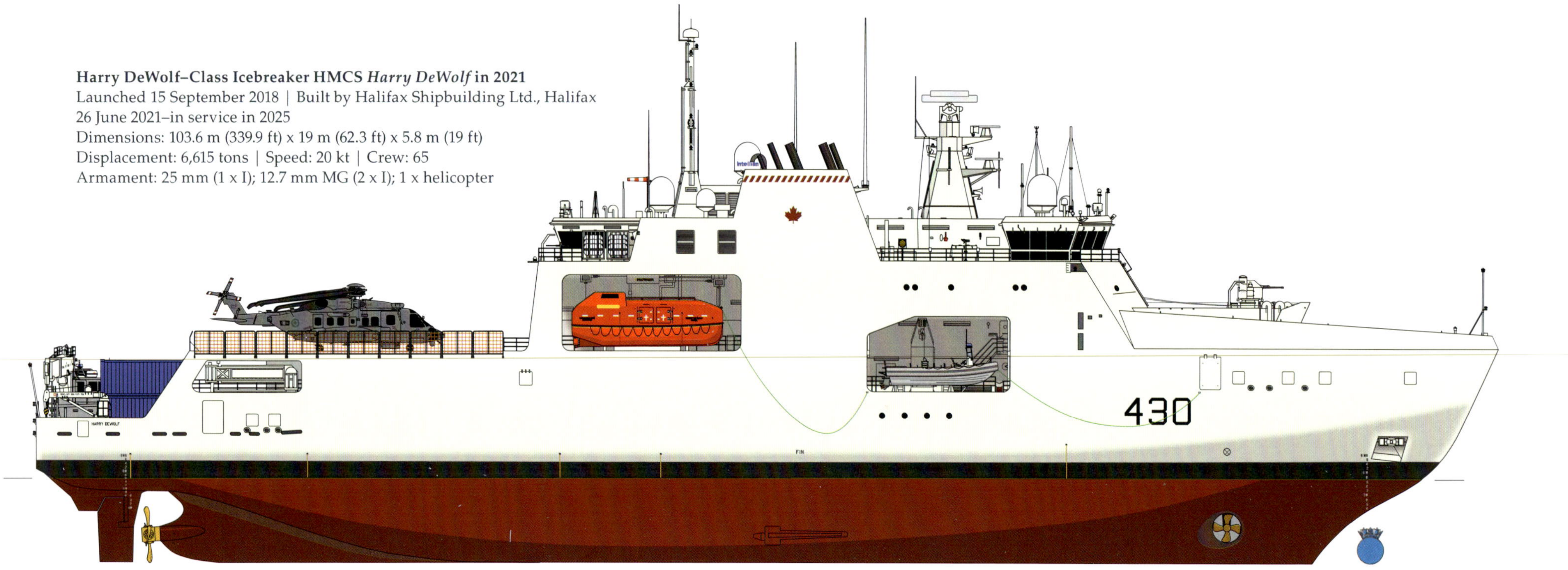

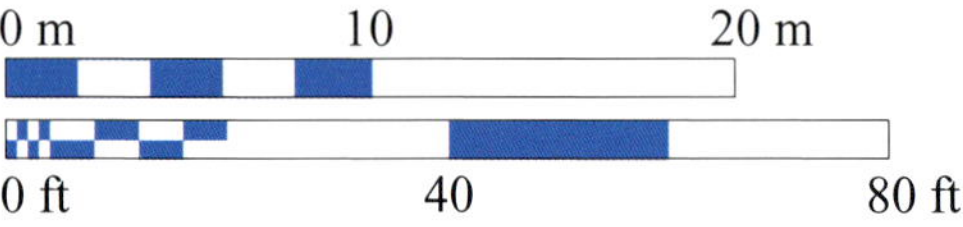

HARRY DEWOLF–CLASS ARCTIC AND OFFSHORE PATROL VESSELS

The Conservative government of Prime Minister Stephen Harper came to office in 2006 determined to address a variety of issues toward which they felt previous ministries had paid only lip service. In military matters, the clear priority was the ongoing campaign in Afghanistan. But a close second was the notion of bolstering Arctic sovereignty. The new minister of national defence was Gordon O'Connor (a retired armoured corps brigadier general with much field and headquarters staff experience), and it was not long before he directed the RCN to begin an investigation into the acquisition of an ice-capable patrol ship. He even provided the model on which to focus the search: the Norwegian Coast Guard vessel NoCGV *Svalbard*. The naval staff was not keen on the notion, its procurement priorities being the mid-life refit of the Halifax-class frigates and finding a replacement for the Iroquois-class destroyers. The naval staff also pointed to the previous experience with *Labrador* as evidence that the mainly constabulary functions applicable in the Arctic were more rightly the preserve of Canada's own Coast Guard. The Coast Guard, for its part — focused more on safety of shipping (ice-breaking and vessel escort) and support for scientific research — balked at assuming the armed presence demanded by the government (for a fuller discussion of the division of Canadian maritime responsibilities between Navy and Coast Guard, see the Naval Association of Canada Briefing Note #22 in Further Reading). With

Robert Hampton Gray rolled out after final assembly in August 2024, the "tape" demonstrating where the prefabricated sections have been joined.

the constabulary missions seeming to drop between the cracks of the two services, meeting the political desire for "grey hulls" therefore fell to the Navy.

The Conservatives had been heartened by how quickly they were able to set in motion the acquisition of a range of equipment to deploy to Afghanistan, such as CC-177 Globemaster and CC-130J Hercules transport aircraft, CH-147F Chinook medium-lift helicopters, and M777 155-mm howitzers. However, their thought that a similar "Military/Commercial off the Shelf" purchase of a clutch of Svalbards should also take a relatively short time soon fell afoul of the DND–Public Works procurement process. The official announcement of the project to acquire six to eight armed naval icebreakers, dubbed "Arctic/Offshore Patrol Ships" (A/OPS, soon refined to AOPV) was made on July 9, 2007, but the first ship would not be commissioned until 2021, fully a decade and a half after the initial direction and indeed six years after Harper had been defeated by Justin Trudeau's Liberals in the 2015 general election.

In fairness to "the process," acquisition of an entirely new and largely untried capability is very different from purchasing battle-proven options such as those listed above. Indeed, *Svalbard* was relatively "new," having entered service only in 2002, and defining the Canadian SOR quickly identified that the conditions and expectations for RCN employment demanded a quite different ship from that used by the Norwegians. Major issues were the need to embark a large helicopter, the ability to operate in open-ocean sea states in the "off season" (that is, the Canadian winter months, when the Arctic is largely inaccessible), and the strong Coast Guard recommendation for conventional twin-shaft propulsion better suited to Canadian multi-year ice conditions than the rotatable Azipods fitted in *Svalbard*, which typically encountered only first-year ice. Additionally, the project was put "on hold" while the government introduced the framework for its National Shipbuilding Procurement Strategy that would determine which shipyard would be contracted to design and build the ships. In October 2011, it was decided that all combat warship construction would be performed by Irving Shipbuilding in Halifax, Nova Scotia, and that the AOPV included in this category would be prioritized over the new CSC destroyer-frigate replacement that had yet to be defined.

In the meantime, BMT Fleet Technology was contracted in 2008 to progress the preliminary design work. Although the company's sketches of the Canadian vessel bore superficial semblance to its Norwegian forebear, it was radically different in detail and capability. To begin, since the Norwegians (and the Danes in Greenland, for that matter) have no requirement to break multi-year ice for their shipping purposes, the Canadian AOPV hull had to be strengthened to navigate in such conditions as often encountered in the waters of the Canadian Arctic archipelago — indeed, although sometimes dismissed by critics as a "slush breaker," the AOPV is a true Polar Class 5 icebreaker. For that reason as well (as noted above), the AOPV is powered by four diesel generators producing power for two electric propulsion motors that drive fixed-pitch propellers — with the bow thruster, this set-up makes the vessel extremely manoeuvrable, which is important for operating in remote areas far from tug support. Then the open-ocean operating prerequisite necessitated other changes to the hull, such as slightly slimming it and adding retractable side stabilizers to make it a better sea-keeper in the wider range of conditions to be encountered in the Atlantic and Pacific Oceans, and for that matter, the Caribbean (which also required attention to internal environmental aspects such as air conditioning, along with heating). It has an enlarged and strengthened helicopter deck and hangar for operating the CH-148 Cyclone, albeit without a Beartrap-type recovery and traverse system. And it is fitted with a large operations room and stowage compartments to embark a range of emergency response teams and special operations forces. While "armed," the AOPV are not intended to engage in combat, although the remote-operated BAE Mk 38 25-mm Bushmaster high-velocity chain gun mounted on the fo'c'sle is deadly against close-range fast-manoeuvring surface craft (firing 180 rounds per minute, effective out to 2,500 m [8,200 ft]). The vessel embarks a variety of smaller boats, including a 12-metre (39-ft) landing craft and an 8.5-metre (27.5-ft) Multi-Role Rescue Boat that offers an over-the-horizon capability in support of rescue and tactical operations. It can also operate a range of unmanned aerial vehicles, and there is room for containerized payloads such as underwater survey equipment, as well as a vehicle bay for pickup trucks, all-terrain vehicles, and snowmobiles. A 20-tonne

Harry DeWolf (left) berthed near the museum ship *Haida* at the Naval Reserve division HMCS *Star* in Hamilton Harbour, November 16, 2023.

East Coast			West Coast		
Name	**Pennant**	**Commissioned**	**Name**	**Pennant**	**Commissioned**
Harry DeWolf	430	June 26, 2021	*Max Bernays*	432	May 3, 2024
Margaret Brooke	431	Oct 28, 2022	*Robert Hampton Gray*	435	[2025]
William Hall	433	May 16, 2024			
Frédérick Rolette	434	June 13, 2025			
Canadian Coast Guard					
Sermilik Glacier		[2027]	*Donjek Glacier*	[2027]	

crane is fitted to facilitate the loading and unloading of all this equipment.

In the year before the Conservatives lost office in 2015, in a departure from the previous practice of naming patrol vessels for birds and mammals, the government directed that the ships be named for Canadian naval heroes, which has proven popular nonetheless. The lead ship, *Harry DeWolf*, was launched on September 15, 2018, and after three years of extensive sea and weather trials was finally commissioned as an HMC Ship on June 26, 2021. Not unlike her predecessor, *Labrador*, almost immediately *Harry DeWolf* was dispatched on an ambitious operational deployment to demonstrate her potential. She sailed from Halifax on August 3 to participate in that year's Operation Nanook deployment to the eastern Arctic, having embarked for trialling a new antisubmarine underwater listening device called the Towed Reelable Active-Passive Sonar. Continuing west through the Northwest Passage and the Bering Strait, she docked briefly at Esquimalt on October 4, 2021, sailing again on October 24 to pass through the Panama Canal into the Caribbean Sea to engage in Operation Caribbe; she seized almost 3,000 kg (6,600 lbs) of cocaine in that anti-drug task. Having repeated *Labrador*'s 1954 feat of circumnavigating North America in a single season, HMCS *Harry DeWolf* returned triumphantly to Halifax on December 16, 2021.

Building upon that initiative, the second ship of the class, *Margaret Brooke*, departed Halifax on January 10, 2025, for another epic deployment. In the words of the Navy press release, she was "bound for the South American and Antarctic regions … [on a mission to] include the conduct of foreign diplomacy and Antarctic scientific research."[66] That four-month cruise saw her become the first Canadian warship to deploy to the southern polar continent; returning home through the Panama Canal to complete a circumnavigation of South America made for another feat not accomplished since the training voyages of the cruisers in the 1950s. To top it off, having participated in the fall 2024 Operation Nanook, this deployment enrolled *Margaret Brooke* in the very small group of warships to have crossed both the Arctic and Antarctic Circles within a twelve-month period.

The remainder of the class have begun to enter service with tentative coastal allocations as listed in the table above. Another two vessels — unarmed — have been contracted for delivery to the Canadian Coast Guard by 2026–27. There are no indications that the six in RCN service will repeat *Labrador*'s fate of being transferred to the Coast Guard to join them.

Margaret Brooke operating in Admiralty Inlet, Antarctica, during Operation Projection, March 2, 2025.

FURTHER READING

"Arctic and Offshore and Patrol Vessels," Naval Association of Canada, Naval Affairs Briefing Note #14, updated October 2024, navalassoc.ca/wp-content/uploads/2024/11/BN-AOPV.pdf.

"The Canadian Coast Guard and the RCN: Roles and Responsibilities," Naval Association of Canada, Naval Affairs Program Briefing Note #22, updated September 2022, navalassoc.ca/wp-content/uploads/2024/11/BN-CCG.pdf.

"Frontline Report: NSPS Projects Status and Future Direction," *FrontLine Defence* 12, no. 3 (2015–16).

Corey Gleason, "HMCS *Harry DeWolf* Transits the Arctic, 2021," in *Northwest Passages: Navigating the Canadian Arctic from* Gjøa *to* Harry DeWolf, eds. P. Whitney Lackenbauer and Adam Lajeunesse (University of Calgary, Centre for Military and Strategic Studies, 2025), 479–89.

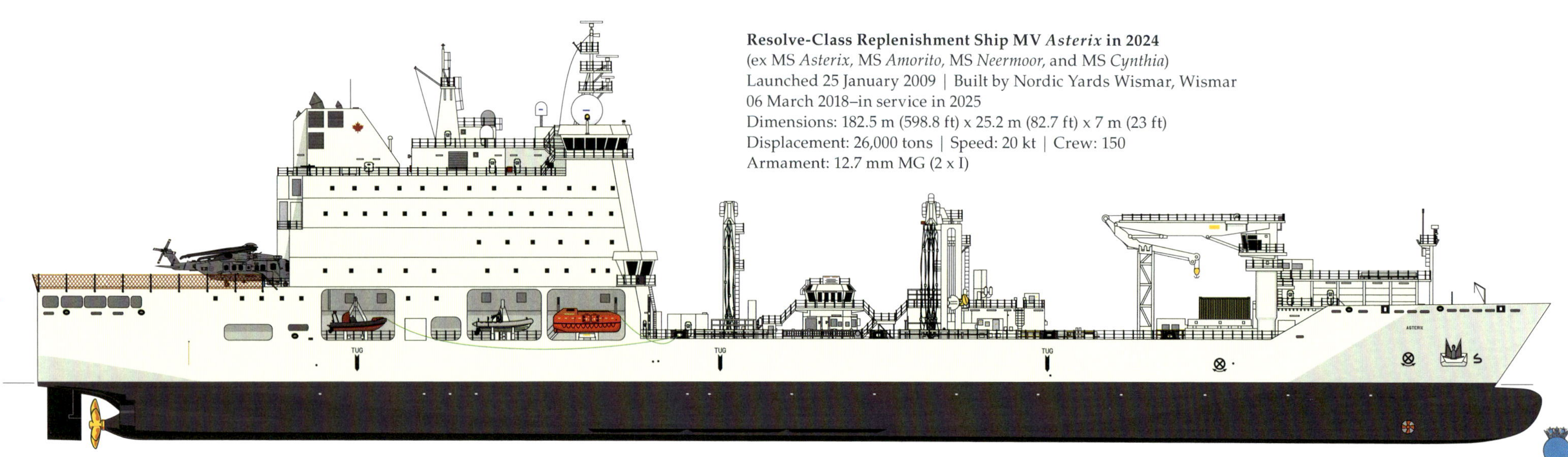

Resolve-Class Replenishment Ship MV *Asterix* in 2024
(ex MS *Asterix*, MS *Amorito*, MS *Neermoor*, and MS *Cynthia*)
Launched 25 January 2009 | Built by Nordic Yards Wismar, Wismar
06 March 2018–in service in 2025
Dimensions: 182.5 m (598.8 ft) x 25.2 m (82.7 ft) x 7 m (23 ft)
Displacement: 26,000 tons | Speed: 20 kt | Crew: 150
Armament: 12.7 mm MG (2 x I)

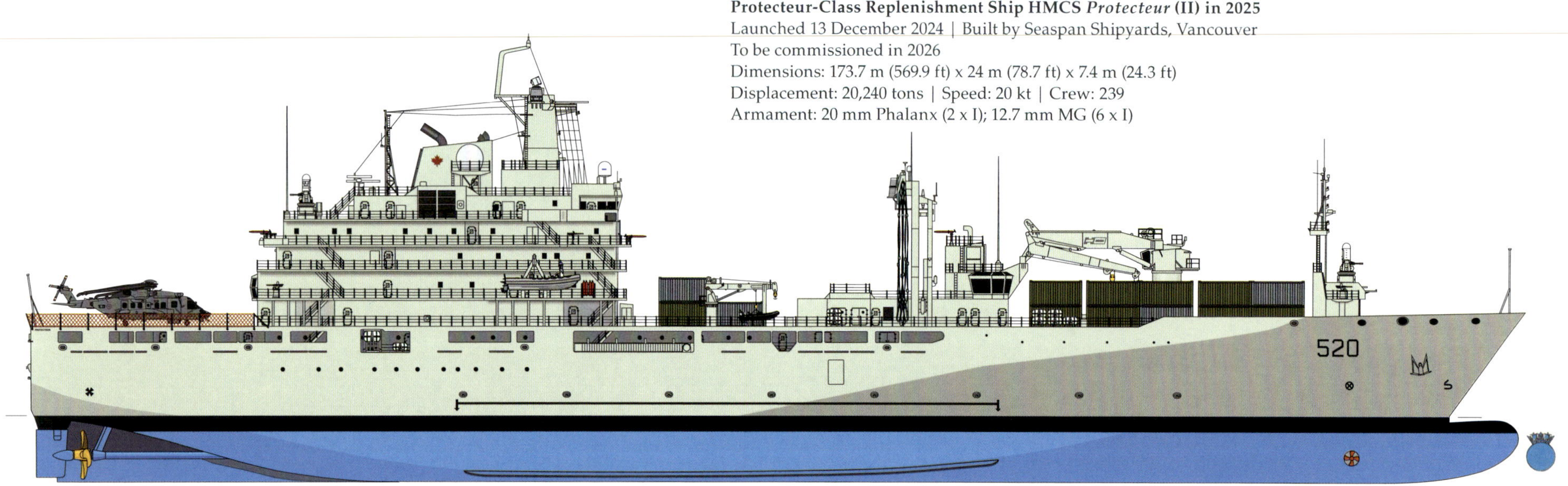

Protecteur-Class Replenishment Ship HMCS *Protecteur* (II) in 2025
Launched 13 December 2024 | Built by Seaspan Shipyards, Vancouver
To be commissioned in 2026
Dimensions: 173.7 m (569.9 ft) x 24 m (78.7 ft) x 7.4 m (24.3 ft)
Displacement: 20,240 tons | Speed: 20 kt | Crew: 239
Armament: 20 mm Phalanx (2 x I); 12.7 mm MG (6 x I)

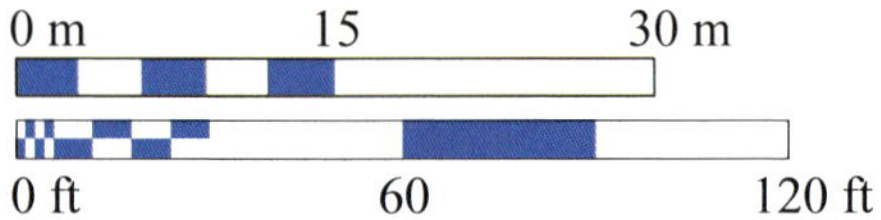

46

JOINT SUPPORT SHIPS: *ASTERIX* AND THE PROTECTEUR CLASS

The need for a replacement for the Navy's original "tankers" (see Chapter 35) was a major observation in the post-deployment assessments of the Navy's performance in the Gulf War of 1990–91. *Protecteur* (AOR 509) had executed her envisioned operational support role admirably but at the price of having to depart the wartime patrol area and make several unscheduled returns to port to rectify a worrying number of arising mechanical defects. Richard Greenwood, a retired rear admiral and former chief engineer of the Navy, writing an "Engineer's Outline of RCN History (1970–2014)," noted:

> A timely operational support ship (OSS) replacement for HMC Ships *Protecteur* and *Preserver* would have started planning in 1989, with contract definition commencing in 1992, contract let in 1994, and delivery between 1998 and 2002. As it was, the tortured history of this requirement is illustrative of requirements formulation as both the pivot and the Achilles heel of the ship design process.[67]

Admiral Greenwood then takes his readers through the alphabet-soup quest of the 1990s and early 2000s to define the AOR replacement project: the SMART ship (Strategic Multi-Role Aid and Replenishment Transport); the MRSV (Multi-Role Support Vessel); and the ALSC (Afloat Logistics Support Concept). Finally, in 2003 the

Frigate *Toronto* manoeuvring alongside *Asterix* during Navy acceptance trials in January 2018, with another frigate in the background, waiting to come alongside.

planning staffs settled upon "JSS" (Joint Support Ship) as the title for the project. Even then, it was only after Stephen Harper's Conservative government took office in 2006, aiming to renew the fleets for both the Navy and the Coast Guard, that the process began to move forward, with JSS becoming a main plank of the National Shipbuilding Procurement Strategy (later shortened by the Trudeau Liberals to simply "National Shipbuilding Strategy," or NSS). Finally, in June 2013, Vancouver's Seaspan Shipyard was identified under the NSS to build two ships as Military off the Shelf variants of the German Berlin-class replenishment ship. Initial construction, however, did not commence until 2018, with a formal contract signed only in 2020, and the first ship not expected to enter service until 2027.

In the meantime, the long-suffering tankers experienced the near-concurrent mechanical misfortunes that resulted in their being withdrawn in 2015. Facing a critical loss of its vital UNREP capability, the Navy investigated a variety of options that would bridge the gap until the new ships could be built. They quickly settled upon the short-term rental of the Chilean AOR *Almirante Montt* while a contract was negotiated with Chantier Davie Shipyard of Quebec to convert a commercial vessel for lease to the RCN as an "interim AOR." Under the rubric "Project Resolve," Davie engaged a group of recently retired naval officers with AOR expertise to seek out a ship that could be fitted with many of the capabilities present in both the legacy and future classes of AOR/JSS. They settled on the container ship M/V *Asterix*, originally built in Germany in 2010 as the *Cynthia* and having dimensions and tonnage very nearly identical to the former *Protecteur*. Taken in hand to commence the conversion in October 2015, *Asterix* was stripped down to the hull and her entire topsides were converted to be a state-of-the-art AOR, not dissimilar to the former Protecteur class, with four liquid refuelling stations, solid stores cargo and transfer, ammunition storage and transfer, aviation, medical, and support to shore-based operations if required.

The implementation of *Asterix* was not without controversy, owing to the high-profile criminal prosecution of the former commander of the RCN, Vice Admiral Mark Norman, who had initiated the investigation into leasing the interim AOR. Negotiation of the contract with Davie was occurring through the summer 2015 general election, and on gaining office, in November, the Trudeau Liberals attempted to cancel it (after work had commenced). Admiral Norman was accused of trying to undermine the new government's efforts by leaking sensitive information relating to the procurement of *Asterix*. Having been appointed vice chief of the defence staff in the meantime, in June 2016, he was relieved of that command in January 2017 and subsequently charged with breach of trust. Although the charges were eventually stayed in 2019, and Norman received an all-party apology in the House of Commons, the legal process tainted an otherwise successful program (and ended a promising career).

In the end, the Liberals had to give approval for the contracted project, the conversion progressed through 2016, and the vessel was relaunched in July 2017. Builder's trials were followed by those with the Navy early in 2018, and the *Asterix* was accepted by the RCN in Halifax on March 6, 2018, on time and within budget. The charter arrangement is that the ship is operated by Federal Fleet Services, which provides a civilian crew of thirty-six to drive it. It also delivers "hotel services" for up to 114 military personnel who comprise the embarked Naval Replenishment Unit that works the UNREP gear and performs other operational duties, such as communications. The ship immediately set out on a busy program, eventually arriving in Esquimalt in December 2018, in the meanwhile (according to statistics recorded by Federal Fleet Services) having had "zero downtime, 51,062 nautical miles [94,566 km] travelled, 20 million litres of fuel delivered in 132 supply operations to forty ships with twenty Allied nations, participated in Exercises RIMPAC [Rim of the Pacific] and Keen Sword (US), Kakadu (Australia) and KAEDEX (Japan), and supported naval patrols in Southeast Asia and off the Korean peninsula."[68]

Despite her controversial conception and entry into service, MV *Asterix* went on to be arguably one of the most reliable and capable vessels in the RCN of the early twenty-first century. Supporting RCN and allied deployments in the Atlantic and Pacific, the "interim AOR" has certainly fulfilled the terms of the charter arrangement. At the time of writing (spring 2025), with construction of the Protecteur class still under way, *Asterix* has been in service for a full eight years and will continue to support the RCN for at least another two years, until the new *Protecteur* is fully operational.

The construction of the two modified Berlin-class ships contracted with Seaspan finally progressed apace. Even before first steel was cut, in 2013, the Conservatives initially named them to mark the bicentennial of the War of 1812 battles Châteauguay and Queenston Heights. In 2017, the Liberals changed those to perpetuate the immediate AOR forebears (which had been scrapped in the meanwhile, making the names once again available to be used). The naming ceremony for the first of the new class, *Protecteur* (second of name), was held on December 13, 2024. She is to be delivered for fitting out and trials through 2025 to 2026, commissioning in 2027, with her sister *Preserver* (third of name) to be completed in that year and entering service soon after. This new Protecteur class is 21,600 tons displacement (3,000 tons less than the original class and more than 4,500 tons smaller than *Asterix*). They will have only two stations (one on each side), which can be used for either liquid refuelling or solid stores heavy jackstay transfer (that is, not both on one side at a time). But that sacrifice is made to provide deck space for up to 60 TEU (20-ft equivalent units) of containerized cargo, not available in the previous class. Several of these containers will hold sections for assembly of a pair of large "sea-to-shore connectors" (self-propelled barges) for use where adequate port facilities might not exist. The helicopter capacity will see hangar space and maintenance facilities for two CH-148 Cyclone helicopters (which are much larger than the previous Sea Kings). Critically, the new vessels are double hulled to meet updated environmental stewardship requirements. Unlike *Asterix*, they are crewed by a full naval complement and armed with two CIWSs for self-defence in high-threat environments.

FURTHER READING

Douglas Campbell, *The Canadianization of the Joint Support Ship: From Mature Design to a Unique Canadian Solution* (Canadian Global Affairs Institute, March 2021), d3n8a8pro7vhmx.cloudfront.net/cdfai/pages/4648/attachments/original/1616098421/The_Canadianization_of_the_Joint_Support_Ship_From_Mature_Design_to_a_Unique_Canadian_Solution.pdf?1616098421.

"Frontline Report: NSPS Projects Status and Future Direction," *FrontLine Defence* 12, no. 3 (2015–16).

Richard W. Greenwood, "An Engineer's Outline of Canadian Naval History, Part 3 (1970–2014)," *The Northern Mariner/Le marin du nord* 24, nos. 3 and 4 (Summer & Autumn 2014): 273–95, tnm.journals.yorku.ca/index.php/default/article/view/255/237.

Dave Perry, "A Narrative History of the NSS from Conception to the CSC RFP," Research Paper, Naval Association of Canada (March 2021), navalassoc.ca/wp-content/uploads/2021/05/NSS-History-NAC-Perry.pdf.

"Project Resolve," Wikimedia Foundation, last modified September 26, 2023, 22:46 (UTC), en.wikipedia.org/wiki/Project_Resolve.

PART 2
SHIPBORNE AIRCRAFT

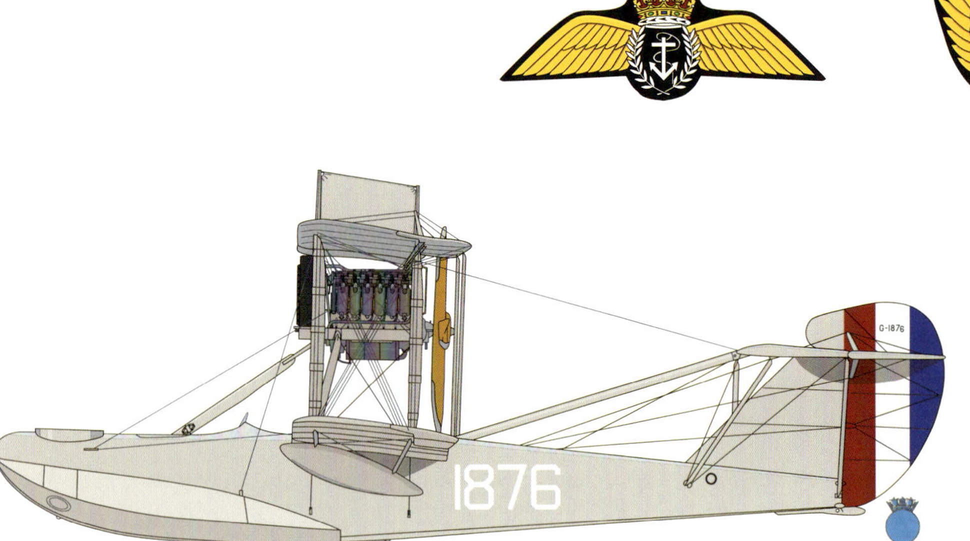

Curtiss HS-2L
2,917 kg | 133 km/h
11.9 m (39 ft) x 22.6 m (74.2 ft) x 4.4 m (14.4 ft)
Dartmouth Naval Air Station, 1919

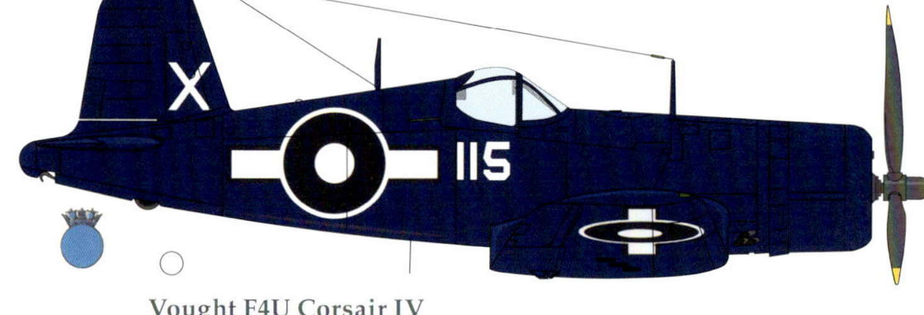

Vought F4U Corsair IV
4,238 kg | 717 km/h
10.3 m (33.8 ft) x 12.5 m (41 ft) x 4.5 m (14.8 ft)
1841 NSA, HMS *Formidable*, August 1945

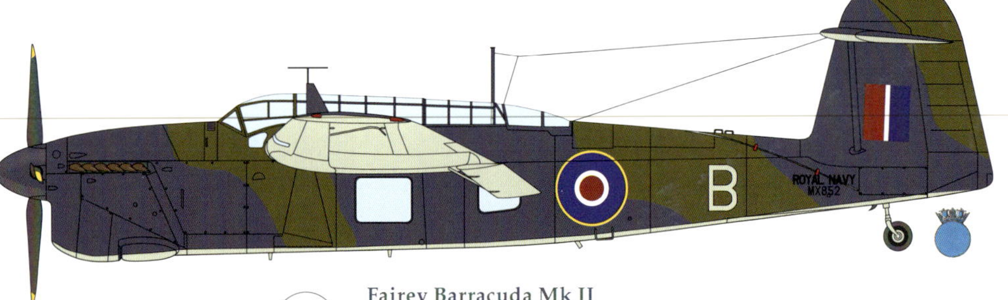

Fairey Barracuda Mk II
4,241 kg | 367 km/h
12.1 m (39.8 ft) x 14.99 m (49.2 ft) x 4.6 m (15.1 ft)
825 Squadron, RNAS Rattray Head, U.K., August 1945

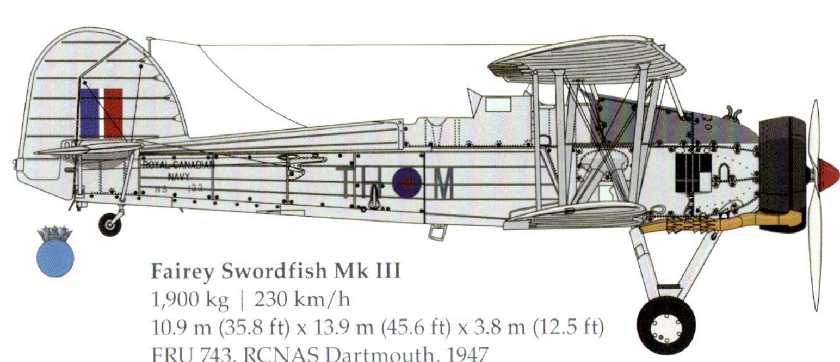

Fairey Swordfish Mk III
1,900 kg | 230 km/h
10.9 m (35.8 ft) x 13.9 m (45.6 ft) x 3.8 m (12.5 ft)
FRU 743, RCNAS Dartmouth, 1947

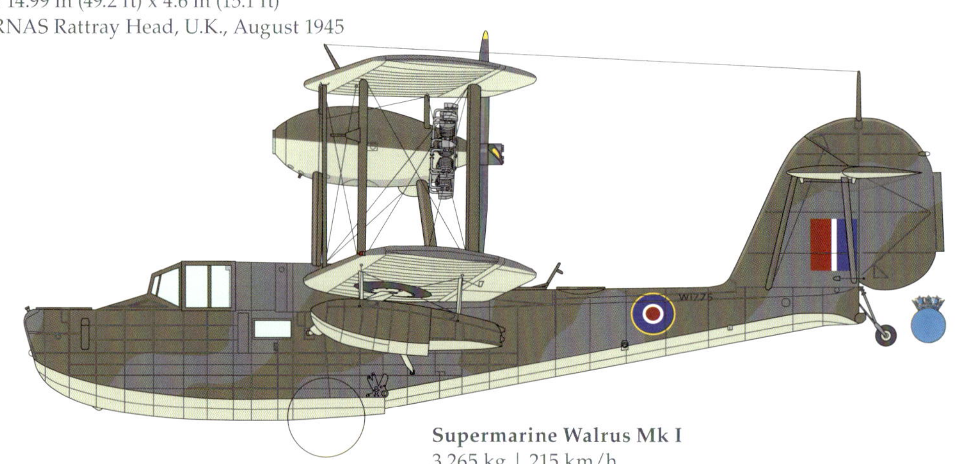

Supermarine Walrus Mk I
3,265 kg | 215 km/h
11.5 m (37.7 ft) x 14 m (45.9 ft) x 4.6 m (15.1 ft)
FRU 743, RCNAS Dartmouth, 1947

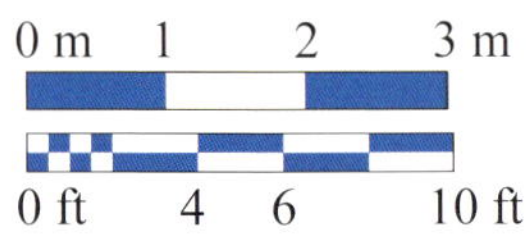

48 ORIGINS: THE RCN AIR BRANCH, SHORE ESTABLISHMENTS, AND MISCELLANEOUS AIRCRAFT

Grand, year-long celebrations marked the centennials in 2010 of the founding of the RCN and, in 2024, of the RCAF. In contrast, the centenary of the establishment of the Royal Canadian Naval Air Service (RCNAS) — Canada's first permanent air force — passed in 2018 practically unremarked, aside from a few social media posts by "today in naval history" aficionados and a day-long "Shearwater 100" historical workshop on August 1 in a small corner of the base (see a report on the proceedings by John Orr in Further Reading). The event attracting greater attention that day was a ceremony marking the fifty-fifth anniversary of the arrival of the first CHSS-2/CH-124 Sea King helicopters. That distinct understatement should probably not be unexpected, as the fledgling RCNAS did not long survive the Armistice that abruptly ended the Great War. It was, however, a benchmark first step on the fitful journey toward the formation of the RCN's Air Branch, which would serve the Navy through the two decades following the (also unexpected) end of the Second World War until the integration and unification of the CAF in the mid-1960s. The background to the RCN Air Branch is not generally well understood, even though it is fundamental to appreciating the types of aircraft acquired and operated by the Navy, and so a summary is presented here.

Aviation was in its infancy and its applications in the maritime domain were practically unknown when war broke out in the summer of 1914. As noted by RN official historian Captain S.W. Roskill (see Further Reading), the Admiralty struggled to define a purely "naval" role for aviation but nonetheless unilaterally established the Royal Naval Air Service (RNAS) in April 1915. In addition to rudimentary shore-based maritime patrol and scouting operations in support of the fleet, the RNAS was tasked with land-based fighter operations on the Continent, as well as the air defence of Great Britain, which could be approached only across water.

In 1915, Admiral Kingsmill authorized recruiting in Canada for service overseas in the RNAS as a logical contribution to the expanding naval war effort. In his encyclopedic *Collishaw & Company* (see Further Reading), Allan Snowie chronicles the stories of the 943 Canadians who answered the call. There was no thought at first that they might return for a future Canadian naval air service, but any potential for that was precluded when the RNAS was combined with the Royal Flying Corps to create the Royal Air Force (RAF) on April 1, 1918. Their ranks, however, included several names familiar as future RCAF chiefs of the air staff in the Second World War and the postwar period: Air Marshals L.S. Breadner, Robert Leckie, and Wilf Curtis; another — Raymond Collishaw — would remain in the RAF until retiring as an air vice marshal toward the end of the Second World War. Their adopted vision of air power would colour the early Cold War debate over control of fixed-wing maritime aviation (to be discussed in Chapter 55).

The first suggestion that a Canadian naval air service should be established arose from the same circumstances that led to building the Battle class and the other trawlers and drifters discussed in Chapter 6: namely, an early-1917 assessment that a major German U-boat campaign could hit North American waters in the summer. The U-boats failed to materialize at that time, fortunately, as neither the British nor the Americans (newly entered into the war in April 1917) were able to provide the necessary aviation assistance, and the Canadian government determined it would be too costly to undertake independently. But a renewed and more credible U-boat threat the next year did spur the USN to engage in a scheme to protect the convoys that would be bound for Europe in the summer of 1918, loaded with troops and equipment of the American Expeditionary Forces.

In late April 1918, Captain Walter Hose, as the then-captain of patrols on the Atlantic Coast, met in Washington with American and British naval officers to work out plans to set up air stations at Halifax (Dartmouth), Sydney, and Cape Sable in Nova Scotia, and Cape Race in Newfoundland, from which would be based dirigibles, seaplanes, and kite-balloons to be supplied and operated by the USN until the Canadians were ready to take over. On May 3, 1918, just a month after the demise of the British naval air service, the Canadian Cabinet approved these various measures to begin the organization of a Canadian naval air arm, and the RCNAS was formally established by Order in Council

PC 2154, dated September 5, 1918. The RN had already loaned a former RNAS officer, now Lieutenant Colonel John Tulloch Cull, RAF, to be appointed as the director of the RCNAS to oversee the administrative effort.

Then, in early August, the first USN airmen began to arrive to construct a seaplane base at Baker Point, near Eastern Passage (Dartmouth, Nova Scotia), and to assemble their crated aircraft. Lieutenant Richard E. Byrd of the USN Reserve Flying Corps — later famous as a polar explorer — was appointed commanding officer of U.S. Naval Air Station Halifax and hoisted "Old Glory" on August 19, 1918. A few days later, on August 25, one of his Curtiss HS-2L flying boats made two flights "over a startled Halifax."[69] Within the month, on September 21, the air station at North Sydney also reported ready for operations.

Initially, only four aircraft were assigned to each of Dartmouth and North Sydney. Given the limitations that the HS-2L could remain airborne for only four hours while cruising at 60 knots, patrols averaged one flight per day from each location, aiming to escort outward-bound convoys 65 miles (105 km) to sea and meeting inward-bound ones some 80 miles (130 km) out. This meant the aircraft were not a factor in countering the alarming German attacks on the Grand Banks fishing fleets that summer, although they did assist in deterring attacks on convoys, which did not suffer any losses in Canadian waters (rerouting many through the Strait of Belle Isle, north of Newfoundland, was also a factor).

Meanwhile, recruiting and training to the target strength of one thousand personnel for the RCNAS proceeded apace, giving confidence in it being a fully fledged fighting force by spring 1919. The signing of the Armistice, however, put a halt to all plans in progress, and the RCNAS was "discontinued" on December 5, 1918 — Conservative Minister of the Naval Service C.C. Ballantyne purposely used that word in a letter to the deputy minister on that date: "I wish it understood that the RCNAS is not abolished, and the action that is now being taken is only until such time as the government decides on the details and policy of a permanent Air Service."[70] When the USN personnel departed at the end of November, they left behind their dozen HS-2Ls and twenty-six spare Liberty engines. These were initially taken over by the Canadian Air Board, a short-lived (1919–22) department of the Dominion government, charged with supervising all matters connected to aeronautics and forerunner to the RCAF.

The Air Board undertook the acquisition of three more sets of HS-2Ls, amounting to twenty-three additional aircraft. None of the thirty-five survived past 1928, most being turned over to civil or provincial use in a multitude of roles. The most famous of these, dubbed *La Vigilance*, became Canada's first "bush plane" before subsequently crashing in a northern Ontario lake in September 1922 while operated by Laurentide Air Service. It was eventually salvaged in the late 1960s and used as the basis for a reconstruction that is now displayed at the Canada Aviation and Space Museum in Ottawa (see Leslie Hutchison in Further Reading).

A year after the RCNAS was discontinued, Admiral Jellicoe's report (discussed in Chapter 7) recommended

RN FAA Corsairs (several of them flown by Canadians) and Avengers (with a lonely Walrus reconnaissance aircraft) ranged on the deck of the fleet carrier HMS *Formidable* with the British Pacific Fleet, summer 1945.

that a notional Canadian naval force should contemplate manning an aircraft carrier along with battle cruisers and other fleet units. In response, the Canadian naval staff drafted Occasional Paper Number 24, dated January 26, 1920, and titled "Remarks on a Canadian Naval Air Force." But none of that came to pass. The RCN was severely reduced after the Washington Naval Disarmament Treaty of 1922, and the fate of any future naval air development was settled by the establishment in 1924 of the RCAF and the allocation of all Dominion air assets to its control, effectively changing the status of the RCNAS from "discontinued" to "abolished." Stuart Soward notes, "Considerable interest was generated in Canadian naval circles in 1934 by the design of a small, high-speed aircraft carrier with a catapult launch system and a complement of seven seaplanes," but Depression budget constraints again put an end to "such progressive thinking in aviation matters."[71]

Instead, it would be the pressures to provide better convoy protection in the Second World War Battle of the Atlantic that would stimulate the next drive for Canadian naval aviation. An August 1943 scheme proposed by Captains Lay and DeWolf led to RCN manning of the British CVEs HM Ships *Nabob* and *Puncher*, intended to complement Canadian Escort Groups in the "air gap" of the central North Atlantic (see Chapter 21). But the naval staff saw that as only the first step toward the formation of a Canadian naval air service modelled upon the RN FAA. A Directorate of Naval Air Division was established in April 1944, and the acquisition of the CVLs for service in the war against Japan progressed through that year (as discussed in Chapter 24). But whereas the escort carriers had RN FAA air squadrons embarked, the Canadian light fleets were envisioned to carry RCN air squadrons.

The manning for these future squadrons accordingly proceeded apace. A small number of RCNVR officers serving in the British fleet had volunteered for flying duty in the FAA; by August 1943, these numbered twenty-nine (twenty-six pilots and three observers). Among them was a Sub-Lieutenant Robert Hampton Gray, who would famously earn a posthumous Victoria Cross flying a Corsair fighter-bomber off the British fleet carrier HMS *Formidable* (former official naval historian Michael Whitby surveys the FAA experience in his three-part "Navy Blue Fighter Pilot" series listed in Further Reading).

Another nineteen officers and twenty-nine ratings were known to have volunteered directly into the FAA as "RNVR (A)," and arrangements were made with the Admiralty in August 1943 for these to transfer to the RCN when required. At the same time, the RN also agreed to undertake training of an additional thirty pilots and twenty-five observers for the RCN, and "an unspecified number of telegraphist air gunners and air maintenance artificers."[72]

By the spring of 1945, the RCN began to form the four squadrons to be embarked in its CVLs, HMC Ships *Warrior* and *Magnificent* — one fighter and one torpedo-bomber-reconnaissance (TBR) squadron for each of them — with the commissioning of ships and associated squadrons anticipated in September and November 1945, respectively. For a variety of reasons, not nearly enough Canadian naval aircrew had been trained, so the numbers were brought up to strength with the influx of 550 ex-RCAF flyers who had volunteered for Pacific service and now (again for complicated reasons not necessary here) were transferred through the RNVR(A) to the RCN. This allowed the formation of 803 Fighter Squadron as the first RCN air unit to be achieved on June 15, 1945, and 825 TBR Squadron soon after, on July 1. The second TBR unit, 826 Squadron, was activated on August 15, and finally, 883 Fighter Squadron formed on September 18, 1945 (it should be noted that initially, all these were formed as part of the RN FAA but would be transferred into the RCN). The aircraft flown by these squadrons will be discussed in the next two chapters, and a full listing of RCN air squadrons is in Appendix C.

While that activity was reaching its apex, however, there came the sudden collapse of Japan with VJ-Day on August 15 and the formal surrender on September 2, and the Canadian government consequently decided in October to reduce the armed services to interim postwar force levels. The commissioning of *Warrior* was slowed until January 1946, and that of *Magnificent*, as the second carrier, was deferred indefinitely. Demobilization of "hostilities-only" volunteers concurrently led to manning issues for the naval air squadrons, leading to the disbanding of 826 and 883 in February 1946. As Stuart Soward again recounts, "a group of fifty ex-RCAF pilots and twenty ex-RNFAA aircrew became the core expertise in the RCNAS [*sic*]"[73] (himself being one of these latter number). The future could not have looked bright, other than when institutional recognition was finally achieved on December 19, 1945, with Cabinet approving the formation of a naval air component in cooperation with the RCAF (the terminology "Air Branch" would appear later in 1946; notably, neither of the terms "Fleet Air Arm" nor "Naval Air Service" are applicable in the postwar RCN experience). Authorized at approximately 11 percent of the Navy's peacetime strength, that translated to start into some 1,120 officers and ratings to crew the squadrons, the air complement of the carrier, any shore establishments, and an air staff at Naval Service Headquarters — a very thin margin on which to maintain the orderly operation of an ostensibly vital component. But as naval recruiting ceilings were raised through the 1950s, the Air Branch accordingly increased in size, and at its height by the time of unification had nearly doubled, to just under 2,200 all ranks.

Coincident with the commissioning of *Warrior* in Belfast on January 26, 1946, 803 and 825 Squadrons were also commissioned into the RCN, and an RCN roundel for display on the aircraft was authorized as of that date (a stylized red sugar maple leaf, slightly different from the red silver maple leaf of the RCAF, on a white disk surrounded by a blue ring). When the carrier arrived in Halifax Harbour on March 31, 1946, the squadron aircraft

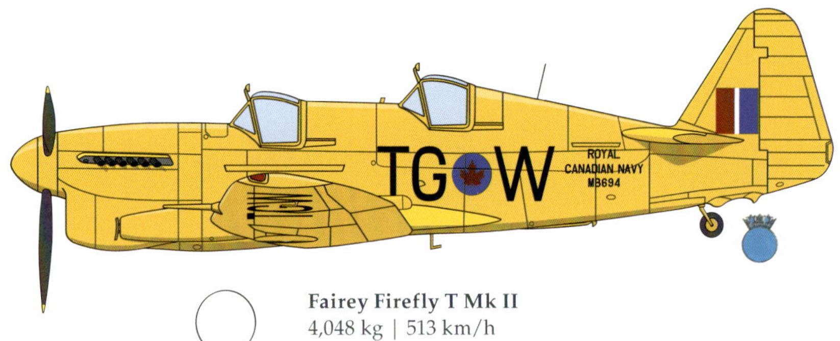

Fairey Firefly T Mk II
4,048 kg | 513 km/h
11.4 m (37.4 ft) x 13.6 m (44.6 ft) x 3.8 m (12.5 ft)
FRU 743, HMCS *Shearwater*, 1950

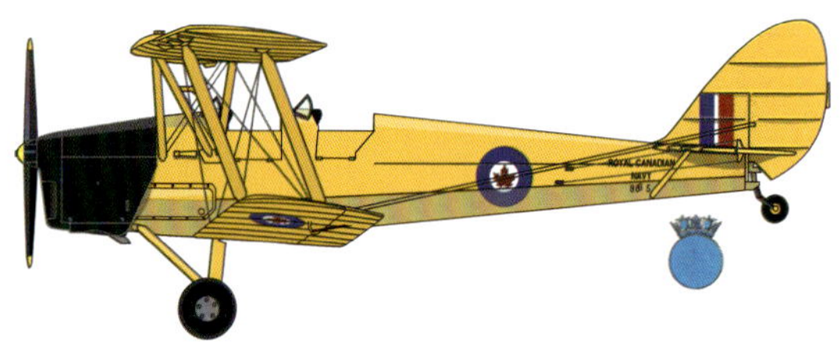

De Havilland Tiger Moth DH.82C
533 kg | 175 km/h
7.3 m (24 ft) x 8.9 m (29.2 ft) x 2.7 m (8.9 ft)
VT 40, HMCS *Shearwater*, 1956

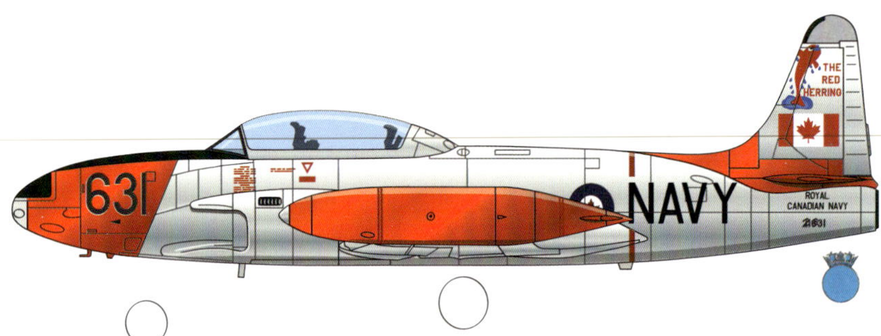

Lockheed/Canadair T-33 Silver Star
3,830 kg | 920 km/h
11.5 m (37.7 ft) x 12.9 m (42.3 ft) x 3.6 m (11.8 ft)
VU 32, HMCS *Shearwater*, 1966

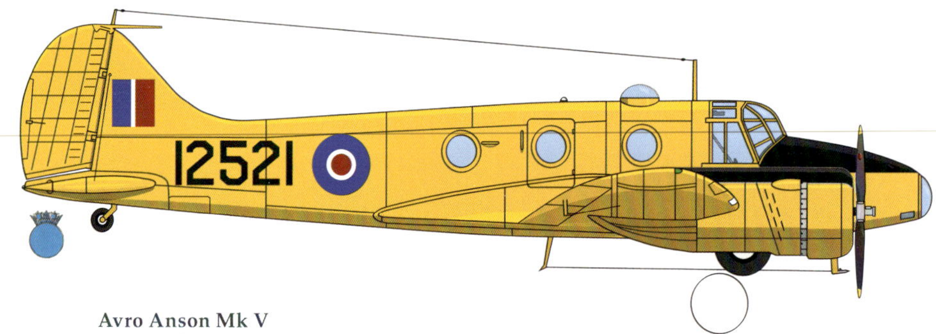

Avro Anson Mk V
2,438 kg | 302 km/h
12.9 m (42.3 ft) x 17.4 m (57.1 ft) x 4 m (13.1 ft)
FRU 743, HMCS *Shearwater*, 1951

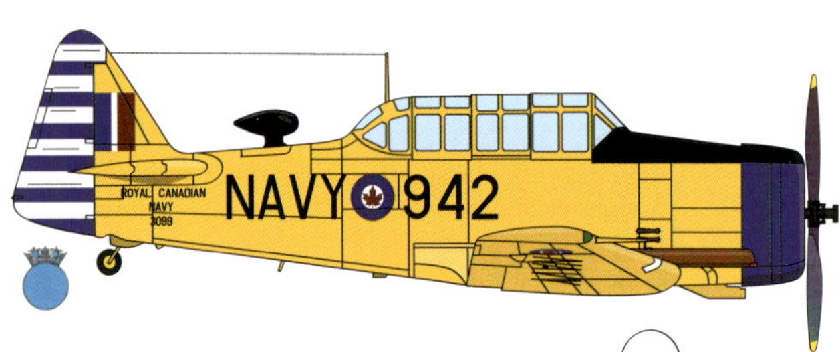

North American Harvard Mk 2A
1,885 kg | 290 km/h
8.8 m (28.9 ft) x 12.8 m (42 ft) x 3.5 m (11.5 ft)
VC 924, HMCS *Tecumseh*, 1958

Beechcraft Expeditor 3NM
2,800 kg | 370 km/h
10.4 m (34.1 ft) x 14.5 m (47.6 ft) x 2.9 m (9.5 ft)
VC 920, HMCS *York*, 1960

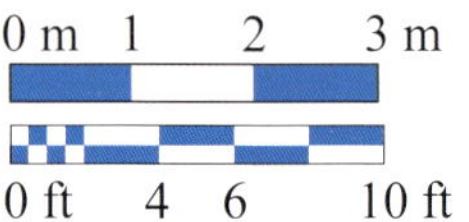

flew off for their new base at the Naval Air Section of RCAF Station Dartmouth. In recognition that the Air Branch was too small to fully support itself, a joint RCN/RCAF committee had been struck to examine common postwar requirements, the thrust being that other than special maintenance needs for the unique types of aircraft required to fly off carriers, the Air Force would provide all administrative, basic training, and logistical support. This was not always a happy arrangement, and as the Air Force (facing its own postwar retrenchment issues) reduced its strength in Dartmouth to consolidate in RCAF Station Greenwood in the Annapolis Valley, the naval air squadrons were soon the majority occupants, especially after 883 and 826 were reformed in 1947. Finally, the decision was taken to transfer control of the facility to the RCN, and on December 1, 1948, the Navy's first airfield — including the Baker Point site where the RCNAS was to have formed — was commissioned as HMCS *Shearwater*. The name was chosen as one of a "seabird" previously in use by the RCN (serving as the submarine depot ship from 1915 to 1919).

The need for a Canadian naval air shore establishment on the West Coast arose with the winter deployment of *Warrior* in early 1947. Once again, the RCN was able to turn to the RCAF. In October 1939, the Air Force had established an aerodrome at Patricia Bay, north of Victoria, where the sheltered waters of the Saanich Inlet next to adjacent flat land allowed for the set-up of a combined seaplane–landplane base relatively close to the dockyard at Esquimalt. It was a fairly busy site during the war, divided into three sections: the West Camp, maintained as an RCAF station; the East Camp for an RAF unit (No. 32 Operational Training Unit); and an RCAF Seaplane Base. Following the war, the seaplane base fell into disuse, and other than the temporary support to *Warrior*'s aircraft flying out from it, so did the land airfield as the RCAF consolidated up-island at Comox. In May 1948, control of the airfield was passed to the Department of Transport, which in 1950 redesignated the former East Camp as Victoria International Airport. When VU 33 was formed on November 1, 1954, as a lodger unit of HMCS *Naden* to support ship gunnery practices and radar calibration, the RCN refurbished the West Camp to house that squadron, along with the VC 922 Naval Air Reserve Composite Squadron tendered to *Malahat*. The "military side of Pat

A pair of VU 33 T-33 Silver Stars on the ramp at Patricia Bay, c. 1963. In the background, far left, the tails of a pair of CS2F Trackers are just visible behind the nose of an RCAF CC-106 Yukon passenger aircraft. Note the variation of the maple leaf in the roundels of the T-33s and differing tail "flag" insignia amongst all the aircraft.

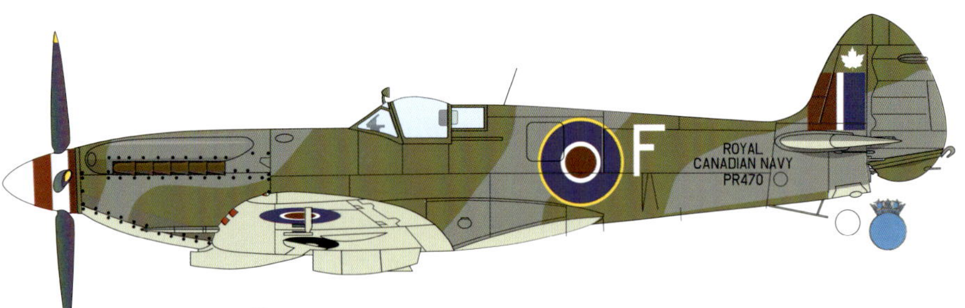

Supermarine Seafire Mk XV with Tail Hook
2,267 kg | 594 km/h
9.8 m (32.2 ft) x 11.2 m (36.8 ft) x 3.3 m (10.8 ft)
803 Squadron, HMCS *Warrior*, 1946

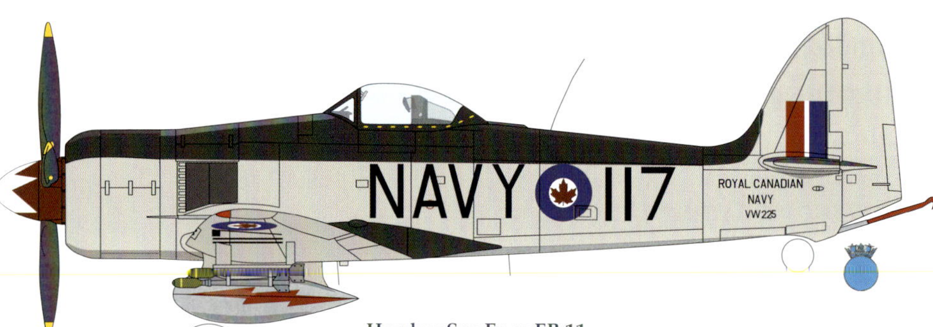

Hawker Sea Fury FB 11
4,190 kg | 740 km/h
10.4 m (34.1 ft) x 11.7 m (38.4 ft) x 5 m (16.4 ft)
VF 870, HMCS *Magnificent*, 1953

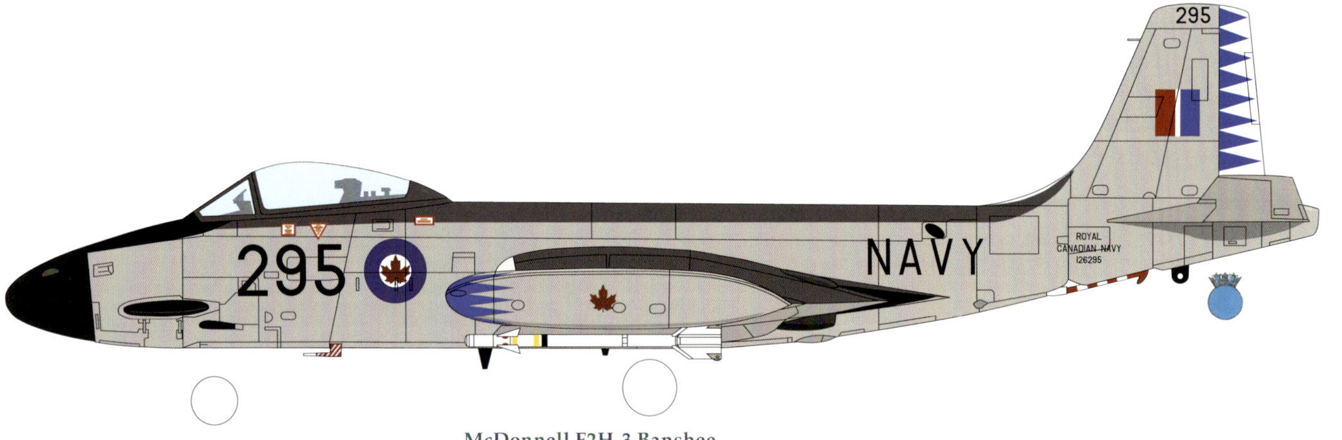

McDonnell F2H-3 Banshee
5,980 kg | 933 km/h
14.7 m (48.2 ft) x 13.7 m (44.9 ft) x 4.4 m (14.4 ft)
VF 870, HMCS *Bonaventure*, 1960

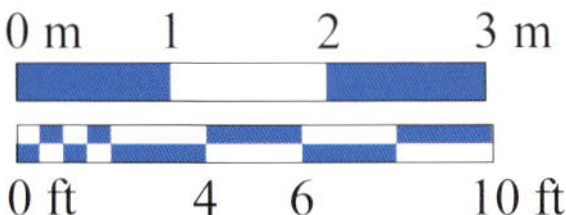

NAVAL FIGHTERS: THE SEAFIRE, SEA FURY, AND BANSHEE

In the summer of 1945, planning for employment of the Canadian aircraft carriers *Warrior* and *Magnificent* as elements of the BPF — to assist in clearing the seas for the climactic Allied invasion of the Japanese home islands — dictated that the aircraft they would embark fall into two broad categories: fighters for air defence of the fleet and escorting other aircraft and TBR types for strikes against shipping and targets ashore. The specific makes within those categories were determined through a variety of interrelated factors comprising the capabilities and limitations of both the ships and the aircraft. Basically, these came down to solving the following calculation: "How many aircraft could be launched from the limited space available?"

The primary consideration was the length of carrier deck. The next was the forward speed the ship could generate when turned into the wind, then combined with the acceleration thrust of the aircraft to achieve takeoff speed within the deck space. At the time, aircraft takeoff speeds were low enough that most carrier launches — even from British light fleets and escort carriers — were "free deck": Although hydro-pneumatic catapults were fitted, they were more cumbersome than the later steam catapult and "used under special but infrequent conditions."[74] The dimensions of the aircraft determined how many could be carried, stowed in the hangar below with wings folded, and ranged as well on unused areas of the flight deck. Most critical was the all-up weight of the aircraft, which in circular fashion affected not only the rate of takeoff acceleration but was also a limiting factor in respect of the load stress that the flight and hangar decks could withstand. Aircraft built to bear the stresses of rapid acceleration and high-impact, sudden deceleration of arrested landings tended to be heavier than their land-based counterparts, and high-performance fighter aircraft could achieve takeoff acceleration in a shorter distance.

With all that in mind, in the summer of 1945, the selection open to the RCN among Allied aircraft built for the unique circumstances of carrier operations proved to be rather limited. With no domestic aircraft design capacity, Canada could turn only to Britan and the United States. American-built aircraft, however, were effectively unavailable owing to the exclusions of Lend-Lease (of which Canada was not a part). With respect to fighter aircraft options, that precluded the most capable type then in operation: the Chance-Vought Corsair Mark IV familiar to Canadian airmen, such as Robert Hampton Gray, flying them from the large British fleet carriers. By the process of elimination, for the Canadian CVLs, that left only the one modern British type then in service — the Supermarine Seafire Mk XV.

The Seafire was not a natural shipboard aircraft. It was a modification of the land-based veteran Spitfire of the Battle of Britain, and by the summer of 1945, the basic design was a decade old, although it had been improved through progressive "marks" to incorporate new technologies as they became available through the war. The notion of adapting a navalized version of the Spitfire first occurred in 1938, in recognition of the poor performance of the existing interwar FAA fighters, such as the biplane Gloster Sea Gladiator (another adaptation of a land-based design) and the Blackburn Skua (at least a monoplane designed for shipboard use, but not at all nimble, and more effective as a dive-bomber). In addition to the Seafire's exceptional aerial performance, a main advantage in adapting it was its low weight; distinct disadvantages were its rather limited range and its closely paired, outward-retracting landing gear, which made it quite unstable in shipboard operations. The first Seafire Mk Ib (based on the Spitfire Mk Vc) weighed in at 7,100 lbs (3,220 kg) loaded* and entered general service from late 1941. It and succeeding variants saw action in British carriers throughout the European theatres, but the FAA's decided preference was for more rugged American models obtained through Lend-Lease, like the Grumman Martlet (7,420 lbs/3,360 kg), Wildcat (7,050 lbs/3,200 kg), and Hellcat (15,415 lbs/6,990 kg), culminating with the Corsair (12,100 lbs/5,490 kg). The latter two, however, were too heavy for the decks of the British CVLs introduced from late 1944, therefore focusing interest on equipping the CVL with Seafire variants — and thus again narrowing the option for the Canadian carriers.

* For consistency and the purposes of argument, the text refers to fully loaded weight at takeoff, whereas the profile drawings give the weights empty. The table in Appendix B provides both for select aircraft (all ship-borne and shore-based patrol types).

The Seafire Mk XV (7,950 lbs/3,600 kg) was a naval version of the Rolls-Royce Griffon-powered Spitfire Mk VII. Armed with two 20-mm cannon and four .303-inch machine guns, it promised to be a match for the dwindling Japanese fighter force and indeed was already enjoying success in action embarked in the CVLs of the BPF. When the two RN FAA squadrons identified for transfer to the RCN and embarkation in the Canadian CVLs began forming in Scotland in the summer of 1945, 803 Squadron (destined for *Warrior*) was equipped with twelve of the type, and 883 Squadron (*Magnificent*) with sixteen. The end of the war led to deferral of the commissioning of *Magnificent* and her air squadrons, so when *Warrior* commissioned in January 1946 and sailed for Halifax in March, she embarked a load of thirty-two Seafires, but only 803 Squadron as a formed fighter unit (along with a TBR squadron, discussed in Chapter 50). Three other aircraft arrived by separate means, making a total of thirty-five eventually taken on in RCN inventory. The Seafires did not deploy in the carrier for her winter 1947 cruise to the West Coast owing to a supercharger problem that grounded the fighter fleet until April 1947. When 883 Squadron reformed in May, it assumed Seafire operations from 803 so the latter could begin conversion to the next-generation fighter (meaning the RCN only ever had one Seafire-equipped squadron in commission at a time). By the end of 1948, all Seafires had been withdrawn from front-line Canadian service. Although *Warrior* had served in the RCN on loan from the British and had to be returned in exchange for her successor, the Seafires had been provided at no cost in partial settlement of British war debts to Canada and therefore had no such requirement for return. A few were kept on for static training purposes, but all were struck off strength by 1954. Only one known Canadian example remains, at the Naval Museum of Alberta in Calgary.

The deferred acquisition of *Magnificent* until 1948 as the replacement carrier (discussed in Chapter 24) allowed for her to be improved from the original Colossus-class configuration to that of the Majestic class, primarily to enable the operation of heavier aircraft. By that time also, the British had finally enjoyed the entry into service of a respectably high-performance homegrown naval fighter design. The Hawker Sea Fury was in development at war's end, the prototype having flown on February 21, 1945. It was also an adaptation of a land-based design, but while the RAF cancelled its orders at the end of the war, the RN continued with the seagoing version on the basis that it promised to be a significant leap in performance over the Seafire. And indeed it was. Weighing 11,820 lbs (5,360 kg) fully loaded and powered by a Centaurus XVIII radial engine driving a five-bladed propeller, it also compared favourably with its postwar American contemporary, the Grumman Bearcat (13,460 lbs/6,100 kg), as the apex of piston-engine fighter design, and the two types are often still seen competing in civilian air races. That power-to-weight ratio provided remarkable takeoff thrust, and their widespread landing gear was much better suited for carrier operations.

The Bearcat, however, was being reserved for service in the USN and not yet available for foreign sales, although Patrick Martin reports the Americans were

A flight of Sea Fury FB.11, each armed with a dozen 3-inch rockets for "air-to-mud" training at RCAF Station Rivers, Manitoba.

willing to sell to the Canadians the surplus Hellcats that the Bearcat was replacing, "at a fraction of the price" of the Sea Fury.[75] But the RCN was impressed that the latter was a much better aircraft than the aging Hellcat, and seemingly also that the British were willing to provide the Canadians their first batch straight from the initial production lots. As such, when 803 Squadron arrived in Belfast in the fall of 1947 for conversion training, they were presented with thirteen of the F.10 version, making the Canadians "the first operational squadron anywhere to be equipped with Sea Furies."[76] By the time the squadron sailed for Canada in *Magnificent* on May 25, 1948, these had been replaced with the slightly better FB.11 version, with a total of twenty-seven of the type embarked. After their arrival in Dartmouth, Nova Scotia, 883 Squadron also completed its conversion to the type by November 1948.

Over the coming years, the RCN purchased seventy-four Sea Fury FB.11 in six batches, the deliveries coordinated with returns of *Magnificent* to European waters. The last batch of nine was taken on strength on November 5, 1953, in Glasgow after the conclusion of the NATO Exercise Mariner. That large total number was driven in part by the high attrition rate of the type, with twenty of them being lost in various collisions, crashes, or ditching at sea, eight of which killed the pilot. The main differences of the FB.11 over the earlier version were a slight enlargement and strengthening of the airframe for better shipboard handling and improved armament capacity of four 20-mm cannon and a pair of 500-lb (230-kg) general purpose bombs, or 90-gallon drop-tanks that gave a range of 1,040 miles (700 miles without); later provision was made for twelve 60-lb (27-kg) rockets in underwing racks. Its primary Canadian service was as a fleet air defence fighter, but annual "air-to-mud" ground attack training was conducted at RCAF Station Rivers in Manitoba or the army's Camp Gagetown in New Brunswick. In the spring of 1953, an arrangement was reached with the RN for VF 871 to deploy to Korea in the ground attack role, to be embarked — ironically enough — in HMS *Warrior*, which by then had been modified to operate heavier aircraft. However, with the signing of the Korean armistice in the summer of 1953, that deployment was cancelled. The ground attack role was not out of place: After the formation of NATO in 1949, *Magnificent* with her air group constituted Canada's primary military commitment to Allied collective defence of Europe for the next five years, until the army was able to commit a brigade to Europe following the Korean War, and the RCAF could build up its eventual four fighter wings on the Continent.

The last Canadian Sea Fury launched from *Magnificent* on June 19, 1956. They were all struck off strength within the year, some being sold for civilian use and a few retained for display in museums across the country, but most were sold to West Germany as spare parts for its reconstituted (but not seagoing) naval air arm. Britain had manufactured a total of 864 Sea Fury in various marks, mostly as the primary fighter for the RN until replacement by jet aircraft from the mid-1950s. The type also saw service with the RAN until 1962 and a few other navies in smaller quantities.

As early as 1951, the RCN decided to join the jet age by acquiring the McDonnell F2H Banshee as the eventual successor to the Sea Fury, and this follow-on Canadian naval fighter unambiguously reflected the symbiosis between growing aircraft capabilities and the need for matching carrier reconfiguration. The type had been in development for the USN since the end of the war, with the prototype flying in January 1947. A rapid process of test, evaluation, and redesign resulted in the production F2H-2 configuration flying in August 1949. Deliveries to the American fleet commenced soon after, and the type first saw combat in the Korean War in the summer of 1951. It was revolutionary in many respects, having a twinjet, tricycle gear configuration, a pressurized cockpit, and an ejection seat. The powerful Westinghouse J34 turbojets each developed 3,250-pounds (14.5 kN) thrust, providing a maximum sea-level speed of 580 mph (930 km/h), 120 mph (190 km/h) faster than the Sea Fury. Initial armament was four 20-mm cannon with underwing hardpoints for six 500-lb (230-kg) bombs.

A Banshee of VF 870 in flight over Halifax Harbour, armed with a pair of Sidewinder air-to-air missiles.

The closest British equivalent was the single-engined Hawker Sea Hawk, which entered service in 1953, but with slightly lower performance than the Banshee and without the engine redundancy felt necessary for long-range over-water operations (the RCN would trial a Sea Hawk in April 1957 during acceptance trials for *Bonaventure*, and the type would operate off her sister Dutch and Indian CVLs). The trade-off was in takeoff weight: Where the Sea Hawk had a maximum not much different from the Sea Fury, at just under 12,000 lbs (5,500 kg), a Banshee fully loaded with more fuel and weapons weighed double that, at 25,200 lbs (11,400 kg).

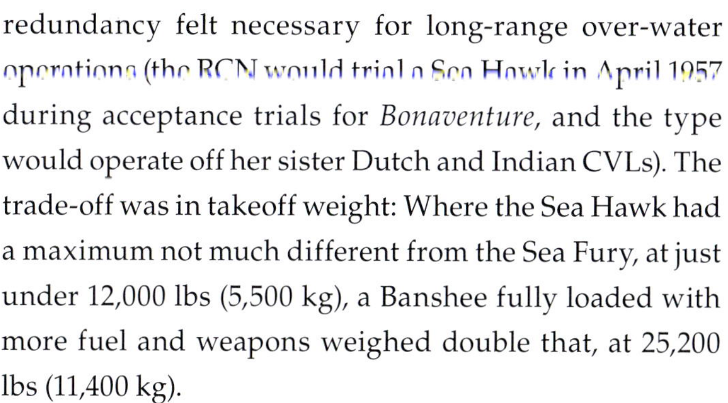

As well, jet aircraft had much higher takeoff speeds than piston-engined aircraft — the Banshee needed 130 mph (210 kph), nearly double that of a Seafire, for example, and not achievable on any carrier deck without catapult assistance. With all that in mind, in 1952, the RCN initiated an order with McDonnell for sixty aircraft to be delivered between 1954 and 1959, the plan being to equip two squadrons with sixteen aircraft each, and a further twenty-eight for attrition over the expected

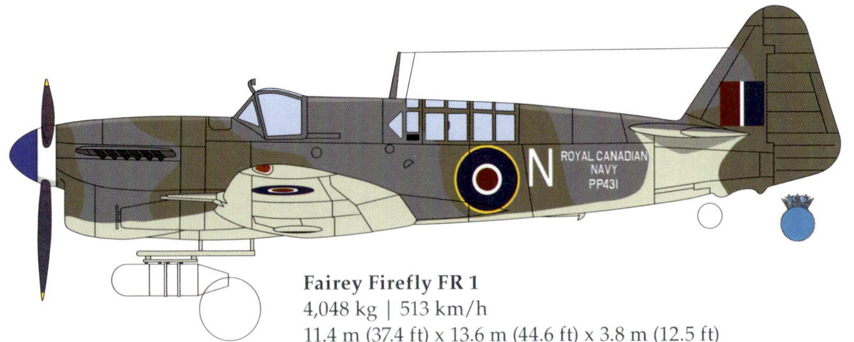

Fairey Firefly FR 1
4,048 kg | 513 km/h
11.4 m (37.4 ft) x 13.6 m (44.6 ft) x 3.8 m (12.5 ft)
825 Squadron, HMCS *Warrior*, 1946

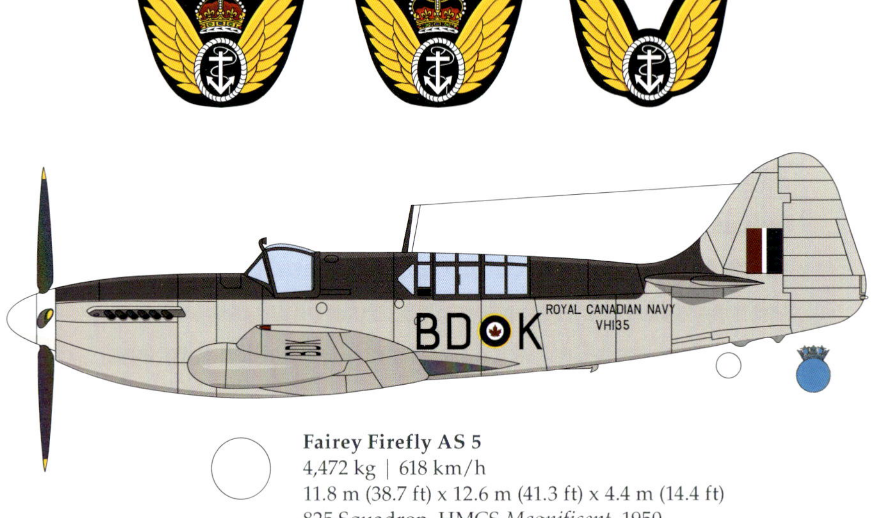

Fairey Firefly AS 5
4,472 kg | 618 km/h
11.8 m (38.7 ft) x 12.6 m (41.3 ft) x 4.4 m (14.4 ft)
825 Squadron, HMCS *Magnificent*, 1950

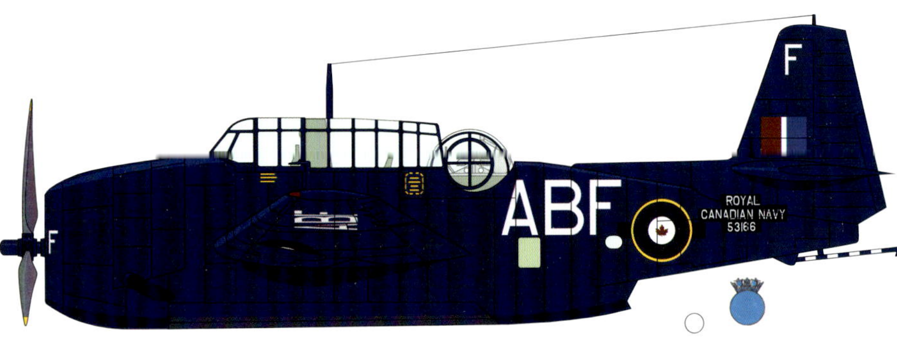

Grumman Avenger TBM-3E
4,782 kg | 444 km/h
12.2 m (40 ft) x 16.5 m (54.1 ft) x 5 m (15.4 ft)
VS 881, HMCS *Magnificent*, 1951

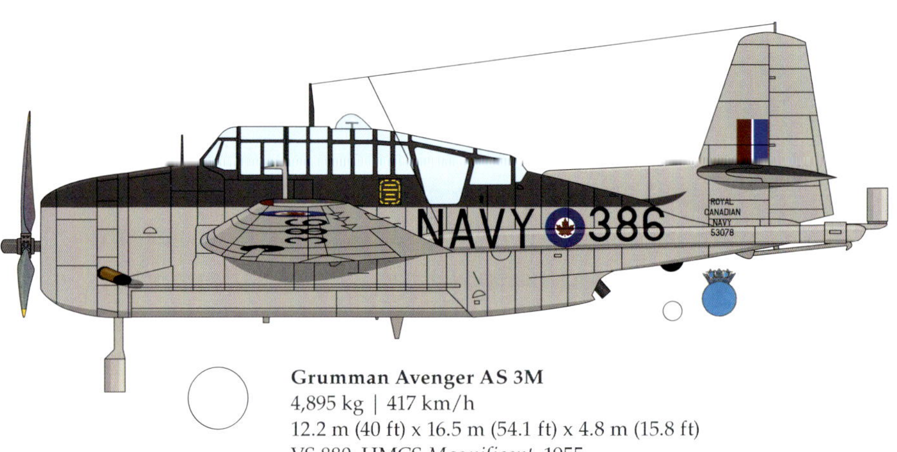

Grumman Avenger AS 3M
4,895 kg | 417 km/h
12.2 m (40 ft) x 16.5 m (54.1 ft) x 4.8 m (15.8 ft)
VS 880, HMCS *Magnificent*, 1955

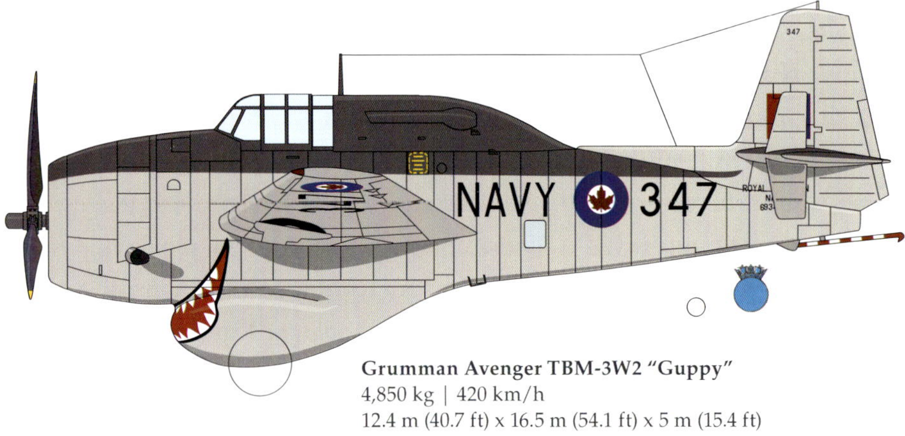

Grumman Avenger TBM-3W2 "Guppy"
4,850 kg | 420 km/h
12.4 m (40.7 ft) x 16.5 m (54.1 ft) x 5 m (15.4 ft)
VS 880, HMCS *Magnificent*, 1956

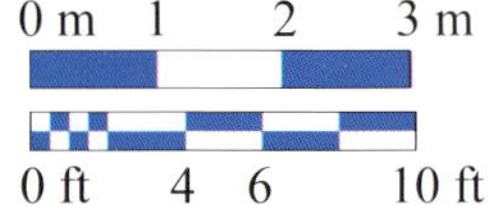

CARRIER-BORNE STRIKE AND ANTISUBMARINE AIRCRAFT: FIREFLY AND AVENGER

When looking at the aircraft embarked for operations from Canadian aircraft carriers, it is common to focus initially — as we have done here — upon the high-performance fighter types. But doing so fails to appreciate that those were employed to protect the other types embarked for the primary function as the offensive striking power of the carrier. Initially these were for the TBR role against enemy shipping and targets ashore. As such, when 825 and 826 Squadrons began forming in the spring of 1945 (initially as units of the RN/FAA) for deployment in *Warrior* and *Magnificent*, respectively, they began training with the Fairey Barracuda Mk II, then the torpedo and dive-bomber workhorse of the British fleet. The RCN was familiar with the Barracuda at a distance, both from it having equipped FAA squadrons embarked at different times in the escort carrier *Puncher* and from it having executed carrier-borne attacks against German warships in occupied Norwegian waters (such as the *Tirpitz* in Kåfjord), with Corsair-flying Canadians in the FAA providing top cover for them. Although the other Canadian-manned CVE, *Nabob*, typically embarked the primary American torpedo-bomber type, the Grumman Avenger (discussed below), the restrictions of Lend-Lease dictated — as with the Seafire for the fighter squadrons — that the British-built Barracuda would be the most likely choice open to the Canadian fleet.

The Barracuda had been designed to pre-war specifications and was showing its age. A new wartime design — the Fairey Firefly — had begun entering FAA service in mid-1944, but it was prioritized for service in the RN. With the end of the war, it became available for service in the Canadian fleet, and in November 1945, 825 Squadron (by now commissioned as an RCN unit) re-equipped with the Firefly FR.1; 826 Squadron would get them in February 1946, albeit just in time to be disbanded at the end of that month. The "FR" type designator suggests it was intended for "fighter-reconnaissance" duties, but operations in Norwegian waters and the Pacific had proven the Firefly's limitations as a fighter while being rather good in the strike role, hence its acceptability to the Canadians for that purpose. When *Warrior* sailed for Canada in March 1946, she had twenty-one FR.1 loaded onboard. Another seven were shipped separately in the RN escort carrier HMS *Queen* in October 1946, and one more arrived by a "method [that] remains an enigma,"[78] making a total of twenty-nine Firefly FR.1 brought into "Canadian" inventory (that is noted in quotes, as they were first taken on RCAF charge further to the inter-service agreement then in place and not transferred formally to RCN inventory until July 12, 1947).

Given the supercharger problem that grounded the Canadian Seafire fleet, the Firefly FR.1 formed the principal air group embarked in *Warrior* for most of her Canadian commission, including for the cruise to the West Coast over the winter of 1946–47, during which they also operated ashore from Patricia Bay. Like the Seafire, the Firefly had been provided by the British for no payment as partial settlement of their war debt with Canada. The FR.1 remained in RCN service through the acquisition of *Magnificent* until the summer of 1950, after which they were disposed of via Crown Assets to Sweden and then sold on to the Imperial Ethiopian Air Force. In 1993, a number of these were spotted by a Canadian military attaché in Asmara, Eritrea. Arrangements were made to return two of them for restoration and display at the Canada Aviation and Space Museum and at the Shearwater Aviation Museum. Despite the passage of time, the restoration has yet to be completed, and they remain in storage at the Ottawa museum.* (The story is related on the Ingenium web page in Further Reading.)

By the time *Magnificent* was identified as the replacement for *Warrior*, the RCN had come to appreciate that the nature of the Cold War Soviet threat was changing. Just as the naval staff turned to the indigenous design of the St. Laurent–class antisubmarine DDE, the Air Branch also began the shift of operational focus from TBR to ASW. The most promising initial type seemed to be the Firefly AS.5, which the RN was developing from the improved fighter-reconnaissance variant FR.IV. This was a redesigned airframe from the original FR.1, with a more powerful Griffon engine and visually distinguished by a four-bladed propeller, the air intake relocated from the

* This episode has a direct connection to this book, as that attaché was Colonel John Orr, and the then-director of the Canada Aviation and Space Museum was Christopher Terry, both of whom are close friends of the authors and have generously assisted in the preparation of the air-related chapters in this book.

chin position to the wing roots, and clipped wing tips for better performance and hangar stowage. The AS.5 was adapted for the specialized antisubmarine role with the four wing-mounted 20-mm cannon removed to make space and weight for a load of sonobuoys, an AN/ARR-3 sonobuoy receiver, and four 450-lb (200-kg) depth charges. The AS.5 was still undergoing trials when *Magnificent* was ready to sail for Canada, so the RN loaned the Canadians a dozen of the FR.IV variant for type conversion training until they became available, and Maggie sailed from Belfast on May 25, 1948, with those twelve aircraft in addition to the twenty-seven Sea Fury fighters discussed in Chapter 49. Two of the FR.IV were lost in accidents, but the remaining ten were returned to the RN in January 1949 once the eighteen purchased examples of the Firefly AS.5 were available. Those were assigned to 825 Squadron, while 826 continued to operate the FR.1. The AS.5, however, "proved far from ideal in the antisubmarine role,"[79] and was retired from Canadian use in November 1951. Four had been lost in RCN service, another was reduced to spares, nine were sold back to the RN, and the remaining four were passed to the Royal Netherlands Navy under the NATO Military Defense Assistance Plan.

In seeking a replacement for the unsatisfactory Firefly AS.5, the Air Branch looked first for a now-preferred American source, but the USN's first purpose-designed antisubmarine aircraft, the Grumman Guardian, would not enter service until September 1950, and then, disappointingly, would prove to be underpowered and under-armed. As for a more traditional British option, the RN's Fairey Gannet was taking too long to develop (and would not begin to enter service until 1953). Just how the initiative to develop an indigenous design originated has been lost to time, but sometime in 1949, the RCN Air Branch identified the Grumman Avenger airframe as suitable for adaptation to the antisubmarine role.

A Fairey Firefly FR.1 readies for a catapult launch from *Warrior*.

Nicknamed the "Turkey," the Avenger had been the workhorse of the wartime American carrier strike fleet as well as seeing extensive service in British carriers (an FAA squadron equipped with the type had been embarked in *Nabob*). The USN developed an antisubmarine variant to be borne in its Bogue-class escort carriers, designated the TBM-3. Fitted with the first examples of an omnidirectional broadband sonobuoy (which localized a contact solely on audio intensity), and armed with rockets and depth bombs, they accounted for twenty-five U-boats and eight Japanese submarines. The late-production TBM-3E model was fitted with an AN/APS-4 search radar in an underwing pod and a retractable ventral magnetic anomaly detector (MAD) boom, although the latter was removed when the type was declared surplus to USN needs and put in storage soon after the war. In the late 1940s, someone in the RCN learned that these aircraft were available at a very low cost, and, although in very rough shape from hasty placement into storage, they had the space and weight to be adapted to carry a tailored suite of equipment augmenting the dated American antisubmarine fit.

In March 1950, Minister of National Defence Brooke Claxton authorized the RCN to purchase seventy-five of the ex-USN Avengers, and the first of them arrived at *Shearwater* on May 12, with the last following by October 1950. The RCAF had opposed the purchase on the grounds that the NATO alliance already had sufficient carrier-borne antisubmarine forces and that Canadian offshore antisubmarine requirements could be met adequately within the tight Canadian defence budget allocation by RCAF maritime patrol aircraft. The Chiefs of Staff Committee, however, recognized that the deal the RCN had negotiated with the Americans was quite affordable and that NATO did not have sufficient carrier-borne forces; nor did the RCAF yet have a suitable maritime patrol aircraft in its inventory (this inter-service doctrinal dispute will be pursued in Chapter 55, on the early evolution of shore-based RCAF long-range patrol aircraft).

The newly acquired Avengers immediately went into use unmodified from the USN TBM-3E standard, including the distinctive dorsal ball turret, the AN/APS-4 search radar in a pod under the starboard wing, and overall glossy sea-blue paint finish. They formed the initial deployment of Avengers as replacements of the Firefly AS.5 aboard *Magnificent* during February and March 1951 to Bermuda. Meanwhile, the RCN had contracted the Canadian division of the Fairey Aviation Company, located adjacent to *Shearwater*, "to undertake design of the ASW conversion,"[80] and in November 1950, VX 10 began testing the first two prototype AS 3. The complete transition to the antisubmarine configuration was accomplished progressively over the next two years, with the first of the conversions entering service in March 1951.

At the risk of simplifying the range of variants in RCN service at any time, most received the "basic" AS 3 conversion, while twenty-two airframes received the ultimate AS 3M configuration and were operational by the summer of 1955. They incorporated a wide range of modifications from the TBM-3E standard. Visually, the dorsal ball turret was replaced with a rearward extension of the "glasshouse" canopy; a pair of electronic countermeasures "cans" extended below the engine cowling and aft from the tail cone; a sonobuoy chute was fitted where the wartime ventral MAD had been housed (and removed); and a new MAD boom fitted along the port fuselage could extend rearward behind the tail. Up to 2,000 lbs (907 kg) of bombs, depth charges, or homing torpedoes could be carried in the internal bomb bay, and rockets on underwing racks. A variety of tactical, communications, and navigation electronic equipment was fitted (Jerry Proc describes the full array, including several photographs, on his web page; see Further Reading). The main elements of these were an AN/UPD-501 direction finder, an AN/ASQ-8 recorder for the MAD, an AN/ARR-3 sonobuoy receiver, and an early version of Links 11/16 to relay tactical information to the carrier and other ships. A planned late conversion to AS 3M2 configuration with further electronic upgrades and a distinctive "camel-back" glasshouse was entering trials when the replacement Trackers began to be accepted, and only two aircraft were so modified. In 1953, when delivery of the Fairey Gannet in the RN was still delayed, the USN supplied the FAA with a hundred TBM-3E under the Military Defense Assistance Plan, and their conversion to AS.4 standard appears to have been influenced by the Canadian configuration.

The RCN ordered a second batch of 50 Avengers from the USN in 1952 for a total of 125, making it the most numerous aircraft type in the RCN inventory. Eight of these had received the airborne early warning TBM-3W2 "Guppy" conversion (not to be confused with the similarly abbreviated conversions the Americans were undertaking at roughly the same time to extend the service life of their wartime diesel submarine fleet, as discussed in Chapter 34 regarding the Canadian West Coast submarines). With a bulbous under-nose AN/APS-20 radar, designed to detect the masts of a snorkelling submarine theoretically out to 20 nm (37 km), the Guppy proved especially effective working in conjunction vectoring an AS 3M "Scrapper" onto a radar target from which the AS 3M could then attack the dived contact without further assistance. The Canadian Avenger Guppy-Scrapper pairings never had occasion to prove their effectiveness in wartime, but in successive exercises achieved a high kill rate against modern Allied conventional submarines (the nuclear-powered submarine had not yet appeared on the scene).

The Guppy also had the capability to provide airborne early warning for directing Sea Fury fighters embarked in the carrier. However, the airborne early warning function was not viewed as central to RCN operations, as the threat shifted to submarines firing long-range antiship missiles, which were considered to be beyond the range and below the detection envelope of the AN/APS-20, and that capability died with retirement of the Guppies.

A good in-flight image of a fully configured Avenger AS 3M.

For the critical early Cold War years from 1950 to 1957, the Avenger formed the backbone of the RCN's carrier-borne antisubmarine capability, and the unique equipment fit of the AS 3M established the Canadian Naval Air Branch's enduring reputation as a premier sub-hunting force in NATO. All variants of the Turkeys were gradually withdrawn from service with the arrival of the Tracker as their replacements. The last official flight of an RCN Avenger was for a target-towing with VU 32 on June 13, 1960. Many had been cannibalized over the years for spares to keep the fleet running, or "burnt to cinders ... during firefighting training."[81]

Another large number were sold surplus and converted to civilian use for insect-spraying and firebombing, in which activity several are still engaged. The Shearwater Aviation Museum has two — one on static display in an air park and the other inside the museum. A flyable example in RCN colours (albeit obtained from USN surplus and never itself in Canadian service) is maintained by the Canadian Warplane Heritage Museum in Hamilton, Ontario.

FURTHER READING

"Fairey Firefly FR.1," Ingenium, Canada Aviation and Space Museum, accessed December 12, 2024, ingeniumcanada.org/aviation/artifact/fairey-firefly-fr1.

Rene J. Francillon, *Grumman Aircraft Since 1929* (Naval Institute Press, 1989).

Roger A. Holler, "The Evolution of the Sonobuoy from World War II to the Cold War," *U.S. Navy Journal of Underwater Acoustics* (January 2014): 322–46.

Patrick Martin and Leo Pettipas, *Royal Canadian Navy Aircraft: Finish and Markings, 1944–1968* (pub. by author, 2021).

Leo Pettipas, *The Fairey Firefly in the Royal Canadian Navy* (Canadian Naval Air Group, 1987).

Leo Pettipas, *The Grumman Avenger in the Royal Canadian Navy* (Canadian Naval Air Group, 1988).

Jerry Proc, "Canadian Avenger AS3 A/S Aircraft," last modified July 25, 2023, jproc.ca/rrp/rrp3/avenger.html.

a smaller carrier. As such, it would also prove to be a perfect match for other operators of similarly modified British CVLs, such as Argentina, Australia, Brazil, and the Netherlands, along with other shore-based forces. In all, Grumman manufactured 1,185 S2F Tracker aircraft for the USN and for export to nine allied navies around the world.

Those acquired for the RCN, however, were built in Canada, where the government was determined to expand the domestic aeronautics industry. De Havilland Aircraft of Canada was selected as the prime contractor to assemble them under licence at a new plant it established in Downsview, Ontario. The first De Havilland–built aircraft was accepted on October 12, 1956, and the last of a production run of ninety-nine airframes was handed over on October 28, 1960. Designated the CS2F, the main external difference of the RCN version was it was 18 inches shorter to better fit in the tight hangar space of the Canadian aircraft carrier (although, as noted, those manufactured by Grumman seem to have served without difficulty in other navies).

The RCN Trackers were being manufactured at the same time as the RCAF was accepting the P2V Neptune into service and as Canadair in Montreal was constructing its own CL-28 Argus long-range patrol aircraft (see Chapters 55 and 56). Despite the ongoing disagreement between the services over which of them would exercise operational control of shore-based maritime fixed-wing aircraft, they did cooperate on complementing the sensor and weapons fits for them. As such, the first Canadian production run of forty-two Trackers, designated the CS2F-1, included the now-standard MAD gear in a boom extending from the rear of the fuselage, a broad-frequency radar direction-finding receiver, and a powerful 70-million-candlepower searchlight mounted under the starboard wing. The search radar in the Tracker (originally an American AN/APS-38A, later replaced with the Canadian AN/APN-502) differed in being located in a retractable ventral "dustbin" radome rather than in the nose, but the sonobuoy fit mirrored that of the Neptune: the new "Julie" explosive echo ranging (EER) type. Although the Tracker weapon's payload of 4,800 lbs (2,200 kg) was about half that of the Argus, it had the same general internal bomb bay and underwing hard point arrangements to carry a similar variety of depth bombs, torpedoes, and sonobuoys. As good as the AS 3M Avenger had proven in RCN service, the Tracker was a quantum advance in capability when it began to replace them aboard Bonnie after her arrival in Canada in 1957.

That capability would be improved further after the Navy and the Air Force agreed upon the operational control structure designated Maritime Command in 1959 (see Chapter 55). A major consequence of this arrangement was that the Navy's Trackers could thereafter be assigned to the prosecution of submarine contacts detected through SOSUS. Upon being vectored to a search area, the challenge of localizing the contact was accomplished with the newly fitted AQA-3 "Jezebel" Low Frequency Analyzer and Recorder (LOFAR) for the onboard processing of passive discreet frequency sonobuoy signals. Concurrently, VX 10 undertook a development and evaluation project to test a tactical navigation system, the

Anti-Submarine Warfare Tactical Navigation System, designed in the ASW Lab of the U.S. Naval Air Development Center in Johnsville, Pennsylvania. The potential of the new display system (dubbed "ASWTNS") was proven conclusively in a major 1959 fleet exercise during which a VX 10 Tracker "carried out the first continuous real-time tracking of a submerged, unrestricted, high-speed, nuclear attack submarine," for over fifty-two minutes of continuous detection[82] (see "ASWTNS," "Jezebel and Data Relay," and "USS *Skipjack* Is Detected by a Tracker" by Leo Pettipas in Jerry Proc's link in Further Reading).

The bulky AQA-3 processor, the ASWTNS, and a variety of other electronic equipment advances were incorporated into what became the second production run of another fifty-seven aircraft that were designated the CS2F-2. The airframe was no different, and as these new models rolled off the assembly line from January 1960, the older ones they replaced were put in storage for spare parts. Two of these were converted to Carrier Onboard Delivery configuration by stripping them of all antisubmarine equipment, strengthening the floor to create space for up to six passengers, and adding tie-down points for cargo. Another seventeen were transferred to the Royal Netherlands Navy under the NATO Military Defense Assistance Plan.

In 1964, Fairey Aviation of Canada was contracted to perform a mid-life modification program to the Tracker fleet to incorporate a further variety of modifications trialled by VX 10, along with an updated ASWTNS and the more advanced AQA-4 Jezebel processor. All this equipment was retrofitted to forty-five of the second Tracker production batch, which, although still not a new airframe, were given the new type designation CS2F-3. The first of these became operational in July 1964, and the last in April 1968.

A pair of Trackers in RCN livery.

Less than two years later, in anticipation of *Bonaventure* being paid off as a cost-saving measure following unification of the CAF, Tracker 1534, the VU 32 Carrier Onboard Delivery aircraft, performed the last fixed-wing launch from Bonnie on December 12, 1969 — Allan Snowie relates the stirring events of the day, conducted in the confined waters of Bedford Basin, with the catapult unserviceable and the massive ship manoeuvring to create enough wind for a free deck launch (see Further Reading). With the demise of the carrier, the Trackers were assigned ashore and given the CAF re-designation CP-121 to fly sovereignty patrols off both the East and West Coasts. The complete fleet of aircraft were stripped of their antisubmarine equipment, new communications gear and radars were installed to suit the new role, and they were fitted to fire the Bristol Canada–developed CRV-7 air-to-ground rockets. After another two decades of steadfast service, the last Trackers were struck off strength in 1989.

As *Bonaventure*'s air wing typically embarked eight and no more than ten Trackers at a time, far more of the aircraft were acquired than could be fully utilized. Many ended their days as training platforms for ground technicians, and several examples remain as static outdoor displays at present-day air bases. A large number were sold off for civilian use fighting forest fires and spraying for insect control; many are still in service, including turboprop conversions. Good-quality specimens in RCN markings are maintained by the Canada Aviation and Space Museum in Ottawa and the Shearwater Aviation Museum in Dartmouth, Nova Scotia, and one has been kept in flying condition by the Canadian Warplane Heritage Museum in Hamilton, Ontario.

FURTHER READING

Peter Charlton, *Nobody Told Us It Couldn't Be Done: The VX10 Story* (pub. by author, 1993).

Peter Charlton and Michael Whitby, eds., *Certified Serviceable: Swordfish to Sea King* (CNATH Book Project, 1995).

Rene J. Francillon, *Grumman Aircraft Since 1929* (Naval Institute Press, 1989).

Patrick Martin and Leo Pettipas, *Royal Canadian Navy Aircraft: Finish and Markings, 1944–1968* (pub. by author, 2021).

Jerry Proc and Leo Pettipas, "CS2F Tracker in Canadian Service — Electronics Suite," last modified August 31, 2013, jproc.ca/rrp/rrp3/tracker_equipment_details.html.

J. Allan Snowie, *The Bonnie: HMCS* Bonaventure (Boston Mills, 1987), 274.

Robert M. Stitt, "Willing Tracker: The Grumman S2F Tracker in Canadian Service, Part 1," *Air Enthusiast*, no. 61 (January/February 1996): 40–51, jproc.ca/rrp/rrp3/tracker_willing_tracker_pt1.pdf.

Dave Tate and Bill Upton, "De Havilland Canada CS2F/CP-121 Tracker: RCN/CAF," Serials 1587/12187 (Canada Aviation Museum Aircraft [n.d., 2000]).

Sikorsky HO4S-3
2,380 kg | 180 km/h
12.9 m (42.3 ft) x 16.2 m (53.2 ft) x 4.5 m (14.8 ft)
HU 21, HMCS *Buckingham*'s trials, 1956

Piasecki HUP-3
1,782 kg | 161 km/h
9.7 m (31.8 ft) x 10.7 m (35.1 ft) x 3.8 m (12.5 ft)
HU 21, HMCS *Labrador*, 1955

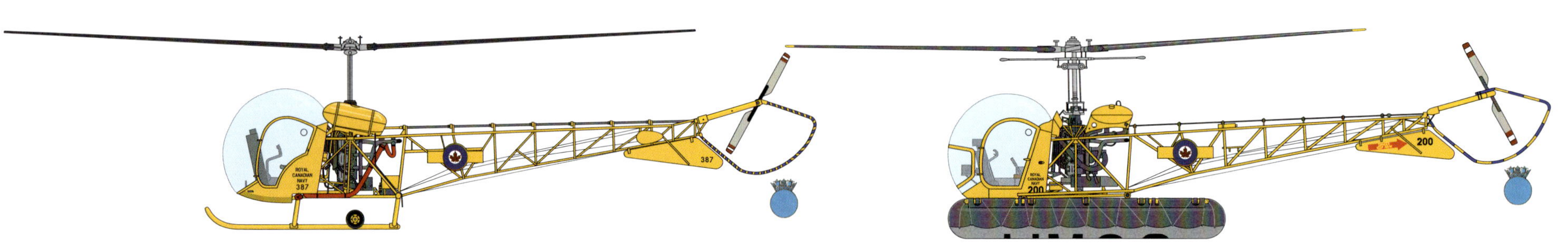

Bell HTL-6
858 kg | 169 km/h
9.6 m (31.5 ft) x 11.3 m (37.1 ft) x 2.8 m (9.2 ft)
HU 21, HMCS *Shearwater*, 1962

Bell HTL-4 on Floats
858 kg | 169 km/h
9.6 m (31.5 ft) x 11.3 m (37.1 ft) x 2.8 m (9.2 ft)
HU 21, HMCS *Labrador*, 1957

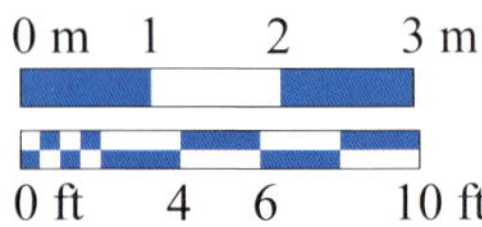

52

EARLY NAVAL HELICOPTERS

Anyone familiar with the *M*A*S*H* productions — either the hit 1970 movie or the long-running television series (1972–83), set notionally in the year 1951 — will be aware that the Bell 47 helicopter (the voiceless but ubiquitous co-star of the plotline) was the battlefield casualty evacuation workhorse of the Korean War. Few readers, however, are likely to appreciate that this was also the year the RCN acquired three of the same type as its first helicopters. Rotary-wing flight was still very much in its infancy, and that role was only one of the many uses that promised to benefit from the new-found ability to take off and land vertically from a small space lacking a full-length runway.

Helicopters had only limited use during the Second World War, as the technology was still in development, and the different types that were trialled typically suffered from being underpowered. The Bell 47 that entered production in 1946 was the first design both light enough and with the requisite power to get airborne successfully, and it was also simple enough to serve as a good introduction to the novel contraption. It was an immediate commercial success. In addition to the thousands manufactured by parent company Bell, it was built under licence in Italy, Japan, and Great Britain, serving extensively in civilian use and the air arms of more than thirty nations in many versions.

The three received into RCN inventory in August 1951 were of the type designated by the USN as HTL-4 (Helicopter Training Light), having a 200-horsepower (150-kW) vertically mounted six-cylinder Franklin 0-335 engine, and were used in the training role as well as a variety of light utility functions. Over the years, the Navy

A "Horse" makes a heavy-weather landing onboard Bonnie's flight deck, while the Tribal-class destroyer *Huron* steams nearby as "plane guard."

acquired additional models with slight improvements, for a total of thirteen of the general type. The only regular shipboard use was two embarked in *Labrador* to conduct ice reconnaissance and survey support, in which they proved exceptionally useful until both crashed during a survey mission in the ship's final naval season of 1957 (the second crashed while attempting to rescue the first, fortunately without injury to any of the crews). The others were sold to civilian interests in 1965, except for one transferred to what is now the Canada Aviation and Space Museum, where it remains on display.

Impressed with the other potential uses for rotary-wing technology, soon after accepting those first Bell HTL, the Canadian Navy placed its next utility helicopter order in December 1951. The Sikorsky HO4S-2 (similar to the S-55 operated by the RCAF) was a much larger aircraft with greater load-carrying capacity, the additional cabin space achieved by locating the nine-cylinder Pratt & Whitney R-1340 radial engine (600 hp/450 kW) in the nose, driving a transmission shaft angled back and up to the rotors. The RCN ordered three of them to fly from the aircraft carrier *Magnificent* in the "plane guard" rescue function, standing by in the event of a crash during fixed-wing launch and recovery operations, which relieved an escorting surface warship for more operational tasks.

The USN had begun experimenting with the HO4S to pursue an entirely new purpose — hunting and attacking submarines by fitting the helicopter to carry a dipping sonar and torpedoes — but found this early variant to be underpowered. The RCN Air Branch, however, was intrigued with the concept, and in November 1953 made a submission to the Chiefs of Staff Committee to form an antisubmarine helicopter squadron consisting of ten Piasecki H-21 (a tandem-rotor medium-lift helicopter already ordered by the RCAF). The Air Force saw this as a challenge in the continuing disagreement over control of maritime aviation and managed to get the submission rejected — fortunately, as it transpired, given that the H-21 (derisively nicknamed the "flying banana") experienced development problems. Meanwhile, the USN had progressed to the HO4S-3, re-engined with a 700-hp (520-kW) Wright R-1300 radial with sufficient lifting power equal to the task. The RCN promptly ordered ten of these — dubbed the "Horse" in a phonetic rendering of the alphanumeric designation — for delivery in the summer of 1955. Along with two of the original models upgraded to the same standard, they were assigned to HS 50, commissioned on July 5, 1955, "as an experimental squadron to evaluate the role of the helicopter in ASW using the AN/AQS-4 dipping sonar," to get around Air Force objections.[83] After conducting shore-based trials from *Shearwater* over the next few months, HS 50 embarked in *Magnificent* in April 1956 to put the dipping Horse through its paces at sea. While it gave up the antisubmarine role with arrival of the Sea King from mid-1963, the Horse continued in the plane guard role until the carrier *Bonaventure* was retired in 1970. Examples are preserved on exhibit at the Shearwater Aviation Museum and the Canada Aviation and Space Museum.

The early 1950s saw great conceptual innovation in the RCN, and even as the first of the novel St. Laurent-class DDEs were building (see Chapter 25), the air staff in Naval Service Headquarters turned to examining the potential for operating a helicopter from an escort-sized vessel as a means of increasing its detection and weapons delivery ranges against the fast and deep-diving nuclear-powered submarine. In retrospect, it is remarkable how quickly the investigation progressed. The Prestonian-class frigate *Buckingham* was fitted temporarily with a large steel landing pad placed above its Squid mortar wells to begin flight trials with an HO4S-3 in September 1956. These confirmed the operational feasibility of the concept but revealed the limitations of the structural strengths of both the ship (too small to adequately support the weight aft) and the aircraft (the undercarriage of the Horse could not withstand the loads imparted to it by the rolling and pitching of the deck). For a second series of tests, the platform was modified slightly and, in October 1957, installed in similar temporary fashion on the stern of the new DDE *Ottawa*, and a larger S-58 (having stronger undercarriage) on loan from the RCAF was embarked for a six-week transatlantic voyage in pursuit of heavy weather — which they found.[84] The many lessons learned from this experience — including the principal ones that a hangar was essential for maintenance and shelter, as was a rapid securing device with mechanical assistance for handling the aircraft on deck — were incorporated into the redesigned ISL conversion of the original seven ships, plus the two Annapolis class into the DDH standard, along with development of the Beartrap helicopter hauldown and rapid securing device.

A Piasecki HUP-3 landing on *Assiniboine* during DDH trials, showing the post-conversion quarterdeck layout (hangar with twin funnels, single Limbo mortar mount, and VDS equipment).

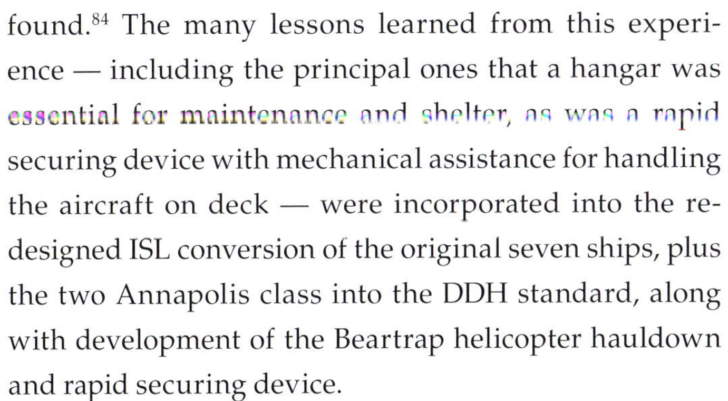

In the midst of all this, the RCN acquired a third type of helicopter — the Piasecki HUP-3 medium-lift utility aircraft, with a tandem rotor blade arrangement and powered by a 550-hp (410-kW) Continental R-975 nine-cylinder air-cooled piston engine. Three were delivered in May 1954, specifically in anticipation for deployment in *Labrador* to supplement the Bell HTL-4 in general utility tasks. First deployed for the icebreaker's second season in 1955, the HUP proved indispensable for the installation of navigational beacons, support of NORAD's

Distant Early Warning line construction, and indeed the rescue of the two HTL-4 that crashed near Pond Inlet, Northwest Territories, in July 1957. Following the transfer of the icebreaker later that year to the Department of Transport, the three HUP remained with the RCN but were assigned ashore. Eventually they were dispatched to VU 33 in Patricia Bay, British Columbia, until struck off strength in February 1964. Serendipitously, all three of these aircraft are preserved as museum exhibits: one each in the Canada Aviation and Space Museum in Ottawa; the British Helicopter Museum in Weston-Super-Mare, England; and the Classic Rotors Helicopter Museum in Ramona, California.

A little remarked distinction shared by all three early rotary-wing types is that examples of each were the first aircraft embarked in the carrier *Bonaventure* while she was undergoing her commissioning trials in the U.K. and before the first Tracker, Banshees, and assorted other RN FAA fixed-wing types. As recorded in Martin and Pettipas,[85] the first to land on Bonnie was HO4S-3 side number "228" from *Magnificent* on February 6, 1957. It was followed a month later, on March 10, by HUP-3 "247" and HTL-4 "200," both from *Labrador*, which was passing nearby on a cruise of northern Europe in advance of her final Canadian ice season.

FURTHER READING

Peter Charlton, *A Monograph on the Integration of Sea King Helicopters and RCN Destroyers — from 1962 to 1966* (pub. by author, 2003).

Peter Charlton, *Nobody Told Us It Couldn't Be Done: The VX10 Story* (pub. by author, 1993).

Peter Charlton and Michael Whitby, eds., *Certified Serviceable: Swordfish to Sea King* (CNATH Book Project, 1995).

TFJ Leversedge, *Canadian Combat and Support Aircraft: A Military Compendium* (Vanwell Publishing, 2007).

Patrick Martin and Leo Pettipas, *Royal Canadian Navy Aircraft: Finish and Markings, 1944–1968* (pub. by author, 2021).

John Orr, "'We Came to Mow Your Lawn': How and Why Canada Acquired the Sikorsky Sea King Helicopter," in *Wings for the Fleet: 50 Years of the Canadian Sea King*, ed. W.A. March, Sic Itur Ad Astra: Canadian Aerospace Power Studies, vol. 5 (Minister of National Defence, 2015), 12–30, publications.gc.ca/collections/collection_2015/mdn-dnd/D4-7-5-2015-eng.pdf.

Robert S. Petite, "Canada's Second World War Helicopter Pilots," *Aviation Quarterly*, no. 3: 7–22, helicopterheritagecanada.com/images/pilots-blog-pdf.pdf.

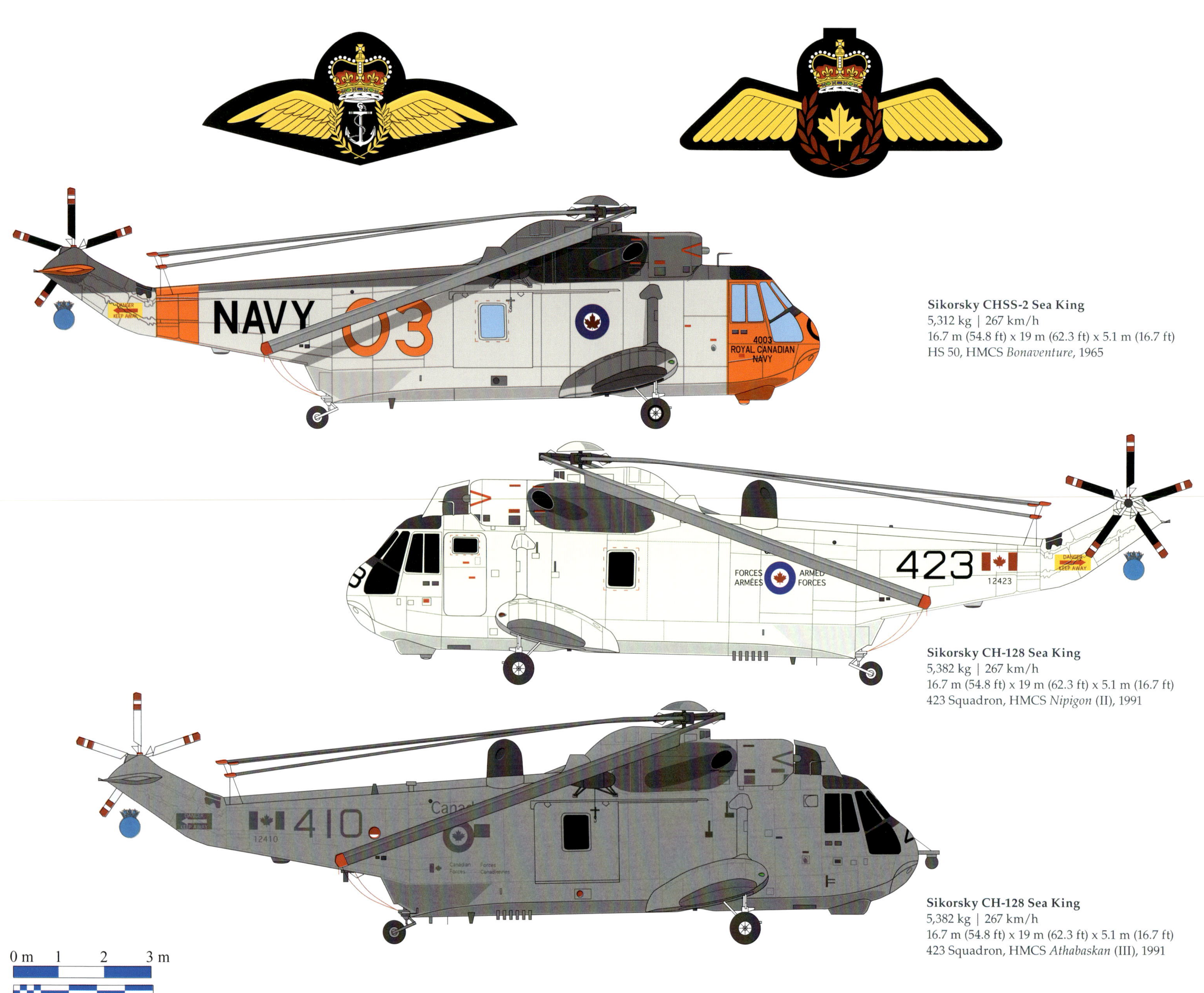

Sikorsky CHSS-2 Sea King
5,312 kg | 267 km/h
16.7 m (54.8 ft) x 19 m (62.3 ft) x 5.1 m (16.7 ft)
HS 50, HMCS *Bonaventure*, 1965

Sikorsky CH-128 Sea King
5,382 kg | 267 km/h
16.7 m (54.8 ft) x 19 m (62.3 ft) x 5.1 m (16.7 ft)
423 Squadron, HMCS *Nipigon* (II), 1991

Sikorsky CH-128 Sea King
5,382 kg | 267 km/h
16.7 m (54.8 ft) x 19 m (62.3 ft) x 5.1 m (16.7 ft)
423 Squadron, HMCS *Athabaskan* (III), 1991

53

CHSS-2/CH-124 SIKORSKY SEA KING HELICOPTER

The Canadian naval investigation into the concept of operating antisubmarine helicopters at sea started from a different premise than its principal American and British allies. Both the USN and the RN had fleets organized around a greater number of aircraft carriers, with the helicopter envisioned as one more asset among several options for the various search and attack functions. The RCN, however, with just a single carrier for the foreseeable future, faced a variety of compounding factors over the course of 1954 to 1955, leading it down a very different evolutionary path that would culminate with operating the large Sea King helicopter from the smaller deck of a DDE.

The first of these factors was the decision to acquire the HO4S-3, with its dipping sonar, to begin operating from the carrier *Magnificent*, although typically only four embarked at a time owing to competition for space with the AS 3M Avengers and Sea Fury fighters in the tight quarters of the CVL. Then came the unveiling of the USS *Nautilus* in September 1954 as the first SSN, threatening to outpace surface warships even as the RCN's new DDEs were still just fitting out (the *St. Laurent* would not commission until October 1955). Something was needed to extend the sensor and weapons range of the escorts to permit them to engage the high-speed deep-diving SSN, and the helicopter seemed to offer a solution. Finally, whereas the USN and RN were content to operate antisubmarine helicopters from their many aircraft carriers, the RCN sought to distribute them also among a number of DDEs, and to combine the search and attack functions into a single rotary-wing airframe that could complement the capabilities of the fixed-wing Trackers that would soon begin to operate from *Bonaventure*.

As described in Chapter 52, the preliminary trials in the frigate *Buckingham* determined that the HO4S-3 already in service aboard the Canadian carriers was unsuitable for the task. The decision then to progress to the next trial stage in the DDE *Ottawa* with an S-58 on loan from the RCAF was driven in large part by the fact that the USN was operating the antisubmarine version of that larger and sturdier airframe, designated the HSS-1 Seabat. In practice, however, its single Wright Cyclone engine proved to be underpowered for an airframe loaded with a dipping sonar and torpedoes and depth charges. The British eventually built a version of the Sikorsky S-58 under licence by Westland with an upgraded turboshaft (jet) engine. This was known as the Wessex and proved to be quite successful in all the British armed services. The USN, however, relegated the Seabat to utility functions.

The Americans instead launched a competition for a compact, all-weather, multipurpose naval helicopter. The first to appear was the Kaman HU2K-1 Seasprite in 1959. Although somewhat smaller than the Seabat (indeed, roughly comparable in capacity to the Horse — see specifications in Appendix B), the RCN was so impressed with the potential for the Seasprite's antisubmarine variant that in December 1960, it placed an initial order for twelve of them. Within a few months, however, the Seasprite encountered difficulties with its preliminary acceptance by the USN as it proved to be overweight and underpowered for the antisubmarine role, and when the purchase cost also suddenly doubled, the RCN cancelled the order. A decade later, the Americans would upgrade the Seasprite with a second engine, changing both to turbines, to the SH2F LAMPS Mk 1 standard (Light Airborne Multi-Purpose System). But in 1961, with the design process well under way for conversion of the ISL DDH, the RCN needed a shipborne helicopter more immediately.

The only other option available was the other entrant in the USN competition, the Sikorsky HSS-2 Sea King. Much larger than any of the previous helicopters at an original maximum takeoff weight of 19,100 lbs (8,665 kg), its revolutionary use of a pair of General Electric T58 turboshaft engines generated more than enough power for the Sea King to complete its acceptance trials in the summer of 1961 with ease (the all-up weight would grow over time to 20,540 lbs [9,320 kg], with engine and transmission upgrades to accommodate additional equipment). This one proved to be a winner. It had a maximum speed of 165 mph (267 kph) and an operating radius of nearly 200 miles (310 km) and could remain airborne for up to three hours. Additionally, the much bigger helicopter came fitted not only with a dipping sonar and capacity for up to 840 lbs (380 kg) of stores and weapons, but also the latest avionics, including a Doppler radar, which, when coupled to the Automatic Stabilization Equipment, enabled the automatic transition to an all-weather day/night hover from which the sonar could be lowered.

In December 1961, the Canadian government approved the acquisition of forty-one of the helicopters, designated the CHSS-2 Sea King, for delivery commencing in 1963. The first four were manufactured by Sikorsky in its Connecticut facility, with the remainder to be assembled in Longueil, Quebec, by United Aircraft Company of Canada (a subsidiary of Sikorsky, now Pratt & Whitney Canada). The first aircraft was accepted by the RCN on May 24, 1963, with deliveries continuing over the next six years. The last arrived on March 27, 1969, meaning the final seven were accepted into the inventory of the newly unified CAF, at which time the type was redesignated the CH-124.

The ISL conversions were progressing concurrently, and the selection of a much larger helicopter required a major mid-course reconfiguration of the originally planned hangar and flight deck. The biggest visual change was the splitting of the single funnel uptake into the paired arrangement familiar to history, one on either side of the forward part of the hangar, to permit sufficient room to stow the helicopter in the narrow space. Also needed were a Tactical Air Navigation system mast, specialized firefighting apparatus, and additional accommodations for the added aircrew. The first ship taken in hand to undergo the procedure had been *Assiniboine*, begun in Esquimalt in June 1962. The changes were now incorporated and the work expedited so she could transfer to Halifax and commence DDH acceptance trials in the summer of 1963. The first onboard Sea King landing was performed on November 27, 1963, with the ship at anchor in Bedford Basin and not using the Beartrap hauldown system. The first actual hauldown "using the wire" followed a week later, on December 2. On proceeding to sea in the next weeks, it immediately became evident that the hangar interior needed further enlarging to facilitate maintenance access to the aircraft and that the ship's hull required underwater stabilizers to alleviate roll induced by the added top weight. These changes again were incorporated into the other ships in progress, and all the conversions were completed by the end of 1966.

To mark the fiftieth anniversary of service, a pair of Sea Kings were painted in their original (closest to the camera) and ultimate schemes.

The Beartrap helicopter hauldown and rapid securing device, an important separate element of the conversion process, was an especially novel and rather complex technology (see diagram on page 300). As John Orr has noted, "[it] proved to be a far more lengthy and complex evaluation than had been anticipated and innovation at the local level was key to reaching a successful conclusion."[86] The result was that the first acceptance of an operational ship hauldown system took place in *Nipigon* only in November 1966, and *Annapolis* was the first DDH cleared for flight operations in April 1967 (different sources provide a range of dates and ships; the authors take John Orr's research in *Perseverance* [page 62] as definitive. See Further Reading).

With that, the Sea Kings quickly became fixtures throughout the fleet, with the caveat that the

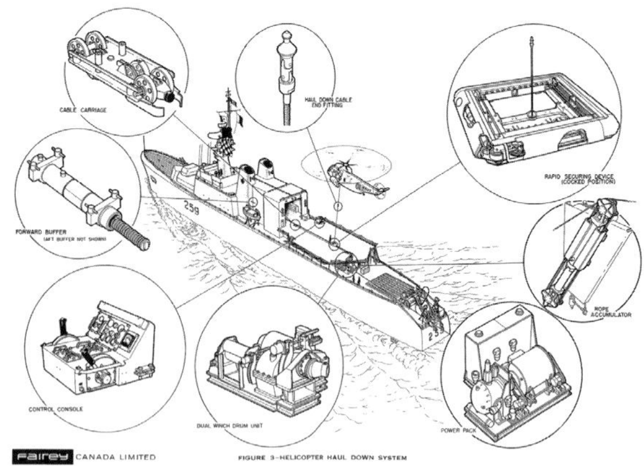

The several elements of the Beartrap hauldown system. Interestingly, the hull number is that of *Terra Nova*, which would be converted to IRE configuration rather than DDH.

post-unification rationalization of the Navy's force structure consolidated all the helicopters and the ships in which they could embark on the East Coast until the late 1980s. Besides being embarked in the aircraft carrier and St. Laurent and Annapolis classes as initially planned, Sea King helicopter air detachments (HELAIRDET) were fixtures through the remainder of the Cold War and well into the twenty-first century in all of the subsequent Iroquois-class destroyers (two per ship), Halifax-class frigates (one per ship), and fleet replenishment ships (two to three per ship, with enhanced onboard maintenance facilities; after *Provider* transferred to the West Coast, she embarked U.S. Naval Reserve Sea King HELAIRDETs on the occasions required).

The introduction of the Sea King established the Canadian Navy as a trailblazer in the DDH concept. The RN began operating the much smaller Westland Wasp helicopter from its similarly sized Leander-class frigates in 1964, but only as a "pony" to carry a torpedo out to a designated target, then having to be instructed when and where to drop it. The RN did operate the Wessex from its large (6,200 ton) County-class guided-missile destroyers commissioned from the mid-1960s, but without a Beartrap equivalent, restricting operations to relatively calm sea states. As discussed above, the USN introduced the LAMPS to its surface escorts only in the early 1970s, and again without a Beartrap equivalent. As such, it was the Canadian Navy that codified the rules and procedures for HOSTAC (Helicopter Operations for Ships Other than Aircraft Carriers) that are used by navies and coast guards around the world to this day.

As naval operations evolved over the years, the Sea Kings underwent a variety of upgrades and modifications from the baseline CH-124 airframe to keep them airworthy and apace with the changing nature of war at sea. In a 2012 presentation, Terry Robbins, a long-time CAF aerospace engineer and then-civilian contractor specializing on the Sea King, said that, to that date, "There have been 813 field level (CF) modifications and 498 contractor level (CD) modifications developed and incorporated into the aircraft."[87] In the early 1970s, the original American sonar and radar were replaced with improved Canadian types, respectively, the AN/AQS-502 dipping sonar (range out to 20,000 yards/18,300 m) and the AN/APS-503 surface search radar (range 70 miles/110 km). Beginning in the mid-1980s, roughly concurrent with the stand-up of the New Shipborne Aircraft project office for its eventual replacement, the Sea King Improvement Program was implemented, incorporating modernized avionics and several safety features. These came to be known as the CH-124A to distinguish them from a parallel program that reconfigured five aircraft as a Helicopter Towed Array Support System to complement the Navy's shift from active to passive sonar expected with the introduction of the Halifax-class frigates — having the dipping sonars removed to be replaced by an onboard passive sonar processor and sonobuoys, this variant was labelled the CH-124B. Then, in the summer of 1990, six other aircraft were speedily converted to a surface surveillance configuration to be deployed for the Persian Gulf War, with the dipping sonar replaced by a variety of equipment, including a forward-looking infrared device, chaff and flare dispensers, missile warning receiver, missile approach warning system, a door-mounted light machine gun, sand screens for the engine intakes, and aircrew-seat armour. Initially known as "the Gulf War mods," consideration was given to designating them as the CH-124C, but as these modifications came to be incorporated fleet wide, that was felt to be unnecessary.

The checkered acquisition process to identify a replacement (see Chapter 54) meant that the CH-124 Sea King served well past its design life. With the introduction of the CH-148 Cyclone, the last Sea King was retired on December 1, 2018. For a full fifty-five years, between 1963 and 2018, it was the shipborne workhorse of the Canadian fleet. In that time, fourteen aircraft and eight aircrew were lost in various accidents. However, notwithstanding the growing number of press reports chronicling its age, the Sea King's safety record actually improved over the years, owing to a combination of "lessons learned," the provision of improved maintenance support, and the dedication of the maintenance crews. Coincidentally, twenty-eight of the type remained on strength at the time of their retirement — a number that will figure in the next chapter, which deals with its replacement. Several examples of the Sea King have been retained at various Canadian naval and military museums, and one stands as a monument at the entrance of the Carling Campus of the National Defence Headquarters in Ottawa.

FURTHER READING

"Beartrap," *Crowsnest: The Royal Canadian Navy's Magazine* 17, nos. 3 and 4 (March–April 1965): 27–29, navalandmilitarymuseum.org/wp-content/uploads/2021/09/CFB-Esquimalt-Museum-Crowsnest-Volume17-Number-03-04-Mar-Apr-1965.pdf.

Peter Charlton, *A Monograph on the Integration of Sea King Helicopters and RCN Destroyers — from 1962 to 1966* (pub. by author, 2003).

Peter Charlton and Michael Whitby, eds., *Certified Serviceable: Swordfish to Sea King* (CNATH Book Project, 1995).

W.A. March, ed., *Wings for the Fleet: 50 Years of the Canadian Sea King*, Sic Itur Ad Astra: Canadian Aerospace Power Studies, vol. 5 (Minister of National Defence, 2015), 12–30, publications.gc.ca/collections/collection_2015/mdn-dnd/D4-7-5-2015-eng.pdf.

Patrick Martin and Leo Pettipas, *Royal Canadian Navy Aircraft: Finish and Markings, 1944–1968* (pub. by author, 2021).

John Orr, "Innovation: Top Down or Bottom Up?", *Canadian Naval Review* 15, no. 1 (2019): 2–4, navalreview.ca/wp-content/uploads/CNR_pdf_full/cnr_vol15_1.pdf — reflections on innovation in developing and maintaining the Sea King/Beartrap/HOTEF.

John L. Orr, *Perseverance: The Canadian Sea King Story* (Sea King 50th Anniversary Committee, 2013).

Aaron Plamondon, *The Politics of Procurement: Military Acquisition in Canada and the Sea King Helicopter* (UBC Press, 2009).

Jeff Tasseron, "Sailing to Byzantium: A Eulogy to the Sea King," *Canadian Naval Review* 15, no. 1 (2019): 5–10, navalreview.ca/wp-content/uploads/CNR_pdf_full/cnr_vol15_1.pdf.

Sikorsky CH-148 Cyclone
7,076 kg | 306 km/h
17.1 m (56.1 ft) x 17.7 m (58.1 ft) x 4.7 m (15.4 ft)
443 Squadron, HMCS *Regina* (II), 2019

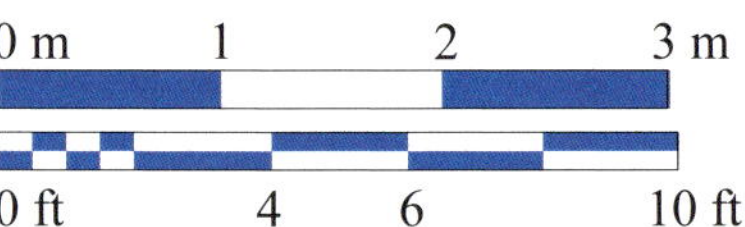

54

CH-148 SIKORSKY CYCLONE HELICOPTER

Astute readers of this section on naval aviation will have noticed the rapid rate of change in the acquisition of new aircraft; typically, a type was in service for only a few years, rarely more than a decade, before being replaced (those who may have missed this pattern can consult the "Years in Service" column in Appendix B). This trend was initiated in part by the need to speedily introduce wartime developments, but it continued for the better part of two decades into the postwar period. There were exceptions: For example, the RCAF's PBY-5 Canso patrol aircraft (see Chapter 55) and DC-3/C-47 Dakota medium transport (not listed in this book) still lumber on in civilian guise, coming up to ninety years after first taking flight in the late 1930s. The brisk replacement trend was especially apparent in new technologies like the helicopter, but again there are exceptions, such as the Bell 47 light helicopter, still going strong today.

By the 1970s, the cycle had stabilized, with airframes and aero-engine technology having reached a point of maturity in development, coincident with new processes, such as non-destructive testing to confirm that the aircraft remained airworthy, and new warfare trends could be accommodated through upgrades to the payload. The Sea King was one of the first postwar designs to break the trend, with ongoing configuration upgrades (described in Chapter 53), although it is possible to argue that, in stretching its operational employment to more than half a century, the point may have been made to excess. (A same-but-different example is the CP-140 Aurora, which, although procured as new-built aircraft, will be seen in Chapter 57 to have

Calgary in post-HCM/FELEX configuration is approached from astern by her CH-148 Cyclone helicopter and a CP-140 Aurora.

descended from the late-1950s Lockheed Electra commercial airframe.)

The Sea King was acquired in the early 1960s in the full expectation it would need to be replaced from 1975. Regular maintenance and inspections to that time, however, continued to confirm that the airframe remained sound and that its service life could be extended for some unknown time. Still, by the early 1980s, it seemed prudent to begin the search for a replacement, and the New Shipborne Aircraft project office was established in 1986, while the Sea King Improvement Project was already being implemented to manage the transition. By then, the ships from which the new aircraft were expected to operate — the CPFs (soon to be designated the Halifax class; see Chapter 40) — were beginning construction, and the late Cold War threat remained the modernizing Soviet nuclear-powered submarine fleet.

In consequence, the SOR identified the need for an aircraft able to fly out to the anticipated shipboard towed array sonar detection range of as far as the third convergence zone (up to 125 miles/200 km), then loiter in the area to localize and prosecute the contact before returning to the mother ship. That effectively called for an endurance of five hours' flight time, a cruising speed fast enough to reach the search area in a timely fashion, and a high all-up weight to accommodate the extra fuel plus a suite of sensors (both an improved active dipping sonar and passive sonobuoy processors) and weapons complementing those in the fixed-wing CP-140 Aurora. The aircraft selected was the three-engine, 12,000 kg (26,500 lb) European Helicopter Industries EH 101, and in 1987 Prime Minister Brian Mulroney's Conservative government committed to acquiring up to fifty of them: thirty-five for the antisubmarine role and the other fifteen in a search-and-rescue configuration. (Other aircraft evaluated were the Sikorsky SH-60 LAMPS III Seahawk, the Aérospatiale Puma, and the NH Industries NH90, none of which fully met the requirement.)

The EH 101 was entering production in 1993 when the purchase became a controversial factor in the Canadian federal election that fall. With the end of the Cold War and the supposed vanquishing of the expected threat, both Mulroney's successor — Prime Minister Kim Campbell — and Jean Chrétien's opposition Liberals campaigned in part on an austerity peace dividend platform, Campbell cutting the maritime order to an arbitrary twenty-eight aircraft (for a supposed saving of $1 billion; she did not touch the fifteen search-and-rescue helicopters) and Chrétien infamously for "zero helicopters." When Chrétien duly won, he immediately cancelled the contract, ostensibly saving

$4.8 billion. However, as tabulated by *Janes Defence* Canadian correspondent Sharon Hobson, "In reality, after all the bills for cancellation costs, the [consequent] Sea King life extension, and the replacement programs are added up, this move saved nothing and effectively eliminated a decade's worth of research and development and industrial investment."[88]

The New Shipborne Aircraft project office was shut down and the procurement renamed the Maritime Helicopter Project. Work commenced to redraft the SOR to reflect the government's view that not only was the Cold War over, but as per the prime minister's election campaign rhetoric, the EH 101 was a "Cadillac" and something more modest would suffice. An interim, descoped SOR was produced but never formally adopted or acted upon. In the meantime, the government remained content to have the Air Force do enough to keep the Sea King airworthy as the aircraft continued to become increasingly difficult to maintain, with diminishing operational capability. The crafting of a clean-sheet-of-paper SOR that considered only the new peacetime needs of the Air Force and the Navy commenced in earnest in 1997 and was approved by DND in July 1999. As reflected in the SOR, the maritime helicopter would support a wide range of missions embodied in DND's force planning scenarios. Broadly, these comprised surface and subsurface surveillance and control operations and a range of utility missions that could be performed anywhere on the globe, including in complex threat environments and demanding weather conditions. Operational research studies were commissioned to establish the required performance levels for the aircraft. This ensured that requirements were developed through a rigorous and well-substantiated process.

The resulting request for proposals to industry was in many respects more robust than that of a decade and a half earlier. AgustaWestland (the renamed owners of European Helicopter Industries) promptly resubmitted an updated version of what was now styled the AW101, a variant of which was in service with the RN as the Merlin (including aboard their Type 23 frigates similar to the Halifax class) as well as with the Italian Navy. But in the end, it lost out to a marinized version of the Sikorsky S-92. Contrary to speculation, then and since, that the competition had been rigged to ensure the AW101 could not be eligible while allowing an unproven aircraft to come out on top, the facts tell a different story. The Sikorsky aircraft was a proven airframe in commercial production, and the modifications for naval use and integration of the military payload were not considered to represent significant risk. The Sikorsky S-92 offering, designated the CH-148 Cyclone by the Canadian Forces, was selected from a field of competitors, following a scoring process that evaluated bids based on performance, price, and Industrial and Technical Benefits. On November 23, 2004, the government of Chrétien's own successor, Liberal Prime Minister Paul Martin, awarded a contract to Sikorsky for twenty-eight aircraft, with deliveries to start in 2009.

Fate, as we know, intervened in a fashion unfriendly to the Cyclone. Another decade of delays unfolded, for issues ranging from engine upgrades, a shift to fly-by-wire control technology, restrictions from U.S. Government International Traffic in Arms Regulations, and changes to the mission package. At one point in 2013, the government of the time — by then, Prime Minister Stephen Harper's Conservatives — threatened to cancel the project owing to Sikorsky's failure to provide the airframe in a timely manner. All this conspired to result in the first batch of six aircraft not being delivered until June 2015. Three years later, in June 2018 — three decades after the original EH 101 contract was let — the Cyclone finally achieved the significant "new" maritime helicopter milestone of initial operational capability, in turn allowing for the long-overdue retirement of the Sea King that fall. The last Cyclone was set to be delivered in fall 2025, although not before one had already been lost: On April 29, 2020, Cyclone callsign "Stalker 22," flying from HMCS *Fredericton* on a routine training mission, crashed into the Ionian Sea, killing the four aircrew and the two ship's officers who were on board for a familiarization flight.

The software fault in the fly-by-wire flight control system that caused the crash would be addressed, but problems continued with integrating the mission package of sensors and processors. At the point in its life cycle when the Air Force would normally be considering a project for a mid-life upgrade, at the time of writing, the Cyclone had yet to complete its full introduction into service, let alone realize its notional potential as one of the most capable maritime helicopters in the world.

FURTHER READING

Gary Garnett and Dave Neil, review of *The Politics of Procurement: Military Acquisition in Canada and the Sea King Helicopter*, by Aaron Plamondon, *Canadian Naval Review* 6, no. 3 (Fall 2010): 41–42, navalreview.ca/wp-content/uploads/CNR_pdf_full/cnr_vol6_3.pdf. See full Plamondon citation below.

Sharon Hobson, "Plain Talk: The Process of (Not) Acquiring Maritime Helicopters," *Canadian Naval Review* 4, no. 4 (Winter 2009): 39–40, navalreview.ca/wp-content/uploads/CNR_pdf_full/cnr_vol4_4.pdf.

Terry Leversedge, *Aircraft of the Royal Canadian Air Force: A Centennial History, 1924–2024* (Minister of National Defence, 2024), publications.gc.ca/collections/collection_2024/mdn-dnd/D2-657-2024-eng.pdf.

National Defence, "Flight Safety Investigation Report for Stalker 22 Accident," news release, June 28, 2021, canada.ca/en/department-national-defence/news/2021/06/flight-safety-investigation-report-for-stalker-22-accident.html.

Aaron Plamondon, *The Politics of Procurement: Military Acquisition in Canada and the Sea King Helicopter* (UBC Press, 2009).

Jeff Tasseron, "Prelude to the Storm: The MH Community Gears Up for the Cyclone," *Canadian Naval Review* 2, no. 1 (Spring 2006): 11–15.

PART 3

RCAF-OPERATED MARITIME PATROL AIRCRAFT

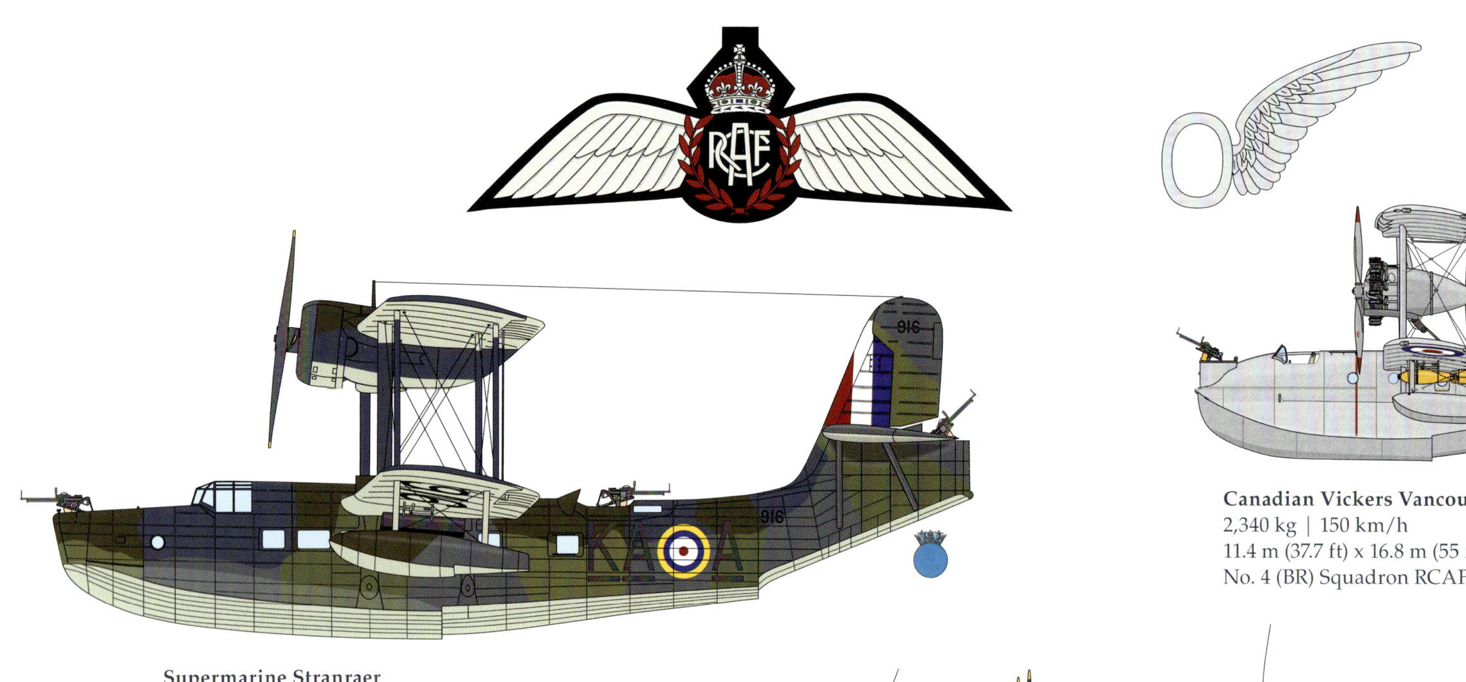

Canadian Vickers Vancouver Mk.IIS/S
2,340 kg | 150 km/h
11.4 m (37.7 ft) x 16.8 m (55 ft) x 4.8 m (16.6 ft)
No. 4 (BR) Squadron RCAF, Jericho Beach, BC, circa 1939

Supermarine Stranraer
5,103 kg | 266 km/h
16.7 m (54.8 ft) x 25.9 m (85 ft) x 6.6 m (21.7 ft)
No. 9 (BR) Squadron RCAF, Bella Bella, BC, 1942

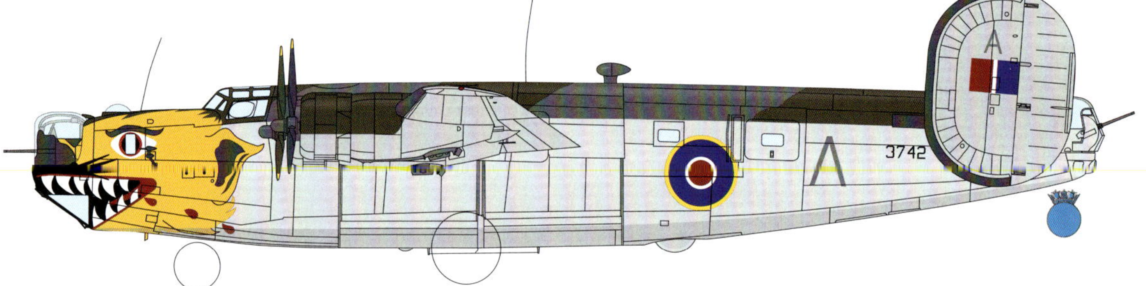

Consolidated B-24 Liberator GR VI
5,103 kg | 440 km/h
19.4 m (63.7 ft) x 34 m (111.5 ft) x 5.7 m (18.7 ft)
No. 10 (BR) Squadron RCAF, Torbay, NF, 1945

Consolidated PBY-5A Catalina/Canso
9,485 kg | 315 km/h
19.5 m (64 ft) x 32 m (105 ft) x 6.4 m (21 ft)
162 (BR) Squadron RCAF, Reykjavik, Iceland, 1944

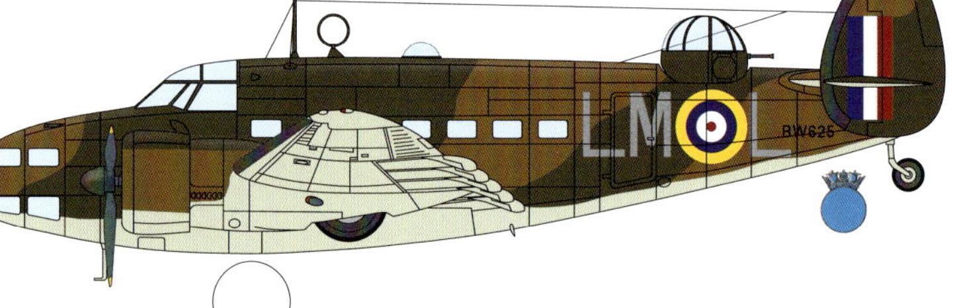

Lockheed Hudson Mk. IIIA
5,275 kg | 396 km/h
13.5 m (44.3 ft) x 20 m (65.5 ft) x 3.6 m (11.8 ft)
113 (BR) Squadron RCAF, Yarmouth, NS, 1942

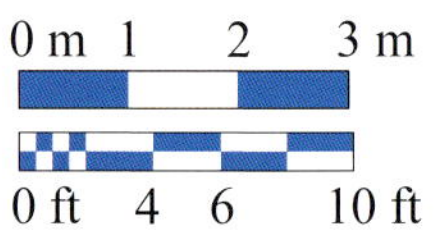

THE EVOLUTION OF MARITIME PATROL: FROM STRANRAER TO NEPTUNE

The close working relationship for patrolling the oceans that exists between the RCN and the RCAF is often looked upon as the model for integrated air–sea cooperation. The truth is that it hasn't always been so. Indeed, as hinted in the several chapters of Part 2 that describe shipborne aircraft, for the first decade and a half of the postwar period, the inter-service doctrinal debate over command and control of maritime aviation was often quite acrimonious, with a counterproductive effect upon the acquisition of the best aircraft types to perform the separate but related shipborne and land-based functions. The subject has attracted surprisingly scant academic analysis and remains deserving of deeper examination than is possible in these pages, but a general survey is essential background to understanding the various aircraft acquisitions by both services.

The establishment of the RCAF on April 1, 1924, was portrayed in Chapter 48 as having been the death knell of a Canadian naval air service, but the fact is that in that era of postwar retrenchment and no apparent viable threat, the new Air Force was itself immediately reduced to non-military functions, administered by a wing commander–ranked director reporting to the army's chief of the general staff (recall at that time the commander of the RCN was also a director-level appointment, elevated to CNS only in March 1928; the RCAF would not get a chief of the air staff until December 1938). Nearly another

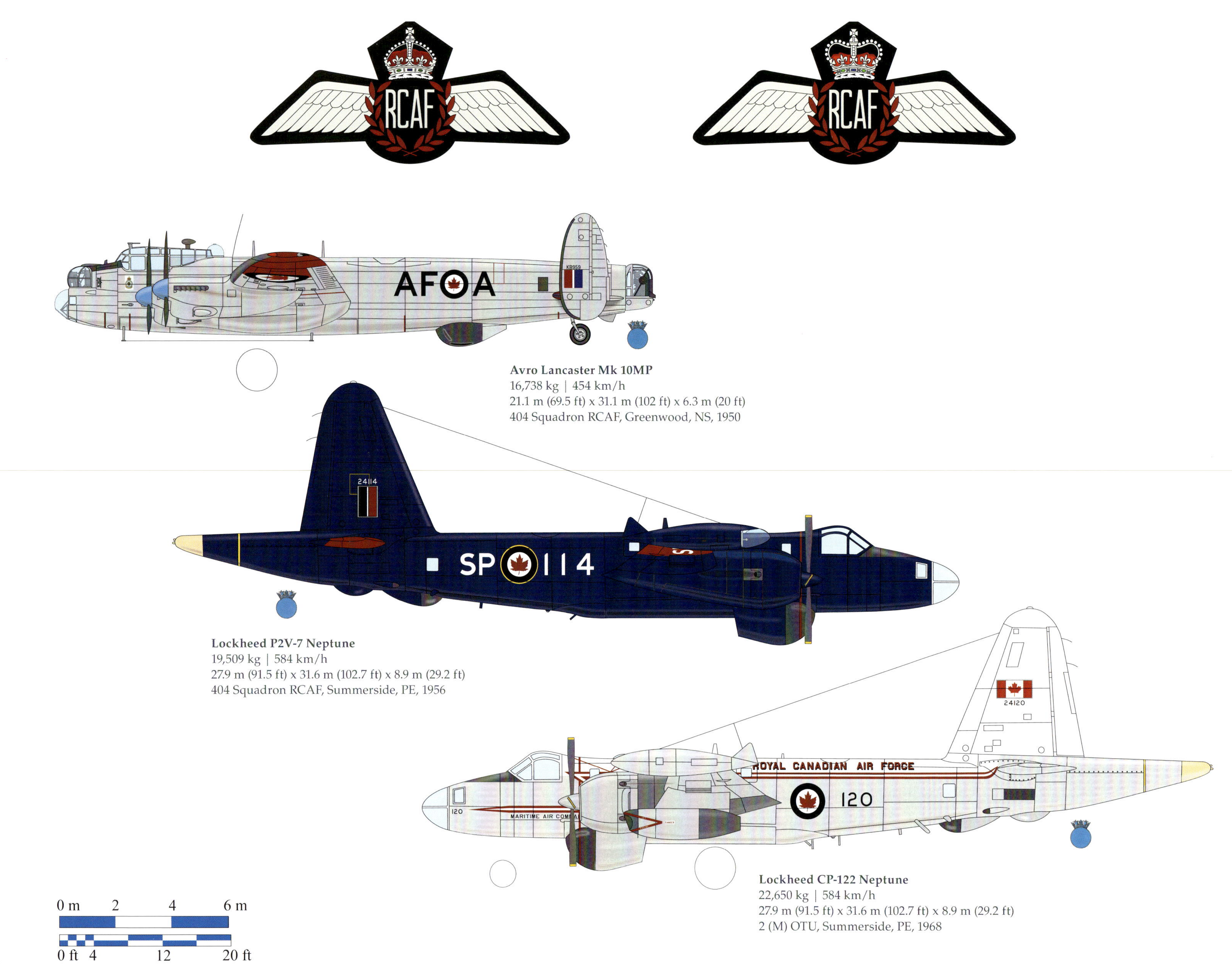

Avro Lancaster Mk 10MP
16,738 kg | 454 km/h
21.1 m (69.5 ft) x 31.1 m (102 ft) x 6.3 m (20 ft)
404 Squadron RCAF, Greenwood, NS, 1950

Lockheed P2V-7 Neptune
19,509 kg | 584 km/h
27.9 m (91.5 ft) x 31.6 m (102.7 ft) x 8.9 m (29.2 ft)
404 Squadron RCAF, Summerside, PE, 1956

Lockheed CP-122 Neptune
22,650 kg | 584 km/h
27.9 m (91.5 ft) x 31.6 m (102.7 ft) x 8.9 m (29.2 ft)
2 (M) OTU, Summerside, PE, 1968

"Protection of Coastal and Sea Lines of Communications and Ports and Harbours," including a "remarkably prescient command and control section ... [that] called for the [re]establishment of a joint RCN-RCAF Headquarters" in which it was allowed the RCN had a "primary interest."[96] At the same time, on November 9, 1950, the Joint RCN–RCAF Maritime Warfare School opened at the Navy's Fleet School in Halifax. Despite these encouraging signs for inter-service cooperation, however, the thrust of the air staff planning was that the RCAF should have responsibility for the management of all aviation assets. This aggravated the inter-service doctrinal dispute, which soon elevated to become a recurring topic of discussion at the Chiefs of Staff Committee (as will be discussed in Chapter 56).

The full evolution of the eventual solution remains to be studied, but the process was presaged by the June 1, 1953, formation within NATO's Supreme Allied Commander Atlantic structure of a Canadian Atlantic Sub-Area (CANLANT), based in Halifax and commanded by the RCN Flag Officer Atlantic Coast. On that same date, the RCAF collected its antisubmarine squadrons into a Maritime Air Command, with the officer in charge designated also as the deputy commander of CANLANT. In due course, this was reflected by the formal establishment of a Canadian "Maritime Command" in 1959 as an integrated RCN–RCAF command structure, with coastal flag officers double-hatted as commanders of Maritime Forces Atlantic and Pacific, respectively, each with a senior RCAF regional commander as his deputy. But the key to resolution was that this Maritime Command* (and subcommands) was set up as an operational structure for tasking purposes only, with the respective services retaining responsibility for procurement and maintenance of stipulated force levels.

After all the acrimony, the services seem to have very quickly fallen into a strong working relationship. The wartime South Street headquarters building was refurbished and reoccupied for the purpose. In 1961, the Deputy Commander of Maritime Command (RCAF Air Commodore Clements) described it in *The Roundel* (the Air Force equivalent of the Navy's *Crowsnest*): "This organization at first glance appears rather complicated. However, in practice it is quite straightforward and has resulted in the best understanding and working arrangements that have ever existed between the RCN and the RCAF in the maritime field."[97] It shifted seamlessly into the integrated CAF structure that went into effect on January 1, 1966, and indeed that MARCOM became the inspiration upon which the structure of the other unified commands would be fashioned.

In the meanwhile, procurement issues continued to unfold. No sooner did the first Lancaster MR 10s enter service than it became obvious the type would have to

* Note that "Maritime Command" would come to be abbreviated as "MARCOM" only after integration of the CAF in 1964. Before then, an admittedly short period of barely a half decade, it was only an inter-service working arrangement. It was nonetheless sufficiently established for the coastal formations to have been accorded badges, the centrepiece of which would become that of the unified MARCOM after 1968; see *Crowsnest*, 13, no. 4 (February 1961): 3, navalandmilitarymuseum.org/wp-content/uploads/2021/09/CFB-Esquimalt-Museum-Crowsnest-Volume13-Number-04-Feb-1961.pdf.

A Lockheed P2 Neptune soon after delivery, in the original midnight-blue paint scheme.

be replaced — the major concerns being the deteriorating condition of the wartime engines and airframes and the diminishing supply of spare parts. In May 1952, Chief of the Air Staff Air Vice Marshal W.A. Curtis sent a proposal to Minister of Defence Production C.D. Howe to introduce the Lockheed P2V-6 Neptune as an interim Lancaster replacement aircraft, pending introduction of a new aircraft type. The Neptune had entered service in the USN in 1947, purpose designed as a medium-range land-based antisubmarine aircraft. It was a large aircraft, having roughly the same dimensions as a Lancaster but driven by a pair of powerful dual-bank eighteen-cylinder Wright Duplex-Cyclone engines that delivered a higher maximum speed (356 mph/572 kph versus 272 mph/438 kph) to arrive in a search area more promptly. Although its range was slightly less than the Lancaster, the Neptune sensor suite came with the distinct improved additions of a more powerful AN/APS-20 search radar, a MAD sensor fitted in a tail boom, and a steerable 70-million-candlepower searchlight mounted in the nose of the starboard tip tank. And of course, there was the fact that it was a new aircraft in service with a host of Allied nations with no operational or logistic interoperability issues. Upon entering service in 1955, its performance on a single engine presented safety concerns, leading to the decision, two years later, to follow the USN by adding a pair of podded Westinghouse J34 jet engines, one under each wing.

It may seem strange that the RCAF did not look to acquiring the Neptune earlier, but that was probably because of the availability of and infrastructure familiarity with the Lancasters before an operational requirement was precisely defined. In the end, twenty-five were acquired, all arriving within six months in mid-1955 and remaining on strength until 1968 — just long enough to qualify for the "new" post-unification CAF type designation as CP-122. Only one example remains, on outdoor display at Greenwood, although it is not Canadian but rather an ex-USN model — silent testimony that, in so many ways, the Neptune does not figure large in RCAF history outside of the small community that actually flew it. But going back to the original request in 1952, the Neptune was only ever conceived as an interim maritime patrol aircraft "pending introduction of a new aircraft type" — that is the subject of the next chapter.

FURTHER READING

Christopher Bell, "The Battle of the Atlantic, the 'Air Gap,' and the Delay in Allocating Liberators to the Royal Canadian Air Force," *The Northern Mariner/ Le marin du nord* 34, no. 2 (Summer 2024): 235–58, tnm.journals.yorku.ca /index.php/default/article/view/1254/1196.

L.J. (Leonard) Birchall, "Early RCN/RCAF Maritime Cooperation," in *Salty Dips*, vol. 2, *"...and All Our Joints Were Limber,"* ed. Mack Lynch (Naval Officers' Association of Canada, 1985), 37–53.

Ernest Cable, "Maritime Air," in *On the Wings of War and Peace: The RCAF During the Early Cold War*, eds. Randall Wakelam et al. (University of Toronto Press, 2023), 325–48.

W.I. Clements, "The Evolution and Current Status of Maritime Air Command," *The Roundel* 13, no. 8 (October 1961): 1–9.

Roscoe Creed, *PBY: The Catalina Flying Boat* (Naval Institute Press, 1985).

WAB Douglas, *The Creation of a National Air Force: The Official History of the Royal Canadian Air Force*, vol. 2 (University of Toronto Press, 1986).

James Eayrs, "Nadir of the Navy," in *In Defence of Canada*, vol. 1, *From the Great War to the Great Depression* (University of Toronto Press, 1964), 270–86.

Richard Goette, "Service Cultures, Personalities, and the Struggle to Establish a Joint Headquarters in Halifax During the Second World War," *The Northern Mariner/Le marin du nord* 33, nos. 3–4 (Fall–Winter 2023): 353–68, tnm .journals.yorku.ca/index.php/default/article/view/1165/1120.

JDF Kealy, "The Development of the Canadian Navy, 1945–67" (DHH SGR II 223).

Samuel Kostenuk and John Griffin, *RCAF Squadron Histories and Aircraft, 1924–1968* (Hakkert, 1977).

Patrick Martin and John Griffin, *Royal Canadian Air Force: Aircraft Finish and Markings, 1947–1968* (pub. by author, 2003).

Richard Mayne, "Cinderella's Star: The CP 140 Aurora and the Evolution of the Royal Canadian Air Force's Modern Long Range Patrol Capability, 1939–2015," *Canadian Military History* 30, no. 1 (2021): 1–34, scholars.wlu.ca /cgi/viewcontent.cgi?article=2050&context=cmh.

Michael J. Neufeld, *Search the Sea: An Illustrated Short History of the Long Range Patrol Aircraft in the Canadian Armed Forces* (LRPA Project, Department of Supply and Services, August 1974).

John Orr, "The Influence of the RCAF on the RCN (Air Branch)," *Canadian Naval Review* 20, no. 1 (2024): 16–21.

John Orr, "Some Policy Aspects of Canadian Involvement in Strategic ASW, 1945–1968," in *People, Policy and Programmes: Proceedings of the 7th Maritime Command (MARCOM) Historical Conference (2005)*, eds. Richard H. Gimblett and Richard O. Mayne, Ottawa (Canadian Naval Heritage Team, 2008), 183–203.

Jerry Proc, "Canadian Lancaster Mk X 10MP and 10MR Aircraft," last modified September 6, 2010, jproc.ca/rrp/rrp3/lanc.html; and "The Canadian Neptune P2V7," last modified November 8, 2009, jproc.ca/rrp/rrp3/neptune.html.

Roger Sarty, *The History of Canada Series: War in the St. Lawrence: The Forgotten U-Boat Battles on Canada's Shores* (Allen Lane, 2012).

Douglas S. Thomas, "'In Cooperation Lies Success': The Early Years of the Maritime Warfare School, 1944–1964," in *People, Policy and Programmes: Proceedings of the 7th Maritime Command (MARCOM) Historical Conference (2005)*, eds. Richard H. Gimblett and Richard O. Mayne, Ottawa (Canadian Naval Heritage Team, 2008), 131–42.

with the more advanced British ASV-21 radar optimized for maritime search and fitted in a smaller, more streamlined chin-mounted radome.

Despite the clear success of the design, the Argus was never exported for use by other Allied forces, which preferred to support their own aircraft industries. The RCAF, however, did subsequently contract Canadair to build an adaptation of the original Britannia airliner for use as a military transport. Designated the CL-44/CC-106 Yukon, it adhered more closely to the Bristol Britannia, retaining the original concept of a pressurized fuselage and powered by four Rolls-Royce Tyne turboprop engines. Entering service in 1960, twelve Yukons were built for the RCAF and twenty-seven for foreign commercial airlines. As an aside, Canadian Pacific Airlines operated six Model 314 Britannias, acquired earlier in 1958 direct from Bristol for its long-haul transpacific operations.

The Argus first flew in March 1957, with deliveries to squadrons commencing in May 1958. It was the mainstay of the RCAF antisubmarine force for more than two decades, until the last was replaced in 1981. They initially operated from East Coast bases at Greenwood, Nova Scotia, and Summerside, Prince Edward Island, before five of the Mk 1s were transferred to 407 Squadron in Comox, British Columbia, on retirement of the Neptunes in 1968. Examples of the Argus are on static display outdoors at Air Force museums in Greenwood, Summerside, Comox, and Trenton, and in the reserve hangar of the Canada Aviation and Space Museum in Ottawa.

FURTHER READING

"Argus Years," 14 Wing Greenwood History, last modified July 18, 2017, canada.ca/en/air-force/corporate/wings/14-wing/history.html.

Cary Baker and Bert Campbell, *The Canadair Argus: The Untold Story of Canada's Cold War Maritime Hunter* (Bryler Publications, 2011).

Ernest Cable, "Maritime Air," in *On the Wings of War and Peace: The RCAF During the Early Cold War*, eds. Randall Wakelam et al. (University of Toronto Press, 2023), 325–48.

Patrick Martin, *Canadian Military Aircraft: Finish and Markings, 1968–2004* (pub. by author, 2004).

Patrick Martin and John Griffin, *Royal Canadian Air Force: Aircraft Finish and Markings, 1947–1968* (pub. by author, 2003).

Richard Mayne, "Cinderella's Star: The CP 140 Aurora and the Evolution of the Royal Canadian Air Force's Modern Long Range Patrol Capability, 1939–2015," *Canadian Military History* 30, no. 1 (2021): 1–34, scholars.wlu.ca/cgi/viewcontent.cgi?article=2050&context=cmh.

Michael J. Neufeld, *Search the Sea: An Illustrated Short History of the Long Range Patrol Aircraft in the Canadian Armed Forces* (LRPA Project, Department of Supply and Services, August 1974).

Jerry Proc, "Argus Aircraft — Electronics Fit," last modified March 28, 2019, jproc.ca/rrp/rrp3/argus.html.

commitments of one to three aircraft detachments in support of missions in diverse locations, ranging from the mid-1990s blockade of the former Yugoslavia, the post-9/11 "war on terror" in the Arabian Sea and over Iraq in support of the Afghanistan mission, the operations in 2011 against Libya in the Mediterranean, ongoing counter-drug operations in the Caribbean, and the embargo against North Korea in the Sea of Japan. A resurgence in Russian nuclear-powered submarine deployments in the late 2010s led to renewed engagement in the antisubmarine mission in Canadian waters and with NATO forces.

With the recent upgrades, and no sign of a replacement aircraft, it was expected that the Aurora's end-of-service timeframe could extend past the 2030s. In late 2023, however, Prime Minister Justin Trudeau's Liberal government announced that the Boeing P-8A Poseidon had been identified as a replacement, with the first scheduled to be delivered as early as 2026. The venerable Aurora fleet could be retired by the end of the 2020s, having completed a near half century of service.

At the time of writing, three Aurora have been withdrawn from service, one being used as a ground test aircraft and two others with time-expired airframes dedicated to outside display at the Comox Air Force Museum and at the Canada Aviation and Space Museum. Of the three Arcturus, one has been preserved as an outdoor display at CFB Greenwood.

FURTHER READING

Charles J. Gauthier, "Long Range Patrol Aircraft," in *Formulation of Defence Policy from 1970 to 1990* (DHH 92/228, Chapter 7), 21–43.

Iain Huddleston, "Changing with the Times: The Evolution of Canada's CP-140 Aurora," *Canadian Naval Review* 11, no. 1 (2015): 10–15.

Patrick Martin, *Canadian Military Aircraft: Finish and Markings, 1968–2004* (pub. by author, 2004).

Richard Mayne, "Cinderella's Star: The CP 140 Aurora and the Evolution of the Royal Canadian Air Force's Modern Long Range Patrol Capability, 1939–2015," *Canadian Military History* 30, no. 1 (2021): 1–34, scholars.wlu.ca/cgi/viewcontent.cgi?article=2050&context=cmh.

Jerry Proc, "CP-140 Aurora," last modified April 1, 2021, jproc.ca/rrp/rrp3/cp140.html.

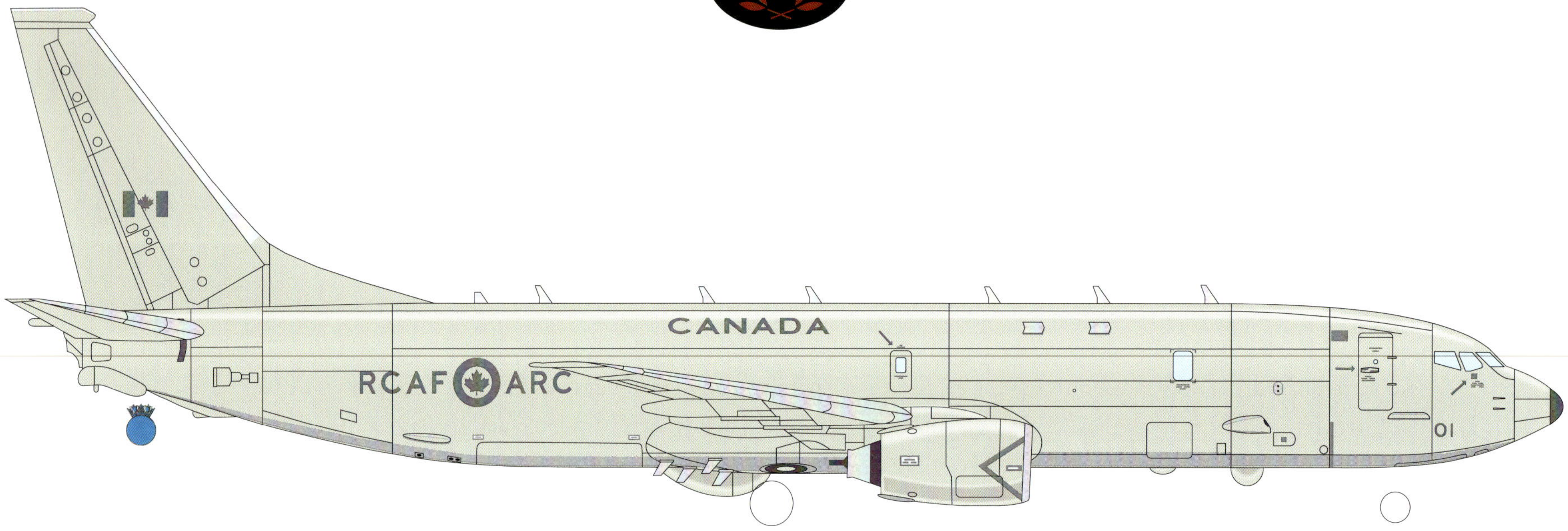

Boeing CP-8A Poseidon
Crew: 9
Length: 39.5 m (129.5 ft)
Wingspan: 37.6 m (123.5 ft)
Height: 12.8 m (42.1 ft)
Empty weight: 85,820 kg (132,300 lb)
Maximum takeoff weight: 85,820 kg (189,300 lb)
Maximum speed: 907 km/h (490 kt or 564 mph)
Cruise speed: 815 km/h (440 kt or 509 mph)
Range: 8,300 km (4,500 nm or 5,200 miles)
Armament: maximum load of 5,670kg (12,700lb) of ordnance

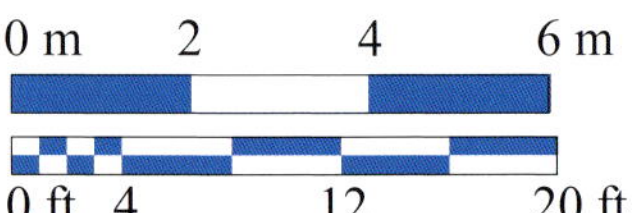

58

CP-8A BOEING POSEIDON

The November 2023 announcement that the RCAF would purchase "up to sixteen" P-8A Poseidon maritime patrol aircraft, with the first of them to be delivered in 2026, came as something of a surprise to Canadian defence watchers. The need to replace the aging CP-140 Aurora had been identified early in the millennium, but the Canadian Multi-Mission Aircraft (CMMA) project was not expected to deliver the first aircraft until well into the 2030s, and a request for information — typically the first in a long sequence of steps in the procurement bidding process — had been issued only the year before.

The decision to sole-source the acquisition and opt for express delivery was rationalized by Justin Trudeau's government because it was "the only currently available aircraft that meets all of the CMMA requirements."[103] That arguably is true, but, in fact, the decision was driven by a variety of additional factors: increasing Allied pressure for Canada to meet the NATO defence spending goal of 2 percent of gross domestic product (Canada was a noticeable laggard at just 1.3 percent); growing appreciation that the Aurora airframes were unlikely to be sustained for another decade and a half; and recognition that the Boeing production line was coming to a close. American State Department approval in June 2023 of the foreign military sale clinched the deal.

Like the Aurora before it, the Poseidon is a derivative of a civilian airliner, in this case the Boeing 737-800, and benefits from being operated by several allied nations, including the United States, United Kingdom, Australia, Germany, Norway, and South Korea. Indeed, to ease transition to the new type, Canadian aircrews have been

FURTHER READING

Canada in Extremis: Rebalancing the Canadian Armed Forces and Rebuilding the Canadian Navy (Naval Association of Canada, May 2024), navalassoc.ca/wp-content/uploads/2024/06/In-Extremis-MR.pdf.

Norman Jolin, "Group Up! A Case for Accelerated Canadian Submarine Procurement," *Starshell* (Spring 2024): 11–16, navalassoc.ca/wp-content/uploads/2024/05/Starshell-May-2024-MR.pdf.

Phillippe Lagassé, "Kicking Canada out of Five Eyes and NORAD?," *Debating Canadian Defence*, March 9, 2025, philippelagasse.substack.com/p/kicking-canada-out-of-five-eyes-and.

National Defence, "Canada Launching Process to Acquire up to 12 Conventionally-Powered Submarines," news release, July 10, 2024, canada.ca/en/department-national-defence/news/2024/07/canada-launching-process-to-acquire-up-to-12-conventionally-powered-submarines.html.

ACKNOWLEDGEMENTS

If the assembling of this book might be likened to the building of a ship, it could not have been launched without the assistance of a full yard of shipwrights covering a broad range of trades and talents. The inventory of acknowledgements must begin by our pointing to the previous publications listed in the Select Bibliography and Further Reading sections as forming the well-laid keel upon which we could frame our efforts. From there, what sustained us through the construction process was the enthusiasm of so many families, friends, and colleagues for our project. And once past the good-natured "slim book" chiding, many individuals and institutions actively facilitated our research. It is with deep appreciation that we recognize the outstanding support we had occasion to call upon.

Our very deep gratitude goes to the RCAF Heritage Fund, enabled by Air Force historian Richard Mayne, as well as to the Naval Association of Canada Endowment Fund for their generous financial support. We benefitted materially from the assistance of several colleagues in the Canadian Nautical Research Society in their different alternate professional capacities: Walter Lewis (team member of the digital heritage advocates at ourdigitalworld.org) performed wonders of restoration to make many of the images usable here; Michael Moir, before retiring recently as head of the Clara Thomas Archives and Special Collections at York University Library (YUL), drew our attention to the wonderful photographic treasures lying dormant in the *Toronto Telegram* newspaper fonds; and Paul Adamthwaite, executive director of the Naval Marine Archive (NMA

Picton, navalmarinearchive.com), provided access to photographs in the Julie Ferguson and Robbie Hughes Collections. Jason Nisenson, the archivist at The Military Museums (TMM) in Calgary, enabled research of the Ken Macpherson photograph collection held there. On the military aviation history side, our long-time friend Terry Leversedge has featured different versions of Karl's drawings in his expanding book series of aircraft profiles (kestrelpublications.com) and assisted in other respects.

The manuscript did not go through a formal academic peer review process, but it sustained the possibly more rigorous examination of a host of naval and aviation practitioners with a historical bent. Former Navy colleagues Colin Darlington, Tom Tulloch, and Ian Yeates read it in whole and provided shrewd observations. John Orr read the air sections (Parts 2 and 3) in their entirety, and, with Ernie Cable and Christopher Terry, who read significant portions, together they ensured we portrayed the aviation aspects accurately — it would have been a slighter (if not slimmer) volume without their input. Military historians Tabitha de Bruin and John Boileau read and provided valuable feedback on earlier versions of segments of this work. Naval architect friends Richard Greenwood and Derek Davis prevented executive branch misrepresentation of structural features and propulsion systems, as did shipmate Norm Jolin on "skimmer" views of "targets" (submarines). Others who provided important cues to further our research include Paul Adamthwaite, Bill Broughton, Stan Brygadyr, Geoff Craven, Jason Delaney, Spencer Fraser, Drew Graham, Ken Hansen, Brian Henwood, Dean Lang, Paul Madore, Michael Moir, Dave Neil, Mark Norman, Clive Orford, William James ("Jim") Pengelly, Allan Snowie, David Soule, and Michael Whitby.

The work to preserve the documentary and physical elements of Canadian naval and military aviation history goes under-appreciated, and we wish to provide a course correction to that by noting certain members of the RCN and RCAF heritage and museum communities who were of special assistance in their various ways: Dean Boettger, John Knoll, and Chris Perry, the small but vital team that constitute the RCN History and Heritage section in NDHQ Ottawa; Jennifer Denty and Jennifer Gamble at the Naval Museum of Halifax; Brad Froggart at the Naval Museum of Alberta; Christine Hines and Lisa Bullen at the Shearwater Aviation Museum; Joseph Lenarcik and Tatiana Robinson at the Esquimalt Naval and Military Museum (ENMM); Rebecca Meunier and Sean Graham at the Directorate of History and Heritage (DHH); and Jeff Noakes and Shannyn Johnson at the Canadian War Museum (CWM). That community is also sustained by a multitude of volunteers, and, at the risk of surely overlooking someone, we want to recognize those who helped in their miscellaneous fashions along the journey: Tim Addison of the Naval Association of Canada, Ottawa Branch; Pat Barnhouse, Ken Bowering, and Tony Thatcher of the Canadian Naval Technical History Association; Mark Bateman; Eric Bramwell; Blaine Duffley; Bill Gard; Clarence Hemeon; Brian Henwood; Randy Hillier; Roger Litwiller; Sandy McClearn; Bill McRitchie; Fred Paradie; Randy Roberts; Roger Sarty; Darren Scannell; Howard Smith; Jacqueline

Vincent (Chislehurst Digitization); and Garry Weir (forposterityssake.ca).

The team at Dundurn has changed entirely since our last book with them, and it has been such a pleasure to see that the tradition of professional collegiality continues under the new management of Meghan Macdonald. The editorial team of Elena Radic, Russell Smith, freelance editor Victoria Bell, and freelance proofreader Rebecca Conolly teased greater comprehension out of the text, while production manager Rudi Garcia brought beautiful visibility to Karl's profile drawings and layout of the other imagery. Thanks also to art director Laura Boyle for the cover design and designer Karen Alexiou for the interior layout, and to publicist Eden Boudreau. We look forward to working with them again in the future.

It might be a cliché, but we cannot express sufficient gratitude to all of those noted above, and of course apologies to anyone we might have inadvertently missed. Any enjoyment the reader gains from the book will gladly be attributed to them, while of course any errors or omissions remain the burden of the authors.

APPENDIX A: PRINCIPAL SHIP CLASSES

(by Type/In-Service Dates)

Class (Name) Type	Years in Service	#	Subtotal by Type	Displacement*	Museum Ship/Remarks
AIRCRAFT CARRIERS			**5**		
Ruler (Bogue) CVE	1943–45	2		15,390	
Colossus CVL (*Warrior*)	1945–48	1		13,350	
Majestic CVL (*Magnificent*)	1948–57	1		15,700	
Improved Majestic CVL (*Bonaventure*)	1957–70	1		16,000	
CRUISERS			**8**		
Apollo (*Rainbow*)	1910–20	1		3,600	
Diadem (*Niobe*)	1910–20	1		11,000	
Arethusa (*Aurora*)	1920–22	1		3,510	HMS *Caroline* (Belfast, NIR)
Prince Armed Merchant Cruisers	1940–45	3		5,700	
Colony (*Québec* & *Ontario*)	1944–58	2		8,800	HMS *Belfast* (London, EN)
DESTROYERS			**60 (+15)**		
RN 1913 M-type	1920–28	2		1,000	
RN 1917 S-type	1928–35	2		1,090	
River (RN Interwar B-H types)	1931–45	14		1,350	
Town (ex-USN Clemson)	1940–45	8		1,100	
Tribal	1942–63	8		2,000	*Haida* (Hamilton ON)
Emergency/Intermediate (RN V- & Cr-type)	1944–63	2		1,730	HMS *Cavalier* (Chatham, EN)
River (DDE/DDH)	1955–98	20		2,300	
Iroquois (DDH 280)	1972–2016	4		5,200	
River (DDG) (TBD)	(TBD)	(15)		(8,000)	
FRIGATES			**82**		
River (RCN Towns)	1943–50	67		1,445	HMAS *Diamantina* (Queensland, AUS) & MV *Christina O* (yacht)
Loch	1944–45	3		1,435	
Prestonian (River frigate conversions)	1954–66	(21)		2,216	Conversions from the wartime River-class frigate construction
Halifax	1990–present	12		4,770	
CORVETTES			**123 (+12)**		
Flower	1940–45	111		950	*Sackville* (Halifax NS)
Castle	1944–45	12		1,010	
Continental Defence Corvette (TBD)	(TBD)	(12)		(TBD)	

APPENDIX B: AIRCRAFT TYPE SPECIFICATIONS

Aircraft Type	Years in Service Canada	#	Operated From	Weight (Empty) kg/lb[a d]	Weight (Loaded) kg/lb[a d]	Stall Spd kts (kph)[b]	Deck Roll/ Runway[c]
CARRIER-BORNE STRIKE/ASW (1)(2)(4)							
Fairey Barracuda Mk II	1945	26	RN various	4,240/9,350	5,715/12,600	61 (113)	510 (155.5)
Fairey Firefly FR.1	1945–50	29	*Warrior*	4,230/9,330	5,490/12,540	63 (119)	540 (164.5)
Fairey Firefly Mk IV	1947–49	12	*Magnificent*	4,470/9,860	6,125/13,500	72.5 (134)	504 (153.5)
Fairey Firefly AS.5	1948–51	18	*Magnificent*	4,390/9,675	7,305/16,100	85 (157)	u/k
Avenger TBM-3E	1950–57	117	*Magnificent*	4,850/10,690	7,404/16,370	68 (126)	500 (152.5)
Avenger TBM-3W2 Guppy	1952–56	8	*Magnificent*	4,850/10,690	7,600/16,760	u/k	u/k
Avenger AS 3M	1955–57	(22)	*Magnificent*	4,810/10,600	7,395/16,300	u/k	600 (183)
DeHavilland CS2F/CP-121 Tracker	1957–89	99	*Bonaventure*/Summerside Comox	7,945/17,500	10,990/24,200	70 (130)	600 (183)
CARRIER-BORNE FIGHTERS (1)(2)(4)							
Chance-Vought Corsair Mk IV	1943–45	n/a	RN various	4,110/9,060	5,490/12,110	63 (119)	475
Supermarine Seafire Mk XV	1945–54	35	*Warrior*	2,800/6,170	3,600/7,950	66 (122)	470
Hawker Sea Fury FB 11	1948–56	74	*Magnificent*	4,100/9,040	5,360/11,820	86 (160)	520
Grumman F8F Bearcat	n/a	n/a	USN various	3,470/7,650	6,105/13,470	98 (181)	400 (122)
F2H-3 Banshee	1955–62	39	*Bonaventure*/*Shearwater*	5,980/13,190	9,530/21,020	108 (200)	n/a (cat)
Hawker Sea Hawk	n/a	n/a	RN various	4,210/9,280	7,325/16,150	105 (195)	n/a (cat)
Douglas A-4 Skyhawk	n/a	n/a	USN various	4,470/9,850	11,115/24,500	100 (185)	n/a (cat)
SHIPBORNE HELICOPTERS (3)(4)(5)							
Bell HTL-4/6	1951–65	13	*Labrador*/*Shearwater*	860/1,900	1,340/2,950	n/a	n/a
HO4S	1952–70	13	*Bonaventure*	2,380/5,250	3,420/7,540	n/a	n/a
Piasecki HUP-3	1954–64	3	*Labrador/Shearwater* Pat Bay BC	1,780/3,930	2,780/6,125	n/a	n/a
Sikorsky HSS-1 Seabat	n/a	n/a	USN various	3,470/7,650	6,035/13,300	n/a	n/a
Kaman HU2K-1 Seasprite	n/a	n/a	USN various	2,335/5,150	4,845/10,680	n/a	n/a
Sikorsky CHSS-2/CH-124 Sea King	1963–2018	41	*Bonaventure*/DDH/FFH/AOR	5,380/11,870	9,320/20,540	n/a	n/a
AugustaWestland EH-101 Cormorant	n/a	n/a	RN various/(RCAF SAR)	6,900/15,200	12,020/26,500	n/a	n/a
Sikorsky CH-148 Cyclone	2018–present	28	FFH/AOR	7,075/15,600	13,290/29,300	n/a	n/a

Aircraft Type	Years in Service Canada	#	Operated From	Weight (Empty) kg/lb[a d]	Weight (Loaded) kg/lb[a d]	Stall Spd kts (kph)[b]	Deck Roll/ Runway[c]
RCAF FIXED-WING MARITIME PATROL (3)(4)							
Supermarine Stranraer	1938–46	40	Dartmouth/Pat Bay BC	5,690/12,530	9,035/19,900	50 (93)	1,320 (402)
Lockheed Hudson	1938–48	247	Various both coasts	5,865/12,930	8,390/18,500	80 (148)	900 (274)
Consolidated PBY-5A Canso	1941–62	224	Various both coasts	9,485/20,910	16,065/35,420	55 (102)	3,590 (1,094)
Consolidated Liberator Mk V	1943–48	148	Dartmouth/Torbay NL	16,780/37,000	29,485/65,000	90 (167)	4,400 (1,340)
Avro Lancaster 10 MR/MP [Maritime Reconnaissance/Patrol]	1950–58	61	Greenwood/Comox	16,000/35,240	27,400/60,000	70 (129)	4,650 (1,417)
Lockheed P2V-7/ CP-122 Neptune	1955–68	25	Greenwood/Summerside Comox	22,650/49,940	36,240/79,900	110 (204)	2,170 (661)
Canadair CL-28/CP-107 Argus	1957–82	33	Greenwood/Summerside Comox	36,745/81,000	67,190/148,000	83 (155)	4,500 (1,372)
Lockheed CP-140 Aurora/Arcturus	1980–present	18	Greenwood/Comox	27,890/61,490	64,410/142,000	133 (246)	6,000 (1,829)
Boeing CP-8A Poseidon	2026/(TBD)	16	Greenwood/Comox/(TBD)	46,600/102,730	85,820/189,200	u/k	8,700 (2,652)

[a] Weights are rounded to the nearest 5 kg/10 lb.

[b] Stall speed (sea level/gear down "dirty") used as the best comparator between minimum takeoff and landing speeds.

[c] Deck roll is the flight deck length in feet (metres) required to take off with a 20-knot wind over deck (not applicable for catapult launches or helicopters); RCAF fixed-wing runway is takeoff distance in feet (metres) with no wind.

[d] This table gives both empty and loaded weights. The chapter text refers to loaded, whereas the drawings use empty.

Sources (in order of consultation):

(1) Norman Friedman, *British Carrier Aviation: The Evolution of the Ships and Their Aircraft* (Naval Institute Press, 1988).

(2) Patrick Martin and Leo Pettipas, *Royal Canadian Navy Aircraft: Finish and Markings, 1944–1968* (pub. by author, 2021).

(3) Patrick Martin and John Griffin, *Royal Canadian Air Force: Aircraft Finish and Markings, 1947–1968* (pub. by author, 2003).

(4) TFJ Leversedge, *Canadian Combat and Support Aircraft: A Military Compendium* (Vanwell Publishing, 2007).

APPENDIX C: RCN/CAF/RCAF NAVAL-MARITIME AIRCRAFT SQUADRONS

Service	In Commission	Location	(Remarks) Aircraft
RCN REGULAR SQUADRONS			
803 Fighter	Jan 26, 1946–May 1, 1951	*Shearwater*	(Redesignated VF 870) | Supermarine Seafire | Hawker Sea Fury
VF 870 Fighter	May 1, 1950–Sept 7, 1962	*Shearwater*	Hawker Sea Fury | McDonnell Banshee
883 Fighter	May 15, 1947–May 1, 1951	*Shearwater*	(Redesignated VF 871) | Supermarine Seafire | Hawker Sea Fury
VF 871 Fighter	May 1, 1951–March 16, 1959	*Shearwater*	Hawker Sea Fury | McDonnell Banshee | (absorbed into VF 870)
825 Torpedo-Bomber/Reconnaissance	Jan 24, 1946–May 1, 1951	*Shearwater*	(Redesignated VS 880) | Fairey Barracuda | Fairey Firefly | Grumman Avenger
VS 880	May 1, 1951– June 9, 1975	*Shearwater*	Grumman Avenger | CS2F/CP-121 Tracker | (integrated into AIRCOM 880 MR Sqn)
826 Torpedo-Bomber/Reconnaissance	May 15, 1947–May 1, 1951	*Shearwater*	(Redesignated VS 881) | Fairey Barracuda | Fairey Firefly | Grumman Avenger
VS 881	May 1, 1951–July 7, 1959	*Shearwater*	(Amalgamated with VS 880) | Grumman Avenger | CS2F Tracker
FRU 743 Fleet Requirements Unit	May 25, 1946–Nov 10, 1952	*Shearwater*	(Absorbed into VU 32) | Supermarine Walrus | Fairey Swordfish | Avro Anson V Fairey Firefly T.1 /2
VH/HU 21 Helicopter Utility	Sept 1, 1951–July 12, 1972	*Shearwater*	(Redesignated HU in April 1955, absorbed into 406 OTU) | Bell HTL 4 & 6 Piasecki HUP-3 | Sikorsky HO4S | Sikorsky Sea King
VU 32 Utility	Nov 10, 1952–July 4, 1992	*Shearwater*	(Initially formed as Fleet Requirement Unit/FRU 743) Fairey Swordfish | Anson V | North American Harvard | Beechcraft Expeditor Lockheed Silver Star | (Duties assumed on disbanding by 434 Sqn AIRCOM/RCAF)
VU 33 Utility	Nov 1, 1954–July 4, 1992	Patricia Bay BC Comox BC	Grumman Avenger | Piasecki HUP-3 | Lockheed Silver Star (Duties assumed on disbanding by 414 Sqn AIRCOM/RCAF)
VX 10 Experimental	Nov 5, 1952–July 1, 1970	*Shearwater*	(Absorbed into Aerospace Engineering Test Establishment [AETE]) Grumman Avenger | CS2F Tracker | Sikorsky Sea King
VT 40 Training	May 1, 1954–May 4, 1959	*Shearwater*	(Absorbed into VU 32) | North American Harvard | Hawker Sea Fury Grumman Avenger | Beechcraft Expeditor | Lockheed Silver Star
HS 50 Anti-Submarine Helicopter	July 4, 1955–Sep 3, 1974	*Shearwater*	(Split into HS 423 & 443, 3 Sept 1974) Sikorsky HO4S | CHHS-2/CP-124 Sea King
NAVAL RESERVE SQUADRONS			
VC 920 (Composite)	May 1, 1953–March 13, 1964	*York* (Downsview)	North American Harvard | Grumman Avenger | Beechcraft Expeditor
VC 921	Sept 30, 1953–March 1, 1959	*Cataraqui* (Kingston ON)	North American Harvard | Grumman Avenger | Beechcraft Expeditor
VC 922	Dec 1, 1953–March 13, 1964	*Malahat* (Victoria BC)	North American Harvard | Grumman Avenger | Beechcraft Expeditor
VC 923	May 1, 1954– March 3, 1959	*Montcalm* (Quebec City)	North American Harvard
VC 924	June 1, 1954– March 4, 1959	*Tecumseh* (Calgary AB)	North American Harvard

Service	In Commission	Location	(Remarks) Aircraft
AIRCOM/RCAF (FROM RCN)			
880 MR Maritime Reconnaissance	June 9, 1975–Sept 1, 1990	CFB Shearwater Summerside PE	(Ex-RCN VS 880) (Moved to CFB Summerside 1981) | CP-121 Tracker
406 Maritime Operational Training Sqn (MOTS)	July 12, 1972–present	CFB Shearwater	(Ex-RCN HS 50) | CH-124 Sea King | CH-148 Cyclone
423 Maritime Helicopter (MH) Sqn	Sept 3, 1974–present	CFB Shearwater	(Ex-RCN HS 50) | CH-124 Sea King | CH-148 Cyclone (Name changed from "HS 423 Helicopter Anti-Submarine Squadron," Jan 30, 1995)
443 Maritime Helicopter (MH) Sqn	Oct 25, 1974–present	CFB Shearwater/ Patricia Bay BC	(Ex-RCN HS 50) | CH-124 Sea King | CH-148 Cyclone | (Squadron changed home station to Patricia Bay, July 10, 1989 | Name changed from "HS 443 Helicopter Anti-Submarine Squadron," Jan 30, 1995)
RCAF (AIRCOM) MARITIME PATROL & UTILITY SQUADRONS (POST–SECOND WORLD WAR)			
404 Maritime Reconnaissance/ Operational Training Unit (OTU)	April 30, 1951–present	Greenwood NS	(Redesignated Maritime Patrol [MP], July 17, 1956, then OTU in 1981 for Aurora) | Lancaster 10 | Lockheed Neptune | Canadair Argus | Lockheed Aurora
405 Maritime Reconnaissance	March 31, 1950–present	Greenwood NS	(Redesignated Maritime Patrol [MP], July 17, 1956) Lancaster 10 | Lockheed Neptune | Canadair Argus | Lockheed Aurora
407 Maritime Reconnaissance	July 1, 1952–present	Comox BC	(Redesignated Maritime Patrol [MP], July 17, 1956) Lancaster 10 | Lockheed Neptune | Canadair Argus | Lockheed Aurora
414 Combat Support	July 4, 1992–Oct 23, 2002	Comox BC	Lockheed Silver Star | Canadair Challenger | (Redesignated 1992 to assume duties of VU 33) | Services contracted out upon disbandment
415 Maritime Reconnaissance	May 1, 1961–present	Summerside PE Greenwood NS	(Redesignated Maritime Patrol [MP], July 17, 1956) Canadair Argus | Lockheed Aurora | (Relocated 1981 to Greenwood NS for conversion to Aurora)
434 Combat Support	July 4, 1992–Oct 23, 2002	Shearwater NS Greenwood NS	Lockheed Silver Star | Canadair Challenger | (Redesignated 1992 to assume duties of VU 32) | (Relocated 1995 to Greenwood NS for fleet rationalization) Services contracted out upon disbandment

Table general notes:

1. The table is organized chronologically by type of aircraft operated, then numerically (with succession redesignations).
2. The four squadrons initially transferred from the RN in 1946 were re-numbered RCN in 1951, when their "original" designations were repatriated to the RN.
3. Soon after, in November 1952, the RCN adopted the USN "V" [heavier-than-air] alphanumeric designation system — that interim period is not accounted for in the table; use was discontinued in 1975.
   USN Squadron Lettering Codes:
   V – heavier-than-air [fixed wing]
   C – composite
   F – fighter
   H – helicopter
   P – patrol
   S – antisubmarine
   T – training
   U – utility
   X – experimental
4. Squadrons were integrated into the CAF on February 1, 1968, and Commonwealth Air Force numbering format was adopted with the establishment of Air Command (AIRCOM) in spring 1975.
5. The title "RCAF" was restored in 2011.

APPENDIX D: WEAPON FITS AND CALIBRE CONVERSIONS[a,b]

Weapon	Weight Projectile, lb/kg	Bore, in	Bore, mm	Ship Classes/Name
Standard machine gun	0.0625/0.028	.303	7.7	Various
.50-cal machine gun	0.225/0.116	.50	12.7	Halifax, Iroquois, Protecteur (I), Kingston
20 mm/70 Oerlikon	0.272/.0.123	.79	20	Various
20 mm Phalanx	0.22/0.1	.79	20	Iroquois (TRUMP), Halifax, Protecteur (I), Protecteur (II)
Mk 38 Bushmaster	0.4375/0.223	.98	25	Harry DeWolf
Vickers QF 1¼-pdr	1.25/0.56	1.46	37	*Canada*
QF 2-pdr Mk VIII	1.81/0.82	1.75	40	Flower, Fairmile D
40 mm/L60 Bofors	2.05/.093	1.575	40	Various
QF 3-pdr Mk I	3.3/1.5	1.85	47	*Canada*, Fairmile B
3-in/50	13/5.9	3.0	76.2	Town
3-in/50	13/5.9	3.0	76.2	St Laurent, Restigouche, Annapolis, Mackenzie, Protecteur (I), Bonaventure
3-in/70	15/6.8	3.0	76.2	Restigouche, Mackenzie
76 mm/62 Compact	14/6.35	3.0	76	Iroquois (TRUMP)
QF 4-in/40 Mk IV	31/14.06	4.0	102	*Aurora*, M-destroyer, S-destroyer
4-in Mk IX	31/14.06	4.0	102	Flower
4-in/40 Mk XIX	35/15.88	4.0	102	River Frigate, Prestonian, Postwar Tribals, Castle
QF 4-in Mk V	31/14.1	4.0	102	Loch, Algerine, Bangor

Weapon	Weight Projectile, lb/kg	Bore, in	Bore, mm	Ship Classes/Name
4.5-in/45 QF	55/24.95	4.5	114	Crescent
4.7-in/45	50/22.68	4.7	120	*Rainbow* (I), River Destroyer, Tribal, V-destroyer
QF 6-in	100/45.4	6.0	152	*Rainbow* (I), *Niobe*, *Aurora*
QF 6-pdr	6.0/2.72	2.2	57	MTB, ML, CD Drifter
6-pdr 7cwt QF Mk 11A	6/5.56	2.244	57	Fairmile D
6-in/50 BL Mk XXIII	112/50.8	6.0	152	*Quebec*, *Ontario*
6-in/45 BL Mk VII	100/45.4	6.0	152	Prince
QF 12-pdr 12 cwt	12.9/5.87	3.0	76.2	*Canada*, 1stWW Trawler, 2ndWW Armed Yacht, Bangor
57 mm/70	5.3/2.4	2.25	57	Halifax
127 mm/54 Compact	69.7/31.6	5.0	127	Iroquois (original)
12.75-in Mk 44	75/34	12.75	324	Improved Restigouche
12.75-in Mk 46	98/44.5	12.75	324	St Laurent, Mackenzie, Annapolis, Iroquois, Halifax
14-in Mark X Torpedo	Warhead: 115/52	14	356	*Rainbow* (I), *Tuna*, *Grilse* (I)
18-in Mk V Torpedo	Warhead: 296/134	18	450	*Niobe* (I)
21-in Mk II Torpedo	Warhead: 515/234	21	533	M-destroyer, S-destroyer, Town
21-in Mk IV Torpedo	Warhead: 515/234	21	533	*Aurora*
21-in Mk V Torpedo	Warhead: 515/234	21	533	Saguenay-Skeena
21-in Mk IX Torpedo	Warhead: 750/340	21	533	River Destroyer, Tribal, V-destroyer, Crescent, MTB G-Type
21-in Mk VIII Torpedo	Warhead: 750/340	21	533	Fairmile D
Mk 14 Torpedo (Steam)	668/303	21	533	*Rainbow* (II), *Grilse* (II)
Mk 18 Torpedo (electric)	595/270	21	533	*Rainbow* (II), *Grilse* (II)
Mk 37 Torpedo	Warhead: 330/150	21	533	Oberon
Mk 48 Torpedo	Warhead: 650/292.5	21	533	Oberon, Victoria

QF = quick-firing
pdr = pounder
cwt = hundredweight

in = inch
mm = millimetre

[a] In increasing order of bore size.
[b] Anti-surface and anti-air weapons; for antisubmarine weapons see listings in main Index.

ACRONYMS AND ABBREVIATIONS

AGOR Auxiliary General Oceanographic Research (intelligence gatherer)

AOPV Arctic and Offshore Patrol Vessel (sometimes S = Ship)

AOR Auxiliary Oiler Replenishment (see also JSS, OSS)

A/S antisubmarine

ASDIC Anti-Submarine Detection Investigation Committee

ASROC Anti-Submarine Rocket (rocket-thrown ASW torpedo)

ASW antisubmarine warfare

ASWTNS ASW Tactical Navigation System

BPF British Pacific Fleet

CADRE Command/Control and Air Defence Replacement

CAF Canadian Armed Forces

CANLANT Canadian Atlantic Sub-Area

CANTASS Canadian Towed Array Sonar System

CASAP Canadian Submarine Acquisition Project

CASSEV Canadian Surveillance and Sovereignty Enforcement Vessel

CCG[S] Canadian Coast Guard [Ship]

CD armed naval drifter

CFAV Canadian Forces Auxiliary Vessel

CFB Canadian Forces Base

CGS Canadian Government Ship

CIWS Close-in Weapons System

CMDO Chief of Maritime Doctrine and Operations

CNS Chief of the Naval Staff

CPF Canadian Patrol Frigate (Halifax-class frigate)

CSC Canadian Surface Combatant

CVE escort aircraft carrier

CVL light fleet aircraft carrier

CWM Canadian War Museum

DDE destroyer-escort

DDH helicopter-carrying destroyer

DHH Directorate of History and Heritage

DND Department of National Defence

EER explosive echo ranging (Julie sonobuoys)

ENMM Esquimalt Naval and Military Museum

FAA Fleet Air Arm (Royal Navy)

FELEX Frigate Equipment Life Extension project

FFH helicopter-carrying frigate

FHE fast hydrofoil escort

NOTES

1 Richard H. Gimblett, "The Many Origins of the RCN," *Canadian Naval Review* 1, no. 1 (Spring 2005): 8.

2 William Johnston et al., *The Seabound Coast: The Official History of the Royal Canadian Navy, 1867–1939*, vol. 1 (Dundurn, 2010), 96.

3 Tane Renata Casserley, "CGS *Canada*: A Canadian Warship in the Florida Keys" (MA thesis, East Carolina University, 2005), 75, quoting the annual report of the Naval Service for the year ending March 31, 1912.

4 Richard H. Gimblett, "Reassessing the Dreadnought Crisis of 1901 and the Origins of the Royal Canadian Navy," *The Northern Mariner/Le marin du nord* 4, no. 1 (January 1994): 48, tnm.journals.yorku.ca/index.php/default/article/view/747/709.

5 William Johnston et al., *The Seabound Coast*, 231.

6 Ken Macpherson and Ron Barrie, *The Ships of Canada's Naval Forces, 1910–2001*, 3rd ed. (Vanwell Publishing, 2002), 9.

7 William Johnston et al., *The Seabound Coast*, 271.

8 For a complete list, see F.J. Dittmar and J.J. Colledge, *British Warships, 1914–1919* (Ian Allan, 1972), 224.

9 Johnston et al., *The Seabound Coast*, 783, n. 161.

10 K.C. Barnaby, *One Hundred Years of Specialized Shipbuilding and Engineering* (Hutchinson, 1964), 97.

11 Macpherson and Barrie, *The Ships of Canada's Naval Forces, 1910–2001*, 201.

12 Ken Macpherson and Marc Milner, *Corvettes of the Royal Canadian Navy, 1939–1945* (Vanwell Publishing, 1993), 13.

13 Macpherson and Barrie, *The Ships of Canada's Naval Forces, 1910–2001*, 204.

14 "The Fishermen's Reserve," *Crowsnest* 12, nos. 7 and 8 (May–June 1960): 21.

15 WAB Douglas et al., *No Higher Purpose: The Official Operational History of the Royal Canadian Navy in the Second World War, 1939–1943*, vol. 2, part 1 (Vanwell Publishing, 2002), 338.

16 James Pritchard, *A Bridge of Ships: Canadian Shipbuilding During the Second World War* (McGill-Queens University Press, 2011), 99.

17 Fraser McKee, "Princes Three: Canada's Use of Armed Merchant Cruisers During World War II," in *RCN in Retrospect, 1910–1968*, ed. James Boutilier (UBC Press, 1982), 137.

18 Gilbert Norman Tucker, *The Naval Service of Canada: Its Official History*, vol. 2 (King's Printer, 1952), 66.
19 Tucker, *The Naval Service of Canada*, vol. 2, 467 and 490.
20 Tucker, *The Naval Service of Canada*, vol. 2, 22.
21 Macpherson and Barrie, *The Ships of Canada's Naval Forces, 1910–2001*, 219–33.
22 Donald E. Graves, "'Hell Boats' of the RCN: The Canadian Navy and the Motor Torpedo Boat, 1936–1941," *The Northern Mariner/Le Marin du nord* 2, no. 3 (July 1992): 31, tnm.journals.yorku.ca/index.php/default/article/view/799/760.
23 Tony German, *The Sea Is at Our Gates: A History of the Canadian Navy* (McClelland & Stewart, 1990), 166.
24 Tucker, *The Naval Service of Canada*, vol. 2, 96.
25 Marc Milner, "Fighting the U-Boats (1939–1945)," in *The Naval Service of Canada, 1910–2010: The Centennial Story*, ed. Richard H. Gimblett (Dundurn, 2009), 98.
26 Thomas G. Lynch, "The Origins of Canadian Carrier Aviation: Canadian-Manned Escort Carriers of the Royal Navy, 1943–5," in *Warship 1994*, ed. John Arthur Roberts (Naval Institute Press, 1994), 132.
27 Lynch, "The Origins of Canadian Carrier Aviation," 133.
28 TFJ Leversedge, *Aircraft Carriers in Royal Canadian Navy Service* (Kestrel Publications, 2023), 8.
29 Leversedge, *Aircraft Carriers in RCN Service*, 12.
30 Richard H. Gimblett, "What the Mainguy Report Never Told Us: The Tradition of 'Mutiny' in the Royal Canadian Navy Before 1949," *Canadian Military Journal* (Summer 2000): 88, navalmarinearchive.com/research/pdf/mainguy_report.pdf.
31 Norman Friedman, *British Cruisers: Two World Wars and After* (Naval Institute Press, 2022), 9.
32 WAB Douglas et al., *A Blue Water Navy: The Official Operational History of the Royal Canadian Navy in the Second World War, 1943–1945* (Vanwell Publishing, 2007), 167–173.
33 Wilfrid G.D. Lund, "Vice-Admiral Howard Emmerson Reid and Vice-Admiral Harold Taylor Wood Grant: Forging the New 'Canadian' Navy," in *The Admirals: Canada's Senior Naval Leadership in the Twentieth Century*, eds. Michael J. Whitby et al. (Dundurn, 2006), 109.
34 Quoted in J.L. Granatstein, "HMCS *Uganda*: The Royal Canadian Navy Ship That Voted Itself out of a War," *The Hub*, June 28, 2022, thehub.ca/2022/06/28/j-l-granatstein-hmcs-uganda-the-royal-canadian-navy-ship-that-voted-itself-out-of-a-war/.
35 "Brief History of HMCS *Algonquin*" (Directorate of History and Heritage 8000 series), 1.
36 Tucker, *The Naval Service of Canada*, vol. 2, 93.
37 Tucker, *The Naval Service of Canada*, vol. 2, 101.
38 Norman Friedman, *British Carrier Aviation: The Evolution of the Ships and Their Aircraft* (Naval Institute Press, 1988), 222.
39 Quoted by Jan Drent, "'A Good, Workable Little Fleet,'" in *A Nation's Navy: In Quest of Canadian Naval Identity*, eds. Hadley et al. (McGill-Queen's University Press, 1996), 205.
40 Lund, "Vice-Admiral Howard Emmerson Reid and Vice-Admiral Harold Taylor Grant," 165 and 169.
41 Peter Kikkert and P. Whitney Lackenbauer, "Setting an Arctic Course: Task Force 80 and Canadian Control in the Arctic, 1948," *The Northern Mariner/le marin du nord* 21, no. 4 (October 2011): 333.
42 "The Venture Story," *HMCS* Venture*, 1954–1968*, accessed October 16, 2024, hmcsventure.com/Venture/Story/VentureStory.html.
43 Sean M. Maloney, "Parry and Thrust: Canadian Maritime Forces and the Defence of North America, 1954–62," *The Northern Mariner/le marin du nord* 18, no. 1 (January 2008): 41, tnm.journals.yorku.ca/index.php/default/article/view/347/328.
44 Jason Delaney, "On the Edge of Hubris: The 1959 Canadian Nuclear Attack Submarine Program," paper

presented at the McMullen Naval History Symposium (2023), United States Naval Academy, Annapolis, MD, 3.

45 Delaney, "On the Edge of Hubris," 4.

46 Julie Ferguson, *Through a Canadian Periscope: The Story of the Canadian Submarine Service*, 2nd ed. (Dundurn, 2014), 271.

47 Quoted in JHW Knox, "An Engineer's Outline of RCN History, Part 2 (1948–68)," in *The RCN in Retrospect, 1910–1968*, ed. James Boutilier (UBC Press, 1982), 326.

48 Ferguson, *Through a Canadian Periscope*, 309.

49 Michael Whitby, "A 'New Look' at Cold War Maritime Defense — The Royal Canadian Navy's Seaward Defence Report and the Threat of the Missile-Firing Submarine, 1955," *Naval War College Review* 73, no. 4, Article 8: 11–12, digital-commons.usnwc.edu/nwc-review/vol73/iss4/8.

50 Kenneth P. Hansen, "Canadian Naval Operational Logistics: Lessons Learned, Lost, and Relearned?," *The Northern Mariner/le marin du nord* 20, no. 4 (October 2010): 378, tnm.journals.yorku.ca/index.php/default/article/view/312/294.

51 Knox, "An Engineer's Outline of RCN History, Part 2," 325.

52 Richard H. Gimblett, ed., *The Naval Service of Canada, 1910–2010: The Centennial Story* (Dundurn, 2009), 160.

53 "HMCS *Bras d'Or* (FHE 400)," Wikimedia Foundation, last modified September 6, 2024, 22:33 (UTC), en.wikipedia.org/wiki/HMCS_Bras_d%27Or_(FHE_400).

54 Isabel Campbell, "Making a Difference in Arctic Naval Research: HMCS *Cedarwood* 1948 to 1956," *Canadian Naval Review* 8, no. 1 (Spring 2012): 10–14.

55 "CNAV *Endeavour*," *Crowsnest* 16, no. 6 (June 1964): 25, navalandmilitarymuseum.org/wp-content/uploads/2021/10/CFB-Esquimalt-Museum-Crowsnest-Volume16-Number-06-Jun-1964.pdf.

56 Quoted in Robert Smol, "Challenge & Commitment Lost: Part 1: Looking Back at the Defence White Paper of 1987 — A Made-in-Canada Policy," *Esprit de Corps* 24, no. 8 (October 12, 2017), espritdecorps.ca/perspectives-1/challenge-commitment-lost-part-1-looking-back-at-the-defence-white-paper-of-1987-a-made-in-canada-policy.

57 Government of Canada, *Challenge and Commitment: A Defence Policy for Canada* (June 1987), 65–66, publications.gc.ca/collections/collection_2012/dn-nd/D2-73-1987-eng.pdf.

58 Bob Blakely, "'This Ain't Your Dad's Naval Reserve Anymore': Sharp-End Missions and Total Force, 1989–2010," in *Citizen Sailors: Chronicles of Canada's Naval Reserve*, eds. Richard Gimblett and Michael Hadley (Dundurn, 2010), 112.

59 Richard W. Greenwood, "An Engineer's Outline of Canadian Naval History, Part 3 (1970–2014)," *The Northern Mariner/Le marin du nord* 24, nos. 3 and 4 (Summer & Autumn 2014): 282, tnm.journals.yorku.ca/index.php/default/article/view/255/237.

60 Marc Milner, *Canada's Navy: The First Century*, 2nd ed. (University of Toronto Press, 2010), 305.

61 Bob Blakely, "'This Ain't Your Dad's Naval Reserve Anymore,'" 118.

62 Ferguson, *Through a Canadian Periscope*, 339.

63 Greenwood, "An Engineer's Outline of Canadian Naval History, Part 3 (1970–2014)," 285.

64 Murray Brewster, "Canada's Submarine Fleet Spent 'Zero Days' at Sea Last Year," *CBC News*, February 11, 2020, cbc.ca/news/politics/submarines-canada-fleet-repairs-canadian-navy-1.5458632.

65 David Peer, "The Orca Project: A Procurement Success," *Canadian Naval Review* 9, no. 2 (2013): 30, navalreview.ca/wp-content/uploads/CNR_pdf_full/cnr_vol9_2.pdf.

66 National Defence/Canadian Armed Forces, "HMCS *Margaret Brooke* departs for Operation PROJECTION 2025," news release, January 10, 2025, canada.ca/en/department-national-defence/news/2025/01/hmcs-margaret-brooke-departs-for-operation-projection-2025.html.

SELECT BIBLIOGRAPHY

OFFICIAL HISTORIES

Appleton, Thomas E. *Usque ad Mare: A History of the Canadian Coast Guard and Marine Services*. Dept of Transport, 1968.

Douglas, W.A.B., Roger Sarty, Michael Whitby, Robert H. Caldwell, William Johnston, and William G.P. Rawling, *A Blue Water Navy: The Official Operational History of the Royal Canadian Navy in the Second World War, 1943–1945*. Vol. 2, Part 1. Vanwell Publishing, 2007.

Douglas, W.A.B., Roger Sarty, Michael Whitby, Robert H. Caldwell, William Johnston, and William G.P. Rawling. *No Higher Purpose: The Official Operational History of the Royal Canadian Navy in the Second World War, 1939–1943*. Vol. 2, Part 1. Vanwell Publishing, 2002.

Gimblett, Richard H., ed. *The Naval Service of Canada, 1910–2010: The Centennial Story*. Dundurn, 2009.

Gimblett, Richard H., and Michael L. Hadley, eds. *Citizen Sailors: Chronicles of Canada's Naval Reserve, 1910–2010*. Dundurn, 2010.

Johnston, William, William Rawling, Richard Gimblett, and John MacFarlane. *The Seabound Coast: The Official History of the Royal Canadian Navy, 1867–1939*. Vol. 1. Dundurn, 2010.

Jolin, Norman H., and John M. Macfarlane. *Canada's Admirals and Commodores/Amiraux et commodores du Canada*. 3rd ed. Maritime Museum of British Columbia, 2016.

Kealy, JDF, and E.C. Russell. *A History of Canadian Naval Aviation, 1918–1962*. Queen's Printer, 1967.

Schull, Joseph. *Far Distant Ships: An Official Account of Canadian Naval Operations in World War II*. King's Printer, 1952.

IMAGE CREDITS

xii Poster reproduced from *The Crowsnest* 12, nos. 7 & 8 (1960): 18–19
2 Photo courtesy Richard H. Gimblett
9 RCN photo CN-3791
10 RCN photo CN-3792
15 RCN photo E-43808
16 RCN photo CN-6732
17 RCN photo CN-3310
21 RCN photo CN-2902
24 Photo courtesy Julie Ferguson collection, NMA Picton
28 RCN photo HS-9811, courtesy ENMM VR993.12.19
30 RCN photo CN-3400
35 RCN photo, courtesy ENMM VR992.84.1
37 RCN photo CN-2855
41 RCN photo E-6546-2, courtesy Macpherson Collection, NMA Calgary
46 RCN photo CN-3896
52 RCN photo GM 0281
57 RCN photo IKMD-03808
59 RCN photo BN-4334
62 RCN photo, courtesy YUL ASC62008
65 RCN photo CN-6142
67 Photo courtesy Clarence Hemeon
70 RCN photo H-583, courtesy the Macpherson Collection, NMA Calgary
72 RCN photo, courtesy YUL ASC62007
76 Gagnon collection
77 RCN photo, courtesy the Macpherson Collection, TMM
82 ENMM photo VR991.320.1
83 RCN photo, via LAC PA-132792
89 RCN photo, via LAC PA-191070
93 RCN photo, courtesy YUL ASC62005
96 RCN photo
100 RCN photo HS-0619-30
103 RCN photo, via ENMM VR991.354.1
108 RCN photo NF-2731
109 RCN photo IXC85-81
113 RCN photo CT-325
114 George Metcalfe Archival Collection, CWM image 19990143-002
118 Gagnon collection
126 RCN photo E7099-6, via ENMM

130 RCN photo, courtesy the Macpherson Collection, TMM
131 RCN photo PMR 98-143
132 RCN graphic CN-6031, courtesy YUL ASC61748
138 RCN photo CT-416
139 RCN photo BVC68-18, courtesy Robbie Hughes Collection, NMA Picton
144 RCN graphic, courtesy YUL ASC61766
145 RCN photo DNS-33910
146 RCN photo SWC69-2099
155 RCN photo EKS-1354
156 RCN photo CS-43
160 RCN photo
164 George Metcalfe Archival Collection, CWM image 19650068-009_58
168 RCN photo ETC85-3218
172 RCN photo CS-553
176 RCN photo O-736
177 RCN photo IXC86-76
180 RCN photo EKS-1941
184 RCN photo, courtesy Julie Ferguson Collection, NMA Picton
188 RCN photo, via ENMM VR2002.1.258
192 RCN photo IXC88-009
193 RCN photo IHC-90-002-8
194 RCN photo ETC93-1111
198 RCN photo HSC-71-326
199 RCN photo
206 RCN photo HSC81-4770
212 RCN photo
216 Combat Camera photo
217 DND image
226 RCN photo HS030001r01
232 RCN photo HS030282d08
233 RCN photo SWC-2005-0425-019a
238 RCN photo
239 RCN image
242 Photo courtesy Sandy McClearn
243 Combat Camera image
245 Canadian Armed Forces image, Corporal Connor Bennett
248 MIL-Davie image
254 RCN artist conception
262 Photo courtesy Randy Hiller
265 RCN photo, courtesy ENMM VR997.164.004
272 RCN photo SW70-1572, courtesy Shearwater Aviation Museum
273 RCN photo, courtesy ENMM VR996.24.112
279 RCN photo, via LAC PA-141275
281 RCN photo, courtesy Shearwater Aviation Museum
287 RCN photo EKS-637
292 RCN photo HS-66400-130
293 RCN photo EKS-1318
299 RCAF photo HS2010-0360-002
300 RCN graphic
304 Combat Camera photo
311 RCAF photo, via LAC PA-133573
312 RCAF photo, via LAC PA-064660
313 RCN photo, via LAC PA-107907
315 RCN photo O-13240
318 RCAF photo RNC-23
323 RCAF photo PCN-734
326 RCAF photo
329 RCAF photo

GENERAL INDEX

See Index of Ships and Aircraft for individual ships, aircraft types, aircraft manufacturers, and ship builders.